HOLMAN
New Testament Commentary

HOLMAN
New Testament Commentary

John

GENERAL EDITOR
Max Anders

AUTHOR
Kenneth O. Gangel

HOLMAN
REFERENCE

NASHVILLE, TENNESSEE

Holman New Testament Commentary
© 2000 B&H Publishing Group
Nashville, Tennessee
All rights reserved

ISBN 978–0–8054–0204–9

John / Kenneth Gangel
    p.   cm. — (Holman New Testament commentary)
Includes bibliographical references.
ISBN 0–8054–0204–7(alk. paper)
1. Bible. N.T. John—Commentaries.   2. Bible. N.T. John—
Commentaries. I. Title.   II. Title: John.   III. Series
226.6'07—dc21   98–39365
                                                                      CIP

12 13 14 15 16   17 16 15 14 13

To my mother,
Rose Marie Gangel,
long in heaven.
A Swiss immigrant,
converted when I was
three years old,
who taught me the
essentials
of the gospel
and foundations of
Christian theology.

Contents

Contents

Editorial Preface

Today's church hungers for Bible teaching, and Bible teachers hunger for resources to guide them in teaching God's Word. The Holman New Testament Commentary provides the church with the food to feed the spiritually hungry in an easily digestible format. The result: new spiritual vitality that the church can readily use.

Bible teaching should result in new interest in the Scriptures, expanded Bible knowledge, discovery of specific scriptural principles, relevant applications, and exciting living. The unique format of the Holman New Testament Commentary includes sections to achieve these results for every New Testament book.

Opening quotations from some of the church's best writers lead to an introductory illustration and discussion that draw individuals and study groups into the Word of God. "In a Nutshell" summarizes the content and teaching of the chapter. Verse-by-verse commentary answers the church's questions rather than raising issues scholars usually admit they cannot adequately solve. Bible principles and specific contemporary applications encourage students to move from Bible to contemporary times. A specific modern illustration then ties application vividly to present life. A brief prayer aids the student to commit his or her daily life to the principles and applications found in the Bible chapter being studied. For those still hungry for more, "Deeper Discoveries" take the student into a more personal, deeper study of the words, phrases, and themes of God's Word. Finally, a teaching outline provides transitional statements and conclusions along with an outline to assist the teacher in group Bible studies.

It is the editors' prayer that this new resource for local church Bible teaching will enrich the ministry of group, as well as individual, Bible study, and that it will lead God's people to truly be people of the Book, living out what God calls us to be.

Holman Old Testament Commentary Contributors

Vol. 1, Genesis
ISBN 978–0-8054-9461-7
Kenneth O. Gangel
and Stephen Bramer

Vol. 2, Exodus, Leviticus, Numbers
ISBN 978–0-8054-9462-4
Glen Martin

Vol. 3, Deuteronomy
ISBN 978–0-8054-9463-1
Doug McIntosh

Vol. 4, Joshua
ISBN 978–0-8054-9464-8
Kenneth O. Gangel

Vol. 5, Judges, Ruth
ISBN 978–0-8054-9465-5
W. Gary Phillips

Vol. 6, 1 & 2 Samuel
ISBN 978–0-8054-9466-2
Stephen Andrews

Vol. 7, 1 & 2 Kings
ISBN 978–0-8054-9467-9
Gary Inrig

Vol. 8, 1 & 2 Chronicles
ISBN 978–0-8054-9468-6
Winfried Corduan

Vol. 9, Ezra, Nehemiah, Esther
ISBN 978–0-8054-9469-3
Knute Larson and Kathy Dahlen

Vol. 10, Job
ISBN 978–0-8054-9470-9
Steven J. Lawson

Vol. 11, Psalms 1-72
ISBN 978–0-8054-9471-6
Steven J. Lawson

Vol. 12, Psalms 73-150
ISBN 978–0-8054-9481-5
Steven J. Lawson

Vol. 13, Proverbs
ISBN 978–0-8054-9472-3
Max Anders

Vol. 14, Ecclesiastes, Song of Songs
ISBN 978–0-8054-9482-2
David George Moore and Daniel L. Akin

Vol. 15, Isaiah
ISBN 978–0-8054-9473-0
Trent C. Butler

Vol. 16, Jeremiah, Lamentations
ISBN 978–0-8054-9474-7
Fred M. Wood and Ross McLaren

Vol. 17, Ezekiel
ISBN 978–0-8054-9475-4
Mark F. Rooker

Vol. 18, Daniel
ISBN 978–0-8054-9476-1
Kenneth O. Gangel

Vol. 19, Hosea, Joel, Amos, Obadiah, Jonah, Micah
ISBN 978–0-8054-9477-8
Trent C. Butler

Vol. 20, Nahum, Habakkuk, Zephaniah, Haggai, Zechariah, Malachi
ISBN 978–0-8054-9478-5
Stephen R. Miller

Holman New Testament
Commentary Contributors

Vol. 1, Matthew
ISBN 978–0-8054-0201-8
Stuart K. Weber

Vol. 2, Mark
ISBN 978–0-8054-0202-5
Rodney L. Cooper

Vol. 3, Luke
ISBN 978–0-8054-0203-2
Trent C. Butler

Vol. 4, John
ISBN 978–0-8054-0204-9
Kenneth O. Gangel

Vol. 5, Acts
ISBN 978–0-8054-0205-6
Kenneth O. Gangel

Vol. 6, Romans
ISBN 978–0-8054-0206-3
Kenneth Boa and William Kruidenier

Vol. 7, 1 & 2 Corinthians
ISBN 978–0-8054-0207-0
Richard L. Pratt Jr.

**Vol. 8, Galatians, Ephesians,
Philippians, Colossians**
ISBN 978–0-8054-0208-7
Max Anders

**Vol. 9, 1 & 2 Thessalonians,
1 & 2 Timothy, Titus, Philemon**
ISBN 978–0-8054-0209-4
Knute Larson

Vol. 10, Hebrews, James
ISBN 978–0-8054-0211-7
Thomas D. Lea

Vol. 11, 1 & 2 Peter, 1, 2, 3 John, Jude
ISBN 978–0-8054-0210-0
David Walls and Max Anders

Vol. 12, Revelation
ISBN 978–0-8054-0212-4
Kendell H. Easley

Holman New Testament Commentary

Twelve volumes designed for Bible study and teaching to enrich the local church and God's people.

Series Editor	Max Anders
Managing Editors	Trent C. Butler & Steve Bond
Project Editor	Lloyd W. Mullens
Marketing Manager	Greg Webster
Product Manager	David Shepherd

Introduction to

John

More than fifty years ago, the New Testament scholar Merrill C. Tenney entitled his commentary on the Fourth Gospel, *JOHN: The Gospel of Belief.* An apt theme to be sure, and one which captures the essence of the apostle's purpose. With profundity wrapped in simplicity John sets forth his case. His Gospel is not always chronological like Luke, yet it is logical and highly theological. From the manifestation of the Word in chapter 1, to the post-resurrection appearance to the disciples in chapter 21, we find John emphasizing over and over again the excellence and eternality of the Son of God.

In this series, we emphasize practical exposition—not literary and exegetical detail—so comments on introductory material will be brief. For full coverage of background materials, see the Introduction to Gerald Borchert's work in *The New American Commentary.*

AUTHORSHIP

Historically, few have challenged the concept of Johannine authorship of the Fourth Gospel. As early as A.D. 180, Theophilus referred to John as the author, and ten years later Irenaeus used 100 quotes from the Fourth Gospel, mentioning John. At the turn of the century in A.D. 200, Clement of Alexandria used John's name frequently in connection with this Gospel. And Tertullian cited passages from almost every chapter, attributing them to the apostle. Opponents of this view have usually come from theological camps outside mainline orthodoxy, such as the Gnostics.

Internally, the author of this book refers to himself as "the disciple whom Jesus loved" (13:23; 19:26; 21:7,20,24). He was clearly an eyewitness to Jesus' earthly ministry, knew Jewish life well, and was Jesus' intimate friend to whom the dying Lord committed his mother (19:25–27). Whether the son of Zebedee actually wrote the scroll is certainly a matter open to question. We do not challenge Peter's authorship of the epistles which bear his name, even through we know Silas helped with the text (1 Pet. 5:12). Borchert spells it out for us: "When all of the arguments both internal and external are set together, there seems little reason to reject the idea that the son of Zebedee was the towering figure and the authentic witness involved in the writing of this Gospel. I would not think it necessary that he himself was the actual scribe."

DATE OF WRITING

Most conservative scholars place the development of John's Gospel toward the end of the first century about A.D. 90. However, as in many arguments of this type, one's view of authorship colors one's view of date. Scholars have argued that the more highly developed theology of the Fourth Gospel suggests that it originated later, but that is hardly definitive. Other scholars, particularly those who deny Johnannine authorship, set a date somewhere in the second century.

So there are those who want to date this book earlier than the fall of Jerusalem (A.D. 70) and others who would like to see it dated well into the second century. My own inclination is to adopt the traditional view of an aged John writing some sixty or seventy years after the resurrection of Jesus.

That we are right in regarding the Gospel of John as the fourth and last of the Gospels is clear not only from the fact that in the majority of manuscripts it is found in this position, but also from patristic references. Clement of Alexandria, for example, who died in A.D. 212, stated on the authority of the elders of an earlier age that John wrote his Gospel last of the evangelists. If the work was published during the last days of the life of John the son of Zebedee, as the evidence suggests, it can be confidently dated in the last decade of the first century, probably at its close. Irenaeus stated that John survived until the reign of the Roman emperor Trajan, which began in A.D. 98.

PURPOSE OF JOHN

Luke wrote for an individual (Theophilus). Matthew and Mark targeted Jewish audiences with their record of Jesus' life and work. John wrote for the world, living as he did at the end of fifty years of church history, knowing that the gospel had already permeated the entire Mediterranean world. Indeed, he stated his purpose clearly: "Jesus did many other miraculous signs in the presence of his disciples, which are not recorded in this book. But these are written that you may believe that Jesus is the Christ, the Son of God, and that by believing you may have life in his name" (John 20:30–31).

The Gospel of John radiates faith. I like to say that John offers the motto, "Believing is seeing." John focused on Jesus' teaching, avoiding most of the miracles and all of the parables. Writing with a clear grasp of Jewish culture, his logic appealed to Greek readers as well as he set forth an evangelistic theology. John carefully selected his material and unashamedly targeted unbelievers. Four ideas emerge in the theme verses quoted above:

Sign: The miracles of Jesus were not just demonstrations of power, but signs of Jesus' person and authority. The Greek word *semeion* connects the sign with what it signifies. This accounts for John's unique selection of the miracles of Jesus which he chose to record.

Selection: John chooses certain signs of the many in order to accomplish his purpose. Traditionally, seven miracles can be found in John, although some interpreters count as many as ten.

Significance: John intended his historical, theological record to produce thinking conviction that would lead to changed lives.

Salvation: John's favorite word for new birth in Christ is *life*, as we will see repeatedly in this study.

John wrote this Gospel so that the Holy Spirit could produce faith in the hearts of those who could not have an earthly, eyewitness experience like his own.

STYLE OF JOHN

For several decades theologians have been "finding the historical Jesus." Actually, the search is not that difficult since four ancient writers have provided ample material. This particular Gospel, however, sets the history in a theological setting. John adds a geographical flavor, identifying numerous sites around first-century Palestine to connect history to the culture of the day. He uses simplicity, repetition, and great detail. He arranges his material carefully to offer interpretive analysis to his readers.

Several "keys" fall into our hands throughout this book. We could probably identify the *key verses* in the passage we noted as the purpose statement (20:30–31). We shall soon discover that the *key chapter* is the first. I also suggest that the *key thought* in the book comes to us in John 1:18—"God the One and Only." The *key words,* which are many, include "believe," "life," "word," and "world."

Do we find intentional structure in this Gospel? Several patterns have been suggested, though attributing any of them to John's intentionality seems out of the question. They do, however, help us grasp the material a bit more efficiently.

For example, the Fourth Gospel could be outlined on the basis of *Christ's relationship to earth:* "I came from the Father and entered the world; now I am leaving the world and going back to the Father" (16:28).

- From the Father (1:1–18)
- Into the world (1:19–12:50)
- Leaving the world and going to the Father (13:1–21:25)

On the basis of *Passovers* (though it is impossible to absolutely discern the number of Passovers in the text):

- Life up to the first Passover (1:1–2:12)
- First year of ministry (2:13–4:54)
- Second year of ministry (5:1–6:71)
- Third year of ministry (7:1–12:50)
- From the last Passover to the end of the crucifixion week (13:1–21:25)

On the basis of the *prologue division,* a system which allows 1:1–18 to set the pattern for the entire book:

- Revelation (cf. 1:1–4 with 1:19–6:71)
- Rejection (cf. 1:5–11 with 7:1–12:50)
- Reception (cf. 1:12–18 with 13:1–19:42)

On the basis of the *testimony about Christ:*

- The testimony of the evangelist (1:1–14)
- The testimony of the Baptist (1:15–36)
- The testimony of the first disciples (1:37–51)
- The testimony of the public ministry (2:1–12:50)
- The testimony of the private ministry (13:1–17:26)
- The testimony of his death (18:1–19:42)
- The testimony of his resurrection (20:1–21:25)

Martin Luther said that if we should lose all the books of the Bible except two—John and Romans—Christianity could be saved. Perhaps, but inspiration and application of the whole Bible is the goal of evangelical Christianity. Nevertheless, this book is special with its wonderful portrait of Jesus, the Savior of the world. An old story suggests that an agnostic was challenged by Henry Clay Trumbell to study the Gospel of John. After emerging from his skeptical analysis, the man told Trumbell, "The one of whom this book tells is either the Savior of the world or He ought to be."

John 1

The Lamb of God

"*V*eiled in flesh the godhead see;

Hail the incarnate Deity,

Pleased as man with men to dwell,

Jesus, our Emmanuel."

Charles Wesley

GEOGRAPHICAL PROFILE: BETHANY

- Name means "house of unripe figs"
- The modern city is called el Azariyeh
- Suggested site of ruins claims to include the tomb of Lazarus and the house of Simon the Leper

GEOGRAPHICAL PROFILE: BETHSAIDA

- Name means "house of fishing"
- Located on the Sea of Galilee close to Capernaum
- Rebuked by Jesus for unbelief (Matt. 11:20–23; Luke 10:13–15)
- Not to be confused with Bethsaida on the east side of the Sea of Galilee where the feeding of the five thousand and the healing of the blind man took place (Mark 8:22)

PERSONAL PROFILE: JOHN THE BAPTIST

- Born six months before Jesus to Zachariah and Elizabeth
- Appointed by God to be Jesus' forerunner
- Last of the Old Testament prophets, first of the New Testament prophets
- Jesus' cousin beheaded by Herod the Great

PERSONAL PROFILE: ANDREW

- The name means "manly"
- Son of Jonas, brother of Simon Peter
- Friend of Philip, who was also from Bethsaida

- Never mentioned in the Bible after Acts 1:13

PERSONAL PROFILE: SIMON PETER

- Simon was his original name; Peter (rock) was a name given by Jesus
- A fisherman from Bethsaida
- The only disciple we know was married (Mark 1:30; 1 Cor. 9:5)
- With James and John, part of Jesus' "inner circle" (Mark 5:37; 9:2; 14:33)
- Leader of the Jerusalem church in the early chapters of Acts

PERSONAL PROFILE: PHILIP

- The name means "lover of horses"
- Philip the apostle of the Gospels should not be confused with Philip the evangelist of Acts 6, 8, and 21
- Probably the first disciple of John the Baptist
- Not mentioned in the Bible after Acts 1:13

PERSONAL PROFILE: NATHANIEL

- The name means "God has given"
- Praised by Jesus for his integrity
- Also known as Bartholomew

 I N   A   N U T S H E L L

John wastes no time in introducing Jesus to his readers as the Word of God, the Son of God, and the Lamb of God. Unlike the writers of the three Synoptic Gospels, John introduces Jesus at the age of thirty and includes no information about his birth.

The Lamb of God

I. INTRODUCTION

Confusing Pictures

*D*uring the years I pastored my first church, my wife spent some time each week tutoring a young girl who had fallen behind in her reading at school. Since Linda was from a Christian family, part of the reading centered in Bible story books. One day Linda asked a penetrating question about the pictures she found in those books: "How do I tell the difference between Jesus and God? They both look alike to me."

The artists, of course, had included all pictures of Jesus since God the Father is Spirit and cannot be shown by anything but symbols such as light or sound. But Linda had learned that Jesus was God, so she kept looking for pictures of both of them throughout her books. A natural mistake, and one which reinforces John's point throughout this book and especially the early verses of this first chapter.

In the first eighteen verses of his book, John introduces the Lord. He begins by proclaiming that Jesus reveals God the Father and tells us that when he came to earth, God's Son showed the human race what the Father was like—eternal, personal, and the source of all life. The word *life* appears no fewer than thirty-six times in this Gospel along with several other key words. We could say that *life* establishes the central theme for the book.

We need only read the first verse of the Bible (Gen. 1:1) to understand the central issue of life, and it centers on the reality of God. If there is a God (and there is), and if that God has spoken in history (and he has), then the most important thing in the world is to find out what he has said.

The Gospel of John is a loved and familiar book, but many who can quote important verses from its pages have a less-than-satisfactory grasp of its important theology. Yet John wasted no time in introducing the key question: "Who is Jesus Christ?"

In his presentation of Jesus as the Son of God, John started out with creation. Everything that was ever made was made through him; and without him, nothing has ever been created. Jesus was the source of power in the original physical creation and in the spiritual creation by which people are brought to new life in Christ.

Do not forget that key word *life*. John used it frequently in his Gospel, and he also used it thirteen times in his first epistle and seventeen more times in Revelation. Here in this Gospel we have more than twenty-five percent of all New Testament references to life. John wanted to make sure that everyone knew life is possible only through the Son of God.

II. COMMENTARY

The Lamb of God

> **MAIN IDEA:** *Jesus Christ is the heart and core of the gospel. Christianity is not a philosophy of life; it centers in a person who is the core of everything Christians believe.*

A Revelation of the Lamb (1:1–5)

> **SUPPORTING IDEA:** *Like his heavenly Father, Jesus reveals eternality, personality, deity, creativity, life, and light.*

1:1–2. Some interpreters have translated the opening phrase of this Gospel, "Before there was a beginning, the Word had been." Indeed, the familiar repetition of Genesis 1:1 almost looks as if John wrote a Gospel of two beginnings—a creation account that parallels physical birth and spiritual rebirth. But it is important to notice that we are dealing with two *beginnings*, not *creations*. The central focus of this verse is eternality. Like his heavenly Father, Jesus always was and therefore existed at the beginning of time.

It is interesting that John should call Jesus **the Word** rather than some other name to introduce his book—interesting, but not surprising since the Jews often referred to God in such terminology. The doctrine at stake here is the deity of Christ. Jesus is God, and John wanted to make that point immediately. In fact, this prologue (vv. 1–18) begins and ends with a strong statement of this doctrine.

The term **Word** (*logos*) would have been familiar to the Greeks as well. Their understanding centered on ultimate reason or the rationale of the universe rather than the personal God revealed to Abraham and his descendents. John claimed that the God of creation, the ultimate mind of the universe, had taken on human form; he had become *incarnate*.

The Bible allows no place for atheism and no room for doubt about how God has spoken—through the Word. Before there was a beginning, the Word had been coequal with God throughout all eternity. But what did the apostle mean by **with God?** The Greek word is *pros* which literally means "toward," implying a face-to-face relationship. John would have neither atheism nor unitarianism. He told us later in his Gospel that the Godhead consists of a trinity, but here in verse 1 we learn plurality.

So Jesus, the Word, is eternal and personal. Nothing can separate the heavenly Father from his Son. Verse 2 merely emphasizes verse 1. I like the way Gary Vanderet puts it: "John intends that the entire book be read in light of this verse. The deeds and the words of Jesus are the deeds and words of God" (Vanderet, *Prelude to Deity*).

1:3. Unlike the Gospel writers before him, John tells us that Jesus participated in creation and again states his case twice for emphasis. Surely this is a deliberate link with Genesis, and it sets the stage for other New Testament Scriptures which show us Jesus' involvement in creation: "For by him all things were created: things in heaven and on earth, visible and invisible, whether thrones or powers or rulers or authorities; all things were created by him and for him" (Col. 1:16). "In the past God spoke to our forefathers through the prophets at many times and in various ways, but in these last days he has spoken to us by his Son, whom he appointed heir of all things, and through whom he made the universe" (Heb. 1:1–2).

Creation is a foundational doctrine of the Christian faith. Virtually every other aspect of theology rests upon our understanding of God as the origin of all life and of the role Jesus Christ, the Word, in creation. John could hardly say it more clearly: **without him nothing was made that has been made—**everything from subatomic particles to galaxies. Only God who created all things can redeem them. Creation is the foundation stone of the gospel. Christ could not have been created, for he created all things. There was a "historical Jesus," but this terminology refers only to his thirty-three years on earth. His life had no beginning, and it will have no end.

1:4. Here we find the first appearance of our key word—**life.** The revelation of the Lamb was also the revelation of life. No fewer than thirty-six times in John, we find the word *zoe.* Jesus Christ the Creator provides physical life; Jesus Christ the Redeemer provides spiritual life; and Jesus Christ the Savior provides eternal life. In verse 4 John also introduced another key word—**light.** The life becomes the light of men. Notice these positive terms. What a wonderful contrast to death and darkness.

In the Word, God's person and power were revealed to humanity. Here again we see a reference to creation since, in the Genesis account, light was the first evidence of God's creative work. God is always the source of light and life. Christ the Son, the Creator, provides life and light to humanity. He alone is the life-giver and the light-bearer. John is getting ready to write new lyrics to an old melody, "With you is the fountain of life; in your light we see light" (Ps. 36:9).

1:5. In this verse John picked up a common first-century theme, the symbols of light and darkness representing good and evil. The word **understood** might be rendered "overcome." All the forces of Satan tried to prevent life and extinguish the light—but they could not.

These five verses tell us that Jesus came to the world with a message of hope, and he came from heaven where he had lived eternally with the Father.

Often I find myself humming the theme of the television miniseries *Winds of War* which aired in the mid 1980s. Based on the Herman Wouk book, the series ran for a total of eighteen hours. This theme played over and over again—in the key of D minor. John's key words are like that, especially "life" and "light." The word rendered "understood" in the NIV is translated "seizes" in Mark 9:18 and "overtakes" in John 12:35. God sent his light into the world, but mankind did not understand it, could not grasp it. But the world will never be able to defeat it.

B Purpose of the Lamb (1:6–13)

SUPPORTING IDEA: *Eternal life and heavenly light come to those who trust Jesus and are born again from above.*

1:6–7. We've already noted the recurring themes of life and light; here is another—**witness**. In order for John the apostle to introduce the Son of God historically, he had to first introduce John the Baptist. We should notice, however, that John emphasized the *function* of the Baptist, not his *identity*. Luke tells us much more about John the Baptist's birth and life; John focuses on why he came and who sent him.

A good witness does not attract attention to himself but to the person or facts which he represents. The Greek word for "witness" by John in this Gospel appears only three times in Mark and only once in Luke. The verb (usually rendered "testify") shows up thirty-three times in John and only once each in Matthew and Luke. All this points up the uniqueness of each account and particularly the intensity with which John will seek to fulfill his purpose. As Tenney puts it, "Although vv. 6–8 seem alien to the general content of the text, they are not irrelevant. As the Word came to bring the heavenly light to humanity, so John came to speak from a human level and to awaken people to their need of God's revelation" (Tenney, *EBC*, p. 31).

How interesting that John the apostle should write about John the Baptist and tell us he was **sent**. He used a verb form upon which the word *apostle* is built. Actually, both men were apostles in the functional sense because they were sent from God with a message to people who needed to hear it.

As implied above, the words **witness** and **testify** are essentially the same word from which we get our English word *martyr*. John used it often, accounting for forty-seven out of seventy-six times the word appears in the New Testament.

1:8–9. John had no problem using repetition to make a point. Though John the Baptist's message was enlightening, he was not the **true light**. We have created virtually every kind of artificial light possible for special effects on television and films. But nothing can compare with watching God's sunrise or sunset, or perhaps staring from the blackness of an Arizona desert into the night sky at stars and planets God has made. Jesus is the **true light**, not some imitation.

But what does it mean to say that Jesus **gives light to every man . . . coming into the world?** The intended contrast between the Master and the messenger strikes us dramatically: John was a man, Jesus is God; John was a witness, Jesus is the Word; John was a servant, Jesus is the Son. The last phrase of verse 9 surely refers to the incarnation of Jesus, though some have interpreted it to mean the conscience God provides every human being, or even the natural revelation everyone can see. The structure of the verse, however, favors a reference to Christ's birth even though the past tense seems awkward in this context. A major theme of this section is regeneration, and these first four verses provide its announcement.

1:10–11. Immediately after describing the announcement, John tells us about apathy toward the message of regeneration. The **world** (*kosmos*) is another of John's theme words; he used it seventy-seven times. With the device of repetition, John taught incarnation, creation, and rejection all in one verse (v. 10). Depravity and blindness thwarted God's efforts to reach out to his own creation—and still do. As Marcus Dods declared,

> There He was, the Creator Himself, that mysterious Being who had hitherto kept Himself so hidden and remote while yet so influential and supreme; the wonderful and unsearchable Source and Fountain out of which had proceeded all that men saw, themselves included— there at last He was 'in the world' He Himself had made, apparent to the eyes of men, and intelligible through their understanding; a real person whom they could know as an individual, whom they could love, who could receive and return their expressions of affection and trust. He was in the world, and the world knew Him not (Dods, p. 25).

In verse 11, the first appearance of the word **own** appears in the neuter gender and the second is masculine. What significance could such a distinction have for interpretation? One possibility is that Jesus came to earth, the place he had created, and the second tells us that the people who lived there turned him away. He was not welcomed or accepted.

1:12–13. Early in his book, John established the heart of the gospel, still two chapters away from the famous John 3:16. From the announcement of regeneration followed by apathy the apostle introduces the acceptance of regeneration.

Like most things in life, there is a right way and a wrong way to respond to God. The right way (and the only meaningful way) is to believe the gospel, receive the Savior and accept new birth as a result. The wrong way somehow links a relationship to God with human qualities such as physical birth, self-determination, or the choice of another person. In John's theological vocabulary, **believed** and **received** are synonymous when it comes to the gospel. Patrick Henry once said, "The most cherished possession I wish I could leave you is my faith in Jesus Christ, for with Him and nothing else you can be happy, but without Him and with all else, you'll never be happy" (cited in Detzler, p. 39).

Ⓒ Incarnation of the Lamb (1:14–18)

> **SUPPORTING IDEA:** *Incarnation is an important doctrinal term meaning that a spirit God took on human flesh in the form of Jesus.*

1:14. This may be the most important verse in the Bible on the doctrine of the incarnation. John went back to verse 1 to pick up one of his favorite themes, **the Word.** God became human; God showed us his glory; God offered us grace and truth; God literally "tabernacled" among us. Remember the tabernacle in the center of the camp? It represented the place of the law, the abode of God, the source of revelation, the site of sacrifice, and the focus of worship. Now in the new covenant, Jesus provides all these.

And not only was Jesus here, but he demonstrated **the glory of the One and Only.** Other prophets, including John the Baptist, were sent from God, but the Word came directly from the Father's presence. Borchert reminds us of some important implications: "This text makes it absolutely clear that the mission of the Logos was unique in the history of the world. *This uniqueness of the Son makes it impossible for Christianity to be a syncretistic religion.* In our mission to the world we cannot say 'Jesus and Caesar' or 'Jesus and Buddha,' and so forth. Our confession is Jesus, the one and only! The early Christians suffered and died because they refused to recognize any other pattern than that which was revealed in Jesus Christ" (Borchert, p. 121).

Finally, we cannot pass lightly over the wonderful phrase, **full of grace and truth.** John used the word **grace** again in verses 16 and 17, then never mentioned it for the rest of his Gospel! He used **truth** many times, but here the combination grabs us. Jesus perfectly blended two of the most important qualities of the divine nature and displayed them in human personality.

1:15–16. The full expression of John the Baptist's comparison between himself and his Lord does not appear until chapter 3, but the phraseology of verse 15 answers the question, "When did the incarnation occur?" Historically, many conservative Bible scholars place the date at 4 B.C., but that is hardly the point of this passage. The incarnation occurred at a specific point in God's plan for the world. Paul spelled it out clearly in his letter to the churches of Galatia: "But when the time had fully come, God sent his Son, born of a woman, born under law, to redeem those under law, that we might receive the full rights of sons" (Gal. 4:4–5). In time Jesus followed John the Baptist, but in importance he holds the preeminence.

At this point in his narrative theology, John the apostle could not hold back a testimony to God's grace: **We have all received one blessing after another.** Various Bible translations and paraphrases render this phrase differently:

- *NIV:* "one blessing after another"
- *KJV:* "grace for grace"
- *LB:* "blessing upon blessing heaped upon us"
- *NLT:* "one gracious blessing after another"

1:17. The contrast between law and grace forms a major portion of Pauline theology, but we get a thumbnail sketch here from John. Moses provided a standard of righteousness—that no one could meet. Then the Prophet whom Moses promised (1:25) came, and he brought a standard of righteousness centered in grace and truth. Like John the Baptist and John the apostle, Moses was a servant. But Jesus is the Son. This verse drives the dividing spike between the old and new covenants, introducing a new way of God's dealing with humankind.

1:18. This verse takes its place beside verse 14 as key passages on the incarnation, telling us that Jesus is the exclusive explanation of the Father. But did not Moses see God (see Exod. 33)? Not in this sense. Moses saw what theologians call a "theophany"—God's appearance in some temporary form. Now, John tells us, he has taken on human flesh and will live among people on earth. Some New Testament experts have translated the phrase, "God only begotten." John left no stone unturned, no argument unclarified. Jesus is the very essence of God and, according to this verse, his purpose in coming to earth was to exegete, to interpret, to explain the heavenly Father.

Numerous Bible passages remind us that Jesus came to feel what we feel, to show us what God is like, to prioritize human life—and all of that is true. But ultimately he came to die. And as John's Gospel will show, the incarnation became the gateway to the cross.

Ⓓ Forerunner of the Lamb (1:19–28)

SUPPORTING IDEA: *Believing is seeing, a message which begins with John the Baptist, now introduced as the key witness, the forerunner of the Messiah.*

1:19–22. Picture the rugged prophet John the Baptist storming up and down the desert, telling people the Messiah is coming. He wore animal skins and ate locusts and wild honey, hardly a refined rabbi with the proper credentials. So formal religious investigation gets under way. The phrase "the Jews" appears nearly seventy times in this Gospel. Sometimes it is used favorably, but more often it expresses hostility. The priests represented the Sanhedrin and the Levites guarded the correctness of temple worship. All the delegates had a simple question for John the Baptist: "Who are you?" Lest anyone confuse the messenger with the Messiah, John quickly told them, **I am not the Christ**. "Christ" (*christos*) is simply the Greek equivalent of the Hebrew *Messiah*. Both words mean "anointed."

Then they give him two other suggestions to deny, **Elijah** and **the Prophet**. No portraits of Elijah hung in first-century museums, but John may have reminded his contemporaries of the verbal descriptions in 1 Kings. More than likely, however, this dialogue referred to Malachi 4:5–6: "See, I will send you the prophet Elijah before that great and dreadful day of the LORD comes. He will turn the hearts of the fathers to their children, and the hearts of the children to their fathers; or else I will come and strike the land with a curse."

The Prophet probably referred to Moses' promise in Deuteronomy 18:15: "The LORD your God will raise up for you a prophet like me from among your own brothers. You must listen to him."

1:23. We can hardly imagine the shock the Jerusalem delegation must have felt upon hearing this rugged mountain man quote Isaiah 40:3 to describe himself. Think back to Isaiah's warnings about the future rise of Babylon with the sharp break in the narrative which begins at chapter 40 to describe the future restoration of Israel. Here is the context for John's answer:

> Comfort, comfort my people, says your God. Speak tenderly to Jerusalem, and proclaim to her that her hard service has been completed, that her sin has been paid for, that she has received from the LORD's hand double for all her sins. A voice of one calling: "In the desert prepare the way for the LORD; make straight in the wilderness a highway for our God. Every valley shall be raised up, every mountain and hill made low; the rough ground shall become level, the rugged places a plain. And the glory of the LORD will be revealed, and all mankind together will see it. For the mouth of the LORD has spoken (Isa. 40:1–5).

So John was Elijah after all (Matt. 11:14; 17:10–13). He fulfilled the prophecy of Malachi as the forerunner who would proclaim the coming of the king.

1:24–28. Enter the Pharisees, often depicted in the New Testament as the bad guys in the black hats (though there were notable exceptions like Nicodemus and Joseph of Arimathea). They were not satisfied with John's answers; they wanted a picture I.D.—particularly because John was not just preaching. He was also baptizing people without proper credentials.

John's response rings as one of the great statements of history which our text will amplify in verses 31–34. Water baptism for John's disciples was a ritual act of cleansing demonstrating repentance and anticipation of the Messiah. But already in their very midst he had come. John considered himself unworthy to do the chores of the lowest household slave—loosen Jesus' sandals.

John the Gospel writer was not as concerned with geography as Luke. But he let his readers know where it all began. We should not confuse this **Bethany** with the hometown of Mary and Martha (11:1) just outside Jerusalem. John designated it as the Bethany on **the other side of the Jordan**, east of the river.

The answers of John the Baptist offer us three important lessons as Christians: (1) We are not the focus of the witness; (2) we are not the light; and (3) we proclaim belief in Jesus.

E Appearance of the Lamb (1:29–34)

SUPPORTING IDEA: *Having explained his own ministry, John the Baptist affirmed Jesus' ministry.*

1:29. What a revelation and proclamation of the gospel! Imagine the scene as Jesus approached the area of Bethany and John spotted him in the distance. We have come to the second day of John's narrative, and we will see yet one to come in this first chapter. The first biblical mention of the Lamb appears in Genesis 22 when Abraham went to the altar to offer his son Isaac. Leviticus 14 talks about lambs as a guilt offering. John came back to it in Revelation as a triumphal title for the conquering Lord. Tenney says, "It combines in one descriptive term the concepts of innocence, voluntary sacrifice, substitutionary atonement, effective obedience, and redemptive power like that of the Passover Lamb (Exod. 12:21–27)" (Tenney, *EBC*, p. 38).

The full expression **Lamb of God** is found only here and in John 1:36. But the emphasis on substitutionary atonement and the universal offering of salvation and forgiveness of sin form the heart and core of the gospel. As we think about the theme of substitutionary atonement, our minds again rush back to the prophet Isaiah:

> Who has believed our message and to whom has the arm of the LORD been revealed? He grew up before him like a tender shoot, and like a root out of dry ground. He had no beauty or majesty to attract us to him, nothing in his appearance that we should desire him. He was despised and rejected by men, a man of sorrows, and familiar with suffering. Like one from whom men hide their faces he was despised, and we esteemed him not. Surely he took up our infirmities and carried our sorrows, yet we considered him stricken by God, smitten by him, and afflicted. But he was pierced for our transgressions, he was crushed for our iniquities; the punishment that brought us peace was upon him, and by his wounds we are healed (Isa. 53:1–5).

1:30–31. John 1:30 is a restatement of John 1:15, emphasizing again John the Baptist's claim of the priority of Christ. John admitted that he did not know his own cousin was the Messiah until Jesus' baptism in the desert.

1:32–34. The baptism of Jesus (see also Matt. 3:13–17; Mark 1:9–11; Luke 3:21–22) took place before this announcement of John 1. The purpose of his baptism, according to Jesus himself, was to fulfill all righteousness—to demonstrate his consecration to the heavenly Father and approval by him. God had obviously given John a direct revelation, telling him that when he saw the dove come down during the baptism he would know the Son of God. Dods treats the union of the Son and Spirit in the charming language of an earlier day:

> Why was the Spirit needed in a personality of which the Word, who had been with God and known God, was the basis? Because the humanity of Christ was a true humanity. Being human, he must be indebted to the Spirit for all impartation to His human nature of what is Divine. The knowledge of God which the Word possesses by experience must be humanly apprehended before it can be communicated to men; and this human apprehension can only be arrived at in the case of Christ by the enlightenment of the Spirit . . . By the Spirit He was enlightened to speak of things divine; and this Spirit, interposed, as it were, between the Word and the human nature of Jesus, was as little cumbrous in its operation or perceptible in consciousness as our breath interposed between the thinking mind and the words we speak to declare our mind (Dods, I, pp. 49–50).

John the Gospel writer continues chapter 1 in high drama. The first people who saw Jesus as the Messiah observed him not in monarchial splendor, but as a Lamb. John the Baptist tells us this Lamb came to take away the sin of the world, that he first revealed himself to Israel, and that he is the Son of God. How easy it would have been to speak in lofty theological language of Old Testament themes. But John wanted no misunderstanding among his hearers, either disciples or religious leaders, so he affirmed what he knew: **I have seen and I testify that this is the Son of God.**

🄵 Followers of the Lamb (1:35–51)

SUPPORTING IDEA: *It is important for us to remember that people come to Christ through us, not by us and certainly not to us.*

1:35–39. John's Gospel does not say much about the calling of Jesus' disciples, but the remainder of chapter 1 introduces several of them. The spotlight falls on two of John's followers, quite possibly one of them the author of these words. Upon hearing their leader announce the second time that Jesus was God's Lamb, they both left John and followed Jesus, only to have their motives challenged. **Rabbi** was a term of great respect, acknowledging Jesus as a master teacher.

The text seems to suggest that these two disciples spent the evening with the Lord (the tenth hour would have been 4 P.M.)—an evening which led to their affirmation that he was indeed the Messiah. The evening also led to witness, since Andrew began his ministry with family evangelism by bringing his brother to Jesus.

1:40–42. Jesus, these disciples would learn, sometimes issued shocking statements. The first thing he did with Peter was to change his name. **Cephas,** the Aramaic form, became **Peter,** the Greek version. Both names mean "rock." Andrew was the first disciple to follow Jesus, but he is never mentioned first in any list of the disciples in the New Testament. Peter, on the other hand, rose to dominance in the Jerusalem church. He was hardly a rock when Jesus called him, but he became that after Pentecost.

1:43–49. Philip went off to find another friend, telling Nathanael about their discovery, and mentioning Nazareth in his announcement. Nathanael asked a question which, though probably intended quite innocently at the time, has become a cliché among Bible students: **Can anything good come from there?**

Philip wasted no time arguing the point. He took Nathanael (also called Bartholomew in the New Testament) directly to Jesus. Again Jesus stunned a future disciple with his first words. He affirmed Nathanael as a genuine student of the Torah—a righteous Jew taught to live in accordance with all the light he had.

Upon learning about the Lord's omniscience—having known his exact location even before Philip found him—Nathanael, like John the Baptist, declared Jesus the Son of God and added, "You are the King of Israel." The phrase **under the fig tree** was used in rabbinical literature to describe meditation on the law. Nathanael had apparently been reading Genesis 28. Jesus contrasted Jacob's guile with Nathanael's integrity.

1:50–51. The last two verses of chapter 1 seem difficult to understand. Had Nathanael been reading about Jacob's dream under the fig tree? Is this why Jesus referred to the open heavens? Should we view this as a future prophecy? Tenney suggests that "he himself was to be the new medium of revelation, a surer link between heaven and earth than the ladder which for the errant Jacob meant a way to God" (p. 82). Whatever the interpretation, Jesus indicated that Nathanael's old covenant faith must now center in him, the focus of the new covenant. Jesus referred to himself as the **Son of Man,** a term he used more than eighty times. This title emphasized his humanity and suffering as well as the perfection of his human nature.

John 1 describes five men who met the Lord and the Lamb. All different. All believers. All models. What great lessons they teach us. We learn that witnessing is everybody's responsibility. We also learn that witnessing begins at home, either in one's own family or hometown, not necessarily by going to another country. A third lesson is that witnessing promotes the Lord, not ourselves or some personal agenda. And finally, these early disciples show us that witnessing is both verbal and specific.

During one of my pastorates, I conducted a Thursday evening visitation program, after which those of us who went out sharing the gospel would come back and describe our experiences. On one occasion I asked the group, "What did you pray as you left the building and started out to knock on doors?" One young man responded in refreshing candor, "I prayed nobody would be at home."

How often we feel that way. Witnessing sometimes seems so difficult, such an imposition on people who do not want to hear what we have to say. Yet we must learn to start at home and, without wasting words, direct people to Jesus. Like John the Baptist, we must say to our modern world, "Look, the Lamb of God!"

> **MAIN IDEA REVIEW:** *Jesus Christ is the heart and core of the gospel. Christianity is not a philosophy of life; it centers in a person who is the core of everything Christians believe.*

III. CONCLUSION

Father and Sons

Fathers and sons have a special relationship. I never experienced that from a son's point of view, but I treasure the relationship I have with my son. He is a Bible teacher too. In recent years I have invited him to speak with me at Bible conferences. Sometimes he will substitute for me in a teaching or preaching opportunity. Our theology and approach to Scripture are nearly identical, so I know he will say what I would have said had I been there—and perhaps even say it the way I would have said it.

John describes a relationship like that in this chapter. Jesus Christ the Word, the Lamb, the Son of God, came to earth to bring humanity the message of his Father. In chapter 14 he told his disciples, "Anyone who has seen me has seen the Father. How can you say, 'Show us the father'? Don't you believe that I am in the Father, and that the Father is in me? The words I say to you are not just my own. Rather, it is the Father, living in me, who is doing his work" (14:9b–10).

But Jesus also came to make sure the message of the Father came through with no error. As the Book of Hebrews declares, "In the past God spoke to our forefathers through the prophets at many times and in various ways, but in these last days he has spoken to us by his Son, whom he appointed heir of all things, and through whom he made the universe. The Son is the radiance of God's glory and the exact representation of his being, sustaining all things by his powerful word" (1:1–3a).

Thirty years ago I wrote the biography of Dr. Walter L. Wilson, a prominent physician and evangelist during the years after World War II. Much of the information came through personal interviews, but Dr. Wilson went to heaven while the book was being written. So the manuscript was affirmed and corroborated by Walter L. Wilson, Jr., representing his father and pronouncing that the message about his father was indeed true.

John the Gospel writer did not wait until chapter 3 or 4 to take us into the temple; in chapter 1 we have already entered the Holy of Holies. This first chapter contains more theology than some congregations hear in a year. May God grant us the understanding to grasp it and to let it impact our lives.

PRINCIPLES

- Jesus Christ is God in human flesh.
- Jesus Christ is the foremost revelation of the Father.
- Jesus Christ is God's provision for our sin.
- Jesus Christ is our teacher and king.

APPLICATIONS

- Be sure people understand you are only a messenger, not the message itself.
- Understand the theology of the Lamb.
- Make sure you treat others with grace and truth.
- Be ready to follow Jesus anywhere.

IV. LIFE APPLICATION

Sparrows in Winter

Paul Harvey tells about a raw winter night on which a farmer heard a thumping sound against the kitchen door. He went to a window and watched as tiny, shivering sparrows, attracted to the warmth inside, beat in vain against the glass storm door.

The farmer bundled up and trudged through fresh snow to open the barn for the struggling birds. He turned on the lights, tossed some hay in a corner, and sprinkled a trail of saltine crackers to direct them to the barn. But the sparrows hid in the darkness, afraid of him.

He tried various tactics: circling behind the birds to drive them toward the barn, tossing crumbs in the air toward them, retreating to his house to see if they would flutter into the barn on their own. Nothing worked. He had terrified them; the birds could not understand that he was trying to help them.

He withdrew to his house and watched the doomed sparrows through a window. As he stared, a thought hit him like lightning from a clear blue sky: *If only I could become a bird—one of them—just for a moment, then I would not frighten them so. I could show them the way to warmth and safety.* At the same moment, another thought dawned on him: *He had grasped the whole principle of the incarnation.*

A man's becoming a bird is nothing compared to God's becoming a man. The concept of a sovereign being as big as the universe confining himself to a human body is too much for some people to believe (cited in Swindoll, *The Tardy Oxcart,* pp. 294–95).

We began this chapter by quoting a few lines by Charles Wesley. The text first appeared in 1739 and was altered numerous times before it took its present form in George Whitefield's *Collection of Hymns for Social Worship* in 1753. The hymn tune was adapted from the second movement of Felix Mendelsshon's *Festgesang, Opus 68,* composed in 1840. This magnificent combination of text and tune provides not only a Christmas hymn but an exercise in New Testament doctrine every time we sing it. The message of John's first chapter fills homes and churches every December with the songs of the people of the Lamb.

V. PRAYER

Father, thank you for Jesus our Creator and Savior. May his life and light shine through us, even though the darkness around us may not understand it. Amen.

VI. DEEPER DISCOVERIES

A. Word (1:1–3)

Appearing some 330 times in the New Testament, the word *logos* is familiar to many people who have never studied Greek. John used it no fewer than sixty-five times in his writings, forty of those found in this Gospel. The noun refers to a message or pronouncement, either oral or written. John used it to refer to the Old Testament, or the words of Jesus, or to Jesus himself. Henry Blackaby spells it out: "Thus, the primary use of *logos* is to denote divine revelation in some form or another. John used the term in its most exalted sense when he personified *logos* to refer to Christ. The *Logos* eternally existed as God (the Son) and with God (the Father)—He was in fact the Creator (John 1:1–3)—but He became a human being (v. 14), Jesus of Nazareth, so that He could reveal the Father and His will for humanity (v. 18)" (Blackaby, p. 2).

B. Life (1:4)

Ever been to a zoo? The word *zoo* and all the other words built around it (like *zoology*) are based on the Greek word *zoe,* which is also sometimes used as a woman's name. Detzler tells us how it was applied by the ancient Greeks: "In ancient Greece the word referred to the natural life which is shared by animals and people. Aristotle used it to describe the procreative processes whereby life is multiplied. In classical Greek it meant any self-movement, in contrast with mechanical movement. Plato extended the word to mean both mortal and immortal life. The Stoics felt that one should live in accordance with the life principle of the universe. For Plato, life could be divided between the here and the hereafter" (Detzler, p. 216).

But like many Greek words, *zoe* takes different meanings in the New Testament where it appears 260 times. All life comes from God the Creator, but different kinds of *zoe* must be acknowledged—physical, spiritual, and eternal. All forms of life come through the power of Jesus who described himself by saying, "I am the way and the truth and the life. No one comes to the Father except through me" (John 14:6).

C. Light (1:4–5)

In addition to *zoo* and its cognates, your vocabulary surely contains the words *photograph* and *phosphorus,* to name just two English words springing from the Greek word *phos.* We find this word in the New Testament seventy-two times, almost half of them in the Gospel of John. Satan represents darkness; Jesus represents light. The bad news is that we live in a world of darkness. The good news is that the darkness cannot overwhelm the light. One significant segment of our book carrying the message of light appears in the words of Jesus himself.

Here are those verses in Peterson's paraphrase: "This is the crisis we're in: God-light streamed into the world, but men and women everywhere ran for the darkness. They went for the darkness because they were not really interested in pleasing God. Everyone who makes a practice of doing evil, addicted to denial and illusion, hates God-light and won't come near it, fearing a painful exposure. But anyone working and living in truth and reality welcomes God-light so the work can be seen for the God-work it is" (John 3:19–21, *The Message*).

D. World (1:10)

Here is another Greek lesson, and this time the English word sounds exactly like its Greek ancestor. The universe is often called the "cosmos" from the Greek word *kosmos.* The ancient Greeks used this word to describe a building or a city or even a culture. This common word for "world" appears 188 times in the New Testament, often referring to the earth and its inhabitants, the sinful society alien to God's truth. Hence we get the concept "worldliness." Pastors often remind us that even Christians can be "worldly" in the sense that they can focus their attention on possessions and entertainment rather than God's Word and the work of the Holy Spirit in their lives. The characteristic of the lost world is precisely the darkness we discussed above.

Boice puts it this way: "Why was it that the world did not know and recognize the Lord Jesus Christ when He was present? The first answer to that question is that the world did not want Him. We know from experience that if a man does not want to see a truth (or an injustice either, for that matter), he will not see it. So, in exactly the same way, men and women did not recognize the Lord Jesus Christ primarily because they did not want to recognize Him" (Boice, I, p. 63).

E. Born of God (1:13)

Non-Christians commonly associate the term *born again* with believers, but in actuality the word *again* does not describe the process adequately. John 1:13 talks about being "born of God" and John 3:3 about being "born again." Both phrases refer to a second birth. Peter spoke twice of being born again, using the word *anagennao* (1 Pet. 1:3,23), but John used only the word *born* without the prefix *ana*. Probably some of our modern grasp of the term comes from Chuck Colson's testimony book entitled *Born Again*.

The evangelist George Whitefield once wrote to Benjamin Franklin, "As you have made a pretty considerable progress in the mysteries of electricity, I would now honestly recommend to your diligent unprejudiced pursuit and study the mysteries of the new birth."

VII. TEACHING OUTLINE

A. INTRODUCTION

1. Lead Story: Confusing Pictures
2. Context: Writing about A.D. 90, John looked back more than six decades to approximately A.D. 26 or 27 and the beginning of Jesus' public ministry. In one sweeping chapter he pulled together the doctrines of creation, incarnation, and regeneration; introduced the Lamb of God to his readers; and described the gathering of Jesus' first disciples. John 1 is one of the most doctrinally rich chapters in the Bible.
3. Transition: Following on the heels of the three synoptic Gospels in the arrangement of New Testament books, John introduced a different way of looking at the life of Jesus with greater focus on Jesus' message than the events of his earthly life.

B. COMMENTARY

1. Revelation of the Lamb (1:1–5)
   a. Revelation of eternality (1:1a)
   b. Revelation of personality (1:1b)
   c. Revelation of deity (1:1c–2)
   d. Revelation of creativity (1:3)
   e. Revelation of life (1:4)
   f. Revelation of light (1:5)
2. Purpose of the Lamb (1:6–13)
   a. Announcement of regeneration (1:6–9)
   b. Apathy toward regeneration (1:10–11)
   c. Acceptance of regeneration (1:12–13)
3. Incarnation of the Lamb (1:14–18)
   a. What is the incarnation? (1:14)
   b. When did it occur? (1:15–16)
   c. Why did God design it as he did? (1:17–18)
4. Forerunner of the Lamb (1:19–28)
   a. Examination by the Jews (1:19–22)
   b. Explanation by John (1:23–28)
5. Appearance of the Lamb (1:29–34)
   a. Recognition by John (1:29–31)
   b. Baptism by the Spirit (1:32–34)
6. Followers of the Lamb (1:35–51)
   a. John and Andrew (1:35–40)
   b. Simon Peter (1:41–42)
   c. Philip and Nathanael (1:43–51)

C. CONCLUSION: SPARROWS IN WINTER

VIII. ISSUES FOR DISCUSSION

1. How can your family and church focus all year long on the importance of the incarnation?
2. Name some ways Christians "follow" the Lamb today.
3. How was the baptism of John the Baptist different than Christian baptism today?

John 2

The Master of Weddings and Worship

I. **INTRODUCTION**
Family Breakdown

II. **COMMENTARY**
A verse-by-verse explanation of the chapter.

III. **CONCLUSION**
Lessons from a Sheep's Tail

An overview of the principles and applications from the chapter.

IV. **LIFE APPLICATION**
Prince of the Outcasts

Melding the chapter to life.

V. **PRAYER**
Tying the chapter to life with God.

VI. **DEEPER DISCOVERIES**
Historical, geographical, and grammatical enrichment of the commentary.

VII. **TEACHING OUTLINE**
Suggested step-by-step group study of the chapter.

VIII. **ISSUES FOR DISCUSSION**
Zeroing the chapter in on daily life.

Quote

"*F*ellowship and worship, then, is genuine Christianity freely shared among God's family members. It's sad to think of how many Christians today are missing that kind of closeness. Sermons and songs, while uplifting and necessary, provide only part of a vital church encounter. We need involvement with others too. If we roll in and out of church each week without acquiring a few grape juice stains, we really haven't tasted the sweet wine of fellowship."

A n n e   O r t l u n d

GEOGRAPHICAL PROFILE: CANA

- Mentioned four times in the Gospel of John (2:1–11; 4:46–54; 21:2) and nowhere else in Scripture
- Some locate the modern site at Kefr-Kenna near Nazareth
- At Cana Jesus announced the healing of the nobleman's son (John 4:46)

GEOGRAPHICAL PROFILE: CAPERNAUM

- Headquarters of Jesus' ministry in Galilee
- Site of many of Jesus' miracles
- Home of Matthew
- Location of the discourse on the Bread of Life and many other teachings (Mark 9:33–50)

PERSONAL PROFILE: MARY

- The mother of Jesus is referred to twice in this Gospel, but not by name (2:1; 19:25)
- Descendent of David in the tribe of Judah
- Not to be confused with at least five other Marys mentioned in the New Testament

John 2

IN A NUTSHELL

In celebration or convocation, Jesus must be the focus of our lives.

The Master of Weddings and Worship

I. INTRODUCTION

Family Breakdown

*I*n August of 1996, publishers released a new magazine entitled *Divorce*. It has become an increasingly popular piece since there are now more than a million divorces a year in the United States. Many staff members of the new magazine, including editor Gloria Sheppard, came from marriage magazines such as *Bride* and *Wedding*. One ad in the premier issue featured a special service to remove an ex-spouse's image from a couple's photos.

Such is life in the early twenty-first century, yet we still celebrate weddings with all the enthusiasm and pomp we have come to expect. But a culture of single parents, pregnant teenagers, and general moral instability sets a dark backdrop for the success of marriage unions not grounded in faith and commitment.

Sociologist Daniel Yankelovich spells it out:

> Americans suspect that the nation's economic difficulties are rooted not in technical economic forces (for example, exchange rates or capital formation) but in fundamental moral causes. There exists a deeply intuitive sense that the success of a market-based economy depends on a highly developed social morality—trustworthiness, honesty, concern for future generations, an ethic of service to others, a humane society that takes care of those in need, frugality instead of greed, high standards of quality and concern for community. These economically desirable social values, in turn, are seen as rooted in family values. Thus the link in public thinking between a healthy family and a robust economy, though indirect, is clear and firm (cited in Anderson, p. 118).

In light of the strong biblical call for family stability in both Old and New Testaments, we should not be surprised at the way John began the narrative of Jesus' public ministry. The first miracle took place in a very natural setting, one of the timeless celebrations of human history. Pressures and joys combine on such occasions and Jesus did not shy away from social events. He and the disciples were probably invited to this wedding because of Mary's relationship to the family. Just two days after John the Baptist announced Jesus as the Lamb of God, Jesus showed up at a wedding which became the stage and background curtain for the changing of water to wine.

II. COMMENTARY

The Master of Weddings and Worship

MAIN IDEA: *Jesus clearly understood that his purpose on earth was to bring glory to the Father.*

 ### A The Master and His Mother (2:1–4)

SUPPORTING IDEA: *Weddings create opportunities for families to glorify God and witness their faith.*

2:1–3. Many commentaries invest endless pages in an exploration of the chronology at the beginning of John 2. **The third day** from when? Possibly three days after Philip and Nathanael had become disciples of Jesus. Or perhaps three days after Jesus' departure from the place of his baptism. The exact identification seems unimportant, but we should note that less than a week went by between Jesus' appearance in the desert and the miracle at Cana.

Jesus' mother had been invited to this event and Jesus accompanied her. The Lord was always welcome among those having a good time in the right way. Running out of wine represented a social disaster much greater in the first century than it would today. Disgrace, humiliation, insult—all these and more would be brought upon the family with such carelessness as to allow this to happen. Wedding celebrations in that day sometimes lasted nearly a week, so the wine supply was a major consideration.

This small town was the home of Nathanael, who might have known the host family as well as the bride and groom. A major lesson surfaces even in these early verses: weddings create opportunities for families to focus on Jesus.

2:4. After the remark of Mary to Jesus ("they have no more wine"), the Lord's response gives rise to even more confusion among commentators. Did he rebuke Mary for her implied request? Was he relieving her of responsibility by saying in effect, "I'll take care of it"? Did he receive her statement and respond with another question which might be interpreted as, "What would you like me to do?"

The Greek text literally reads, *What to me and to you, woman?* Jesus was probably not saying, "This is not our problem; let them figure it out." Perhaps he wanted to emphasize to Mary that they had come into a new relationship with her remark. This may be the first time that she had asked her son for help on a public occasion. For Jesus it was his first opportunity to work under the heavenly Father's authority and through the Holy Spirit's power to produce a miraculous sign.

The last part of verse 4 seems to explain the first part—**My time has not yet come.** The word translated **time** in the NIV is actually *hora*, the common word for *hour*. These two terms are used somewhat interchangeably in John. Four times more in this Gospel we are told that Jesus delayed something or that his enemies could not seize him because his time had not yet come. But as he approached the time of his death on the cross, Jesus prayed, "Father, the time has come" (John 17:1).

Mary had carried the stigma of Jesus' miraculous birth for thirty years. It was only natural she would want some public revelation that her son was the Messiah. Jesus seemed to be saying, however, "What you expect out of this will not occur yet. I'm on a divine timetable and the revelation of my purpose will not happen today." But God's timetable for the Lamb did allow him to begin giving evidence of his calling by performing this local miracle.

B The Master and His Method (2:5–8)

SUPPORTING IDEA: *Weddings create opportunities for service to God.*

2:5. This timeless spiritual principle lives on through two thousand years of church history: **Do whatever he tells you.** Mary's faith stood strong; she knew that Jesus could do whatever was necessary in the situation as long as the servants obeyed. This is probably true in any family or congregation which has, in some way, run out of spiritual wine. If we as servants obey and trust the power of Jesus, God is capable of any results. Of this verse Archbishop Trench writes, "Luther bids us here to imitate her faith, who, nothing daunted by the semblance of a refusal, reads between the lines of this refusal a better answer to her prayer; is confident that even the infirmity which clave to it shall not defeat it altogether; is so confident of this, as to indicate not obscurely the very manner of its granting" (Trench, p. 110).

2:6–7. Notice the phrase, **six stone water jars . . . each holding from twenty to thirty gallons.** These containers held a total of at least 120 gallons. The servants were told to fill them with water, and they did so—**to the brim.** Such washing pots were used in religious ceremonies, but they were about to enter a new phase of operation. Tenney clarifies the magnitude of the liquid refreshment created on this occasion: "The combined capacity of the water pots was about 150 gallons. Reckoning a half-pint to a glass, these vessels would contain about 2,400 servings of wine—certainly enough to supply a large number of people for several days. In quality and quantity the new-made wine more than satisfied the needs and taste of those who attended the feast" (Tenney, *EBC*, p. 83).

2:8. From these jars Jesus chose the servants to **draw some out and take it to the master of the banquet.** Not to the waiters nor the maitre'd, but to the master. These servants knew they were handling water when the host asked for wine. We have to conclude that the water became wine somewhere between the kitchen and the head table at the banquet. This demonstrates great faith and obedience on the part of these servants. Despite misgivings, they followed through on Mary's words.

Let us back up for a moment and talk again about this **master of the banquet**. Tenney suggests "toastmaster," a word we would today associate with master of ceremonies. The important idea, regardless of title, helps us see these servants making a public commitment, not discussing matters with their manager in the back room. They marched out with the "water." When the public reception of what Jesus had accomplished was obvious to many at the party, it was wine.

The Master and His Miracle (2:9–11)

SUPPORTING IDEA: *Weddings create opportunity for us to glorify God.*

2:9–10. John carefully drew the narrative to indicate that the master tasted the wine and, probably much to the amazement of the trembling servants, pronounced it the best of the evening. Many interpreters have pondered whether Jesus created intoxicating wine, and arguments have been raised on both sides. The word *oinos* is of no help since it is used for both intoxicating and non-intoxicating wine. We can hardly imagine, however, that people who had been drinking throughout the evening would not immediately recognize a switch from normal wine to grape juice.

Perhaps we must simply recognize that the culture of the day accepted and even demanded drinking on occasions like this. The most we can say here is that this passage cannot support abstinence, but verse 10 hints at the importance of moderation. Whatever we believe or do not believe about the use of alcoholic beverages will have to draw support from some other passage.

Just as this wedding ran out of wine, humankind ran out of fellowship with God in the Garden of Eden. When sin entered the world, the celebration ceased—but Jesus came to restore our reason to celebrate. Wine is even used sometimes in Scripture as a picture of joy: "Wine that gladdens the heart of man, oil to make his face shine, and bread that sustains his heart" (Ps. 104:15).

Just as the banquet master said that most people brought out the best wine first and the cheap wine once senses were dulled, in the same way the world throws its best pictures of sin at us to trick us, then the cheap stuff comes along. Eventually the joy and pleasure the world offers through sin runs out. But God's joy lasts forever and he saves his best blessings for last. As Christians we always have more to look forward to because heaven reminds us that God saves the best wine for the end of the party.

2:11. The results of the first miracle? Two things happened: Jesus **revealed his glory** by this miraculous sign, and **his disciples put their faith in him.** Certainly they had some faith before this event, but now it was strengthened, solidified, and stabilized. Now they were ready to follow him anywhere.

We should never ignore the little ways in which Jesus did his miracles, especially when we read the word *sign* (*semeion*) as we do here in verse 11. The ceremonial washing of hands for which these jars had always been used was put aside and replaced with something new. The Lamb came to fulfill the Mosaic Law and exchange it for higher law—the law of grace. He would fulfill ceremonial cleansing with complete, spiritual, and eternal cleansing of his own blood on the cross.

The disciples surely did not understand this part of the sign at the moment. But when Jesus held a cup of wine at the Last Supper and said, "This cup is the new covenant in my blood, which is poured out for you" (Luke 22:20), we wonder if any of them remembered the wedding in Cana where old covenant water became new covenant wine.

What a fitting picture of Christ's submission. The continual need for cleansing water reminded the Israelites that they were constantly unclean. But Jesus would offer his cleansing blood as the wine that would satisfy forever.

And what a wonderful sign for us. We do not need animal sacrifices and ceremonial cleansing water because Jesus has poured out his blood as the final and perfect sacrifice for our sins. We have complete forgiveness and cleansing because we've been washed in the blood of the Lamb. This is no trivial miracle to satisfy the thirst of partygoers but a clear symbol with a magnificent message. Christ transformed temple-cleansing water into eternal-saving wine. To those of us who have no wine of our own, he offers his blood for eternal life.

D The Master and the Market (2:12–16)

SUPPORTING IDEA: *Worship is not commercial activity; it is connecting with the Father in spirit and in truth through Jesus Christ the Lamb.*

2:12. John made a clear transition in his narrative as he showed us Jesus and his disciples heading to Capernaum, and from there on to Jerusalem for the Passover—the first such festival mentioned in the Lord's three-and-one-half-year ministry. We may assume that up to this point Jesus had maintained a comfortable relationship with his family but now he left them in Galilee and his disciples took the place of his mother and half-brothers as his constant companions.

The body of all New Testament passages taken together tells us that Mary and Joseph had other children after the supernatural birth of Jesus. Some have suggested that these **brothers** were former children of Joseph by a first marriage. This position is intended to uphold the perpetual virginity of Mary, but it is not supported by Scripture. In the words of Morris, "The most natural way of taking [brothers] is to understand children of Joseph and Mary. This is called the 'Helvidian' view (from Helvidius, a fourth century theologian who advocated it). The expression occurs several times in the Synoptic Gospels, and never with any qualification such as would be expected if the words were to bear any other meaning. The view is supported by appealing to the statements that Joseph 'knew her not till she had brought forth a son' (Matt. 1:25) and that Jesus was Mary's 'firstborn son' (Luke 2:7)" (Morris, p. 187).

2:13–14. It was April and the great feast of the Passover was in session for one week in Jerusalem. What a different scene there than in Jesus' home town of Nazareth or the other surrounding small towns of Cana and Capernaum. This was "the big apple," and the Lord did not like what he saw. The feast included the eating of the Passover Lamb which commemorated the passing of death over the Israelites before their departure from Egypt. Sometimes known as the Feast of Unleavened Bread, Passover was held in the first month of the sacred year, the seventh month of the civil year.

The merchandise described in verse 14 was required for sacrifices. Worshipers had traveled from great distances, and the availability of sacrificial animals was essential to temple worship. So what was the problem? The key phrase appears at the beginning of verse 14—**in the temple courts**—the place where Gentiles could pray. Furthermore, in Jesus' day, these concession stands had become "cash cows," an insult to the Father and a desecration of the Father's house.

2:15–16. Though we would not respond the same way, we should also be upset by the crass commercialism of some religious activity in churches and on radio or television. But we are startled to see the gentle Lamb make a whip and drive the merchants out of the temple.

Interpreters do not agree on whether the Lord actually used violence on the merchants, suggesting that perhaps the scourge was only the sign of authority, or perhaps only used on the animals. But certainly he knocked over the tables. There seems to be a miraculous element in one man overcoming a large group of merchants, who must have been determined to protect their businesses.

The central problem with this text is not whether it contains a miracle, but the unusual placement of the event by John at the beginning of Jesus' ministry. The Synoptic writers connect the cleansing of the temple to Jesus' last visit to Jerusalem at the time of his death (Matt. 21:10–17; Mark 11:15–19; Luke 19:45–46). We have three choices here: (1) John is right and the Synoptics are wrong; (2) there were two similar occasions, one recorded only by John and the other only by the Synoptics; or (3) John has rearranged his material for theological purposes.

Assuming serious Bible students would reject the first option, I hasten to note that no less a scholar than Tenney chooses the second: "It is not at all improbable that He may have cleansed the temple twice, two Passovers apart, and that the second so enraged the hierarchy that their animosity toward Him exploded into drastic action. Interfering with their privileges once was impudent, twice would be inexcusable" (Tenney, p. 44).

Borchert, on the other hand, calls this the greatest historical problem in John and says, "The familiar argument of two cleansings is a historiographic monstrosity that has no basis in the texts of the Gospels" (Borchert, p. 160).

Both Tasker and Morris, eminent scholars of the Gospel of John, agree with Tenney. I find myself drawn to Borchert's argument, particularly in view of the emphasis all students of John must see in the compelling power of his purpose. As Borchert puts it

> Why should John have to write his Gospel as a modern newspaper reporter? His purpose was not to report but to proclaim and persuade (20:30–31). He was a great inspired artist and theologian who organized his episodes from the life of Jesus in such a way as to bring people to faith in Jesus as the Son of God. What is more, the evangelist viewed the story of Jesus in its entirety from a *postresurrection perspective*. The evangelist even told us what he was doing in this very section (2:22). At the time of writing, Jesus was not then living on earth and facing death; He was reigning in power with God (Borchert, p. 161).

Ⓔ The Master and His Meaning (2:17–22)

SUPPORTING IDEA: *Worship cannot be relegated to a building like the temple; it centers in the person of Christ himself.*

2:17. This verse seems curious, and we wonder why the disciples happened to remember Psalm 69:9 on this occasion. Certainly the reference of that verse to Christ would indicate a messianic realization, and he had just referred to the temple as "my Father's house." We learn here a certain holy concern for the sanctity of places of worship even though place is not the central issue. Israel had zeal without knowledge; now God was going to demand a blend of those two important qualities.

2:18–21. Since Jews required signs (1 Cor. 1:22), that is exactly what they did here, only to hear Jesus say, **Destroy this temple, and I will raise it again in three days.** That magnificent building had been started by Herod in 20 B.C., and this conversation took place in approximately A.D. 26. The construction process would still go on for thirty-seven more years until its completion in A.D. 63. The temple would stand complete for only seven years before being destroyed by the armies of Titus in A.D. 70. These words would not be forgotten by the crowds, however, and mockers would repeat the charge as Jesus hung on the cross (Matt. 27:40; Mark 15:29).

Like the water turned into wine, the new would again replace the old. This time, the system of worship would be replaced. As Tasker points out:

> The mission of Jesus was far from being merely negative and destructive. He had come to make possible a more direct approach by men to God in a purer worship by offering His own body in sacrifice, an offering whose acceptance by the Father as an all-sufficient atonement would be signified by His resurrection on the third day. All believers who accepted His sacrifice would become part of His body and so enabled to offer themselves, in Paul's words, 'A living sacrifice, holy, acceptable unto God' (Rom. xii., I). This is the truth conveyed in the somewhat enigmatical words recorded by John as Jesus' answer to the demand by the Jews for a sign (Tasker, pp. 63–64).

As happened so often during his earthly ministry, Jesus was misunderstood and misinterpreted. Taken by surprise with the answer in verse 19, the Jews could only apply it in their limited understanding to the temple beside which they were standing at that moment. But the Lord spoke of his resurrection. The building was not the issue, but his body. Sometimes in such language the contrast is with the temple and the literal body of Jesus. In our day we must make this distinction between a church facility and the people of God who use it.

2:22. John spoke for the other disciples when he observed that they did not think much of this phrase at the moment but remembered it later after Jesus' resurrection. Only then did they believe the Scripture and the words Jesus had spoken. But worship is always related to the words of Jesus and never linked with a building, as much as we like to think in Old Testament terms of a special "temple where we meet God." We will see this with greater clarity in chapter 4. This Gospel always presents Jesus in light of his resurrection, which is what we should expect, knowing when John wrote. He had seen the effects across nearly five decades of the preaching of an empty tomb around the Mediterranean world. John wasted no time inserting the doctrine of resurrection alongside creation, incarnation, and regeneration.

But what **Scripture** did they believe after the resurrection which they somehow linked with the promise of Jesus? According to Morris, "In the singular 'scripture' usually refers to a single passage. If this is the case it is not easy to identify the passage in mind. It may perhaps be Ps. 16:10, which is interpreted as the resurrection in Acts 2:31; 13:35. Or it may be Isa. 53:12, which is not unfairly understood of the resurrection for it speaks of the activity of the Servant after His death. There is a reference to being raised on the third day in Hos. 6:2, but this does not seem at all relevant to the resurrection of Christ" (Morris, p. 204).

I suggest we not worry about a specific passage here, at least as we consider application in our own lives. Knowing a specific "proof text" is not nearly as productive in overall Christian life and service as our dependence upon the Bible and its authoritative and infallible message of God's truth. Boice lays it on the line: "How does it stand with you? Do you approach things scripturally as God wants you to? Or are you still trying to puzzle out God's truth with your own weak faculties of reasoning? The Bible tells us that we will only advance spiritually and that we will only hear God's voice as we approach Him through the pages of His book" (Boice, I, p. 219).

F The Master and His Motive (2:23–25)

SUPPORTING IDEA: *Not all faith is saving faith; God honors only faith that selects the right object.*

2:23. This verse contains a key word in our Gospel as we read about Jesus' **signs.** Numerous miracles took place at this time, but the description of them does not fit John's purpose. As we have already seen, John emphasizes the message of Jesus rather than his miracles. Nevertheless, miracles led people to believe in his name. It sounds like a great evangelistic effort, as though the band of disciples was building rapidly in the big city. All the sign-miracles of John were revelations of Christ's glory, and the disciples often did not understand their spiritual significance.

The word *semeion* ("sign") appears sixteen times in John's Gospel and twenty-three times in his entire writings. Two other words describe miracles in the New Testament: *dunamis* ("power") and *teras* ("wonder"). "The distinction between the three terms is one of emphasis: *semeion* refers to the purpose of the miracle; *dunamis* refers to the source that enables someone to perform the miracle; and *teras* refers to the reaction of the crowd when a miracle was performed. John's favorite term for Jesus' miracles was *semeion* (*dunamis* does not occur and *teras* occurs only once, 4:48), for he emphasized the purpose for these miracles: they revealed who Jesus was so that people would believe in Him (20:30–31)" (Blackaby, p. 6).

But we're about to see a significant difference between the belief of verse 22 and the belief of verse 23.

2:24–25. John 2:24 is one of the most important verses in this Gospel because it reminds us that in the New Testament the word *believe* does not always mean that a person has placed genuine faith in Jesus. The spectators in Jerusalem must have exercised only intellectual assent—perhaps agreeing that Jesus might be some significant prophet who has come among the people. But the Lord looked right into their hearts and saw their motives. Their faith had been placed in his works rather than in his person. Therefore, he would **not entrust himself to them.** The Greek text is helpful at this point since the verb "believe" (*episteuo*) appears in three consecutive verses (vv. 22–24).

The disciples believed Jesus' words and the Scripture only after his resurrection. The people in Jerusalem claimed to believe, but Jesus did not believe their belief. The NIV translation for **would not entrust** is the same essential root as the words translated "believed" in the two previous verses. The past tense indicates ongoing action in verse 24. Jesus continuously did not trust their claims to faith. The second verb of the verse (**knew**) is in the present tense, indicating that he knew the hearts of all people all the time. This includes modern believers.

For emphasis, John repeated that thought in verse 25. The Lord looks at our hearts to examine whether what we say we believe really represents our inner selves. Borchert sums it up nicely in the context of this Gospel:

> When John wrote this Gospel, he knew that Jesus performed many signs and that people said they believed. John also knew that Jesus died and that while he had no intention of abandoning the believers (14:18), they could not avoid abandoning him. For John, then, there was good reason for Jesus not to believe people's believing. Thus, when we read the stories of John, we must not treat them simply as stories from the past. They are also in fact living portraits of humanity in every era. Accordingly, we need to understand that the living Jesus does not believe everyone's believing because *he knows* what is in them. Those words ought to stand as a warning to everyone (Borchert, p. 168).

MAIN IDEA REVIEW: *Jesus clearly understood that his purpose on earth was to bring glory to the Father.*

III. CONCLUSION

Lessons from a Sheep's Tail

Abraham Lincoln, known for his homespun humor, once asked, "How many legs would a sheep have if you called a tail a leg?" Someone answered, "Five," to which Lincoln replied, "No. Calling something a leg does not make it so."

And calling *believing* "saving faith" does not make it saving faith. In the context of Scripture, saving faith has three essential elements: intellectual assent, spiritual appropriation, and personal commitment. It would appear that here we see only the first in the crowds, though the disciples have certainly moved on to some spiritual appropriation. Their personal commitment developed slowly through the years they walked with the Lord.

And let us not forget the faithful obedience of the servants in the first part of chapter 2. Nothing is said about spiritual change in the Cana account, but at the very end we learn that the result on the part of his disciples was that they "put their faith in him" (2:11).

So we have two definitive signs leading to declared faith. At the wedding feast people saw a sign of glory—Christ's creative power to transform; a sign of joy—Christ's ability to turn humiliation into celebrations; and a sign of calling—Christ's commitment to the purposes and timing of the Father.

In Jerusalem we see a sign of anger—Christ's attitude when he sees what has happened at the temple; a sign of power—Christ's action with the money-changers in cleansing the temple; and a sign of authority—Christ's prophecy of the resurrection.

PRINCIPLES

- We should glorify God in all aspects of our lives, including public worship and public parties.
- We should never overlook an opportunity for ministry to others through the normal events of our lives.
- We must never limit worship to a building, no matter how large or imposing it might be.
- We best honor the Father by recognizing the authority of the Son.

APPLICATIONS

- "Do whatever he tells you."
- Think about how Jesus has "revealed his glory" in you.
- Never confuse true worship with the crass commercialism of media religion.
- In worship, concentrate on faith—not format.

IV. LIFE APPLICATION

Prince of the Outcasts

There is an old story about the Prince of Wales visiting India when that country was part of the vast British Empire, upon whose domain it was said that the sun never set. The caste system prevailed at that time, and local officials had erected barriers in the first city that the prince visited. After greeting local officials, he commanded, "Take those barriers down." In the next city ten thousand people gathered to welcome him under a banner carefully lettered in English—"Prince of the Outcasts."

Jesus the Lamb, Jesus the Messiah, Jesus the Son of God is the ultimate prince of the outcasts. An outcast rejected by his own people, he stands as heaven's prince welcoming men and women, boys and girls of all colors and races to approach the throne of heaven's King through the crucified and resurrected prince. And the Gospel of John is the story of how he removed all barriers to that access.

Jesus is the master of weddings and worship, and both cry out for his involvement in our lives. A relationship to the Prince comes not through form or formality, but through faith and freedom. To those who struggle with religious legalism, skepticism, agnosticism, or just plain ignorance of truth and grace, he says, "Take those barriers down."

V. PRAYER

Father, thank you for every opportunity you give us to show visible grace—at home, at church, or at parties. Amen.

VI. DEEPER DISCOVERIES

A. Miracles in John (chs. 2,4,5,6,9,11)

Almost every commentary you read will list seven miracles in the Gospel of John:

1. Turning water to wine (ch. 2)
2. Healing of the official's son (ch. 4)
3. Healing of the invalid man at Bethesda (ch. 5)
4. Feeding of the five thousand (ch. 6)
5. Walking on the water (ch. 6)
6. Healing the man born blind (ch. 9)
7. Raising Lazarus (ch. 11)

All Bible students agree that Jesus' resurrection was a miracle. But they do not list it with his miracles because it was performed by the Father and Jesus' earthly body was the object rather than the initiator of the miracle. But two others remain in question. The NIV Study Bible, for example, lists eight miracles, including the miraculous catch of fish (21:1–11). I tend to agree, though that would be a minority viewpoint.

I raise this issue here in connection with chapter 2 because some interpreters have suggested that the cleansing of the temple was a miracle which—when we include Jesus' resurrection—would bring the total to ten rather than seven.

The number is of small importance except when we compare John's list with the three Synoptics and review again his purpose. Matthew records twenty-one miracles, Mark twenty, and Luke twenty-one. So we find John at less than one-half the level of the other writers (whose materials he had in hand when he wrote). This emphasizes John's careful selection process and his emphasis on message rather than miracles.

Nor should we forget that John's focus on regeneration shows us that spiritual miracles are more important than physical miracles. Writing in 1904, long before the modern signs-and-wonders movement, Archbishop Richard C. Trench makes the point in the quaint vocabulary of his day.

> While then it does not greatly concern us to know *when* this power was withdrawn, what does vitally concern us is, that we suffer not these carnal desires after miracles, as though they were certainly saints who had them, and they but imperfect Christians who were without them, as though the Church were inadequately furnished and spiritually impoverished which could not show them, to rise up in our hearts; being, as they are, ever ready to rise up in the natural heart of man, to which power is so much dearer than holiness. There is no surer proof than the utterance of sentiments such as these, that the true glory of the Church is hidden from our eyes—that some of its outward trappings and ornaments have caught our fancy; and not the fact that it is all-glorious within, answering to the deepest needs of the spirit of man, which has taken possession of our hearts and minds. It is little which we ourselves have known of the miracles of grace, when *they* seem to us poor and pale, when only the miracles of power have any attraction in our eyes (Trench, p. 61).

B. "My Time Has Not Yet Come" (2:4)

This phraseology (see also 7:6,8,30; 8:20) depicts the Lamb moving inexorably to the slaughter. No other human being had any idea that the cross lay three and one-half years beyond the changing from water to wine, but Jesus walked a straight line from the moment of his baptism to the triumph of his resurrection. And he kept trying to explain to the disciples how their understanding of timing could not match the Father's. Finally, beginning the last week of his life Jesus said, "The hour has come for the Son of Man to be glorified" (12:23) and just a few verses later, "Now my heart is troubled, and what shall I say? 'Father, save me from this hour'? No, it was for this very reason I came to this hour" (12:27).

Two important concepts merge in this terminology found throughout John—purpose and timing. Jesus knew exactly why he was in the world and he was committed to the Father's schedule. This timing could not be altered by Pilate, Herod, Satan, or even the well-meaning disciples.

C. The Best Wine (2:10)

Since evangelicals are widely divided on the use of alcohol as a beverage, perhaps particularly wine, interpretation of John 2 must endure some wide swings of opinion. The same Greek word *oinos* appears in verses 3,9–10. In verse 10 the master of ceremonies adds the adjectives "choice," "cheaper," and "best," though, in fact, "good" and "choice" in the NIV text are exactly the same Greek word (*kalon*).

Some interpreters are scandalized by the idea that Jesus could have made wine that was intoxicating. But the context clearly implies that the new wine was no different than the old wine in terms of its effect. It was actually higher in quality. As I indicated in the "Commentary" section, any argument for total abstinence must be made from other passages because it can be neither developed nor inferred from the record of John 2.

Apart from the textual issue, however, there is the cultural issue. Acts 2 brings up the issue of drunkenness, certainly well-known in first-century Palestinian society. The scoffers in Jerusalem said about the Spirit-baptized believers, "They have had too much wine" (Acts 2:13), and Peter replied, "These men are not drunk, as you suppose. It's only nine in the morning!" (Acts 2:15). At this point we face a problem since the word in Acts 2:13 is *gleukos,* used only once in the Bible. But we have no doubt about the meaning of the scoffers when we couple their words with Peter's response.

Both Paul and Peter pick up on the idea of drunkenness and Spirit-control, highlighted in the familiar passage in Ephesians, "Do not get drunk on wine, which leads to debauchery. Instead, be filled with the Spirit. Speak to one another with psalms, hymns and spiritual songs. Sing and make music in your heart to the Lord, always giving thanks to God the Father for everything, in the name of our Lord Jesus Christ" (Eph. 5:18–20).

But ours is a different culture. The average first use of alcohol occurs at age twelve and "ninety-three percent of all teenagers in the United States have had some experience with alcohol by the end of their senior year of high school, and six percent drink daily" (Anderson, p. 99). Anderson goes on to review the situation among adults.

> The social costs of alcohol are staggering. Alcoholism is the third largest health problem (following heart disease and cancer). Often alcohol-related medical problems begin before birth. More than forty thousand babies are born at risk each year because their mothers drank alcohol during pregnancy.
>
> There are an estimated ten million problem drinkers in the American adult population, and an estimated 3.3 million teenagers are problem drinkers. Half of all traffic fatalities and one-third of all

traffic injuries are alcohol-related. Alcohol is involved in sixty-seven percent of all murders and thirty-three percent of all suicides.

Alcohol is also a prime contributor to the breakdown of American families. A high percentage of family violence, parental abuse and neglect, lost wages, and divorce are tied to the abuse of alcohol in this country. In a George Gallup poll, nearly one-fourth of all Americans cited alcohol and/or drug abuse as one of three factors most responsible for the high divorce rate in this country (Anderson, p. 101).

So, as is often the case in handling Scripture, balance is the key. Careful teachers and preachers will avoid making any case for abstinence from this passage while at the same time pointing out the staggering negative impact of alcohol abuse in today's world.

D. Passover Feasts (2:13)

Usually considered the most important of the Jewish feasts, Passover linked up with the Feast of Unleavened Bread to form a double festival. Passover was one day and the Feast of Unleavened Bread extended seven days beyond in a celebration to which the Mosaic Law assigned all male Jews by requirement (Exod. 23:17; Deut. 16:16). Such an attendance demand applied as well to the Feast of Weeks (Pentecost) and the Feast of Tabernacles. These pilgrimage festivals brought hundreds of people to Jerusalem as noted particularly in the Passover connection with Christ's death and the coming of the Holy Spirit at Pentecost.

This citation from Brown pinpoints the significance of feasts in the life of Israel at the time of Jesus:

What in the Synoptic Gospels is tacitly assumed rather than explicitly stated, becomes in the Fourth Gospel a main theme: Jesus is not merely a Jew among Jews; He represents rather the true Israel. Therefore, He demonstrates in His life, suffering and death the proper festal celebration. Through Him the meaning of the traditional festivals returns with a new, final significance and is offered afresh to the Jews in this renewed form . . . woven into, as it were, the fabric of the recurring festivals of Israel, He presents Himself with His discourses as their secret, and yet revealed, centre and climax. In each case the discourse centres on the 'I Am' words. The significance of this with the structure of John is even shown statistically by the fact that 15 of the total of 25 occurrences of the word *heorte* in the N.T. are found in this Gospel (Brown, I, p. 628).

E. Herod's Temple (2:19–20)

Herod the Great ruled from 37 B.C. to A.D. 4, and the temple represented the most ambitious example of his many building projects. He never saw its completion (A.D. 64), but John had seen it and knew all about how the armies of Titus sacked Jerusalem in A.D. 70. The Court of the Gentiles where Jesus encountered the salesmen was just inside the portico and outside the sacred enclosure of the temple. Jesus had been here before—when he was twelve years old. Here, when he was only eight days old, he had met Simeon and Anna possibly in the women's court on the east side. Today the Dome of the Rock stands over the site because the temple has never been rebuilt.

VII. TEACHING OUTLINE

A. INTRODUCTION
1. Lead Story: Family Breakdown
2. Context: Immediately after the introduction of the Lamb of God by John the Baptist, Jesus and his disciples appeared at a wedding in Cana to mark the beginning of his ministry in Galilee. After a stop in Capernaum, John played his trump card of resurrection by introducing an event which happened later in Jesus' life but which John decided to describe as part of his foundation. We must repeatedly remind ourselves that John deals with a theological rather than a chronological handling of the events of Jesus' life.
3. Transition: Chapter 2 forms a bridge between the doctrine of regeneration in chapter 1 and the experience of regeneration in chapter 3. Verses 23–25 represent an important transition, contrasting the false-believing people at the feast with the true believer, Nicodemus.

B. COMMENTARY
1. The Master and His Mother (2:1–4)
2. The Master and His Method (2:5–8)
3. The Master and His Miracle (2:9–11)
4. The Master and the Market (2:12–16)
5. The Master and His Meanings (2:17–22)
6. The Master and His Motive (2:23–25)

C. CONCLUSION: PRINCE OF THE OUTCASTS

VIII. ISSUES FOR DISCUSSION

1. How can we witness visible grace more effectively at public events like weddings and worship?
2. How can we practice more complete obedience to the Master?
3. In what ways do we make sure our faith is real—not false like that of the people in Jerusalem at the Passover feast?

John 3

Eternal Life

"*The* truest end of life is to know the life that never ends."

William Penn

GEOGRAPHICAL PROFILE: AENON

- The word in Aramaic means "springs"
- Possibly located in the hills southeast of Mount Karison near the northern border of Judea

PERSONAL PROFILE: NICODEMUS

- A Pharisee and member of the seventy-elder Sanhedrin which ruled the Jewish people
- Defended Jesus in the Sanhedrin (John 7:50–52)
- Assisted Joseph of Arimathea with Jesus' burial
- Name means "victor over the people"
- Never again mentioned in the New Testament after John 19

PERSONAL PROFILE: PHARISEES

- Jewish sect that used oral law and tradition in their teaching
- Minority party in the Sanhedrin
- Theologically conservative by comparison with the Sadducees
- Major opponents of Jesus' teaching
- Numbered about six thousand during the time of Jesus
- Middle-class businessmen, merchants, and tradesmen

IN A NUTSHELL

"*For* God so loved the world that he gave his one and only Son, that whoever believes in him shall not perish but have eternal life."

Eternal Life

I. INTRODUCTION

Same Text—Same Sermon

*M*any believe Dwight L. Moody was the greatest evangelist of the nineteenth century. Born in 1837, he was led to Christ by his Sunday school teacher, Edward Kimball, at the Mount Vernon Congregational Church in Boston. Later he moved to Chicago and became a successful businessman. In 1860 he decided to spend his full time in Sunday school and YMCA work. He became a national figure in 1873 while on a two-year tour of the British Isles. His visit included a four-month series of meetings in London attended by more than two and one-half million people. Before his death in December of 1899, Moody had traveled more than one million miles and preached to more than one hundred million people.

On one occasion in Chicago, Moody's home base, he had asked Henry Moorhouse to substitute for him during a week while he was out of town. As the story goes, Moorhouse preached every night for that full week on one verse—John 3:16—and every night people came to Christ and throughout the week the crowds increased.

Is there a verse anywhere in the Bible more well-known and loved than this? How poignantly it states that eternal life is not earned by begging, crying, praying, working, or joining! Salvation comes as a free gift when we believe what God has said. For almost two thousand years people have been adding to the gospel. But the truth still rings clear today—"Whoever believes in him shall not perish but have eternal life." This chapter proclaims God's love and God's gift, the uniqueness of Jesus, salvation by faith and reprieve from eternal judgment—and they are all included in one poignant sentence in this key verse.

The verse looms as the centerpiece of the gospel, perhaps the high-water mark of God's love for sinners shown at the cross. The concept of eternal life waves over this chapter like the American flag over the Pentagon or the U.S. Capitol. The adjective "eternal" is always used in John's Gospel of life. It refers to the age to come, the time that never ceases. The great Greek scholar B. F. Westcott once said of eternal life, "It is not an endless duration of being in time, but being of which time is not a measure."

But the chapter contains much more than just the sixteenth verse. Indeed, it represents one of the great theological chapters of this deeply theological book.

John opens with what appears to be a deliberate contrast between the inadequate faith of those described at the end of chapter 2 and the righteous heart of Nicodemus, a Pharisee ready to believe. Nicodemus means "conqueror of the people," but on this night, he would be conquered by the power of the Savior.

II. COMMENTARY

Eternal Life

MAIN IDEA: *Our response to the Son of God determines our destiny.*

A Conversation with Nicodemus (3:1–15)

SUPPORTING IDEA: *Philosophy and religion can be complicated, but the gospel is simple, yet profound enough to stun the intellect of a learned Pharisee.*

3:1–2. It is useless to speculate why Nicodemus came to Jesus at night, though interpreters have invested a great amount of ink in doing so. He was obviously prompted by miracles which he had seen and, as a guardian of theology, he had an obligation to investigate further. Jesus was always surrounded by people in the daytime, so a late-evening meeting would have been a logical choice. We should not infer that Nicodemus was afraid or embarrassed to be with Jesus.

The text does not suggest Nicodemus's motive, but John does emphasize his personal subordination to one he already understood had authority from God. When Nicodemus called Jesus **Rabbi**, this member of the Jewish ruling council placed himself in the role of learner. The conversation which unfolded led him to eternal life. The Pharisees were legalistically bound to every aspect of the law and had made ridiculous interpretations and applications (such as not traveling beyond a thousand yards on the Sabbath).

Nicodemus was rich, he was highly educated, he was interested in spiritual matters, he had a solid grasp of Old Testament Scripture—but he knew something was missing in his life. A theologian approached a carpenter and graciously acknowledged him as a teacher from God *because of the signs.* This common misperception of the gospel appears throughout John's book because Jesus repeatedly emphasized that the signs were indicators of the real message. Borchert observes, "Thus Nicodemus' mere reliance on signs at this stage became an excellent example of the type of believing that is not really sufficient. Jesus understood the nature of genuine believing and knowing, and he recognized a façade or pseudo-knowledge when he encountered it (2:23–24). Nicodemus actually did not realize what he was saying about knowing!" (Borchert, p. 171).

3:3. If we view these first fifteen verses of chapter 3 as a series of questions and answers, the first question might look like this: "Are you here to bring in the kingdom?" And Jesus' first answer is, "You will never see the kingdom without being born again."

Nicodemus demonstrates that religious training without spiritual insight is useless. Jesus wasted no time getting to the heart of the problem. He told the teacher he must be **born again** or from above (*anothen*), a word which appears again in verses 7 and 31. This popular expression can be applied to almost anything in our day. A football team gets a new coach, and sportscasters tell us it is *born again*. A company languishing in bankruptcy issues new stock and shows profit under a new CEO, and we read that it is *born again*. Buildings get a renovation, changing their appearance and function, and people say they have been *born again*.

The actual words describe a garment torn from top to bottom. Unless God changes our hearts his way, from the inside out, any discussion of the kingdom is useless. All devout Jews connected the Messiah with the kingdom; Jesus drove to the heart of the matter immediately.

Nicodemus had not mentioned the **kingdom**, but the Lord knew his true interest. As we noted in connection with chapter 1, the word translated **again** really means "from above." In other words, to belong to the heavenly kingdom, one must be born into it just as one is born into the earthly kingdom. Morris offers a helpful paragraph on the concept of the kingdom.

> "The kingdom of God" is the most common topic of Jesus' teaching in the Synoptic Gospels. As such it has attracted a great deal of attention, and the literature on the subject is enormous. Most modern students hold that the term "kingdom" is to be understood in the dynamic sense. It is "reign" rather than "realm." It is God's rule in action. We are probably not meant to put much difference between seeing and entering (v. 5) the kingdom. But it will be appropriate that Jesus speaks here of seeing it. So far from entering into the kingdom and enjoying all its privileges, the man who is not reborn will not even see it. This passage incidentally is the only one in this Gospel which mentions the kingdom of God . . . But John frequently speaks of eternal life, and for him the possession of eternal life appears to mean very much the same thing as the Synoptic Gospels mean by entering the kingdom of God (Morris, pp. 213–14).

3:4. Now the second question surfaces: **How can a man be born when he is old?** Do we understand this as a literal question or a figure of speech suggesting something like "I'm too old to change?" Since Nicodemus was still unaware that Jesus was speaking in the spiritual realm, I favor taking his response literally. The physical world is often unexplainable just like the spiritual world, and Jesus later used the wind as an example to make that point. A person cannot respond to spiritual truth in natural ways.

Though the metaphor may have changed somewhat, Nicodemus could have heard this message even before Jesus' public ministry began. John the Baptist had preached that the king was already in their midst, but they would not experience the kingdom just because they were children of Abraham. Jews had compelled Gentiles to be baptized in order to participate in the nation, and John warned them that the Jews needed the baptism of repentance. The rite of Jewish baptism for proselytes does not necessarily depict the new birth Jesus proclaimed. But it contained the idea of washing away one's old and defiled life in order to emerge as a new person. But Nicodemus could not make the connection; he was stuck on a physical wavelength.

3:5. The second answer must have hit Nicodemus directly between his theological eyes: **no one can enter the kingdom of God unless he is born of water and the Spirit.** Verse 3 deals with the source of the new birth, and verse 5 talks about the process. We understand what it means to be born of the Spirit. This is the regeneration which he provides at the time of faith in Christ. What does it mean to be born of water? We can choose from a variety of interpretations.

1. *Baptism of repentance:* In this interpretation the text would say, "being born of John's baptism is not enough; you must also be born of the Spirit" (Tenney and Godet).

2. *Christian baptism:* No less a scholar than Westcott argues for baptismal regeneration from a text like this. Borchert and Luther do not, but they see the water as the act of baptism.

3. *Physical birth:* Many interpreters would say that the context picks up on Nicodemus' reference to the breaking of water at physical birth (Oderberg).

4. *The Word of God:* Texts like Titus 3:5 and Ephesians 5:26 which link water and the Word seem attractive here (Boice).

5. *The Spirit:* The Greek word *kai* translated here (and commonly) as **and** can also mean "even." Proponents of this view bring in passages like John 7:37–39 to link water with the Spirit.

After reviewing a variety of choices, Morris sums up a reasonable position: "Nicodemus was a Pharisee. He was used to this way of speaking. The allusion would be natural for him. We should accordingly take the passage to mean being born of 'spiritual water,' and see this as another way of referring to being born 'of the spirit.' Jesus is referring to the miracle which takes place when the divine activity re-makes a man. He is born all over again by the very Spirit of God. As John is fond of using expressions which may be taken in more ways than one, it is, of course, not impossible that he wants us to think of the other meanings as well. But the main thrust of the words surely has to do with divine re-making" (Morris, p. 218).

3:6–7. Though the Holy Spirit was active in the Old Testament text, nowhere in Judaism could one find the role of the Holy Spirit in personal regeneration. Upon hearing the word **flesh**, Nicodemus might have remembered the words of Genesis 2:23–24, "The man said, 'This is now bone of my bones and flesh of my flesh; she shall be called "woman," for she was taken out of man.' For this reason a man will leave his father and mother and be united to his wife, and they will become one flesh."

Apparently in the Genesis passage *flesh* indicates total being. But by the time we get to the New Testament, it seems narrowed to human nature. Paul's writing is particularly helpful on this subject since we see the perspective through the eyes of another Pharisee. My friend Bob Pyne has some helpful paragraphs on the subject: "In Galatians, Paul used the term 'flesh' to describe a Spirit-less attempt at righteousness (represented most prominently by circumcision), and in Romans 8:9 he described unbelievers as 'in the flesh.' His use of the term in these other contexts helps explain why Paul could say in Romans 7:18 that 'nothing good dwells in me, that is, in my flesh.' Apart from the Spirit, unbelievers are, so to speak, nothing more than unanimated, dead flesh. Nothing is good about that condition. They experience only depravity and service to sin (7:25)" (Pyne, p. 187).

So Nicodemus should not have been shocked by the message of the new birth. There is, however, a surprise in the Greek text. The first time **You** appears in verse 7 it is singular as in verses 3 and 5. Obviously Jesus was talking directly to Nicodemus. But in the last phrase of verse 7, the **You** becomes plural saying, in effect, "all of you." The new birth was not just for Nicodemus. The movement from flesh to spirit, from world to kingdom, from death to life is a necessity for every human being.

3:8. In this fascinating conversation, Jesus moves from the metaphor of birth to that of breeze. Human effort can only produce human results (John 1:13), but the *pneuma*—that is a different story. This is a spiritual mystery known only to God and explainable only in terms that humans can grasp. The words *wind* and *spirit* are derived from the same Greek word. God brings the breeze when and where he chooses. This is a spiritual prototype for the way God brings people to faith.

This verse guards against a physical dependence for the new birth such as the water of baptismal regeneration or another accompanying phenomenon. Sights, sounds, and smells are irrelevant. Nor are the time and place of new birth essential, though many people can point to both. Regenerational reality comes from the presence of the Holy Spirit. We are not improved caterpillars but by faith have become spiritual butterflies.

A verse like this challenges our modern dependence on quick fixes and guaranteed formulas. Sociologists explain why churches grow and die, why behaviors flourish or die. But their formulas fail to describe the faith of a lifetime.

The word connection between *wind* and *spirit* works in both Greek (*pneuma*) and Hebrew (*ruach*). Borchert picks up on how all this inner mystery turns into theological truth:

> In these characteristics of the wind there was provided to Nicodemus and the reader of John an example of how believers in Christ appear to outsiders. First-century outside observers probably knew little of how Christians became followers of Jesus, and they understood little concerning their eschatological destinies. But what they could sense was the presence and work in these children of the Spirit in the midst of pagan and Jewish societies. What they saw and heard from the Christians who were present in their societies was telling as to how they formulated their understanding of Christianity (cf. John 13:35). Their lives were a witness to an unseen reality. Is this picture not an appropriate word for today? (Borchert, p. 177).

3:9–11. Nicodemus raised a third question: **How can this be?** or, "What does all this mean?" and Jesus began an answer which said, in effect, "It means that eternal life only comes through personal faith in the cross." As a student of the Old Testament, Nicodemus should have understood something about new birth (Isa. 44:3; Jer. 31:31–33; Ezek. 36:25–16).

The text stops us in verse 11 when we encounter the word **we.** Does this refer to Jesus and John the Baptist? Jesus and the disciples? Nicodemus's understanding of the prophets? We encounter a plural pronoun four times in this one verse, then abruptly in verse 12 Jesus went back to the use of the singular **I.**

Some commentators do not even deal with this point, and others take a variety of views. Dogmatism is unwarranted in such a case, of course, but the unique appearance of the plurals surely requires some explanation. This sounds to me like "teacher talk." In verse 2 Nicodemus called Jesus "a teacher who has come from God" and in verse 10 Jesus responded by saying, **You are Israel's teacher.** Perhaps the verse could be paraphrased this way: "Teachers tell the truth, instruct from their own knowledge, and describe things they have seen. Why then do religious leaders like you, used to this kind of procedure, not recognize the reality of changed lives you have seen among disciples and followers."

The word *people* is an unfortunate addition in the NIV text, especially in view of modern lingo in which the phrase "you people" is often taken as ethnically derogatory. The beginning of verse 11 offers the third double-amen statement in this conversation (cf. vv. 3,5). It provides emphasis on what follows, denoted not so much by the word order of the sentence as by the special expression rendered in the KJV as "verily, verily." Today we might say, "Listen up."

3:12–13. What are these **earthly things** of which Jesus had been speaking? Perhaps basic regeneration, without which no other **heavenly things** could be understood. Included in that spiritual list would have been such doctrines as the incarnation, the virgin birth, and the coming kingdom in which Nicodemus was so interested. Some interpreters take **heavenly things** to refer to the conversation with Nicodemus while **earthly things** could have meant earlier teaching, but that is pure speculation. Tenney thinks "earthly things" refers to physical phenomena like earth and wind.

Whatever the exact meaning of the terms, there is no doubt about the source of authority. Since only Jesus himself had been in heaven before coming to earth, he speaks with authority. Tenney offers a great line here: "Revelation, not discovery, is the basis for faith" (Tenney, *EBC*, p. 48). Some Jews of Nicodemus's day taught that great saints would attain heaven by their godliness and righteous living. But no one ever sees heaven apart from the new birth.

Several manuscripts include the words "who is in heaven" at the end of verse 13, but we can find little textual support for that addition. Jesus' favorite designation of himself was Son of Man, which we have already seen in the last verse of chapter 1. The phrase appears eighty-one times in the Gospels and is used only by Jesus, quite possibly recited from Daniel 7:13–14. As this Gospel emphasizes his deity, so this phrase emphasizes his perfect humanity. Verses like this remind us of John 14:6, strongly emphasizing the exclusivity of the gospel.

3:14–15. John G. Payton, missionary to the New Hebrides, searched the local language to find a satisfactory word for *believe*. One day after a hunt he fell exhausted into a lawn chair outside his tent. One of the natives observed, "It's good to stretch yourself out and rest when you're tired." Immediately Payton seized on the words "stretch out and rest" and translated the New Testament word for *believe* in that way.

This section ends with an interesting reference to Numbers 21 and the serpent of brass. Obviously Jesus referred to the cross, and the key words appear in verse 15—**in him.** But why the reference to the brass serpent? This illustration from the Old Testament life of Moses shows us that the cross provides a cure from the poison of sin, deliverance from the death of sin, and removal of the condemnation of sin.

The words **lifted up** appear twice more in this Gospel (8:28; 12:32), and each time they emphasize the centrality of the cross and the message of salvation. The sin in the desert was rebellion, and Israel needed to show faith and obedience by looking to the pole (Num. 21:9). As Tasker expressed it, "Similarly, Jesus, the heavenly Son of man made flesh, is destined to be lifted up for all to see. He will hang on a cross like a condemned criminal. But his subjection to that particular form of death will not be due to some mischance. He will die in that way, precisely because it is in that way that God has chosen to reveal His love for sinners" (Tasker, pp. 68–69).

At the end of the paragraph we find the words **eternal life** from which the title of this chapter is taken. It comes at us again at the end of verse 16. Certainly the adjective refers to the duration of life with God (it lasts forever), but it also describes quality, contrasting Christian faith with nihilism and futility. According to Morris, "Eternal life is life in Christ, that life which removes a man from the merely earthly. As we see from the earlier part of this chapter it originates in a divine action, in a man's being born anew. It is the gift of God, and is not the achievement of man" (Morris, p. 227).

B Contrast Between Believers and Unbelievers (3:16–21)

SUPPORTING IDEA: *The deepening and growing experience of imperishable life is given to whomever believes in him. God's wonderful gift cannot be earned or inherited.*

3:16. Is there a verse anywhere in the Bible more well-known and loved than this one? How poignantly it states that eternal life comes not because of anything we do. Salvation comes as a free gift when we believe what God has said. For almost two thousand years people have been adding to the gospel, but the truth still rings clear today—**whoever believes in him shall not perish but have eternal life**. Nicodemus had superb religious training but very little spiritual insight. He could not grasp Jesus' statement that a person must be born from above to experience eternal life.

Four times in three verses (vv. 16–18) Jesus uses variations of the word *believe*, perhaps the most important key word in John's Gospel. The Son of God classified the entire human race into two groups—those who believe and are not condemned, and those who do not believe and are condemned already.

The gospel begins with God's love, penetrates through the cross and the empty tomb, and results in eternal life for those who believe. Morris declared, "In typical Johannine fashion, 'gave' is used in two sentences. God gave the Son by sending Him into the world, but God also gave the Son on the cross. Notice that the cross is not said to show us the love of the Son (as in Gal. 2:20), but that of the Father. The atonement proceeds from the loving heart of God. It is not something wrung from Him. The Greek construction puts some stress on the actuality of the gift: it is not 'God loved so as to give,' but 'God loved so that He gave'" (Morris, p. 229).

Nicodemus would have believed firmly that God loved Israel, but not much in Jewish theology allowed for God to love the world. This is new revelation, the new covenant breadth of the gospel. Jesus had just evoked one Old

Testament image in the Pharisee's mind (the snake in the desert), and now he touched on another—the aged Abraham sacrificing his only son on the altar (Gen. 22:2).

We've already explored the word *believe,* so crucial to the message of the gospel and the record of John. But two other words call for attention in this splendid verse. To describe God's love for the world John chose the verb *agapao* for the first time in his writings. He used it thirty-six times, more than twice as many as any other book of the New Testament except his first epistle in which he used it thirty-one times. But the gospel does not center in God's love, but rather what he gave on the cross—the death of his Son. The Bible does not allow us to merely acknowledge that Christ died for the world; saving faith requires a recognition that he died for each of us individually.

The words **one and only** translate *monogenes,* which appears again in verse 18. John had already used it in 1:14,18 and used it again in 1 John 4:9.

The verb **perish** speaks of eternal death in contrast to eternal life. It represents the opposite of preservation, since death is the opposite of life. Those who refuse God's gift are alienated from Him without hope for both the present and the future. A person need not sin blatantly to perish. One may simply fail to act positively in receiving God's gift. When applied to Judas in John 17:12, we learn that the one who perished was the son of perdition, or in the NIV, the one "doomed to destruction," a play on the word *apoleo.*

A word needs to be said here about the section that includes verses 16–18. If we take these verses separately in our study, they form a single unit of thought in the text and each verse depends upon the others (though many who could quote verse 16 would not be able to recite verses 17–18 with equal accuracy). Verse 16 tells us that God gave his Son, verse 17 explains why, and verse 18 emphasizes the result.

Yet another point requires mention here. Red-letter editions of the Bible identify Jesus speaking throughout this chapter in response to Nicodemus. However, many scholars believe that the Lord's words end at the end of verse 15 and that verses 16–21 represent the words of John. As Tasker puts it, "It is a reasonable assumption that verses 16 to 21 are not part of Jesus' words to Nicodemus, but comments by the evangelist, as Jesus in speaking of the first Person of the Trinity refers to him as 'Father' not as 'God'" (Tasker, p. 69).

In Tenney's view, "The words may be the author's condensation of Jesus' utterance, but were doubtless based on what He said on this occasion. Possibly he was present at the interview, though he was not mentioned as being included in it" (Tenney, *The Gospel of John,* p. 89).

3:17–18. Did all this happen for judgment and condemnation? No. That was never God's purpose. Notice how central Jesus is to the passage. Verse 15 emphasizes the words "in him" and they appear again in verses 16–18, while verse 17 talks about God's saving the world **through him.** Every human being has a choice—eternal life or eternal death. And as the Bible describes it, to perish is not to cease existence, but to experience utter failure, futility, and loss—an eternity without God.

Somebody once said that the world could be divided into two groups— those who divide the world into two groups and those who do not. If that is the case, God is definitely in the former category for he divides the saved and the unsaved clearly in these verses. The saved believe and are not condemned; the unsaved do not believe and are condemned. And let us not miss the word **already.** We exist in a state of condemnation by birth—our sin natures inherited from Adam.

We enter physical life in a state of spiritual death and then our sin natures compound the problem with sinful behavior. As Pyne points out, "Because of the sinfulness of our hearts, we tend to run from God rather than to Him. We cannot produce works of righteousness apart from His Spirit, for we act in accordance with our own desires, and our desires are evil. Even if we could fulfill God's law, we could never overcome the guilt already incurred by our sinful acts in the past. As a result, we cannot save ourselves" (Pyne, pp. 190–91).

3:19–21. Now we see the verdict. People reject Christ because of evil deeds and because they hate the light. God does not label their deeds evil because they love darkness; they love darkness because that is their very nature. Five times John mentioned **light,** a word he had already introduced in chapter 1. Boice illustrates this by using the familiar image of a father and small child throwing a ball. No matter how close they stand to each other, the child's awkward throw goes awry. The problem is not the distance between them but the child's aim. Well-meaning people, even those who seek righteousness in their own understanding, fail—that is why we need the cross.

We dare never forget how Isaiah put it: "All of us have become like one who is unclean, and all our righteous acts are like filthy rags; we all shrivel up like a leaf, and like the wind our sins sweep us away. No one calls on your name or strives to lay hold of you; for you have hidden your face from us and made us waste away because of our sins" (Isa. 64:6–7).

We talk about "giving the invitation" but God demands repentance. What possible excuses keep people from Christ? Failure to understand their need? No time for hearing the truth? Insufficient evidence to affirm the gospel? This passage tells us they refuse light because it shows up the darkness in their own lives. The contrast of our text continues:

- Believers possess eternal life but unbelievers do not.
- Believers are not condemned, but unbelievers are condemned already.
- Believers live in the light while unbelievers live in the darkness.

The last phrase of this paragraph should encourage all of us. Those who practice the truth, who continuously live in the light of God's spirit, demonstrate that their righteousness has been brought about by God. Paul emphasized this point to Christians in Ephesus: "For it is by grace you have been saved, through faith—and this not from yourselves, it is the gift of God—not by works, so that no one can boast" (Eph. 2:8–9).

John has been writing about changed lives, the message of Jesus to Nicodemus. Salvation is the work of God internally through the Holy Spirit, but it demonstrates itself outwardly in godly living. Boice expands a story from the life of Harry Ironside which originally appeared in *Random Reminiscences*. I paraphrase it further here.

Early in his ministry when Ironside lived in the San Francisco Bay area, he conducted a meeting for the Salvation Army. At the end of the sermon, a well-known socialist handed Dr. Ironside a card on which he had written, "Sir, I challenge you to debate me with the question, 'Agnosticism vs. Christianity' in the Academy of Science Hall next Sunday afternoon at 4:00 P.M. I will pay all expenses."

Ironside read the card aloud, then agreed to the debate on certain terms. First, that the socialist bring to the debate a man whose life had been wrecked by sin but now redeemed for righteousness and goodness because of agnosticism. Second, that he would bring a woman wrecked by sin, an outcast prostitute, who had been rehabilitated and now lived a virtuous, happy life because of agnosticism. Ironside agreed to bring one hundred such people saved by the power of Jesus Christ whose lives would be "present-day proof of the truth of the Bible." As the story ends, the man left the hall unwilling to take up such a challenge. This chapter describes that kind of transformation.

Ⓒ Confirmation of John's Witness (3:22–36)

SUPPORTING IDEA: *Humble witnesses for the Savior proclaim his gospel, and people's response to the Son of God determines their destiny.*

In the NIV arrangement, three paragraphs remain in this chapter. And they confer John's mission and his message. Competition between John's disciples and those of Jesus was not encouraged by either leader. Such diversionary activity would take away from the main event—God sent his Son into the world to bring salvation to the lost. Twenty-three times in this book John records references by Jesus to the one who sent him.

3:22–23. An argument was about to break out between two ministry teams regarding the popularity of one of the leaders. Jealousy seemed to be the motive and in the context of the times we can certainly understand the event. Remember, in the New Testament we still find adherence to John's baptism twenty years after Jesus' resurrection. Two different baptismal groups, headed by two different leaders, baptizing in two different cities—both claiming messianic connections. Two things seem important in the text: (1) John's ongoing baptism was hardly competitive because he still proclaimed Jesus and presumably attracted even more people to the Lamb, and (2) although verse 23 talks about Jesus baptizing, we learn in John 4:2 that he supervised the activity and the disciples themselves did the baptizing.

What kind of baptism was this? Probably not Christian baptism since it took place before the crucifixion, resurrection, and coming of the Holy Spirit at Pentecost. According to Morris, "More probably it represents a continuation of the 'baptism of repentance' that was characteristic of John the Baptist. Both Jesus and his first disciples had come from the circle around John, and it may well be that for some time they continued to call on men to submit to the baptism that symbolized repentance . . . The tense of the last two verbs is continuous and we might give the force of it as 'they kept coming and being baptized'" (Morris, p. 237).

3:24–26. Why did not John tell us more about the Baptist's imprisonment as the Synoptists did (Matt. 14:1–12; Mark 6:14,29; Luke 3:19–20)? That event simply did not fit his purpose. John the apostle dealt with John the Baptist only insofar as the latter served the introduction and explanation of Jesus Christ. John and Jesus both understood this perfectly. Writing as we have seen with the benefit of lengthy hindsight, the apostle John could put the whole thing in perspective for his readers.

But the **argument** was real. According to the Dead Sea Scrolls, people at the time were interested in the finer points of ceremonial purification. John the Baptist hardly observed the finer points of anything. Petty bickering over church ritual has been a blind spot in the behavior of Christians since the days of Jesus. The very one who wrote these words, while still in his younger days, said to the one of whom he wrote, "Master . . . we saw a man driving out demons in your name and we tried to stop him, because he is not one of us" (Luke 9:49). Jesus replied to John the apostle, "Do not stop him . . . for whoever is not against you is for you" (Luke 9:50).

This competition was encouraged neither by Jesus nor John. We would do well to notice that envy or jealousy over someone else's popularity, especially in ministry, can never advance God's kingdom but only deteriorate our spiritual lives.

We find the designation **Rabbi** in verse 26 interesting, since this is the only place in the Gospel it is applied to anyone other than Jesus. As Borchert points out, "The disciples of John the Baptist were obviously concerned to protect the popularity and prestige of their teacher, and they wanted the Baptizer to counter Jesus' growing popularity by taking some affirmative action on his own behalf. Disciples of teachers are often more zealous for their teacher's perspectives than the teachers themselves, and thus history is replete with many examples of the excesses of disciples, as in the case of the Arminians and Calvinists" (Borchert, p. 190).

3:27–28. What kept this popular prophet so humble? We see in this passage his awareness of God's sovereignty, of his own unworthiness, and of the preeminence of Christ in the world. This response by John almost becomes a standard Christian principle: **man can receive only what is given him from heaven.** The principle certainly applies to John, whose disciples seemed to have wanted his status elevated. It applies to Jesus, about whom many still had questions, but whose greatness John constantly affirms. And it applies to us, who dare not exercise authority or leadership in ministry beyond what God has gifted us and called us to do. The word **heaven** in this context refers back to God, since throughout this Gospel John saw everything as coming from the hand of the Father.

3:29–30. The bride/bridegroom theme introduces the church, although this Gospel says little about that important New Testament theme. The bride (the church), including the disciples who were then following John, belonged to the bridegroom (Christ). John described himself as the friend of the bridegroom, delighted to see him claim his own. Surely John 3:30 is one of the great verses of the Bible: **He must become greater; I must become less.**

This wedding scene builds on Old Testament imagery of Jehovah as the husband of Israel (Isa. 54:5; 62:4; Jer. 2:2; 3:20; Ezek. 16:8; Hos. 2:19). Now in the new covenant, the Messiah becomes the bridegroom of the church. This important theme radiates through the New Testament (2 Cor. 11:2; Eph. 5:32), culminating in Revelation 19:7–8. In the words of Calvin, "Those who win the Church over to themselves rather than to Christ faithlessly violate the marriage which they ought to honour."

So the bride and bridegroom imagery is well established in both the Old Testament and the New Testament. As the friend of the bridegroom, John emphasized his delight and joy rather than jealousy over Jesus' arrival and instant popularity. It is said of the pioneer missionary, William Carey, that when he was close to death he turned to a friend and said, "When I am gone, don't talk about William Carey; talk about William Carey's Savior. I desire that Christ alone might be magnified."

3:31. In the words of Tozer, "A spiritual kingdom lies all about us, enclosing us, embracing us, all together within reach of our inner selves, waiting for us to recognize it. God Himself is here waiting our response to His Presence. This eternal world will come alive to us the moment we begin to reckon upon its reality" (Tozer, p. 52). That is what this verse offers—the understanding of God, both Father and Son. All human beings, including John the Baptist, are **from the earth** and belong **to the earth.** But twice John told us that Jesus, who had his origin in heaven, **is above all.** Hear Eugene Peterson's paraphrase of verse 31: "The One who comes from above is head and shoulders over other messengers from God. The earthborn is earthbound and speaks earth language; the heavenborn is in a league of his own. He sets out the evidence of what he saw and heard in heaven. No one wants to deal with these facts. But anyone who examines this evidence will come to stake his life on this: that God himself is the truth" (*The Message*).

3:32–33. John expected an avalanche of faith from the nation of Israel. They had waited four hundred years for a revelation from God and many more centuries for the coming of the promised Prophet. Isaiah could not have been more clear in his predictions, and John's own personal witness was as bold and lucid as he could make it. Almost no one responded—but the few who did affirmed God's truth. The word **truthful** at the end of verse 33 demonstrates its emphatic sense by its placement in the sentence. Truth is one of John's major themes, and all truth originates with God.

3:34–35. No fewer than twenty-three times in this Gospel Jesus refers to the one who sent him, and John describes that in this paragraph. We find here a strong Christology developed either by John the Baptist or John the apostle (interpreters are not in agreement on who speaks in vv. 31–36). The matter of authorship aside, consider the central themes:

- Jesus comes from above; he is sent from God (vv. 31,34).
- Jesus is above all; he has all things in his hand (vv. 31,35).
- Jesus speaks things he has seen and heard from the Father (vv. 31,34).
- Jesus gives the truth to those who receive him (v. 33).
- Jesus gives the Spirit to those who trust in him (v. 34).
- Jesus is loved by the Father for he is the Son (v. 35).
- Jesus can communicate life which is everlasting (v. 36).

The intimacy between the Father and the Son guarantees Jesus' complete authority for universal reign. He speaks the **words of God**, this time not *logos* but *rhema*—a message offered by a living voice. The Bible is the Word inscripturated; Jesus is the Word incarnate.

Verse 34 is a trinitarian statement—Father, Son, and Spirit all appear in the same short verse. Borchert points out: "The idea that the Spirit was not given in a limited or measured way (*Ek Metrou*, 3:34) is here applied particularly to Jesus because of his unique relationship within the godhead. But that idea of the unlimited Spirit is applicable to believers in a derivative sense by the act of Jesus in passing on the Holy Spirit (cf. 20:22)" (Borchert, p. 194).

3:36. Before moving on with his narrative of Jesus' ministry and message, John wanted to state one more time the essence of the gospel—believing people receive eternal life; rejecting people receive **God's wrath**. What is the wrath of God? By his very nature which is perfect, God opposes the disobedience and rebellion which come from unbelief.

The word *orge*, from which we get our English word *orgy*, describes the anger of disapproval. It can arise gradually and is usually guided by reason and understanding. Hundreds of passages in the Bible refer to God's wrath. Morris quotes Hodgson: "The wrath of God and divine punishment are essential elements in a doctrine which is to face the facts of evil and retain a fundamental optimism. The belief that God has sworn in His wrath that men who do certain things shall not enter into His rest enables the Church to open its worship each day with the words, 'Come let us sing unto the Lord. Let us heartily rejoice in the strength of our salvation'" (Morris, p. 250).

Any approach to God apart from Jesus Christ is futile. Religions, cults, and civic groups miss the message of the Bible when they talk frequently about God but do not want to disturb the pluralistic harmony of their members by emphasizing Jesus Christ. God allows no approach to himself apart from his Son. Whoever rejects the Son has forfeited eternal life and receives instead the wrath of God. This is what the Bible means when it says life is in the Son.

MAIN IDEA REVIEW: *Our response to the Son of God determines our destiny.*

III. CONCLUSION

Lunchbox Evangelism

In one of my favorite *Peanuts* cartoons, Peppermint Patty says to Linus, "I would have made a good evangelist." The skeptical Linus responds, "You? An evangelist? How could that happen?" Peppermint Patty explains: "You know the kid that sits behind me in school? I convinced him that my religion is better than his." An increasingly befuddled Linus ponders, "How did you do that?" Says Peppermint Patty, "I hit him with my lunchbox."

John 3 may be one of the most evangelistic passages of the entire Bible, proclaiming the gospel repeatedly in numerous words and ways. But John was not trying to convince anybody whose religion is better; he wanted to demonstrate how the Son of God continues to fulfill the plan of God on earth by bringing new birth and life to those who believe.

Verse 30 is one of the great transition passages of the New Testament. The Old Testament prophet must fade (the present tense verb literally means "continuously decrease"), while the new covenant Prophet must continuously increase. Evangelism is the proclamation that God's Son has come to earth to die for the sins of humanity and that rejection of that gift leads to judgment and wrath. As we have seen, the message is profoundly simple yet still obscure to millions two thousand years after John introduced Jesus to the world.

Part of the problem comes when we try to tack on to evangelism modern accoutrements to make it happen. We use big advertising campaigns, large tents, a variety of contemporary music approaches, and even some manipulative gimmicks (such as "altar counselors" moving forward at the beginning of an invitation hymn to simulate spontaneous response to the invitation). All this is part of cultural accretion, and God has used it all in one way or another.

On the other hand, none of it is evangelism, but merely the party wardrobe (sometimes the grave clothes) of the message. As Inrig observes:

> Some Christians have suggested that true evangelism is "power evangelism," in which resistance to the Gospel is overcome by the demonstration of God's power in supernatural events. This, we are told, makes receptivity to Christ's claim very high. In fact, it has even been suggested that people who do not experience such power are less likely not only to believe but to move on to a mature faith. But the Lord's words suggest something very different. True power evangelism involves not the doing of miracles but the proclamation of God's truth in Scripture, which is able to make people "wise for salvation through faith in Christ Jesus" (2 Tim. 3:15) (Inrig, pp. 133–34).

PRINCIPLES

- We cannot respond to spiritual truth in natural terms.
- People reject the gospel because they love darkness.
- Faith is God's command, not his request.
- The purpose of witness is to affirm by speaking the truth.

APPLICATIONS

- Let Jesus be your spiritual teacher.
- Show others that you are a lover of light.
- Never forget your own unworthiness when compared to Jesus.
- Accept and proclaim the gospel, thereby certifying that God is truth.

IV. LIFE APPLICATION

Night Landings

Intense interest captured my mind as I listened to the former naval pilot tie his experience in carrier landings with his Christian faith. Never before had I heard the metaphor developed in this way; never would I forget it.

I paraphrase loosely when I say that he told us three things make night carrier landing possible. The first is phrenol beam, a light sent up from the carrier to guide the plane in. Our speaker linked this to Jesus, the light of the world, a major theme in the Gospel of John. Picture that pilot seeing the beam come up from his home deck at the end of a long run, low on fuel and surrounded by darkness.

The second guideline is a center strobe which starts off the stern of the carrier and goes through the center of the landing area. The angle of landing looks right only if the pilot lines up his plane with the strobe. Here the aviator drew a parallel with the Scriptures which give us the information about landing correctly on God's ship of salvation—not from the side, not at an awkward angle, but straight down the middle—following the strobe line of the gospel.

Finally, as the pilot puts all these pieces together, he stays in radio contact with the landing signal officer who guides him in. The landing signal officer has only one mission—to keep the pilot focused on the phrenal beam and the strobe line. Here we see the Holy Spirit, said our speaker, who focuses our attention on Jesus and the Scriptures.

A powerful analogy! And one John might have warmed to immediately. That is what this chapter is about: how the Holy Spirit uses the message of God to point to the Son of God and draw believers to him.

V. PRAYER

Father, we come to you through Jesus, the only access you have provided. Thank you that life instead of wrath may be ours because you loved him and through him you have loved us. Amen.

VI. DEEPER DISCOVERIES

A. Rabbi (3:2,26)

The word that appears in our English Bible is a transliteration of the Greek word, used as a title of honor and respect in addressing religious leaders. Apparently it came into the language just about a hundred years before the time of Christ. *The Dictionary of Christ and the Gospels* suggests "that Saint John regarded it as a comparatively modern word, and not universally known in his time, seems evident from the fact that he deemed it necessary to explain its meaning" (p. 467).

A similar term, *Rabboni*, appears in John 20:16 when Mary recognized Jesus in the garden, a title perhaps more emphatic and honored even than *Rabbi*. Jesus was called *Rabbi* by his disciples, by a blind man, by a Pharisee, and by Judas. The term appears several times in this Gospel before the exclamation by Mary in the garden, but never again after that moment. Gariepy observes, "It is not enough that we ascribe to Christ those titles of respect and tradition. We, too, must know Him as our risen Lord. We, too, have a mandate and a mission to proclaim the Good News from a personal experience, 'I have seen the Lord.' Only a vibrant encounter with the resurrected Christ and a recognition of His mighty power leads us to know Him as He truly is and to share His message with others. In that discovery is our destiny" (Gariepy, pp. 103–04).

B. Flesh and Spirit (3:6–7)

Although we have dealt with this some in the text, additional treatment may be useful here. The word for "flesh" is *sarx*, which denotes mortality and earthly creation and connotes frailty and weakness. This is a physical understanding, not to be confused with Paul's theological treatment of the sinful nature using such words as "fleshly" or "carnal." John emphasizes the difference between earthly and heavenly and how eternal life can come.

As Borchert puts it, "The flesh of itself is unable, because of its frailty, to attain the destiny of eternal life, but the Spirit is the empowering means of life (cf. John 6:63). In the Old Testament the hope of the eschatological era was tied to the coming days of the Spirit (e.g., Joel 2:28–29; Ezk 36:26–27) and the expectation of Israel centered on the coming of the One who would embody the presence of the Spirit (e.g., Isa 61:1; cf. John 1:31–32; Lk 4:18)" (Borchert, p. 176).

The term *spirit*, on the other hand, contained significant understandings of Greek philosophy and Jewish theology. We recognize the Greek word *pneuma* from English words like *pneumonia* and *pneumatic* which have to do with breath and air. Even the Greeks regarded air as the bearer of life. In the Old Testament the *spirit* kept human beings alive (Ezek. 37:8) and also referred to the Spirit of God (Isa. 32:15–20).

The word appears 370 times in the New Testament to describe the inner personality of human beings (Rom. 8:16), good and evil spirits which indwelled the universe (Matt. 8:16), and the third person of the Trinity (as John uses it almost exclusively). Puritan writer Thomas Watson once said, "We may read many truths in the Bible, but we cannot know them savingly, 'til God by His Spirit shines upon our soul . . . He not only informs our mind, but inclines our will" (cited in Detzler, p. 359).

In my own Bible study in earlier years I profited greatly from the translations and comments of the New Testament scholar Kenneth S. Wuest. Here is a paragraph picking up the theme of new life in Christ through the Spirit: "The teaching here is that man, in his totally depraved condition, cannot be improved. Reformation will not change him into a fit subject for the kingdom of God. The flesh is incurably wicked, and cannot by any process be changed so as to produce a righteous life. What that person needs, Jesus says, is a new nature, a spiritual nature which will produce a life pleasing to God, and which will be a life fit for the kingdom of God . . . the new birth is a permanent thing, produces a permanent change in the life of the individual, and makes him a fit subject for the kingdom of God" (Wuest, pp. 57–58).

C. The Snake in the Desert (3:14)

Jesus used a simile adapted from Numbers 21, recalling the time when serpents bit the Israelites and they began to die. God sent healing to those who looked at a bronze serpent that Moses had made and placed on a pole.

The primary application centers in the cross, on which Jesus was "lifted up" to pay the penalty for our sin. But it is typical of John to build in a double meaning. Many scholars pick up on the theme of exaltation of the crucified Christ, especially since the glorification of Jesus came through his sufferings. The use of the phraseology "lifted up" in John refers exclusively to the cross. The concept of exaltation ("Let us lift up Jesus in our service this morning") is purely application, not interpretation of the text.

Looking at the snake manifested active faith. It was not sufficient for the Israelites to know that there was a snake on the pole; they had to turn in faith, expecting God's cure. So it is with the cross. It is not enough to know that Jesus was crucified on the cross; one must look to him in faith, accepting God's free gift of salvation.

By this time readers know I am drawn to the flowing narrative of older commentaries which, in their "King James fashion," poetically describe the essence of the gospel from metaphors like this one. Dods will do just fine as an example:

> Christ being lifted up, then, meant this, whatever else, that in His death sin was slain, its power to hurt ended. He being made sin for us, we are to argue that what we see done to Him is done to sin. Is He smitten, does He become accursed, does God deliver Him to death, is He at last slain and proved to be dead, so certainly dead that not a bone of Him need be broken? Then in this we are to read that sin is thus doomed by God, has been judged by Him, and was in the cross of Christ slain and put an end to—so utterly slain that there is left in it not any so faint a flicker or pulsation of life that a second blow need be given to prove it really dead (Dods, p. 124).

To which we can all respond, "Hallelujah!"

D. Son of Man (3:13–14)

In an earlier chapter we cited Charles Wesley's familiar Christmas hymn, "Hark the Herald Angels Sing." In a lesser-known but equally powerful theological text he once wrote:

> Let earth and heaven combine,
> Angels and men agree,
> To praise in songs divine
> The incarnate deity;

Our God contracted to a span,

Incomprehensibly made man (cited in Detzler, p. 357).

The phrase "Son of Man" represents a literal translation of the Aramaic for *man* or *the man*. Jesus applied it to himself eighty-eight times in the Gospels and nobody else ever used it to describe him except Stephen (Acts 7:56) and the Greeks in this Gospel (12:34). The title was also used by the author of Hebrews when he quoted Psalm 8:4 (Heb. 2:6) and by John upon his revelation of Jesus among the seven lampstands (Rev. 1:13) and as the crown prince of heaven (Rev. 14:14).

Witmer offers a helpful explanation:

Since the title had Messianic significance as a result of its occurrence in Daniel 7:13 as interpreted by subsequent Jewish scholars, Jesus' use of it was acclaimed to His identity as Israel's promised Messiah. This involved His ministry as the suffering servant and redemptive sacrifice (Matt. 20:28) who provides eternal life (John 6:53–58), accomplished by His death and resurrection at the end of His first coming. Jesus' exercise of "authority, glory, and sovereign power," is being worshipped by "all peoples, nations, and men of every language" and His eternal kingdom and "everlasting dominion" (Dan. 7:14) will not be realized until His return to earth to establish His Messianic kingdom, but Jesus was conscious of and spoke of His possession of those future Messianic prerogatives (Matt. 16:27–28; 24:30; 26:64). At least some of those Messianic rights were exercised by Jesus in His first coming, including the authority to forgive sins (9:6) and His authority over the Sabbath (12:8) (Witmer, p. 52).

In two of the first three chapters, John appears preoccupied with the nature of the Son of God. He wants his readers to grasp both humanity and deity, with a clear focus on the origin of Christ in heaven with the Father. Certainly the Lord's humanity is more definitively argued in Mark, while John focuses on a central point: Jesus Christ is God. The position of liberal theology proclaims Jesus as a historical figure, a powerful if somewhat misguided personage of the first century whose teachings were misunderstood and which led to the cross. These liberal theologians argue that Jesus never claimed to be God, but the confused Jews and Romans around him became confused and killed him for exactly such a claim.

Evangelicals believe this is the exact reverse of what the New Testament states, particularly the record of John. Jesus claimed to be God because he was God and John affirmed that deity in every possible way. One little book stands out above others in affirming John's message during the heyday of liberal theology. I offer one tasty sample from Sir Robert Anderson's, *The Lord from Heaven:*

No one who accepts the Scriptures as divine is entitled to deny that in His personal ministry, the Lord Jesus laid claim to Deity. And the crucifixion is a public proof that He did in fact assert this claim. For we are told expressly that the reason why the Jews plotted His death was because He not only broke the Sabbath but also called God His own Father, making Himself equal with God. His claim to be "Lord even of the Sabbath" was in itself an assertion of equality with the God of Sinai. And as regards His declaring Himself to be the Son of God, the question is not what these words might convey to English readers today, but what He Himself intended His hearers to understand by them.

And this He made unequivocally clear. The charge brought against Him was one from which, if false, any godly Israelite would have recoiled with horror. But instead of repelling it He accepted it in a way which even common men could understand. For He immediately asserted such absolute unity with God that the Father was responsible for His every act, including, of course, the miracle which they had denounced as a violation of the divine law. He next claimed absolute equality with God as "the author and giver of life"—the supreme prerogative of deity. And, lastly, He asserted His exclusive right to the equally divine prerogative of judgment (Anderson, p. 88).

VII. TEACHING OUTLINE

A. INTRODUCTION

1. Lead Story: Same Text—Same Sermon
2. Context: Set early in the time of Jesus' ministry, the record of his visit with Nicodemus establishes from his own mouth the principles and truths the apostle John proclaimed in chapter 1. As early as verse 3 Jesus said, "I tell you the truth, no one can see the kingdom of God unless he is born again." And at the very end of the chapter the text reminds us of the same truth: "Whoever believes in the Son has eternal life, but whoever rejects the Son will not see life, for God's wrath remains on him" (v. 36).
3. Transition: Apart from the theology of the chapter, John mentioned the issue of baptizing (vv. 22–23) which he expanded at the beginning of chapter 4. Geographically Jesus has moved from Cana in Galilee (2:1–11) to Jerusalem (2:13–3:21) and northeast of Jerusalem to the

desert (3:22–36), setting up John to say in 4:3–4, "He left Judea and went back once more to Galilee. Now he had to go through Samaria."

B. COMMENTARY

1. Conversation with Nicodemus (3:1–15)
    a. First question: "Are you here to bring in the kingdom?" First answer: "You will never see the kingdom without being born again" (3:1–3)
    b. Second question: "How can an old man be reborn?" Second answer: "You need to be born of the spirit" (3:4–8)
    c. Third question: "What does that mean?" Third answer: "It means that eternal life only comes through personal faith in the cross" (3:9–15)
2. Contrast Between Believers and Unbelievers (3:16–21)
    a. Believers have eternal life—unbelievers do not (3:16)
    b. Believers are not condemned—unbelievers are condemned already (3:17–18)
    c. Believers live in the light—unbelievers live in darkness (3:19–21)
3. Confirmation of John's Witness (3:22–36)
    a. The place of witness (3:22–26)
    b. The person of witness (3:27–30)
    c. The purpose of witness (3:31–36)

C. CONCLUSION: NIGHT LANDINGS

VIII. ISSUES FOR DISCUSSION

1. How would you explain the new birth in terms understandable to a person who never read the Bible and never attended church?
2. In your own words, explain how God saved the world through Jesus (John 3:16–18).
3. In what ways can you become less in your life and influence while Jesus Christ becomes greater?

John 4

Good News for Thirsty People

Q u o t e

"*The* Gospel is neither a discussion nor a debate.

It is an announcement."

P a u l   S .   R e e s

GEOGRAPHICAL PROFILE: SAMARIA

- Possibly named after the original source of the site
- Capital city of the Northern Kingdom of Israel (1 Kgs. 16:24)
- The relocation of peoples by the Assyrians after 722 B.C. replaced thirty thousand Jews sent to other parts of the Assyrian Empire and populated the area with foreigners
- Though they absorbed the religion of the Jews, resettled inhabitants insisted their capitol (Shechem) was the holy city rather than Jerusalem
- They constructed their temple on Mount Gerizim in the fourth century B.C.

GEOGRAPHICAL PROFILE: SYCHAR

- Situated on the main road from Jerusalem to Galilee
- Most often identified with the modern site of Askar
- Located close to Shechem and sometimes mistakenly identified with it
- Jacob's Well lies about one-half mile south of the village

- Located on the northwest side of the Sea of Galilee
- One of the best fishing sites on the lake because of springs that flow into the lake at that point
- The name means "town of Nahum" but is likely named for a major donor to its development, not the Old Testament prophet
- The synagogue at Capernaum contained the Seat of Moses which Jesus used to proclaim his message (Matt. 23:2)

John 4

IN A NUTSHELL

John 4 is the tale of two cities and how the gospel came to them. Sychar was insignificant and lay in alien territory while Capernaum had long been a prominent Galilean town. Yet when Jesus visited both, they were never the same again.

Good News for
Thirsty People

I. INTRODUCTION

A Drink from Jacob's Well

*M*ore than twenty-five years ago, our family drove through Israel for two weeks, following something of a triangle pattern from Tel-Aviv northeast to eastern Galilee, south to Jerusalem and back to Tel-Aviv. We had not intended to drive a rental car around Israel just two weeks after the Münich massacre, but our scheduled contact person was seriously ill in a Jerusalem hospital and could not assist us with the trip.

We were seasoned travelers (though the children were only twelve and nine at that point), so it seemed logical to rent a car and strike out on our own, grabbing food and lodging as we needed them along the way.

In the first week we headed south from Galilee to Jerusalem, stopping along the way to visit Jacob's Well. We stayed the night in the Arab city of Nablus, aware that we had chosen an unusual though hardly hostile venue. Tension was great in Israel at that time; armed troops jammed the airport and every major population area. Once as we drove across the Jordan River to search for the ruins of the town of Bethsaida, home of the first disciples, we came over a hilltop and were instantly surrounded by angry Israeli soldiers who insisted on knowing what we were doing there. Our explanation failed to impress them. One young man said, "This is the Golan Heights; turn your car around and leave immediately."

But the people of Nablus seemed to hold no bitterness toward this young and apparently naïve American family who stayed overnight just to visit Jacob's Well. We had no trouble finding it and, amid the olive groves, we all enjoyed a drink from that ancient source. The water was as cool and refreshing as it must have been the day Jesus stopped there almost two thousand years ago.

It may be worthwhile here to reflect a moment on John's apparent fascination with water. In the first chapter he made a great deal out of baptism both in the ministry of John the Baptist and the specific baptism of Jesus. In chapter 2 he recorded the changing of water to wine. In chapter 3 we read about Nicodemus, who was told that "no one can enter the kingdom of God unless he is born of water and the Spirit" (v. 5). Now in chapter 4 Jesus met a woman by a well, and water once again became a major topic of conversation as it commonly would among thirsty people in a desert land.

The fourth chapter of John's Gospel contains two separate but related stories. The central theme that connects them is the gospel message of Jesus and his disciples and the response of people who heard that message.

II. COMMENTARY

Good News for Thirsty People

MAIN IDEA: *The emptiness of the Samaritan woman's life could not be filled with the physical water from a well; after every drink, her thirst would return. But those who have trusted Jesus have within them a bubbling spring, a vigorous stream which guarantees no continuing spiritual thirst. Such is the indwelling presence of the Holy Spirit in the lives of believers.*

A Demonstration of Gospel Witness (4:1–26)

SUPPORTING IDEA: *Every heart contains a God-induced thirst for which the only adequate quenching is the Water of Life provided by Jesus through the Holy Spirit.*

4:1–3. Even as the chapter opens, the potential conflict with John the Baptist rises again, this time over the issue of baptism. As we read the text, we could ask, "Why didn't Jesus baptize?" Perhaps because people might emphasize the ritual more than the spiritual reality—a problem sometimes encountered in today's church. Or perhaps those people baptized by Jesus would be factious and proud. So the text tells us clearly no one could claim that kind of distinction.

The Pharisees were interested in anything that might look like a religio-political movement. They may have assumed that Jesus had now succeeded John in stirring up civil unrest. Some interpreters suggest that the Pharisees were secret admirers of Jesus but could not bring themselves to take the final step of faith because of the chains of tradition. Throughout his Gospel John portrays the Pharisees as theological conservatives who would let nothing disturb the Jewish way of life which had grown up over recent centuries.

Though John was not nearly as interested in geography as Luke, he did remind us of Acts 1:8 as the gospel spread from Jerusalem to Samaria, goaded by some pharisaical threat. Did Jesus and his disciples continue a baptismal ministry? If they did, John had no intention of talking about it for this is the last mention of baptism in this Gospel. He intended to emphasize the power of faith, not the procedure of ritual.

One more thought on these verses focuses on the name **Lord.** At the time when John wrote, the word was an expression of reverence or deity. However, throughout the Fourth Gospel it more likely means "sir" as it is translated throughout this chapter (vv. 11,15,19,49). Morris picks up on this with clarity: "It is also worth noticing that the Evangelist himself speaks of Jesus as 'the Lord' only here and in 6:23; 11:2; 20:20; 21:12. His reserve may be a mark of acquaintance with the primitive state of affairs. We should, however, notice that while the title 'Lord' was not characteristic during the earthly ministry the Lordship of Christ was there. The relationship established during the days of His flesh prepared the way for the full use of the title in later times" (Morris, p. 252).

4:4–6. To avoid comparison and controversy with John's ministry and to move out of the scrutiny of the Jerusalem Pharisees, Jesus and his disciples headed north to Galilee through Samaria. But again a question haunts us when we read that **he had to go through Samaria.** Why? The common way would be to head northwest to Jericho, cross over the river Jordan and not set foot on Samaritan soil at all. But Jesus was led by the Holy Spirit through Samaria precisely for the purpose which unfolds in this chapter. As Tenney puts it, "The words 'had to' translate an expression of necessity. While the term speaks of general necessity rather than of personal obligation, in this instance it must refer to some compulsion other than mere convenience. As the Savior of all men, Jesus had to confront the smoldering suspicion and enmity between Jew and Samaritan by ministering to his enemies" (Tenney, *EBC*, p. 54).

Let us not miss the touch of Jesus' humanity that comes to us when we read the words **tired as he was from the journey.** As Borchert points out, "It is absolutely crucial to recognize that all the Gospel writers were fully aware of the humanity of Jesus. The strategic Christian doctrine of the incarnation is not merely a theological assertion about the deity of Jesus; it is equally a theological assertion about his humanity. Heretical tendencies result when either element is omitted or submerged. Jesus was really a mortal who experienced the bodily weaknesses of being human, even though he did not suffer the human curse of sin (cf. Heb 4:15)" (Borchert, p. 201).

4:7–9. The conversation which ensued at this point was initiated and concluded by Jesus. He spoke seven times and the woman spoke six times. About noon the woman came to the well, obviously a social outcast since that hot hour would have been an unlikely time to lug a heavy water jar back into the city. It reminds us of the young women who were helped by Moses at another well about the same hour (Exod. 2:15–17). Not all interpreters agree on the hour, some suggesting that John may have been using the Roman time-reckoning system which would be about 6:00 P.M. or, as some argue, about noon. That seems so highly speculative as to be useless, since John consistently reflects the viewpoint of a Palestinian Jew throughout the entirety of this Gospel.

After having dealt with the way to Galilee, Jesus' question opens a long section of the chapter which deals with the truth of personal salvation. The woman reminded him that Jews and Samaritans had no social dealings. This situation dated back to 722 B.C. when the Assyrian captivity was concluded by Sargon, who resettled nearly thirty thousand people from Samaria to other points in the Assyrian Empire. They were replaced by captives from other countries, and a pluralistic culture of sorts developed. Any Jew would become ceremonially unclean by using a vessel handled by a Samaritan.

Notice that the last phrase of verse 9 is a parenthesis, indicating that it contains John's comment, not a part of the woman's response to Jesus. Jesus broke through two levels of prejudice. The person with whom he spoke was not only a Samaritan but a woman. For a Jewish man to speak to a Samaritan woman was unheard of, and she probably had never experienced a similar conversation. She represents an oppressed minority, still a common reality in much Middle Eastern culture. But Jesus was neither racist nor sexist. He knew that his question would lead to far more than an exchange of words and water.

4:10–12. Jesus cut right to the basics and offered **living water**. This confused the woman since she had no context for moving from physical to spiritual water. The expression **gift of God** appears only here in the Gospels, but it has become a vital part of modern Christian vocabulary. The gift of God is living water, the water of life, life itself through the Holy Spirit. Once again Morris helps our interpretation: "Jesus is speaking of the new life that He will give, a life connected with the activity of the Spirit. Notice that, although Jesus calls Himself 'the Bread of Life' (6:35), He does not refer to Himself as the living water. Living water rather, symbolizes the Spirit, whom He would send, than the Christ Himself. Oderberg shows that in a number of Jewish writings water symbolizes teaching or doctrine. It seems likely that the primary meaning here is the Holy Spirit. But, in the manner so typical of this Gospel, there may also be a reference to Jesus' teaching. If so, it will be to His teaching as issuing forth in spiritual life" (Morris, pp. 260–61).

The woman seemed quite intelligent and quickly linked the well with its original digger, emphasizing the Samaritan connection with the patriarchs. Josephus suggests that the Samaritans traced their ancestry back to Jacob through Joseph, Ephriam, and Manasseh.

Boice provides an interesting comparison between Nicodemus of chapter 3 and the Samaritan woman of chapter 4. Here is an abbreviated look at those similarities:

- Both thought they were spiritually secure.
- Both were crudely literal or materialistic in their reaction to Jesus' spiritual teaching.
- Both were spiritually empty and sensed the need for God.
- Both were spiritually lost, and that was the root of all their other problems (Boice, I, pp. 335–37).

4:13–15. The water that the woman had come to draw had to be obtained with hard labor in the sun. If the refreshing water of which this stranger spoke could be made available without all that effort, so much the better. And even that dimension of comparison is important in these verses. Jesus pointed out that the spiritual water of which he spoke is not something for which one strives in difficulty and struggle. Rather, a person receives it as it bubbles up from within.

People who depend only on physical water will be continuously thirsty. Either ignorant or resentful of their God-implanted need for spiritual water, they will always look in the wrong direction for satisfaction. Jeremiah had proclaimed this truth centuries earlier: "My people have committed two sins: They have forsaken me, the spring of living water, and have dug their own cisterns, broken cisterns that cannot hold water" (Jer. 2:13).

What could the woman have meant by her request in verse 15? Deliberate sarcasm? "If you're better than Jacob, make my life easier by producing this amazing water of which you speak." Sincere confusion? "I have no idea what you're talking about, but if you can channel a stream into our village so I don't have to come out here and get the water, I'm all for it." Caustic selfishness? "I have no idea what you're talking about, but if you can produce some kind of water in some magical way, let's see it."

Perhaps we can best see here a sincere but confused appeal from one whose life must have been filled with social suffering. I would link her response with Nicodemus's words in John 3:9: "How can this be?"

4:16–18. Beginning with verse 16, Jesus pushed all metaphors aside and dealt in straight talk. Like this woman, we must recognize our sin and understand that God sees us for what we are. Surely the change in topic must have seemed abrupt, but again the woman did not miss a beat. What she said was true—she had no husband—at the moment. And the fact that she spoke the truth was the very point at which Jesus pinned down the reality.

Family connections were important in the Jewish religion and would soon become a major metaphor for the church. Believers are the bride of Christ who will attend the marriage supper of the Lamb. Husbands are to love their wives as Christ loved the church. Christians are brothers and sisters in the family of God.

Here was a woman who lived outside the boundaries of any religious or cultural standards of her day. A string of five husbands followed by a lover is certainly not unknown in the twenty-first century, but it is hardly common even in our permissive society with its twisted tolerance for evil. In first-century Samaria, such a domestic arrangement was unthinkable.

The gospel has social implications. The first requirement for eligibility to receive living water is a recognition of sin for what it is. In a passage which shows us Jesus' humanity (he was tired and thirsty) we also see his deity. He exercised the divine attribute of omniscience which we have already seen when he said to Nathanael, "I saw you while you were still under the fig tree before Philip called you" (John 1:48). The woman picked up on this immediately and later told her neighbors, "Come, see a man who told me everything I ever did" (4:29).

4:19–20. Embarrassed by Jesus' penetrating analysis of her moral condition, the woman turned the discussion to religion, notably the proper place of worship. She conceded she was no longer talking to a dusty stranger with peculiar ideas about the source of water, but a **prophet**. The Jews had a long line of prophets, and they used the term quite freely. The Samaritans, on the other hand, recognized no prophet after Moses other than the one of whom Moses spoke in Deuteronomy 18:18. It is possible that the woman connected Jesus with the promised Messiah.

To turn the conversation away from her personal morals, she raised what may have been the most important distinction in Jewish and Samaritan theology—the place of worship. Abraham and Jacob had worshiped on Mount Gerizim (Gen. 12:7; 33:20). According to the Samaritans, that was the very place Abraham had offered Isaac on the altar. Samaritans overlooked references to Jerusalem in the historical books (2 Chr. 6; 7:12) and acknowledged only the Pentateuch, so Jerusalem worship meant nothing to them. They had built on Mount Gerizim four hundred years earlier a temple that was destroyed by the Jews around 128 B.C. The appropriate site of worship now became the topic.

4:21–24. In this passage we find one of the strongest worship statements in the New Testament. Ten of John's thirteen uses of the Greek word for *worship* appear in these few verses. We learn immediately that place is irrelevant and that worship is not primarily in body—through physical motions and activities—but **in spirit**. The text does not refer to the Holy Spirit but an attitude of heart which acknowledges God and his sovereignty over our lives. Furthermore, worship must be done **in truth**—honestly, biblically, centered on Christ. This paragraph shows the difference between religion and the gospel: religion describes humankind's search for God; the gospel describes the way God reached down to humanity.

But the repeated phrase **a time is coming** grabs our attention, especially in view of the addition in verse 23—**and has now come.** Is this the same "hour" as the one we encountered in John 2:4? Borchert thinks so and suggests, "The mention of 'hour' here is a Johannine theme which encapsulates the decisive moment in history of the crucifixion and resurrection that transformed and continues to transform human reality" (Borchert, p. 207). Yes, that is the common way the word is used throughout the epistle. But there seems to be something uncommon about this occasion, precisely because of the phrase **has now come.**

Rather than the hour of crucifixion, the emphasis here seems to rest upon the first advent. The Messiah has appeared; the gospel has already been proclaimed;

life and light are available. True believers must stop this mindless, endless, meaningless bickering about sites and sounds of worship. God is not interested in Jews or Samaritans, Presbyterians or Methodists, Calvinists or Arminians. He is interested in worshipers who **must worship in spirit and in truth.**

Nevertheless, honesty and candor required that Jesus correct the woman's theological error: the Samaritans were wrong since **salvation is from the Jews.** But that was an Old Testament argument and a new time has come, bringing with it a new attitude and aura of worship. Temples and tabernacles, mountains and cities were fading symbols of the past, shadows of the spiritual reality who now stood before her. Marcus Dods states the point eloquently:

> Rich music, striking combinations of colour and of architectural forms, are nothing to God so far as worship goes, except insofar as they bring the human spirit into fellowship with Him. Persons are differently constituted, and what is natural to one will be formal and artificial to another. Some worshippers will always feel that they get closer to God in private, in their own silent room, and with nothing but their own circumstances and wants to stimulate; they feel that a service carefully arranged and abounding in musical effects does indeed move them, but does not make it easier for them to address themselves to God. Others, again, feel differently; they feel that they can best worship God in spirit when the forms of worship are expressive and significant. But in two points all will agree: first, that in external worship, while we strive to keep it simple, we should also strive to make it good—the best possible of its kind. If we are to sing God's praise at all, then let the singing be the best possible, the best music a congregation can join in, and executed with the utmost skill that care can develop. Music which cannot be sung save by persons of exceptional musical talent is unsuitable for congregational worship; but music which requires no consideration, and admits of no excellence, is hardly suitable for the worship of God. I do not know what idea of God's worship is held by persons who never put themselves to the least trouble to improve it so far as they are concerned. The other point in which we all will agree, is that where the Spirit is not engaged there is no worship at all (Dods, pp. 156–57).

4:25–26. So the woman had faith after all; like most Samaritans, she waited the coming of the Messiah who would finally put an end to all bickering and confusion about the spiritual life. And since only the Messiah could straighten out religious confusion, there was no further point in talking about husbands or worship or any such complicated questions. But she was hardly prepared for the next statement—the only occasion of New Testament record other than his trial on which Jesus claimed to be the Christ. The literal translation of the Greek text is, "I am the one speaking to you."

The use of *ego eimi* (**I am**) represents an important theological theme in this Gospel. Usually there is a metaphoric connection such as Bread of Life (6:35) or the Good Shepherd (10:14). But here it becomes what Borchert calls "the shocking reality of a confession of the divine-human presence" (Borchert, p. 209). An absolute declaration of deity. "You are waiting for the Messiah? Then you should be interested in this conversation because I have come and am speaking personally to you."

Bible students know how strongly Jesus linked himself with Yahweh of the Old Testament, notably the references in Isaiah 40–55. The announcement of the arrival of a Messiah represents an enormous fulfillment of promise. Jews and Samaritans had waited centuries to hear what this peasant woman heard from the lips of the Son of God. Westcott reminds us how this serves us even in the present hour:

> It cannot have been for nothing that God was pleased to disclose His counsels, fragment by fragment through long intervals of silence and disappointment and disaster. In that slow preparation for the perfect revelation of Himself come in which was most inadequately apprehended till it was finally given, we discern the pattern of His ways. As it was in the case of the first Advent, even so now He is guiding the course of the world to the second Advent. We can see enough in the past, to find a vantage ground for faith; and, when the night is deepest and all sight fails, shall we not still *endure*, like the men of old time, *as seeing the invisible?* (Westcott, p. 27).

B Explanation of Gospel Witness (4:27–38)

SUPPORTING IDEA: *Through honest testimony, people whom God has prepared will understand and believe the gospel.*

4:27–30. The disciples had been in town buying groceries during Jesus' conversation with the woman, but now they returned. Since it was midday, they urged Jesus to have some lunch. The conversion of the woman described in verses 27–30 and the personal concern for Jesus' nourishment expressed by the disciples was followed by personal control that Jesus asserted over the disciples' confusion regarding their mission that day. We've already noted why the disciples would naturally be **surprised to find him talking with a woman.** But spiritual sensitivity and a sense of courtesy overcome their natural Jewish revulsion at this predicament. We can only imagine what Judas thought on this occasion.

A change in the woman is noted by several important elements of verses 28–29:

- She had come to draw water, but she was so excited that she abandoned her water jar.
- She rushed back into town and exclaimed the revelations of her personal life when, just a short time ago, she had come to the well alone, quite likely as a social outcast.
- On the basis of Jesus' omniscience, she raised the question of whether the Messiah had come.

Boice calls her report "the cry of a new life" and somewhat dogmatically draws his conclusion: "What had happened was that the woman had been born again. She is the first clear example in the Gospel. She had come down the hill a child of Adam's race, thinking only of the life she had known and of her very mundane need for more water. Instead she had met the second Adam, Jesus, who had filled her with a desire for a quality of life that she had never dreamed of and who had revealed Himself to her as the One through whom that life is imparted to men and women. As a result of Christ's words the woman believed on Him and became His witness" (Boice, I, p. 380).

The NIV has done a nice job of rendering the woman's question since the original text shows it to be tentative, not rhetorical.

Some question has been raised about the translation of **people** in verse 28 and the corollary pronoun **they** in verse 30. *Anthropos* is the common word for man. Borchert suggests, "I think we have here a woman who probably knew where to find the men of the town, and her story also may well have been their story!" (Borchert, p. 211). Perhaps that pushes the woman's past just a bit too far in this story. If it means *men only,* she may have contacted the elders of the city on what surely was for Samaritans the most touchy theological point of all. More than likely however, *anthropos* means **people** in this context, since Greek contains a more specific term for adult males.

4:31–35. Meanwhile, the disciples had more pressing concerns than the evangelism of an entire town. They showed legitimate concern for their leader and friend, confident that he must be exhausted and hungry. But their spiritual immaturity prohibited them from seeing into the spiritual realities of the situation. Like Nicodemus, they could not make the transfer from the earthly to the heavenly.

Picking up the food metaphor, Jesus pointed the disciples to the immediate opportunity for ministry, fields white and ripe for harvest, a description Christians have always found applicable to their own situation in any age. Interpreters have pondered for centuries what Jesus meant by the words, **open your eyes and look at the fields! They are ripe for harvest.** Perhaps the time was fall and he gestured to actual harvest-ready fields surrounding Sychar. Or maybe the white-robed Samaritans, already out of the city and heading down the hill, represented the harvest of that day.

The venerable Sir Robert Andrews argues that John intended a chronological cue by recording this line. The problem is that scholars differ on whether the harvest was still four months distant or right at hand. Andrews takes the reference as "the only datum we have by which to determine the time of the year when Jesus went into Galilee." But he also reminds us, "Some, however, deny that this reference to the harvest as yet four months distant is of any chronological value, because the expression is a proverbial one, based upon the fact that there is an average interval of four months between the sowing and harvesting" (Andrews, pp. 182–83).

Perhaps the best interpretation minimizes the chronological import and stays with the main storyline which John offered as a video rather than a snapshot. The disciples had just approached Jesus by the well, the Samaritans were on their way out of the city, the topic was food (bread made from grain), so Jesus contrasted the yet-distant grain harvest with the immediate heart harvest. Whether all this was based on a common proverb of the time, we can only guess.

4:36–38. Sowers and reapers are often different people. In this particular instance, the disciples were about to join the harvest at Sychar where they had not previously worked. But who were the **others** who had done **the hard work**? Certainly Old Testament prophets would be included, and perhaps even John the Baptist, whose influence could have spread into Samaria. We find a key companion passage in 1 Corinthians 3:6–8: "I planted the seed, Apollos watered it, but God made it grow. So neither he who plants nor he who waters is anything, but only God, who makes things grow. The man who plants and the man who waters have one purpose, and each will be rewarded according to his own labor."

The Samaritan evangelism project had already begun, and Jesus wanted these disciples to understand the principle of uniting sowers and reapers. The main focus was spiritual, a Samaritan model of a task that would last until Jesus returns. In eternity's efforts, we can allow no competition among those who work in God's fields. Some sow, some reap, but they rejoice together—an appropriate picture of what the church ought to be in collective ministry today. We would love to focus the spotlight on reaping, but there is no reaping without sowing. Sowing is useless unless someone has watered and cultivated, sometimes for a long period of time. Whatever our tasks in the harvest, we must handle them in cooperation with other workers.

C Personalization of Gospel Witness (4:39–42)

SUPPORTING IDEA: *When we cooperate with other believers in faithful evangelistic efforts, God is able to turn hearts toward him.*

4:39–41. We already know the woman had a change of heart and mind that indicated new birth. She had gone back to town to announce her meeting with Jesus. John reported that many Samaritans believed that day **because of the woman's testimony.** But since this is one of John's key words, he wanted to emphasize what actually happened in that town. Preliminary faith that rested on the woman's testimony became solid faith after the Savior had stayed there two days and proclaimed his message.

How did Jesus witness? He was friendly; he asked questions; he showed concern for human need; he faithfully explained the Scriptures; and he emphasized good news for thirsty people. Witnesses are not responsible for converting people; their task is to tell the truth about what they know.

4:42. The corporate announcement at the end of the passage is nothing less than dramatic: **we know that this man really is the Savior of the world.** Remember that **world** (*kosmos*) is one of John's key words, appearing 185 times in the New Testament, 105 of those in John's writings. Earlier the discussion centered on two sites of worship, Jerusalem and Mount Gerizim. Then the talk turned to the coming Messiah, surely still a localized expectation related to Samaritan theology. Now, after two days with Jesus, these new converts understood the gospel very well.

The phrase appears only here and in 1 John 4:14, but it encapsulates John's universal message—"Whosoever will may come." I like Borchert's treatment of the text:

> The expression "Savior of the world" is particularly Johannine. It coordinates magnificently with the baptizer's initial confession of Jesus as the paschal "Lamb of God, who takes away the sin of the world" (John 1:29). John saw Jesus as the answer to the world's need. The people of the world were the focus of God's love in Jesus (3:16). The outcasts of Samaria here articulated the purpose of God because Jesus was their expected *Taheb*, the Savior of the world. Their confession stands as a vivid contrast to the disgust of the Pharisees and the story of the entry into Jerusalem just prior to Passover when in exasperation they finally complained, "The whole world has gone after Him!" (12:19) (Borchert, p. 215–16).

Ⅾ Propagation of Gospel Witness (4:43–54)

SUPPORTING IDEA: *Sometimes God allows us to experience desperate faith in order to move us toward deliberate faith.*

4:43–45. John's purpose in this Gospel was not just to bring people to saving faith, but to increase the faith they already had, to teach Jesus' followers to believe in such a way that they could live life abundantly. It had been an exciting two days in Samaria and now Jesus and his disciples headed north into Galilee, the northern province of his home in Nazareth. In Matthew and

Mark the phrase **own country** refers specifically to Nazareth. John may have been foreshadowing what would come.

Other interpreters, however, suggest that in going north Jesus was leaving Judea, the **own country** represented by Jerusalem where he had already been rejected. But by whom? The first verse of this chapter (4:1) indicates that his ministry in Judea was well received. Nevertheless, Westcott argues for Judea, and Lightfoot identifies **own country** with heaven, to which Morris replies, "This view is much to be preferred to that which sees John as locating Jesus in Judea" (Morris, p. 286). John, however, always saw Jesus as a Galilean (1:46; 2:12; 7:1–4,40–43,52; 19:19). We also know that Jesus was rejected in the Galilean synagogue (Matt. 13:57; Mark 6:4; Luke 4:24), so this seems to be the best choice of the passage.

Perhaps John's major point here contrasted the Galileans' previous attitude with their attitude after the Jerusalem miracles (2:23). John did not make a big point of miracles, although he would unfold a second one before the end of this chapter.

4:46–50a. On this return to Galilee, Jesus also visited Cana (bypassing Nazareth), the location of the water-to-wine miracle recorded in chapter 2. There he encountered a request for help from a royal official who served in the court of Herod Antipas, the tetrarch of Galilee. Some interpreters suggest the man could have been a Gentile centurion, but perhaps not since Jesus directed his early ministry exclusively to Jews. This official had made the journey of twenty-five miles on the basis of Jesus' reputation.

Notice the verbs as John draws a picture of a desperate man. He **heard that Jesus had arrived,** and **he went to him and begged him.** The word describes repeated and persistent pleas. Desperate faith drove him to Jesus and also drove him to his knees.

The Lord's words shock us as they must have shocked the royal official. He did not address the desperate man but spoke in the plural (**you**) to the crowd, accusing them of wanting only more **signs and wonders.** But faith built only on the spectacular is not biblical faith. Perhaps Jesus drew a contrast here between the Samaritans in Sychar who believed because of his message and the Jews in Cana who were interested only in physical miracles.

Before we look at the faith factor, let us clarify a couple of common misunderstandings in this passage. The royal official of John 4 should not be confused with the centurion of Matthew 8 and Luke 7. The town was the same (Capernaum), but in the Synoptics we read about a dying slave rather than a dying son. Many scholars argue that all the Gospel writers drew from a common source and changed the flavor of the story. But John took great pains to establish his eyewitness account and also, writing much later, had opportunity to review all the Synoptic accounts while preparing his own.

Another pointed issue is the phrase **signs and wonders** which has taken on immense popularity in our day. John generally used the word **signs** (*semia*), but this is the only appearance of **wonders** (*terrata*). Borchert writes, "In the ancient world miracles and acts of power were linked to the presence of the miracle worker, but here the healer refused to be present. The story, therefore, is an important illustration of the purpose for which John wrote the Gospel." And again, "Jesus is clearly portrayed in the Gospel as one who seeks to lead persons through stages of inadequate believing to satisfactory believing even if it means denying the person or request" (Borchert, p. 220).

Jesus did not say **you may go** as the NIV translates. The word **go** is imperative, so the man has been commanded by the Savior of the world with a promise of life for his son. But if he left, according to his way of thinking, he would leave behind his one chance for help. Jesus demanded that his faith be desperate enough to trust his word, not just his visible works.

Wonders may produce awe, but words produce faith. Remember John's theme: Believing is seeing. Our modern society assumes everything must be tested by science, explained with logic, or personally experienced. When it passes those tests, it can be identified as reality. But the writer of Hebrews said, "Now faith is being sure of what we hope for and certain of what we do not see" (11:1).

This story is so dramatically human because it is so like life. Any of us who has failed or flunked, been fired or flattened can understand desperate faith. In my view of the passage, Jesus did not criticize the royal official but rather the Galileans who gathered around because **they had seen all that He had done in Jerusalem at the Passover Feast.**

4:50b–54. The man obeyed, persisted, and received the promise of a miracle. Most notable in this section of chapter 4 is the phrase that appears at the end of verse 50: **The man took Jesus at his word.** This kind of faith God constantly rewarded in the New Testament, and particularly in the Gospels. The total trust that Jesus will do what he has promised, a response to the Savior, culminates in faith-behavior—actually doing what Jesus says to do.

Apparently it was too late in the day to begin the trip back to Capernaum, but the next day the royal official set out to cover the twenty-five miles. We can only imagine the anxiety of that seemingly endless trip, but the servants brought the good news before he arrived home. The father asked about the timing of the child's recovery, and his faith was confirmed. Vague and impersonal faith became specific and personal faith. The word **believed** has no direct or indirect object in verse 53, so we assume the royal official **and all his household** exhibited intentional faith in Jesus' person, his deity, and his messianic claims.

Not only did the royal official himself believe, but he shared the entire experience with his family. The concept of "household salvation" is certainly not uncommon in the New Testament, and we are reminded here of the Philippian jailer in Acts 16. Let us keep a good balance here. While recognizing the strong influence of the major male member of a household in first-century Middle Eastern culture, we must also acknowledge that everyone in the house knew how sick the boy was as well as when and why he recovered. In fact, the faith of the members of the household, not having spoken with Jesus as their master did, represents the kind of faith John describes throughout this Gospel.

John did not record any other witnessing done by this man, but the story obviously got back to him so it could be included in the Gospel. A very private miraculous sign moved a petty politician from desperate faith to deliberate faith. Jesus came to save us from sin. But he does not want us to trust him just because we are desperate and have no other choices. He wants us to believe in his word and trust him with every part of our lives.

In a classic work published almost a hundred years ago, Archbishop Trench describes the growth of the noblemen's faith: "But did he not believe already? Was not this healing itself a gracious reward of his faith? Yes, he believed that particular word of the Lord's; but this is something more, the entering into the number of Christ's disciples, the yielding of himself to Him as to the promised Messiah. Of admitting that he already truly believed, there may be indicated here a strengthening and augmenting of his faith. For faith may be true, and yet most capable of this increase" (Trench, p. 131).

> **MAIN IDEA REVIEW:** *The emptiness of the Samaritan woman's life could not be filled with the physical water from a well; after every drink, her thirst would return. But those who have trusted Jesus have within them a bubbling spring, a vigorous stream which guarantees no continuing spiritual thirst. Such is the indwelling presence of the Holy Spirit in the lives of believers.*

III. CONCLUSION

Optimistic Outlook

When asked what he thought about when he struck out, Babe Ruth said, "I think about hitting home runs." When inducted into the Hall of Fame, gold-medal winner Roger Blough had just come off a three-year record of three wins, seventeen losses, and two ties. In accepting the honor, Blough observed, "We won over 75 percent of the games we didn't lose." Genuine faith requires optimism, not related to what we can achieve, but what God will do based on the words of Jesus.

The two marvelous stories of this chapter describe Jesus' intervention in the lives of individuals and the collective life of an entire town. Perhaps it would be useful to review how many times the word *must* has appeared in the last two chapters. In John 3:7 we learned, "You must be born again." In John 3:14 we saw that "the Son of Man must be lifted up." And now in John 4:24 we learn that "worshipers must worship in spirit and in truth."

The Bible records numerous "musts" for the practice of our Christian faith. The gospel does not center in signs and wonders, or even in healing and teaching, but in death and resurrection. An optimistic outlook is always healthy, but optimism is not faith. The kind of faith John has been talking about for four chapters centers in heart conviction that Jesus Christ the Son of God, the Messiah, the Savior of the world can alone provide eternal life.

The Student Volunteer Movement for Missions met in Des Moines, Iowa, in 1920 and voted to drop traditional aspects of its program which had focused on Bible study, evangelism, and foreign missions. Instead it chose to focus on racial injustice, imperialism, and other social issues. Within fifteen years the movement was dead. Thirsty people need more than optimism. They need good news and that good news centers in the only one who can say, "The water I give [you] will become in [you] a spring of water welling up to eternal life" (John 4:14).

PRINCIPLES

- All of us get thirsty, tired, and sometimes disgusted at our personal lives.
- Only the Holy Spirit can provide internal bubbling joy for believers.
- When Christians work together in cooperation rather than competition, entire towns can be reached with the gospel.
- Signs and wonders are exciting, but genuine faith rests in the promises of Scripture.

APPLICATIONS

- When you are thirsty, meet Jesus at the well of the Word.
- Remember that worship is a matter of person, not place.
- Never overlook some service you can do for God now by saying something like, "Four months more and then the harvest."
- Always take Jesus at his word and obey.

IV. LIFE APPLICATION

Parties and Promises

A modern parable tells about a young man who went off to college—let us call him Todd. Todd was a Christian, but he got mixed up with a group of students who would get drunk on weekends—a major problem on many university campuses. Todd did not drink much, but he would pretend to be drunk in order to fit in with the group. One night, the driver was seriously stoned and weaving all over the road on the way back to campus. Todd was frightened out of his wits—but not frightened enough to intervene and take the wheel. He prayed that God would get him home alive and promised he would never get drunk again. His desperate faith worked for the moment; he got home safely.

But a few weeks later, the promise was forgotten; he went out with the same group of friends to get drunk again. But just as he was about to take his first drink, he remembered that hair-raising ride as well as his desperate prayer and God's answer. He walked out of the party, found another ride back to campus, and never drank again. Desperate faith had led him to pray, but deliberate faith led him to a changed lifestyle.

We need to look back and see God's hand at work in our lives. Such a faith-history can give us new strength to listen to God, trust his Word, and follow his direction for our lives. The God who helps us through the desperate times should be the object of our deliberate faith.

- Think of how God honored a time when you made a sacrifice, and have the deliberate faith to sacrifice again.
- Think of how God honored a time when you obeyed him even though it was tough, and have the deliberate faith to obey again.
- Think of a time when God rewarded your patience, and have the deliberate faith to be patient again.
- Remember a time when God rewarded your stand on a conviction, and have the deliberate faith to take a stand again.

I began driving before seat belts were installed in cars. Even after we had them for many years, they were optional equipment. Our children would play in the back of our station wagon with no safety attachments whatsoever. But when seat belt laws were passed, we changed our habits. But imagine a man who survives a terrible accident because of a seat belt. Very likely he now buckles his seat belt regularly, not because of the law, but because he has experienced its lifesaving power.

Jesus came to save us from sin, but he does not want us to trust him just because it is the law or because we're supposed to follow certain religious traditions—not even because we are desperate and have no other choice. The Savior of the world wants us to trust him because we believe his promises are true and because he has never failed us in the past.

V. PRAYER

Father, thank you for the eternal spring of life within us. May we drink daily of its refreshing, life-giving waters in order to keep our spiritual lives healthy and happy. Amen.

VI. DEEPER DISCOVERIES

A. Jacob's Well (4:6)

For twenty years Jacob had lived in Paddan Aram. But when he returned to ancient Palestine he settled near Mount Gerizim and bought some land from Tamor, the father of Shechem (Gen. 33:18–20). Some years later Joseph was buried at this same site (Josh. 24:32). One cannot be sure of the site then or now, but most scholars agree that the original well Jacob dug on his land was the one at which Jesus met the Samaritan woman. Beers says, "In A.D. 670 a visitor wrote that it was 240 feet deep. In 1697 another said it was only 105 feet deep. By 1861, it was only 75 feet deep. The reason for this changing depth is that pilgrims threw pebbles into the well throughout the centuries, gradually filling it in. But water from the well is still pure enough to drink" (Beers, p. 355).

B. Samaritans (4:4)

It all began just after 722 B.C. when the Assyrians resettled the northern kingdom territory with captives from other countries. Theological pluralism ensued. When the remnants of the Israelites returned from Babylon in 539 B.C., they found themselves at odds with the residents of Samaria. In the fourth century B.C. the Samaritans built their temple atop Mount Gerizim and the relationships between these two groups deteriorated further. During the time of the Maccabees the Samaritans dedicated the temple to Zeus Xenios. Bitterness exploded into a full-fledged war during which the temple was destroyed by John Hyrcanus, nephew of Judas Maccabeus.

By the time of John 4, the Samaritans numbered in the hundreds of thousands. The respected *Dictionary of Christ and the Gospels* describes the antipathy, resting its report somewhat on the work of Josephus: "During the period of unrest that followed the deposition of Archelaus (A.D. 6), the Samaritans became so aggressive that they came privately into Jerusalem by night, and, when the gates of the Temple were opened just after midnight, they entered and scattered dead men's bodies in the cloisters to defile the Temple . . . this led to civil war for a time, then to the intervention of the Roman authorities, and ultimately to a decision in favour of the Jews by Claudius himself (A.D. 51)" (p. 558).

So it is not difficult to understand the attitudes that existed at the time of Jesus' visit (about A.D. 29–30). Such information makes even more remarkable the parable of "The Good Samaritan," since in the eyes of Jesus' Jewish contemporaries, there were no good Samaritans.

Today a handful of Samaritans live amid a sea of Arabs who hate them almost as much as they do the Jews. A small community still clusters around

Mount Gerizim, living and working in Nablus, speaking Arabic, and dressing like Arabs. On holy days they still trudge up the slope of Gerizim to perform rituals at the ruins of the ancient temple.

C. God Is Spirit (4:24)

This phrase anchors the worship section of John 4 like the fourth man on a relay team. Foundational to worshiping "in spirit and truth" is an understanding of the nature of the Father. God is not confined to space and time, gender, ethnic origin, or any other human boundaries. Tenney reminds us that this verse "carries one of the four descriptions of God found in the New Testament. The other three are 'God is light' (1 John 1:5), 'God is love' (1 John 4:8,16), and 'God is a consuming fire' (Heb. 12:29) . . . [God] cannot be represented adequately by an abstract concept, which is intrinsically impersonal, nor can any idol depict His likeness since He is not material. Only 'the word become flesh' could represent Him adequately" (Tenney, *EBC,* p. 56).

Passages like this remind us of our own link with God through creation. He made us in his image, and a major portion of that image is our spirituality. Through our spirits we understand God's truth and communicate with God.

D. I Am (4:26)

As noted earlier in the "Commentary" section, this phrase in this context represents an absolute claim to deity. Such statements occur seven times in John's Gospel (4:26; 6:20; 8:24,28,58; 13:19; 18:5). Seven additional times the words link up with a metaphor (6:35; 8:12; 9:5; 10:7,9,11,14; 11:25; 14:6; 15:1,5). We will touch on the metaphors as they appear and particularly in chapter 8. Here we observe the striking finality of the statement. Lewis correctly links it to Exodus 3:14—"I AM WHO I AM."

> God is not merely placing before His people an intriguing piece of religious information; He is telling them something about Himself that is momentous for them. Notice that He does not say, "I am this" or "I am that," but simply, "I am who I am." That is, He is conditioned and defined by nothing outside Himself. He is the unconditioned God: eternal in His being and unbounded in His freedom and resources. Yahweh is the self-existent deity who can be to His people all that He chooses and all that they need. In this covenant context His "I am who I am" really means, "All that I am, I am for you." God in his unfathomable and unlimited being was putting Himself at the disposal of His beloved people: He who was all things in Himself would be all things to them (Lewis, p. 90).

We can hardly place such highly developed theology upon the shoulders of the Samaritan peasant woman, but we have no difficulty sensing the excitement of John's readers when they actually saw the scroll of this fourth chapter. The disciples were not present when these words were spoken, so John did not hear the statement in its initial form. We assume Jesus later told the disciples the story, or perhaps the woman had repeated it numerous times during the two days of ministry in the village. Of course the Holy Spirit guarded and guided John's record.

VII. TEACHING OUTLINE

A. INTRODUCTION

1. Lead Story: A Drink from Jacob's Well
2. Context: John's brilliant arrangement of materials continued to build his case for the perfect humanity and deity of Jesus, the Son of God. He selected his miracles carefully and soon introduced the healing of the man at the Pool of Bethesda, but first he took Jesus on a quick trip back to Galilee with an important stop in Samaria. The chapter closes with the words, "This was the second miraculous sign that Jesus performed" which, in John's system, would not mean the second of all miracles, but the second that appears in John's pattern of theology.
3. Transition: The geographical transition takes us from Jerusalem to Galilee, where Jesus ministered for some time. The theological transition is even greater as we see the gospel proclaimed to the outlaw Samaritans and a politician from Herod's court.

B. COMMENTARY

1. Demonstration of Gospel Witness (4:1–26)
   a. The way to Galilee (4:1–6)
   b. The truth of personal salvation (4:7–18)
   c. The life for a worshiper (4:19–26)
2. Explanation of Gospel Witness (4:27–38)
   a. Personal conversion (4:27–30)
   b. Personal concern (4:31–33)
   c. Personal control (4:34–38)
3. Personalization of Gospel Witness (4:39–42)
   a. Faith from testimony (4:39–40)
   b. Faith from theology (4:41)
   c. Faith from experience (4:42)
4. Propagation of Gospel Witness (4:43–54)
   a. Return to Galilee (4:43–45)
   b. Request for help (4:46–49)
   c. Response to the Savior (4:50–54)

C. CONCLUSION: PARTIES AND PROMISES

VIII. ISSUES FOR DISCUSSION

1. What is the significance of baptism in your congregation and how does it relate to the baptism John describes at the beginning of this chapter?
2. Describe some ways we humans can know that we are spiritually thirsty.
3. How can you tell if you are worshiping God in spirit and truth in your public worship at church? In your private worship?
4. Where are the ripened harvest fields in today's world?
5. What role do miracles play in the life of God's people today?

John 5

The Light of
the World

I. INTRODUCTION
Pedal for Your Life

II. COMMENTARY
A verse-by-verse explanation of the chapter.

III. CONCLUSION
The Heretical Scales

An overview of the principles and applications from the chapter.

IV. LIFE APPLICATION
The Mahatma and the Master

Melding the chapter to life.

V. PRAYER
Tying the chapter to life with God.

VI. DEEPER DISCOVERIES
Historical, geographical, and grammatical enrichment of the commentary.

VII. TEACHING OUTLINE
Suggested step-by-step group study of the chapter.

VIII. ISSUES FOR DISCUSSION
Zeroing the chapter in on daily life.

"Whatever light men find they doubt it; They love not light, but talk about it."

John Masefield

GEOGRAPHICAL PROFILE: BETHESDA

- A spring-fed pool surrounded by five porches
- Probably located in the northeast part of the city
- In 1888 archeological work uncovered two large pools and five porches and numerous fragments of marble columns
- The same discovery (of a time somewhat after the first century) also found a fresco of an angel in the act of troubling the waters

PERSONAL PROFILE: MOSES

- Member of the tribe of Levi, brother of Aaron and Miriam
- Raised for forty years in Egypt by the Pharaoh's daughter
- Lived forty years in the desert of Midian
- At the age of eighty called by God to deliver Israel from Egyptian bondage
- Died at the age of 120 before entering the Promised Land

IN A NUTSHELL

The central theme of this chapter is captured in verse 24: "I tell you the truth, whoever hears my word and believes him who sent me has eternal life and will not be condemned; he has crossed over from death to life." Once again, Jesus divides all humanity into two groups. The first have received eternal life; the others, condemnation because they have not crossed over the line. The theme of this chapter centers in the unity of the Father and the Son. John typically emphasizes that both life and condemnation are present possessions with eternal consequences. The miracle and the message that follow challenge readers to find life by trusting Christ in faith.

The Light of the World

I. INTRODUCTION

Pedal for Your Life

$\mathcal{B}$icycles are very popular today, with double-figure speeds, all kinds of fancy equipment, laws for the wearing of helmets, and riding paths for bikes. Just one hundred years ago, however, the bicycle was just progressing to the point at which it was powered by pedal cranks and a chain drive—a fascinating gadgetry which intrigued inventors because of its possible other uses.

In 1895, for example, a Frenchman by the name of François Barathon designed a one-person, pedal-driven life preserver for use in case of shipwreck. It consisted of a saucer-shaped metal dish containing an inflatable rubber bag and some machinery.

To survive, the rider was told to sit on the bag which held both him and machine afloat while he turned two sets of cranks, one with his hands and one with his feet. The cranks worked two propellers, the foot-crank placed vertically to keep the strange craft afloat, and the hand-crank pushed from behind to make progress toward shore. For obvious reasons, the pedaling life preserver never quite caught on.

This chapter in John's Gospel also deals with saving life—but not by pedaling. People in our society like to say, "God helps those who help themselves." But John 5 demonstrates precisely the opposite—God helps those who are incapable of helping themselves. The invalid at Bethesda had been rejected by other people who took advantage of his helplessness. Jesus asked just one question, "Do you want to get well?" (v. 6). People need life preservers for life on earth and for eternity. Once again in this chapter, we are told how that is possible.

II. COMMENTARY

The Light of the World

> **MAIN IDEA:** *Salvation comes through sincere and complete faith in the Savior.*

Divine Grace (5:1–9a)

> **SUPPORTING IDEA:** *In this third miracle of John's Gospel, we see proof of Jesus' deity as he moves from near obscurity to open debate with the religious leaders of Jerusalem about the Sabbath.*

5:1–3. As chapter 5 opens, John made a geographical switch from Galilee to Jerusalem and specifically the Pool of Bethesda, a gathering place for invalids. Apparently the pool was located in the northeast corner of the old city. It functioned under considerable local superstition as a place with miraculous healing powers.

John also dropped a vague chronological note when he observed it was feast time. Many interpreters argue this was a second Passover, but Tasker warns, "If we adopt the better-attested reading *a feast* in v. I, which now has the additional support of the Bodmer Papyrus, the reference could be to any feast, and there is no need to assume, as many commentators do, that the chapters have been dislocated, and to attempt to restore the 'original' order by placing chapter iv before chapter v" (Tasker, pp. 84–85).

Many suggestions have been offered as a substitute for the Passover—Pentecost, Purim, Dedication, Trumpets. But two arguments persist: a recognition of this feast as the Passover would stretch the record of John through three and one-half years, a figure commonly preferred by most evangelical Bible scholars for the earthly ministry of Jesus.

Also, it was an important enough feast to draw Jesus back to Jerusalem and we must consider that impact. Borchert indicates that the strong emphasis on Sabbath in this chapter may be the key to recognizing a Passover feast here. He says, "The problem with searching for a name for the unnamed feast is that it involves filling in what is perceived to be a chronological gap in John, failing to realize the theological nature of these festival statements and the cyclical pattern that focuses these chapters on Passover" (Borchert, p. 230).

5:4. The fourth verse has no significant textual support and is therefore omitted by the NIV, although some will be familiar with wording from the KJV describing the angel who would stir up the waters and the hope that the first person in the pool after such a swirling would be healed.

5:5–7. As in Sychar and Cana, Jesus focused on a single individual, this time a man who had been lame for thirty-eight years. He asked the crucial question, **Do you want to get well?** The man responded by raising the obvious problem. He could not get well because he could not get down to the healing pool fast enough. The man had been an invalid for thirty-eight years. Why did Jesus choose him now, and why him from among all the other disabled people gathered around the pool? The only possible answer is God's sovereign grace. In the Father's timing, this was the time, the place, and the way he would heal this man. The length and extent of the man's illness presented no problem for Jesus.

We tend to think that time produces hopelessness. Surely the longer a person is sick, the less likely that he or she will get well. The longer a person has lived in sin, the less likely that person will come to Christ. We have all the statistics to show that we must win people to Christ when they are young or the chances diminish. The argument is sound on the basis of what we know, bolstered by human experience. But God is the master of difficult situations just like this one. What is humanly impossible, God loves to do. Perhaps Jesus intentionally chose the veteran Bethesda-pool invalid to prove his divine grace. Even today God may choose difficult people through whom he will prove his grace.

5:8–9a. These verses describe the miraculous cure. The original question in verse 6 focused on the man's infatuation with magical powers and traditional superstition. If the pool had really been God's healing agent, Jesus could have just helped the man in the water first after the angelic stirring. But the words **Get up! Pick up your mat and walk** emphasize that Jesus was the source of divine healing, not some kind of wave pool. When you are really sick, miracle is preferable to magic.

We dare not miss the absence of faith here. The man did not ask for help; he showed no faith that John reports; and he did not even know who Jesus was. Contrast this miracle with the royal official's son in John 4.

Royal Official	Invalid
Sought Jesus	Jesus sought him
Pleaded for help	Jesus asked if he wanted help
Expressed the miracle privately	Jesus healed publicly
No sin mentioned	Jesus mentioned sin
Man was motivated to believe	Jesus worked without the man's belief

Let us notice too that the Lord's ministry was not primarily social, just as ours is not. He had the power to clean out the entire pool area. Not a single invalid could have survived the power of God. But he healed only one man, and that seems to have been done to form a basis for the message to follow. Throughout this book I will refer to this process as the miracle-message method in which a "selective" miracle lays the groundwork for a sermon. We see it here regarding authority over the Sabbath, in chapter 6 where the feeding of the five thousand forms the basis for the sermon on the bread of life. We also see it in chapter 9 where the healing of the blind man leads to a sermon on spiritual blindness followed by the sermon on the good shepherd in chapter 10, and finally in chapter 11 where the healing of Lazarus leads to a sermon on life.

Hot Springs National Park has warm and relaxing facilities—but no ultimate cure. Yet it has drawn millions to that site. But God does not need "stirring pools" to work in our lives. We do not need crosses around our necks, a saintly figurine on the car dashboard, or even oil on the head for healing. Sometimes God wants us to ask as the royal official did. And sometimes *he* asks for faith before he acts.

But God does not need our help, our permission, or even our faith when *he* chooses to work in our lives or in the lives of our loved ones.

B Divine Warning (5:9b–15)

SUPPORTING IDEA: *Many times religious tradition and political bureaucracy stand in the way when people need life.*

5:9b–10. Jesus performed this miracle on the Sabbath and that became the point of argument in the next four chapters. Why the fuss over a day? Because people want rules, not grace. They want to boast about what *they* did to earn merit from God. This attitude opposes the gospel. Luke mentioned the Sabbath only nine times in Acts, and not once in connection with Christian worship. But the Pharisees could not get over this hurdle which troubled them during the entire time of Jesus' life on earth.

This dramatic healing attracted *the typical reaction* from **the Jews**—a phrase uncommon to the Synpotics but used seventy times in John, usually to describe religious leaders opposing Christ. The New Testament is not anti-Semitic. Jesus wept over Jerusalem and constantly proclaimed the Gospel to any Jews who would listen. Paul went from synagogue to synagogue offering salvation to his own people first.

The Sabbath, of course, was always the seventh day (and is so today) never the first, though we sometimes incorrectly refer to Sunday in this way. This issue dominates the next four chapters of John as the hypocrisy and formalism of religious observance link the first century with our modern time.

This was no accident—Jesus did not just forget it was Saturday. He was not ignorant of the provision that the rabbis had added to God's Sabbath law: "Whoever on the Sabbath brings anything in or takes anything out from a public place to a private one, if he has done this inadvertently, he shall sacrifice for his sins; but if willingly, he shall be cut off and shall be stoned." The scribes had come up with thirty-nine tasks prohibited on the Sabbath. Certainly Jesus knew that healing on the Sabbath would upset the religious leaders. He knew that by commanding the man to carry his mat out of a public place he would anger them even more. So why did he do it? The dialogue rages over the next several chapters, but the central idea has to do with the authority of Jesus as the Son of God.

5:11–13. In these three verses we see how little the man actually knew. This startling stranger had walked into his life, given him back normality in his legs, and then disappeared. The man's reply to the Jews (doubtless the leaders of the Sanhedrin) reflected his willing obedience, reminiscent of the royal official in chapter 4. The exchange betrayed the Jewish leaders' shallow understanding of theology; they focused on the carried mat, not the new legs.

Trench pinpoints this significant difference in the brief conversation:

> The malignity of the questioners reveals itself in the very shape which their question assumes. They do not take up the poor man's words on their more favourable side, which would also have been in the more natural: nor ask, "What man is that which made me whole?" But, probably themselves knowing perfectly well, or at least guessing, who his Healer was, they insinuate by the form of their question that *He* could not be from God who gave a command which they, the interpreters of God's law, esteemed so grievous an outrage against it. So will they weaken and undermine any influence which Christ may have obtained over this simple man—an influence already manifest in his finding the Lord's authority sufficient to justify him in the transgression of their commandment (Trench, p. 272).

5:14–15. The innocent response is followed by the final warning—a brief section of a verse which fits significantly into the miracle-message method John records so carefully. Indeed, John 5:14 must be compared theologically with John 9:3. In the first case, one must conclude that the lameness was caused by sin; and in the second, clearly the blindness was not. The Greek text might better be translated, "Give up sinning." The **something worse** could refer to a physical illness more burdensome than the one the man had carried for so many years, or it might suggest spiritual disaster, even eternal condemnation. Borchert's comments are helpful:

> In this story Jesus found the man in the temple, a place where in his hopeless state he would have found little welcome but in his healed state was now able to enter. Moreover, Jesus addressed him in his healed state: "Stop sinning or something worse may happen to you"(5:14). These words are not meant to be a cause-and-effect statement related to his sickness or paralysis. Such a direct identification between personal sin and illness, which was proposed by the disciples in the story of the blind man (9:2), was firmly rejected by Jesus (9:3). The statement of cause and effect in this story, therefore, must be taken as referring to the eschatological correlation between sin and judgment that undoubtedly is the meaning of "something worse" in Jesus' warning to the paralytic (Borchert, p. 235).

Let us not fail to notice that **Jesus found him**. In our day we talk a great deal about "looking for God" or "finding Jesus" as though the initiative for spiritual contact lies entirely with us. We shall encounter this doctrine several more times in John, but here we take notice of the intentional search by the Savior for a stumbling beggar who had not yet figured out what to do with his new legs.

Ⓒ Divine Authority (5:16–23)

> **SUPPORTING IDEA:** *Healing on the Sabbath brought persecution, but it also gave Jesus an opportunity to display and explain his authority.*

5:16–18. The argument against the healed invalid had to do with his carrying of his mat; now we have advanced to the broader problem of breaking the Sabbath, including work of any kind. Christians worship on the first day because of the resurrection of Jesus on this day. Major New Testament events commonly occurred on the first day—the ascension, the appearances of Christ, the coming of the Spirit at Pentecost, and John's revelation vision. But none of those carry with them any special behavioral laws.

Christians have almost subconsciously carried over some Sabbath legalism to Sunday. The first day of the week rather than the last day has become the day of rest. There is nothing wrong with that, as long as we do not make one of two errors: a false identification of Sunday as the "Sabbath" with all the legalistic judgmentalism we find attached to it in this chapter; or worshiping in an old-covenant way on Saturday to maintain the Sabbath legalism of the Old Testament.

The words *life* or *live* occur eight times in John 5:16–30, but we will deal with that theme in the next section of our study. In this part of the chapter, Jesus called on contemporary religious leaders to accept life through the authority of the Father, through faith in the Father, and by the power the Father gives.

Jesus' answer to the argumentative Jewish leaders begins the long dialogue about the Father throughout most of this Gospel. The Son emulates the Father by **working**, and John uses the common Greek word for work, *ergozomai*. At issue here is the fact that both the Father and the Son have *authority over the Sabbath*. Furthermore, both have worked together in perfect unity and harmony. It would be impossible for the Son to break the Father's law—a law never intended to prohibit works of grace and mercy on the Sabbath.

Verse 18 is one of the key phrases of this book, a major foundation stone in John's theological building. In the last phrase John tells us that Jesus clearly claimed to be **equal with God**. If one considers Sabbath-breaking a serious offense, claiming equality with God must be rank heresy. But this is one of John's great themes (10:30), reflecting what he heard Jesus say over and over. Furthermore, the Jews understood precisely what Jesus was claiming and ultimately killed him for it.

Some modern theologians argue that Jesus never claimed deity and was greatly misunderstood, but that is hardly John's point of view. Veteran theologian Robert Lightner puts it this way: "Christ has existed eternally as the Son of God. Though no specific verse states this truth precisely that way, the evidence pointing in that direction is overwhelming. Whenever the title is used of Him, it speaks of His divine essence. His fierce critics, the Jewish religious leaders, did not fail to make the connection between His repeated claims that God is His Father and His claim for deity, that He is equal with God the Father (John 5:18; 10:30–38; 20:28–31)" (Lightner, p. 61).

5:19–20. The Son of God not only had authority over the Sabbath; this authority was grounded in relationship. As the Lord's argument unfolds, we learn that people must accept life because he, Jesus, carries the authority of the Father. The equality factor explodes in dimensions the Jews must have found mind-boggling. Jesus, equal in nature with God; his goals, identical with God's goals; his will, only subordinate so that people through him could see the Father.

Just a few days before writing these words, I played a tennis match with my son, in mixed doubles competition. Since I taught Jeff to play, and since we have been playing together for over twenty years, his game reflects the way I play. He is taller, stronger, and faster, but our strategies seem eerily the same. Normally in men's doubles I play as his partner and in those matches think only about how we fit together, not about how he plays. Playing as his opponent, however, I try to sense where he will move and hit. I find it surprisingly predictable as I attempt to make up for his speed and strength by thinking what he would do on the basis of what I believe I would do in a similar situation. I suspect he does the same.

That is what Jesus was talking about here. He thinks the Father's thoughts after him and has already shown the Son **all he does**, and continues to show him. All the verbs in verse 20 are present tense, indicating ongoing activity. The **greater things** will be explained in the next section.

5:21–23. Healing a lame man was nothing. The Father has raised the dead and the Son will soon do the same. Indeed, the Father has given judgmental authority to the Son. Anyone who does not recognize that authority in the Son has denied the authority of the Father—the very *authority to give life.* The phrase **who sent him** at the end of verse 23 is used by the Lord only of the Father (4:34; 5:24,30; 6:38–39; 7:16,28,33; 8:26,29; 9:4; 12:44–45; 13:20; 15:21; 16:5).

The impact of all this on traditional religious leaders of the first century must have been staggering, hence the Lord's introductory phrase "to your amazement" (v. 20). Westcott captures the moment: "The full significance of this claim of Christ to 'quicken whom He will' is illustrated by the second of the 'Shemoneh Esreh,' the 'Eighteen [benedictions],' of the Jewish Prayer Book. It is probable that this thanksgiving was used in substance in the apostolic age: 'Thou, O Lord, art mighty forever: Thou quickenest the dead: Thou are strong to save. Thou sustainest the living by Thy mercy: Thou quickenest the dead by Thy great compassion. Thou . . . makest good Thy faithfulness to them that sleep in the dust . . . Thou art faithful to quicken the dead. Blessed art Thou, O Lord, who quickenest the dead'" (Westcott, p. 86).

D Divine Life (5:24–30)

> **SUPPORTING IDEA:** *Life is in the Son, and there is no other way to heaven.*

5:24. In the Greek text our verse begins with the words, *amen, amen,* translated in the familiar KJV with the words "verily, verily." Actually, this entire equality-with-God section began the same way back in verse 19. The theme of this entire section of John's Gospel centers in the unity of the Father and the Son. John emphasized that both life and condemnation are present possessions with eternal consequences.

This verse challenges all readers to trust Christ through faith. Let us remember, too, that hearing and believing are almost synonymous in John's use. The phrase **he has crossed over** appears in the perfect tense, meaning the actual crossing took place some time in the past, but the result continues to the present. In short, salvation is an accomplished fact and an assured position. Like John 3:16, John 5:24 is pure gospel.

5:25. Verses 25–27 talk about spiritual resurrection, life in the Son through regeneration (2 Cor. 5:17; 1 John 5:11ff.). But I can almost hear someone thinking, "Why wouldn't this verse refer to the resurrection at the end of time?" The answer lies in the little phrase, **and has now come.** According to Morris, "This shows that what is primarily in mind is the present giving of life that characterizes the ministry of the Son. In Him the last age is vividly present. Men's eternal destiny is determined by their attitude to Him. Those who are spiritually dead hear His voice, and those who have heard it live. 'Hear,' of course, means 'Hear with appreciation,' 'Take heed'" (Morris, p. 318).

This verse also contains the phrase **Son of God,** so common in our Christian vocabulary that we think it must appear everywhere in the New Testament. But then we think the same thing about the word *Christian* which only appears three times in Acts. And in the same manner, John uses **the Son of God** only three times in this Gospel (10:36; 11:4). Actually, it appears two other times in contexts other than the Lord's direct claim—the Jews' complaint in 19:7 and John's purpose statement in 20:31.

So life (*zoe*) comes through regeneration and a person can claim it now. What is the basis for this broad invitation?

5:26–27. Of all the gifts the Father has given to the Son, eternal life is surely important. Some interpreters believe this life was given after the ascension (Godet), but surely the Son had it eternally and only immortality occurred after his resurrection. John's point centers in more than just the life Jesus possessed. It includes the life that he passed on to believing humanity. Since the life resides in the Son, John directs others to Jesus for this life.

The word **given** in this context refers to permission, privilege, and power. The Father appointed the Son to give eternal life to those who believe. During his time on earth, the Christ gave up the independent exercise of his attributes and placed himself under the Father's direct will. In taking upon himself the position of a human being, Jesus looked to the Father for the authority to give life.

In verse 27 the theme changes to judgmental **authority**, and "Son of God" of verse 25 now becomes again the **Son of Man** (see also 1:51; 3:14). In the Old Testament we know that God is the judge of the earth (Gen. 18:25; Judg. 11:27). This makes this passage all the more dramatic.

Some interpreters point out the absence of the definite article in the reference at the end of verse 27, making it read "Son of Man." Morris disagrees and I concur. He says, "This is Jesus' favourite self-designation. Moreover it gives an excellent reason for judgment being committed to Him. He is the heavenly figure of Dan. 7:14 to whom is given 'dominion, and glory, and a kingdom, that all the peoples, nations, and languages should serve Him: His dominion is an everlasting dominion, which shall not pass away, and His kingdom that which shall not be destroyed'" (Morris, p. 320).

5:28–29. Jesus switched suddenly to physical resurrection and identified a major doctrine of the New Testament—the concept of two resurrections, one for the righteous and one for the wicked. The second resurrection is a resurrection to damnation (Rev. 20:13), but many interpreters believe there are three parts to the first resurrection outlined in Scripture: Christ the firstfruits (1 Cor. 15:20,23); the saints (church) at the rapture; and Old Testament believers at the beginning of the millennium. Passages like this should lay to rest the false doctrine that death ends all life and essentially serves as a cessation of existence. There will not only be resurrection; resurrection will be followed by judgment.

5:30. Having announced this forthcoming event and the major hope of Israel proclaimed in the Old Testament, Jesus reminded his hearers again that he came only as the Father's representative. This verse transitions into the next section about testimony and truth.

Borchert pinpoints the issue for our attention:

> Notice the statements: "By myself," "I can do nothing," "I judge," "I hear," "my judgment," "I seek," "Not to lease myself," "who sent me." Here are eight references in English (nine in Greek) to the first-person singular in a brief thirty-word Greek sentence. It is not difficult to recognize the tremendous shift that has occurred in the text. The movement in language should be a signal to interpreters of that change. In accepting his mission ("sent") as judge, Jesus is portrayed as placing himself on the block of scrutiny for all to examine him. The issue therefore is defined. He claimed to be just, and his defense was that he had not compromised himself by pursuing self-interest. The case was therefore joined: Was he what he claimed to be? That is the question to be answered in the next section" (Borchert, pp. 242–43).

E Divine Testimony (5:31–40)

SUPPORTING IDEA: *Jesus really did not need confirmation from other people, but he provided that evidence to help us gain experiential knowledge of the life that he brings.*

5:31–32. Throughout this section the key word **testify** or **testimony** appears ten times. And Jesus offered four answers to the unasked question he read in the minds of the Jews: "Who will give evidence of who you are?" Jesus admitted that if his own words represented all he could bring to the witness stand, his accusers would have every reason for their doubt and scorn. Nevertheless, any accused man might speak in his own defense if he wished. That is exactly what Jesus did in verses 17–30.

The resumé has been submitted, and it has come not only with references but with the testimony of **another who testifies in my favor.** This probably refers to the Father whom Jesus mentioned several times in his own report. The word translated **valid** means "true." This mention of the Father at the beginning of the testimony list indicates that Jesus believed all his words and actions were already approved and did *not* need any further word. As Tasker puts it, the Father "is the only witness in fact whom Jesus regards as important as far as His own vindication is concerned" (Tasker, p. 88).

5:33–35. From the testimony of Jesus we move to the testimony of John the Baptist, the first entry on the resumé. The Greek grammar implies that John the Baptist was the Jews' own witness, a prophet highly regarded by those who now challenged Jesus' authority. Human testimony should not be necessary, but since they obviously considered it important, we start with **a lamp that burned and gave light.** Our first thought here tends to focus on light. This is no doubt an important component of the metaphor. But the word **burned** may suggest a candle or torch that burned itself out. Devout Jews were happy to see their Elijah, delighted at his message of a coming Messiah. But they cared nothing for what he delivered. Now they are accused of not taking his message seriously.

5:36. The third testimony is the testimony of Jesus' works which should be even stronger in the eyes of the Jews than the prophecy of John. The word appears in the plural (*works*), not **work** as the NIV has it—a term John used frequently to describe Jesus' miracles (5:20; 9:4; 10:25,32,37–38; 14:10–11; 15:24). The word (*erga*) appears twenty-seven times in this Gospel. Even though faith should never rest in the works alone, those works always attest to Jesus' character. Furthermore, God was not hesitant to use words to demonstrate his point (Moses' burning bush; Gideon's fleece; Elijah's burning altar).

5:37–38. Having already introduced the Father earlier in this section, Jesus now added him to the resumé, focusing on his will and his word. The idea of a universal fatherhood of God applies only to creation and humanity.

When it comes to spiritual sonship, the issue is personal faith. Note how the rejection of Jesus is a "catch twenty-two" kind of problem. These denying Jews never grasped the Father's testimony about Jesus because they refused Jesus' testimony about the Father.

5:39–40. The fifth testimony is one you may have in your hands right now—the Scriptures. Some people have quoted this verse as a command: "Search the Scriptures"—but that is not permissible according to the grammar of the text. Jesus essentially told these combatants, "You are serious Bible students and study the Old Testament carefully in order to gain eternal life. Yet you have been unable to see how your Scriptures prophesied my coming and, therefore, refuse the life that I bring."

An open heart and open eyes will produce an open mind—but we begin with an open Bible. Not superstitious reverence, but practical use. Doubts concerning the Bible's authenticity are only about two hundred years old. This should tell us something about the moral and spiritual squalor we see in the modern world.

Nevertheless, these passages also remind us that posting the Ten Commandments on the walls of school classrooms will not produce righteousness. The religious legalism of the first century shows us that. These verses also lead into the final section of this chapter. Tenney raises an important flag as we make this transition: "No less than eighteen unmistakable references to the Old Testament occur in the text of John, most of which are given a direct application to Christ, and there are other allusions in addition. If Moses (and the others) wrote of him, then the testimony would have to be admitted by his enemies as incontrovertible" (Tenney, p. 111).

𝔽 Divine Praise (5:41–47)

> **SUPPORTING IDEA:** *Biblical praise begins by praising God and seeking praise from him.*

5:41–42. The final two paragraphs close the sermon by condemning Jesus' accusers. The people with whom he spoke had studied the Scriptures for several thousand years. From the writings of Moses to the appearance of the Messiah, they revered God's writings, but they never understood them. Indeed, if they had grasped only the Pentateuch they would have been ready to receive Jesus as God's Son and Messiah. They searched to find life and life was in Christ, but they never made the connection. Without the love of God in their hearts, they would be quite willing to accept imposters who claimed only their own testimony and denied Jesus in the face of all the evidence that attested the truth of his message. Verses 41 and 42 remind us of the Lord's reaction to the "believing" Jews at the end of chapter 2: "But Jesus would not entrust himself to them, for he knew all men. He did not need man's testimony about man, for he knew what was in a man" (2:24–25).

The word translated in the NIV as **praise** is *doxa,* the common Greek word for *glory* or *honor.* The word appears three times in four verses, indicating John's emphasis on the rejection of Christ's glory by his accusers.

5:43–44. Bogus messiahs had crowded the Jewish scene for at least two hundred years before Christ. Like some modern religious leaders, they drew attention to themselves—an attitude for which Jesus condemned his own disciples (Luke 22:25). And the attitude continued. As Ken Hughes puts it, "Jesus told them that another would come in His name and that they would receive that one. Subsequent historical accounts tell us that no less than sixty-three messianic claimants attracted followers. People followed them because their claims corresponded with the desires of men. They offered easy victory, political power, and material advantage. Christ offered the Cross" (Hughes, p. 112).

So all the mutual glorification omitted serious worship, never finding **the praise that comes from the only God.** We have no trouble understanding how we must praise God, but how do we receive praise from God? Let us remember the people to whom these remarks were addressed. Pharisees, Sadducees, and Jewish religious leaders of the first century made a big show of public worship, ostentatiously praying and giving in public (Matt. 23:5–7). But the true glory of God was present in Jesus whom they rejected. True glory comes only from God, and this entire discourse has to do with Jesus as the true representative of that glory. In *The Everlasting Mercy,* Robert Harvey Strachan offers more of the verse from which the initial quotation in this chapter is taken.

> A trained mind outs the upright soul,
> As Jesus said the trained mind might,
> Being wiser than the sons of light,
> But trained men's minds are spread so thin
> They let all sorts of darkness in;
> Whatever light men find they doubt it,
> They love not light but talk about it (Strachan, p. 47).

5:45–47. This entire chapter stems from the issue of Sabbath-breaking that John introduced as early as verses 9–10. Therefore, this question of Mosaic Law both begins and ends the chapter. The Jews were proud of their tradition, their knowledge of Scripture, and certainly proud of Moses. But according to Jesus, they really did not believe Moses. If they had, they would have believed and accepted the Christ of whom Moses wrote. Rejecting Moses therefore, they also rejected Jesus.

We can hardly miss the connection between the writings of Moses in verses 45–47 and the emphasis on Scripture in general in verses 39–40. The only contact these people had with Moses was through the Pentateuch, the section of Scripture that Moses wrote. But how and when did Moses write about Christ? Certainly one possibility is the reference in Deuteronomy 18:15 which John has already used in the discussion of religious leaders with John the Baptist (1:21). In connection with these verses you may want to review the text of Deuteronomy 18:14–22.

Tasker sums up the issue like this:

> The tragedy however, was that the Jews had regarded the Mosaic ordinances, particularly those relating to animal sacrifice, as ends in themselves; they were not therefore, ready to welcome Him who was not only the supreme revealer of the divine will, the Prophet who was greater than all the prophets, but also the Priest who alone could fully atone for human sin. The law of Moses could not save sinners and give them eternal life; it could only expose their sinfulness. By such exposure Moses prepared the way for the Son of God who made forgiveness a reality and enabled men to receive praise from God. If the Jews, therefore, really believed Moses; if, in other words, they were really longing for divine forgiveness and for eternal life, they would now be believing in Jesus (Tasker, p. 90).

MAIN IDEA REVIEW: *Salvation comes through sincere and complete faith in the Savior.*

III. CONCLUSION

The Heretical Scales

Down through the years of my ministry I have talked to hundreds of people about the gospel and have found an amazing amount of confusion, even among people who claim to believe the Bible. When asked how they plan to get to heaven, for example, many people respond with the story of the scales. They imagine God (or more likely St. Peter) standing in the anteroom of heaven with a giant scale on which he has already measured the "good things" they have done in life on one side against the "bad things" on the other. Since most people believe their good things outweigh their bad things, they envision the scales tipped slightly in their favor, at which point St. Peter opens the door and issues them into eternal happiness.

And what, one might ask, would be on the "good things" side of those mythical scales? At that point in the conversation people talk about being good neighbors, loving parents, involvement in civic activities, church membership, baptism, and a host of other things they believe God likes.

What they are describing, of course, is the kind of lifestyle God expects of Christians after they have been born again. Actually, the kind of behavior only the Holy Spirit can produce in a life which has already been regenerated by the power of the Son of God. In a sense, they have adopted the attitude of the Pharisees, who applied distorted human measurements to ascertain God's holiness. Most people make the gospel much more complicated than it is; its simplicity tends to throw them into futile humanism.

John the Apostle wrote his Gospel to counteract such heretical notions. Throughout his Gospel he reminded us over and over again of the message Jesus repeated so many times: "I tell you the truth, whoever hears my word and believes him who sent me has eternal life and will not be condemned; he has crossed over from death to life" (John 5:24).

In 1873 Dora Greenwell wrote some poetic verses which were later set to music by William J. Kirkpatrick. He called his tune "Greenwell." Many older Christians have sung the hymn dozens of times.

> I am not skilled to understand
> What God has willed, what God has planned;
> I only know at His right hand
> Is one Who is my Savior!
>
> I take Him at His Word and deed:
> "Christ died for sinners," this I read;
> For in my heart I find a need
> Of Him to be my Savior!
>
> That He should leave His place on high
> And come for sinful man to die,
> You count it strange? So once did I,
> Before I knew my Savior!

PRINCIPLES

- We are never too sick, never too lost, never too sinful for God's power.
- When God chooses to act, he can do so independent of any other source—including us.
- In John, miracles are not produced by faith; they produce faith.
- Open eyes and an open heart can produce an open mind.

APPLICATIONS

- Consider the lives of people you know who could be examples of God's limitless grace.
- Remember that spiritual health is more important than physical health.
- Place your faith in Christ not only for eternal life but for present power for living.
- Study the Scriptures with a view to finding what they say about Jesus.
- Believe God and give him praise.

IV. LIFE APPLICATION

The Mahatma and the Master

During the 1983 Academy Award, ceremony, the outstanding film *Ghandi* walked away with eight Oscars. Ghandi's life was exemplary in many respects and his peace initiatives set the standard for many nonviolent movements of the later twentieth century. He will probably be considered one of the most important leaders of the twentieth century as people continue to reflect on the history of the 1900s.

But the Mahatma did not offer the same message as the Master; Ghandi proclaimed no gospel. In one dramatic scene from the movie, a Hindu man in Calcutta killed a Muslim boy. Ghandi offered him salvation if he would find and raise a Muslim orphan in place of the boy he had killed. A noble gesture to be sure, and typical of Ghandi's altruistic philosophy, but hardly what we find in the first five chapters of John's Gospel.

Humanity has always been drawn to the posture of works salvation—if it is worth having, a person ought to work for it. So earth-designed religions call for special diets, unique patterns of worship, personal sacrifice, memberships and attendance, and often even suffering. But Jesus offered himself and asks us to reject everything we might have to offer and to accept what he has already offered. We could say of the Gospel of John the same thing Jesus said about the Old Testament Scriptures in general: "These are the Scriptures that testify about me, yet you refuse to come to me to have life" (vv. 39b–40).

V. PRAYER

Father, thank you for calling us across the line from death to life. We rejoice that we are now free from condemnation because Jesus bore the penalty of sin for us. Amen.

VI. DEEPER DISCOVERIES

A. Stirring Up the Waters (5:4)

Many Christians are disturbed when translators omit a text that they have read in another version. This time, as we observed earlier in the "Commentary," it is a portion of John 5:3 and all of John 5:4: "From time to time an angel of the Lord would come down and stir up the waters. The first one into the pool after each such disturbance would be cured of whatever disease he had." Almost all contemporary evangelical scholars agree that these words were added later by some editor who wanted to explain why people came to the pool. Many scholars omit it because they accept *earlier* rather than majority text manuscripts. In other words, they assume that the closer we can get to the actual autograph (original writing) of the New Testament, the more accurate the text will be.

But those who choose the Majority Text on which the KJV is based may still accept the angelic miracle. Greene writes three pages on the work of angels in his commentary on verse 4 after saying, "The Scripture does not tell us when the miracle began or when it ceased to be, or whether the angel is seen or invisible when he came down to trouble the water; but this is not important, for if the Holy Spirit had wanted us to know these details they would have been made plain in the Word" (Greene, p. 265).

The HCSB includes the phraseology but puts it in brackets with this note, "Other mss omit the words in brackets." Borchert's extensive work explains the issue thoroughly: "The reader should recognize that vv. 3b–4 (present in the KJV) are a later scribal addition to the story, probably inserted into the text by an early copyist who believed in such mythical manifestations and who sought to support the man's belief pattern by such a statement. In terms of an explanation it is possible that the man's theory here may have been based on the occurrence of an interesting natural phenomenon in which at high water times the pool apparently was infused by a periodic influx of spring water that stirred the pool with excess water. *The question here is not one of the possibility of miracle but of the message of the text* (italics mine)" (Borchert, p. 232).

We treat the question here to emphasize that, especially in a chapter that discusses the authority of Scripture, we should never be thrown off base by human additions or subtractions to the text. Such anomalies do not dilute the doctrine of inspiration.

B. My Father (5:17,19–24,36–37,43)

The unity of the Father and the Son is a major theme in Jesus' teaching and in John's Gospel. We find it emphasized in chapters 5, 14, and 17. We will discuss that at greater length in chapter 14, but here let me offer a sample from interpreters on the relationship Jesus develops in chapter 5.

> The language Jesus uses is thoroughly Rabbinic. He begins with a very strong affirmation of community of action with the Father. It is not simply that He does not act in independence of the Father. He cannot act in independence of the Father. He can do only the things He sees the Father doing (Morris, p. 312).

> Not only was Jesus claiming identity of action with God the Father; He was also claiming equality with God. God the Father and God the Son do the same works with the same motivation and in the same manner (Hughes, p. 101).

> [Jesus'] explanation of His action on the Sabbath, "My Father worketh even until now, and I work," indicated that He made the Father His

pattern, and that He felt that the Father's work constituted sufficient precedent and reason for His. His enemies understood what He meant, for they sought to kill Him because He had assumed the prerogatives of deity in calling God "His own Father." The term *His own* meant particularly His, in a way that could not be applied to anyone else (Tenney, p. 106).

Perfect Sonship involves perfect identity of will and action with the Father . . . Separate action on His part is an impossibility, as being a contradiction of His unity with the Father (Westcott, p. 85).

C. Testimony (5:31–40)

Ten times in ten verses John uses some form of the verb *martureo,* commonly translated by the English words *testify* or *witness.* This chapter contains almost one-third of all the uses in this Gospel; John uses the word a total of forty-seven times in his writings, and it appears twenty-nine more times in the New Testament. To put that another way, John uses the word *witness* almost twice as often as the rest of the New Testament writers combined.

We still think of the words *witness* or *testimony* in conjunction with a legal procedure, and that is just the way it was used in the Greco-Roman vocabulary. It is also the word from which we get our English word *martyr.* The New Testament does not attempt to provide a legal brief, though the dialogue between Jesus and the Jews in this chapter would certainly evoke some courtroom images. So we are not surprised when Jesus talks about witnesses who support his claims.

When writing to Timothy, Paul gave good advice for us to live out today: "So do not be ashamed to testify about our Lord, or ashamed of me his prisoner. But join with me in suffering for the gospel, by the power of God" (2 Tim. 1:8). Peter added a word about our attitude when bearing witness: "But in your hearts set apart Christ as Lord. Always be prepared to give an answer to everyone who asks you to give the reason for the hope that you have. But do this with gentleness and respect" (1 Pet. 3:15).

VII. TEACHING OUTLINE

A. INTRODUCTION

1. Lead Story: Pedal for Your Life
2. Context: Though he treated fewer miracles than any other Gospel writer, John sandwiched three together in the second half of chapter 4, the first part of chapter 5, and the first part of chapter 6. But the words of Jesus between the healing of the paralytic and the feeding of the five thousand grab center stage in this chapter and offer believers life through the Son.

3. Transition: Both salvation and physical healing come through God's grace and faith in Jesus Christ—not by our own efforts, magic, or an appeal to religion.

B. COMMENTARY

1. Divine Grace (5:1–9a)
    a. The crucial question (5:1–6)
    b. The obvious problem (5:7)
    c. The miraculous cure (5:8–9a)
2. Divine Warning (5:9b–15)
    a. The typical reaction (5:9b–10)
    b. The innocent response (5:11–13)
    c. The final warning (5:14–15)
3. Divine Authority (5:16–23)
    a. Authority over the Sabbath (5:16–18)
    b. Authority grounded in relationship (5:19–20)
    c. Authority to give life (5:21–23)
4. Divine Life (5:24–30)
    a. Spiritual resurrection (5:24–27)
    b. Physical resurrection (5:28–30)
5. Divine Testimony (5:31–40)
    a. The testimony of Jesus (5:31–32)
    b. The testimony of John the Baptist (5:33–35)
    c. The testimony of Jesus' works (5:36)
    d. The testimony of the Father (5:37–38)
    e. The testimony of Scripture (5:39–40)
6. Divine Praise (5:41–47)
    a. Acceptance (5:41–44)
    b. Accusation (5:45–47)

C. CONCLUSION: THE MAHATMA AND THE MASTER

VIII. ISSUES FOR DISCUSSION

1. How should we respond when handling a passage like John 5:4?
2. What is the correct Christian understanding of "Sabbath"?
3. How do you interpret John 5:25?

John 6

The Bread of Life

"*It* is a lot easier emotionally to handle the fact that millions of people are starving if we don't see them as individuals."

S t a n   M o o n e y h a m

GEOGRAPHICAL PROFILE: SEA OF GALILEE

- A large inland lake about sixty miles north of Jerusalem
- Begins at the Jordan River in the north and empties into the Dead Sea
- Up to 150 feet deep at points
- In Jesus' time it was surrounded by some thirty fishing villages

GEOGRAPHICAL PROFILE: TIBERIAS

- The capitol city of Herod Antipas, tetrarch of Galilee and Perea
- Built between A.D. 16 and 22
- Ruins include portions of a wall three miles long, a palace, forum, and a great synagogue

PERSONAL PROFILE: JUDAS ISCARIOT

- "Iscariot" is usually taken to mean "a man of Kerioth," an area in the south of Judah
- Mentioned in John 6, 12, 13, and 18
- Betrayed Jesus for thirty pieces of silver

- Married to Jesus' mother, Mary
- A carpenter of Nazareth descended from the line of David
- Spoken to by angels regarding the birth and early childhood of Jesus (Matt. 1:18–25; Luke 2:8–20)
- Probably died some time between the beginning of Jesus' ministry and the crucifixion

John 6

IN A NUTSHELL

*J*ohn 6 records the feeding of the five thousand followed by Jesus' poignant sermon on the bread of life. The chapter ends with the departure of some disciples and the rededication of the Twelve.

The Bread of Life

I. INTRODUCTION

World Hunger

*O*n any given day several hundred million people face hunger. In any given year as many as five million people, mainly children, die from starvation, malnutrition, and related causes. In Brazil, for example, thousands of children gather in the modern capital of that country (Brasilia) where a few years ago five hundred of them were actually chosen to represent the street urchins of Brazilian society. The best estimates indicate at least ten million street children in towns and cities across Brazil, a country of more than 150 million people.

Even in the affluent society of modern America, fourteen million children live in poverty. Twelve million of them suffer from constant hunger, and in parts of the country more than one-fourth of all children never get enough nourishment. A study from the Center on Hunger, Poverty, and Nutrition Policy at Tufts University estimates that 20 percent of American children under age eighteen experience hunger every year. On any given night in the USA, one hundred thousand homeless children live on the streets. People below eighteen are the fastest-growing age group among the homeless.

With electronic gadgetry decorating homes and cars and instant millionaires arising from technology stocks, the glitz and glitter fail to cover the harsh realities of the life of the poor. According to former Senator Daniel Patrick Moynihan, "We may be the first society in history of which it can be said that the children are worse off than their parents."

Chapter 6 of John begins with hungry people, perhaps some of them living in poverty, but all of them expecting to eat. The crowds found Jesus the day after he had fed them with the bread and fish along the shores of the Sea of Galilee. But his opening statement penetrated to their real motives in seeking him: "I tell you the truth, you are looking for me, not because you saw miraculous signs but because you ate the loaves and had your fill" (6:26).

There is another kind of food that should have had higher priority in their thinking. Jesus wanted them to seek him for himself, not for what he could do for them. Eternal life is not the reward of work; it is always and only a free gift.

Just as it is difficult to motivate starving people to think about spiritual things, it is also difficult to motivate people who eat well to transfer their attention to something other than what they are eating. That was the problem with the Samaritan woman, and it occurs again in this chapter with the people in both Galilee and Judea. Jesus was impressed neither with their attention nor their hunger. But he emphasized throughout the chapter that spiritual food and drink come directly from Jesus.

II. COMMENTARY

The Bread of Life

MAIN IDEA: *Water, food, and bread are metaphors that show how spiritual appropriation of the life which Jesus gives is necessary for salvation.*

A Faith Is Expectant Obedience (6:1–15)

SUPPORTING IDEA: *When Jesus is in charge of a situation, available human resources are irrelevant.*

6:1–4. The feeding of the five thousand is the only miracle of Jesus recorded in all four Gospels. Jesus had crossed to the eastern shore of the Sea of Galilee at a time when the Jewish Passover feast was near. If we accept John 5:1 as a Passover, the reference in 6:4 would be the third Passover observance recorded in this Gospel.

This is one of those several examples in John where we see the miracle-message method of Jesus' ministry. Paul told the Corinthians that Jews required a sign, and John reminded us that **a great crowd of people followed him because they saw the miraculous signs he had performed on the sick** (6:2). Some scholars estimate there may have been as many as seven thousand to ten thousand people, since verse 10 talks about five thousand men. As we shall see, this chapter is about faith, but these people wanted food. Jesus talked about spiritual relationship, but the crowds were interested in physical showmanship. They focused on the lunch, not the love; on their bellies, not their beliefs.

Our passage first centers on people in need. As we have already seen, starvation is a stark and unpleasant reality in our modern world. Ten percent of the world's babies die before their first birthday, and one of every four children suffers from malnutrition. Yet the problem of spiritual hunger is even more severe. Like the people gathering on the mountainside in Galilee, millions today need the living bread that only Jesus can provide.

The introduction of the Passover is always significant in the chronological pattern of John's Gospel. He contrasted the rejection in Jerusalem at the end of chapter 5 with the magnificent scene of thousands coming to hear Jesus speak on the shore of the Sea of Tiberias. This body of water actually has four names in Scripture: The Sea of Galilee and the Sea of Tiberias both identified here in our text; the Lake of Gennesaret in Luke 5:1; and the Sea of

Kinnereth (Num. 34:11). Today it is generally called Lake Kinneret, but students of the Bible have difficulty calling it anything other than the Sea of Galilee.

The bread-and-water connection has ancient Israeli roots in the manna of the desert and water from the rock. The entire Exodus experience sets the historic basis for the **Jewish Passover Feast.** Borchert suggests a useful reminder: "Those familiar with the Psalms will also recognize that the two mercies of water control and food supply were very significant to the psalmist (cf. Ps 78:13–30). In Israel's history, stories of food and water are indelibly attached to faith. From the tree of life in the garden, the rescue of Noah in the flood, and throughout their pilgrimage these two symbols are repeatedly rewoven into the fabric of God's dealings with His people. It is understandable then that Paul, thinking like a Jew, also linked these two symbols in his warnings to the Corinthians about their relationship with God (10:1–4)" (Borchert, p. 249).

6:5–9. Remember that Jesus had been doing more miracles than the three John has recorded for us so far. Many people followed him because of their interest in his power and his teaching. This crowd would have been greatly enlarged because of the number of visitors to Palestine for the Passover. Jesus had led his disciples out to this solitary place to have some private teaching time with them, but the crowds followed. Mark tells us in his account that Jesus had compassion on them and taught them late into the day—and he also saw their need for food.

From a picture of people in need we move to a picture of the disciples in confusion. Philip's reply is so typical of what we might say. He looked strictly at the human dilemma, considering only his own resources, and pronounced that the situation was hopeless. This whole inquiry was instigated by Jesus' question: **Where shall we buy bread for these people to eat?** It is typical of John to remind his readers that Jesus already knew what would happen next (v. 6). At first we wonder why Philip was singled out, but then we remember he was a native of Bethsaida, possibly the closest town. If a local convenience store had been open at that hour, Philip would have known about it. Nevertheless, Philip did a quick assessment of what it would cost **for each one to have a bite!**

Westcott starts with the assumption that a denarius was a day's wage and "concludes that 200 denarii would buy 4,800 quarts of barley, or 1,600 quarts of wheat" (cited in Morris, p. 343). Modern currency translations grope for some way to express the enormity of Philip's problem. The Living Bible has Philip say, "It would take a fortune to begin to do it!" To Philip—the task was impossible.

But Andrew had a plan; this fellow-citizen of Bethsaida found a boy carrying a lunch consisting of barley loaves and fish. Like Philip, Andrew had no idea what use that pittance would be. John's record offers so many interesting observations, not the least of which is that the two fish Andrew found were definitely **small**. The word *opsarion* is used only by John, and it emphasizes the insignificance of these tiny sardines.

Two things surface in this portion of our text. First, we see that Jesus Christ was all-sufficient for any need even when his disciples were in confusion. Second, the purpose of the miracle seems clear: to instruct the disciples, to lay a foundation for the sermon on the bread of life, and to feed hungry people.

6:10–13. Like Moses' ancient rod, Samson's donkey jawbone, and David's sling, this simple lunch shows again that seemingly useless things can become important in Jesus' hands. He alone is all-sufficient. Everyone was satisfied, and each disciple had his own personal basket of leftovers as a reminder of the Master's power. The identification of the number of men appears in all four Gospels. We can only guess what the total number of people might have been. Some estimates reach as high as twenty thousand people. What a wonderful picture John paints of Jesus holding those five small barley loaves in his hands as he **gave thanks**. The verb is the word from which we get our word *eucharist,* though this was a simple mealtime blessing, not a religious ceremony.

But why the command to **gather the pieces that are left over. Let nothing be wasted?** Obviously the ample provision is important (Jer. 31:14), and surely a special focus on the role of the disciples. All of them probably doubted that anything could be done to feed this vast number of people. Philip and Andrew just happened to be on the spot to respond publicly.

According to Carson:

> That there were *twelve* baskets is almost certainly significant: The Lord has enough to supply the needs of the twelve tribes of Israel. All four Gospels draw attention to the number. From the time of Hilary of Poitiers (fourth century A.D.), it has been common to argue that the feeding of the five-thousand represents the Lord's provision for the Jews, and the feeding of the four-thousand, with seven baskets left over, represents the Lord's provision for the Gentiles. Certainly the word for "basket" (*kophinos*) used in all four accounts of the feeding of the five-thousand has peculiarly Jewish associations, whereas the "basket" (*spyris*) used in the feeding of the four-thousand (Matt. 15:37; Mark 8:8) does not. It strains credulity, however, to suppose that John saw in the leftovers a symbol of the "food that endures" (6:27) (Carson, p. 271).

Yes, Jesus can supply all our needs. And he often works miracles to provide for us physically. But there is always the need for faith and the intent to teach us to trust him for both physical and spiritual needs. As God provides for our physical needs, we should let down our defenses and allow him to put his arms around us and tame our sinful and rebellious spirits.

6:14–15. No one could deny the miracle, especially those who had enjoyed lunch. Many people were drawn back again to questions posed to John the Baptist in 1:21, particularly the reference to "that prophet" promised by Moses. But Jesus would have none of their political pressure brought on by full stomachs. He slipped again into the hills for rest and worship. Mark told us that he "dismissed the crowd" (Mark 6:45), and John told us that he **withdrew again to a mountain by himself.** He would be no political messiah hustled into battle with the Romans to regain Palestine for Israel.

This passage marks one of the high points of Jesus' popular favor. Since the promise of Deuteronomy 18, the Jews had looked for another Moses, for the great Prophet sent from God. And who better to fulfill that prophecy than this Jesus who gave them a new kind of manna? But the crowd's limited view of the prophet's message and ministry seemed to exclude his spiritual mission. They had no understanding of suffering for sinners and death for forgiveness.

No. Jesus could not accept the popular movement to make him king. The people were ready to offer him worship, but it was false worship. This was one of the things Satan had promised during the temptation in the wilderness—Jesus' own people wanting to make him king.

On their way back to Georgia from south Texas, my son and his family stopped in New Orleans. That city has one of the country's oldest trolleys which carries visitors to the zoo. It looked like a great idea so the whole family—Mom, Dad, and two children—jumped on. Jeff assumed the role of sufficient and dependable leader. He watched his map, looked for landmarks, and told the family when to jump off the trolley. But as they rose to get off, the driver looked right at him and shook his head. "You're going to the zoo, right?" Jeff nodded and offered a feeble "Yes." "Next stop," said the driver. Sometimes we lean on our own maps and fail to consult the source of true authority about what we should do with our lives.

𝕭 Faith Is Willing Trust (6:16–24)

> **SUPPORTING IDEA:** *Jesus meets basic physical needs to show he can also meet basic spiritual needs.*

6:16–18. The Sea of Galilee lies six hundred feet below sea level, and the prevailing winds still blow from the west. According to John, **his disciples went down to the lake.** But both Matthew and Mark specify that Jesus sent his disciples away. We see here a lesson in authority for the disciples. Several of them were fishermen, and this east-west route across the lake toward the town of Capernaum would not have been unfamiliar. But it was dark and the waters were treacherous. This miracle also appears in Matthew 14:22–33 and Mark 6:45–52. Presumably, Jesus had set a time and perhaps even a place where he would meet them on the west coast of the lake.

6:19–21. The distance across the northern end of the Sea of Galilee is about five miles, so they were more than half way across when they saw Jesus walking on the water. He knew their problems with faith and fear; Mark tells us he had been watching them (Mark 6:48). This was no ghost, no mystical apparition brought about by their terrified emotions. His words are so like the Lord: **It is I; don't be afraid.**

This miracle revealed Jesus' authority to the disciples and his purpose of ministry to the crowds. The requirements for help in their distress were simple enough—recognize their own need and take Jesus into the boat. That has *not* changed much in our day. But just seeing Jesus and recognizing him were not enough; they had to take him into the boat. As we shall see in our continuing study of this chapter, intellectual assent must be accompanied by spiritual appropriation and personal commitment to gain eternal life, or—as in this case—to gain physical safety.

Let us not move too quickly over the word **immediately** in verse 21. With little fuss and no intent to make a point, John probably indicated another miracle which few count in numbering the miracles in John. Some interpreters opt for the natural explanation (they were already near shore). Or perhaps the remainder of the voyage seemed as nothing compared to what they had already been through. I stand with Godet's interpretation: "One can scarcely imagine, indeed, that, after an act of power so magnificent and so kingly as Jesus walking on the waters, he should have seated himself in the boat, and the voyage should have been laboriously continued by the stroke of the oar. At the moment when Jesus set his foot in the boat, he communicated to it, as he has just done for Peter, the force victorious over gravity and space, which had just been so strikingly displayed on his own person" (cited in Morris, p. 351).

6:22–24. The final paragraph of this portion of chapter 6 offers us a lesson in purpose for the crowd. Obviously they were confused, never having thought the Lord crossed the lake by walking on the water. They assumed the disciples had gone west across the water and that Jesus was still on the northeastern shore. Unable to find him there, they eventually made their way to Capernaum. What did they want? More food? Another deliberate attempt to force him into political office? Whatever it was, they were hardly prepared for what they heard.

◖C◗ Faith Is Eternal Choice (6:25–33)

SUPPORTING IDEA: *When we place our faith in Jesus Christ, we accept spiritual food that will never spoil and eternal life that will never cease.*

6:25–27. These half-hearted seekers had no penetrating theological question to ask the one they called **Rabbi.** They only wanted to know when he had arrived. But the Lord cut through all the sham of their pretended interest.

As he did with Nicodemus, he answered a question they did not ask. Like many modern North Americans, they displayed materialistic and greedy attitudes, working for **food that spoils** but not for **food that endures to eternal life**. Their words and their behavior portrayed a misunderstanding of God's plan. Like some believers today, they followed Jesus for what they could get out of him—to justify their own prejudice, to support their own politics, to confirm their own culture.

How common in our day to see Christians attempting to substitute spiritual power with some false and useless modern ideal. We look for spiritual power in politics, signs and wonders, size and influence, spiritual warfare, or even the popularity of celebrities. John points us to the cross and to the one who died there, of whom he says, **On him God the Father has placed his seal of approval.**

We should not miss the focus on motive in these verses. They were not wrong to be hungry, and perhaps not even wrong to look for Jesus. But they wanted Jesus for their own purposes, to serve their own ends. This was something like Simon of Samaria who said to Peter, "Give me also this ability so that everyone on whom I lay my hands may receive the Holy Spirit" (Acts 8:19).

6:28–29. The crowd's second question evoked an explanation of salvation. Here it is again: believing is seeing. As good Jews they wanted some way to work in order to gain God's favor, but the Lord pointed them to faith and grace—**to believe in the one he has sent.** The only spiritual work that pleases God is to allow him to work in us through the Holy Spirit. As Tenney puts it, "To Jewish questioners, attaining eternal life consisted in finding the right formula for performing works to please God. Jesus directed them to the gift of God that could be obtained by faith in him. Again there is a similarity to his conversation with the Samaritan woman: 'If you knew the gift of God' (John 4:10). Jesus contradicted directly the presuppositions of his interrogators" (Tenney, *EBC*, p. 75).

6:30–31. Faith? Certainly, if he could prove to them what he claimed. These people were from Missouri, the "show me" state. They agreed with the old adage, "Seeing is believing," but could not grasp the message of Jesus finely tuned in this Gospel—"Believing is seeing." But wait. Were not these the same people who ate the bread just a few hours earlier? Sure. But that was then and this is now. In the great tradition of people steeped in religion but not faith, they quoted a text to prove they were right. Carson claims they wanted even more than Moses provided—a miracle greater than manna! "If Jesus is superior to Moses, as his tone and claims suggest, then should not his followers be privileged to witness mightier works than those seen by the disciples of Moses?" (Carson, p. 286).

6:32–33. Their third question came back to miraculous signs, and the Lord responded in two ways. First, Moses did not give the Israelites manna; it came from God. Second, physical bread was not the issue. Spiritual bread was—the bread of life about whom Jesus would soon speak in detail. The Greek word for bread (*artos*) appears almost one hundred times in the New Testament. The flat loaf of those days was as common as a bagel today.

When Jesus was fasting in the desert, Satan urged him to turn stones into bread (Matt. 4:3–4). He taught his disciples to pray, "Give us today our daily bread" (Matt. 6:11). And now we learn that Jesus himself is the Bread of Life. Manna was the kind of food that perished, even though it was given from the good hand of the Father. But now there was imperishable bread that must be eaten spiritually. It also came down from heaven; it also was given from the gracious hand of the Father; and it also provided life for a dying people.

Jesus had not yet specifically applied the bread to himself, but that was just a breath away. Having known about Moses and eaten of the bread, these people remind us of the British people in the 1700s of whom Edmund Burke said, "And having looked to government for bread, on the very first scarcity they will turn and bite the hand that fed them."

Faith Is Mental Assent (6:34–51)

SUPPORTING IDEA: *The crowds loved Jesus for what they could get out of him, preferably another free lunch. When he spoke again of the Father, they seemed ready to respond, but rejected him more vehemently.*

6:34–37. Faith as mental assent, agreement with the essential message of the gospel, begins with election. The three earlier questions ("When did you get here?" "What must we do to do the works God requires?" "What will you do?") now give way to one of the great statements of the Bible: **from now on give us this bread.** What a wonderful response, if it had been sincerely spoken. The spiritual bread that the Lord can provide is necessary for life, suited for everyone, must be eaten daily, and produces spiritual growth in those who believe it. How appropriate and essential for us to pray daily, **give us this bread.**

Not all of Jesus' teachings in the Bible could be called "sermons," but this one certainly falls into that category. Its title is simple: "I Am the Bread of Life." Its theme rings with candor: "You are inherently selfish and materialistic; try first to seek spiritual and eternal values which you will only find in me." Its proposition is clear: "My Father sent me down from heaven to be your spiritual bread."

All this we have seen in preparation for this potent paragraph which begins in verse 35 where Jesus moved into the deep theology of salvation. The invitation is genuine—whoever comes will never go hungry; whoever believes will never thirst. But as we have already seen as early as chapter 2, the word *believe* does not necessarily mean spiritual appropriation of the gospel.

Seven times in this Gospel John recorded Jesus' announcements about himself, introduced by the words, "I am." Here is the first of these—**I am the bread of life.** When did Jesus actually say, **You have seen me and still you do not believe?** Perhaps many times, but John surely intended us to recall his record of an earlier visit to Jerusalem (John 5:37–40).

Verse 37 is one of the key verses in Scripture on the issue of election. It demonstrates both election and free-will in the same verse. The Father literally gives certain believers to the Son. On the other hand, the gospel always proclaims, "Whosoever will may come." Does God choose us or do we choose him? The only possible answer is, "Yes." These two strands run side by side like two lanes of a super highway throughout the Scriptures.

Tenney expresses it like this:

> How can one be sure that the Father has really given him to Christ? Will he come only to be rebuffed? Jesus made plain that human salvation is no surprise to God. He summons men to himself by his Word and by his Spirit. They can come only at his invitation. The invitation, however, is not restricted to any particular time or place, nor is it exclusively for any one nation, race, or culture. No man needs to fear that he will come in vain, for Jesus said emphatically that he would not refuse anyone. Man does not make his opportunity for salvation; he accepts its free offer. A superficial attachment to God is not enough, for if the desire for salvation is not inspired by God, true salvation will not result (Tenney, *EBC*, p. 76).

This crowd insisted on speaking only of physical bread until Jesus told them plainly, "I am the bread of life." This solemn self-affirmation linked the speaker with Jehovah of the Old Testament, the One who spoke to Moses from the burning bush. Each of the seven "I am" statements in this Gospel links the Savior in some way with the God of the Old Testament.

These verses are not some esoteric philosophical statement offering an abstract idea. They form a personal invitation to participate spiritually in the life of Jesus by trusting him. As Ezekiel "ate the scroll" in the prophetic days of the Old Testament (see Ezek. 3:1–3), so believers today eat the bread of life when they acknowledge that the death of Jesus was on their behalf.

The permanency of the effect is important. Those who eat will *never* be hungry. Those who drink will *never* be thirsty. But the faith that produces this kind of result is not just faith in miracles but a genuine commitment to the person of the miracle worker—Jesus the Son of God.

6:38–40. In these three verses John reminded us that mental assent proceeds to security. The Savior does the Father's will and one aspect of that will is to hold on to all believers, losing none of them. Jesus plumbed the depth of doctrinal debate which has waged for ages. Those who have been given to the Savior have guaranteed resurrection. They will be raised up at the last day. Why? Because that is the Father's will. Everyone who looks to the Son and believes in him will have eternal life. This is the great theme of both John and Paul (Rom. 8:35–39). Eternal life was purchased at the cross and guaranteed at the empty tomb.

We cannot miss John's emphasis on the will of God, a subject of great concern to Jesus. We talk a great deal about the will of God, but our concern is limited when compared with the allegiance to the Father practiced daily by the Lord Jesus. We talk about the Father's will for a new job or perhaps a move to another city. High school students talk about finding God's will for a college or the choice of a career, while young people in love wonder if it is God's will for them to marry.

But there is an absolute plan regarding the Father's will for all people: God wants everyone to believe in Jesus, to have eternal life, and to experience resurrection at the last day. Do we wait until then to find out if God gets his way? Definitely not. There is no question that God's sovereign will shall be accomplished in the lives of people who belong to Jesus. They have life in the Son, and they have it now. Of verse 39 Borchert writes, "This text is undoubtedly one of the strongest assurance texts in the Gospel and is clearly parallel to 17:12, where Jesus indicates that while he was on earth he 'protected' and 'safeguarded' all those who were given to him . . . The great Christian doctrine of the perseverance of the saints is not based merely on human effort but on the confidence that God is active both in the saving as well as in the preserving of those who commit themselves to serve God in Christ" (Borchert, p. 265).

Orville Murphy, a Christian who resides in the Middle East, tells about an Indian Christian who was constrained to witness for Christ on the job. The first day he said to a Pakistani coworker, "Jesus Christ died for you." He was cursed and rejected, but the next day he said it twice, and the third day, three times. Eventually, through the power of the Holy Spirit and the simple message of the gospel, the Pakistani broke down and they wept in each other's arms as former enemies now were united by the cross and the empty tomb.

This text rings off the page like the Magna Carta of the Christian faith. They asked for bread, expecting to eat on a regular basis; Jesus gave them eternal life and the absolute promise of resurrection. Westcott says, "So far from the doctrine of the Resurrection being, as has been asserted, inconsistent with St. John's teaching on the present reality of eternal life, it would be rather true to say that this doctrine makes the necessity of the resurrection obvious" (Westcott, p. 103).

6:41–42. Time for the Jewish leaders to break in again and this time they **grumble**. The word is *gogguzo*, meaning "to murmur or complain." Just minutes ago the conversation had dealt with Moses and manna so we should be reminded of Exodus 16:2,8–9 and Numbers 11:4. The forefathers of these grumblers set a precedent by complaining before the manna was provided and after they received it! They just did not like Jesus' theology. Carson offers an artful comparison:

> "The Jews" in Jerusalem (5:18ff.) were incensed because they recognized Jesus said things that put him on a par with God; these Galilean Jews are incensed because they think they know a fellow Galilean, and take umbrage at his claims. It is not so much his claim to be bread that offends them as his claim to be bread *from heaven,* his claim that he *came down from heaven.* How could this be so, when his family had moved to Capernaum and he was known there . . . ? Parallel suspicions were raised in Nazareth (Mark 6:2–3; Luke 4:22) (Carson, p. 292).

Interesting how the Jews repeatedly stumbled on Jesus' earthly connections. Origin was always a problem for the unbelieving religious leaders, especially the Pharisees. The word for **grumble** describes a sound which goes through a crowd when they are angry at what a speaker has said and want to show their opposition. Perhaps the modern counterpart would be hissing and booing.

6:43–45. Even though there was no formal question, John tells us that **Jesus answered**. Verse 44 is the opposite of the first part of verse 37. All will come, but no one can come unless he or she is drawn, and the automatic result is resurrection. But what is the significance of the citation of Isaiah 54:13 in the middle of verse 45? This is important if we are to maintain balance in this passage. The original Old Testament text describes the new Jerusalem in which "all your sons will be taught by the Lord" (Isa. 54:13).

The context here seems to require the learning of the gospel and a spiritual awareness that creates a desire for truth. Borchert warns, "Salvation is never achieved apart from the drawing power of God, and it is never consummated apart from the willingness of humans to hear and learn from God. To choose one or the other will ultimately end in unbalanced, unbiblical theology . . . Rather than resolving the tension, the best resolution is learning to live with the tension and accepting those whose theological commitments differ from ours" (Borchert, pp. 268–69).

6:46–47. Where does all this information come from? Only from the one who has both seen the Father and brought his message to the world. These verses are very reminiscent of 1:18, "No one has ever seen God, but God the One and Only, who is at the Father's side, has made him known." And the message persists—everlasting life comes through faith. But for John, faith is more a process than a state of being to which one has arrived. It is informed and intelligent, not faith in faith or hope in hope. The dramatic emphasis of verse 47 shows us how important God considers eternal life to be. For the third time in this passage we see the double *amen* (vv. 26,32) and this is a solemn declaration: faith is the road to life.

Have a look at verses 43–46 from *The Message*:

> Jesus said, "Do not bicker among yourselves over me. You are not in charge here. The Father who sent me is in charge. He draws people to me—that's the only way you'll ever come. Only then do I do my work, putting people together, setting them on their feet, ready for the End. This is what the prophets meant when they wrote, 'And then they will all be personally taught by God.' Anyone who has spent any time at all listening to the Father, really listening and therefore learning, comes to me to be taught personally—to see it with his own eyes, hear it with his own ears, from me, since I have it first hand from the Father. No one has seen the Father except the One who has his Being alongside the Father—and you can see *me*" (John 6:43–46, *The Message*).

6:48–51. Jesus offered the gospel of himself as the bread-eating metaphor persisted. Israelites who ate the manna in the desert died; it was only physical bread designed to sustain their lives on earth a bit longer. But the living bread is not like that; it provides eternal life. And then the bombshell: **This bread is my flesh, which I will give for the life of the world.** Certainly this is not a reference to the Lord's supper for there was no "Lord's Supper" as yet. Furthermore, participating in any religious ritual does not produce eternal life; only faith in Jesus' death on the cross and his resurrection can accomplish that.

By this time, mental assent—agreement with the truth of the Gospel—was giving way to spiritual appropriation, the voluntary and personal application of Christ's death to oneself. Yes, the manna came from God, but it was temporary, and those who ate of it still died. Spiritual appropriation of the life of Jesus leads to eternal life—and that is what they should have been seeking, not another free lunch.

The constant repetition of the concept of bread as life seems to roll upon the shores of our minds like breakers from the sea. Surely the Holy Spirit intends John to repeat in print what Jesus emphasized in word. We need constant reminders that an eternal relationship with God surpasses any food necessary for physical life.

Imagine the shock verse 51 must have had on the ears and minds of the hearers that day in Capernaum. One can talk in general terms about eating the bread of life; it is quite another matter to say, **this bread is my flesh.** The word for *flesh* is different from *body* or *self* because it focuses on physical death and clearly points to the cross. There the bread of life was offered by Jesus universally—**for the life of the world.**

It is crucial for us to understand the significance of spiritual appropriation in these verses. Jesus claimed that his death and its atonement for sin are effective only when people reach out and apply that substitutionary sacrifice to themselves in a spiritual sense.

It is interesting that a short verse like this can consist of three complete sentences. And there is an order or design to the sentences. The first states the source of the living bread; the second discusses the manner in which the life is received when one eats the living bread; and the third focuses on how that eating is available through the vicarious death of Christ on the cross. As Morris declares, "It is a strong word and one bound to attract attention. Its almost crude forcefulness rivets attention on the historical fact that Christ did give Himself for man. He is not speaking simply of a moving idea . . . The last words of the verse bring before us once more the truth that the mission of Jesus is universal. He had not come to minister to the Jews only. When he gave his flesh it would be 'for the life of the world'" (Morris, p. 376).

E Faith Is Spiritual Appropriation (6:52–59)

SUPPORTING IDEA: *The eternal life which is in us who believe comes from the appropriation of the death of Jesus for our salvation. Those who feed on Christ will live forever.*

6:52–55. Still focused on earthly interpretations of spiritual realities (the same problem that troubled Nicodemus in chapter 3), the crowd pondered a very human and earthbound question: **How can this man give us his flesh to eat?** The word translated **argue sharply** is *emachonto*, which describes a debate. The indication seems to be that some favored what Jesus was saying while others opposed him. What follows is a paragraph which must be understood spiritually. It tells us first that spiritual appropriation provides initial life. Without the careful textual approach, we can end up with some kind of theological cannibalism. Jesus was talking about the cross—the spiritual act whereby we accept his death on our behalf in order to gain access to his offer of eternal life. In the spiritual sense, that is the real food and the real drink.

These verses focus on the exclusive character of the atonement. The Jews were divided over the process of receiving the gift of Christ's death on man's behalf. But rather than tone down his language, Jesus issued a fourth double *amen.* Then to the eating of his flesh, he added the drinking of his blood—an idea especially abhorrent to the Jews when taken in its literal and physical sense (Gen. 9:4). Both verbs appear in the Greek aorist tense, indicating that spiritual appropriation is done only once.

The Law of Moses had forbidden any drinking of blood on penalty of being cut off from the nation (Lev. 17:10–14). Yet no fewer than three times in the context of this passage our Lord spoke of eating his flesh and drinking his blood. Some interpreters believe the Lord referred to participating in what we call "communion" when he told people to do these things. But there was no such ordinance before the night before his crucifixion. Furthermore, partaking of the elements in the Lord's Supper does not provide eternal life.

The change of verb for **eat** in verse 54 is interesting at the very least; *esthio* switches to *trogo*, typically used in the Greek of the day to speak of crunching or munching. This switch has led some to connect the passage with the Lord's Supper on what appears to be no solid basis. Carson observes, "The language of vv. 53–54 is so completely unqualified that if its primary reference is to the Eucharist we must conclude that the *one* thing necessary to eternal life is participation at the Lord's table. This interpretation of course actually *contradicts* the earlier parts of the discourse, not least v. 40. The only reasonable alternative is to understand these verses as a *repetition* of the earlier truth, but now in metaphorical form" (Carson, p. 297).

Trogo also appears in verses 56–58. Some interpreters have found in its repetition a reference to a continuous appropriation—the consistent feeding on the Lord as a source of life. This may be a secondary application, subordinate to the initial eating and drinking for salvation. One thing seems clear: the central focus is still eternal life, and now that promise is coupled with resurrection. We find such language difficult today; we can imagine the struggle that the citizens of Jerusalem must have had capturing the essence of Jesus' words.

6:56–57. The Lord emphasized that spiritual appropriation provides abiding life. These verses sound like John 15 with their emphasis on remaining in the Lord after initial faith. We eat by trusting the Savior for regeneration; we abide by feeding on him on a regular basis. Eating becomes a metaphor of faith. Greene says, "We know that food and drink keep the physical body alive and cause it to grow, and our food and drink become part of the body. The same is true in the spiritual sense: when we receive the Word of God, the living word, we are appropriating Christ and he becomes part of us, the new creation (II Cor. 5:17)" (Greene, p. 376).

Jesus began talking about the Father in verse 27 and he continued throughout this entire discourse. John would not allow his readers to forget that Jesus had a mission and was, therefore, a "missionary." He was sent by the Father to the world. The terminology of verse 57 changes just a bit to speak no longer of flesh and blood, but just of eating Christ—the present tense feel of chapter 15. We might paraphrase Jesus' words as, "The one who keeps on feeding on me will live because I live within him."

6:58–59. Finally, we learn that spiritual appropriation provides eternal life. The real bread that came down from heaven was not manna but the life of God's Son given on our behalf. Eating the physical bread of the Old Testament ultimately led to death. But eating the spiritual bread of the New Testament, participating in Christ's death at Calvary, provides eternal life.

The invitation has been open from that day to this. The spiritual appropriation of the life of Christ is available to everyone who trusts him, who believes that Christ's death on the cross paid the penalty for the sin of humankind. Boice sums it up with great clarity: "Do you understand the illustration? That is what faith is. That is what it means to eat Christ's flesh and drink his blood. It is to commit yourself to him. It is to accept his promise and pledge on your behalf and to repeat his promise, vowing to be his for eternity. If you have done that, you have done the most important thing there is to be done in this life, regardless of what you may already have accomplished or may yet accomplish. If you have not, you should know that today is the day of salvation. Today is the day of your union with Christ, if you will have it so" (Boice, II, p. 220).

▉ Faith Is Personal Commitment (6:60–71)

> **SUPPORTING IDEA:** *Like the words of Jesus, the words of Scripture are life because they point to the source of eternal life, the death of Christ.*

6:60–63. All so-called followers of Jesus are not true disciples. Many who are called "disciples" cannot tolerate what they consider to be the teaching of cannibalism. Jesus tried to help them understand that a wooden, literal interpretation of his words about flesh and blood would not lead them to the truth. It is the Holy Spirit who explains the spiritual meaning of his words.

We have already learned that faith is mental assent *and* spiritual appropriation. Now Jesus added the component of personal commitment. And personal commitment comes through spiritual truth. In verse 41 we read that "the Jews began to grumble," and now in verse 61 we read that **his disciples were grumbling.** This was not the Twelve who got special treatment at the beginning of verse 67, but many who had attached themselves to Jesus and called themselves "disciples." According to Carson, "At the most elementary level, a disciple is someone who is at that point following Jesus, either literally by joining the group that pursued him from place to place, or metaphorically in regarding him as the authoritative teacher. Such a 'disciple' is not necessarily a 'Christian,' someone who has savingly trusted Jesus and sworn allegiance to him, given by the Father to the Son, drawn by the Father and born again by the Spirit" (Carson, p. 300).

This parallels closely 2:23–25 where all "believers" are not believers. The issue in biblical Christianity is regeneration—heart change produced by the Holy Spirit—not labels, not affiliations, not personal claims, not religious acts or pilgrimages, and certainly not the keeping of religious laws. And let us not miss in verse 60 that the teaching is hard to **accept.**

Jesus did not skip a theological beat over this grumbling. In rapid-fire verses he talked about the ascension and the Holy Spirit. Only those willing to allow God's Spirit to illumine their understanding of God's Word can find in it the very substance of life. As we shall see, John had more to say about the Holy Spirit than the other three Gospels put together. John clearly recorded Jesus' intentional link of resurrection, ascension, and the coming of the Holy Spirit (7:37–39).

But we still struggle with the phrase **the flesh counts for nothing,** especially in view of Jesus' repeated insistence that they eat his flesh. Morris explains, "A woodenly literal, flesh-dominated manner of looking at Jesus' words will not yield the correct interpretation. That is granted only to the spiritual man, the Spirit-dominated man. Such words cannot be comprehended by the fleshly, whose horizon is bounded by this earth and its outlook. Only as the life-giving Spirit informs him may a man understand these words" (Morris, p. 385).

Perhaps the mention of the ascension in verse 62 switches the thought from eating the flesh of Jesus (spiritual appropriation of the cross) to depending on the flesh of humanity (trusting one's own strength for eternal salvation). We are reminded here of 2 Corinthians 3:6, Paul's contrast between the spirit and the letter.

6:64–66. Some of these **disciples** did not believe, and Jesus knew their hearts. This may be a specific reference to Judas's betrayal. Serious hard teaching about the cross and substitutionary atonement is no more palatable to the modern mind than it was to the first-century mind. Personal commitment comes through spiritual truth and heavenly enabling.

We are almost astonished to find Jesus turning again to the subject we have called "election" as an explanation for the unbelief and departure of false disciples. How does one participate in this heavenly bread? How does one come to the Bread of Life in order to receive eternal life? Only because the Father makes it possible.

6:67–71. The half-hearted followers were gone, and only the Twelve were left. When asked whether they also wished to leave, Peter affirmed their faith in Christ's divine appointment. Somehow he understood the exclusivity of Jesus' claim to be the sole source of eternal life. There is no other option.

Personal commitment comes through *individual choice.* Peter's answer became a high-water mark of spiritual insight given him on this occasion by the Holy Spirit. And here we see it again—believing is seeing: **We believe and**

know that you are the Holy One of God. Peter would not understand the full meaning of his own words until after the resurrection. Jesus had just said to the crowd, "the words I have spoken to you are spirit and they are life" (v. 63). Peter affirmed that true disciples agree and accept that conclusion. Morris helps us with the grammar of Peter's response: "The verbs 'have believed' and 'know' are both in the perfect tense and this should be given its full force. 'We have come to a place of faith and continue there. We have entered into knowledge and retain it'" (Morris, p. 390).

Then Jesus singled out the betrayer and calls him a *diabolos,* the actual word used for Satan in other places in Scripture. Judas surely knew his own heart, but he said nothing when Peter affirmed a collective faith in verse 69. Writing much later, John feared some of his readers might misunderstand Jesus' words, so he added the explanation of verse 71.

We must be careful, especially amid so much talk of God's choosing and drawing people to himself, that we do not edge into a theology of reprobation when we find the word **chosen** in connection with Judas. "The text does not say that Jesus determined Judas would become a devil. The servant of the devil performed a task necessary in the opening of salvation to the world (cf. Luke 22:22). But great care must be taken lest God be blamed for the evil of Judas. The biblical message does not blame God for evil. The rebellious heart is to blame. Here Jesus chose Judas, but Judas was a willful devil (6:70)" (Borchert, p. 276).

Peter's rhetorical question seems a good place to end our study of chapter 6: **Lord, to whom shall we go?** To whom indeed. To the multiple bizarre cults all around us today? To the false religions of the world? To the secular ideology of a barbarian and materialistic society? To a careless indifference which postpones eternal questions of eternal life until some more convenient time? To the sickening sadism and sex of a hedonistic society gone mad? Bad choices all. Even in times of our own spiritual weakness, the options are futile. We must stand with Peter and against the crowds that wander off from the message of the cross. Jesus is the only way to the Father and the only source of life.

MAIN IDEA REVIEW: *Water, food, and bread are metaphors that show how spiritual appropriation of the life which Jesus gives is necessary for salvation.*

III. CONCLUSION

The Garden of God's Grace

My seminary theology professor, Dr. Alva J. McClain, used a wonderful illustration to explain the doctrine of election, one which I have repeated hundreds of times throughout my own ministry. He talked about standing outside a beautiful garden, perhaps like the Butschart Gardens on Vancouver Island, or perhaps the Biltmore Estate in North Carolina, or the DuPont Gardens in Delaware. As we stand outside the gate surveying the beautiful array of flowers, we ponder what it might cost to spend two or three hours strolling around the gardens and photographing the beautiful scenery.

About this point, we look up at the stone archway over the gate and read in large letters, "Whosoever Will May Come." Surely it cannot be possible. Places like this are always expensive. But there is no ticket booth, no waiting line, no signs offering different rates for children, adults, and seniors. Assuming the sign means what it says, we enter the garden and begin to peruse its botanical treasures. Before we get too far down the pathways, however, we want to see that welcome sign one more time—inviting us without charge to enjoy this magnificent place. But as we turn, we look up at the interior of the wall and see the wording of the sign has changed. Now it reads, "Chosen in Him from the Foundation of the World."

McClain's point was both brilliant and simple: to unbelievers, the message is a universal call to faith in Jesus Christ; to believers, it is a reminder that God has controlled our eternal destiny from the beginning. To state it theologically, only the elect will come, but those who come demonstrate they have been chosen.

My friend and former colleague Bob Lightner has compressed this complex theology into two terse and understandable paragraphs:

> It seems most in harmony with the totality of Scripture to believe in personal, pre-temporal election as well as a corporate election of the church. God's foreknowledge of human faith and His election both of individuals and the church must be included. He did predestine those He foreknew (Rom. 8:29). And He did choose according to His foreknowledge (1 Peter 1:1–2). We are not told what it was in God's foreknowledge which moved Him to choose. It is going beyond what Scripture says to say it was his knowledge of the sinner's faith which caused him to make the choice.
>
> The precious truths of election and salvation will not make one self-absorbed and unconcerned for the lost if rightly understood and balanced with God's commands involving human responsibilities. His plan is the result of his infinite wisdom and love and is in keeping with his absolute holiness, justice, mercy, and grace (Lightner, pp. 148–49).

PRINCIPLES

- Jesus is sufficient, not just the satisfier.
- Even when our faith is weak, God wants to work in and through us.
- Only those who are willing to allow the Spirit of God to illumine the understanding of God's Word can find in it the very substance of life.
- Jesus is the only way to the Father and the only source of spiritual food.

APPLICATIONS

- Determine to accept and live out the Father's will for your life.
- Allow God to meet both physical and spiritual needs through Jesus.
- Clarify your understanding of how Christians participate in Christ's death.
- Respond to Jesus the way Peter did: "You have the words of eternal life."

IV. LIFE APPLICATION

The Gospel Train

Though I could never find the music today, the words live in my mind from decades of singing gospel quartet music. Indeed, many songs pick up the metaphor of the gospel train but the one I remember says:

I hear da train a comin'; it's comin' 'round the bend.

I hear the car wheels rollin' and rumblin' through the land.

Oh, get on board, little children, get on board, little children,

Get on board, little children; there's room for many a'more.

The song's image seems to place the decision for salvation in our hands. We go to the station, wait in line to buy a ticket, grab the handrail, and pull ourselves on board. Yes, God sent the train, but we had the schedule and took the initiative to get on it.

The picture of John 6, however, is considerably different. As Boice describes the scene, "You are not even on the platform. You are at home. But God comes on the train; He gets off; He goes to your house; He does a miracle in your life. And then he asks you to live for him there, because that is important to him" (Boise, I, p. 179).

There is nothing wrong with songs about the gospel train or the glory train, but let us never back away from the concept of God as the initiator in our eternal life. Many of those old spirituals we used to sing were based more on emotion than theology, but consider the profound words of George W. Chadwick:

> I sought the Lord, and afterward I knew
> He moved my soul to seek him, seeking me;
> It was not I that found, O Savior true;
> No, I was found of Thee.

> Thou didst reach forth Thy hand and mine enfold;
> I walked and sank not on the storm-vexed sea;
> T'was not so much that I on Thee took hold,
> As, Thou, dear Lord, on me.

V. PRAYER

Father, we are humbled when we think that you have included us in your magnificent plan to provide eternal life for all who believe in Jesus. We accept your grace for life now and throughout eternity. Thank you for the Bread of Life that continually nourishes and satisfies our hearts. Amen.

VI. DEEPER DISCOVERIES

A. Believe (6:29,36,40,47,64,69)

John sprinkled his favorite word throughout this chapter. The Greek verb (*pisteuo*) appears 241 times in the New Testament; 107 of those are in John's writings; and 98 in this Gospel. Tenney's title was well-chosen when he called his commentary *John: The Gospel of Belief.*

The word means to trust or have faith and inseparably links to the noun form (*pistis*) which appears 239 times in the New Testament. On average, some form of the word *faith* or *believe* appears twice in every chapter of the New Testament.

In his Gospel, John never used the words *repent, repentance,* or *faith* to describe the way people are saved. Instead, he used *believe* since this term included all these ideas. John preferred the verb form to emphasize the act that is necessary for someone to be saved—total dependence on the work of Another. John did indicate, however, that believing can be superficial; that is, it can be merely intellectual without resulting in true salvation (Jn 2:23–24; 12:42–43; see Jms 2:19). But John's main thrust is that complete reliance upon Jesus the Messiah and Son of God (20:31) for salvation gives eternal life to the person who believes (3:16; 6:47). Jesus used a word play when He said that people must do 'the work of God' for salvation, for His point was that we must not try to work for it at all. We must simply 'believe in the One He has sent' (6:29) (Blackaby, p. 17).

Christians are people of faith, people who have put their trust in Jesus Christ for eternal salvation and spiritual feeding with the Bread of Life here on earth. This act of believing produces faith which has become a hallmark of evangelicalism for two thousand years. This distinct emphasis in John's Gospel has given birth to many powerful quotations. Here is a small sample:

Faith is a living, daring confidence in God's grace. It is so sure and certain that a man could stake his life on it a thousand times (Martin Luther).

The most cherished possession I wish I could leave with you is my faith in Jesus Christ (Patrick Henry).

The soul is the life of the body. Faith is the life of the soul. Christ is the life of faith (John Flavel).

To seek proof is to admit doubt, and to obtain proof is to render faith superfluous (A. W. Tozer).

Faith rests on the naked Word of God; that Word believed gives full assurance (Harry A. Ironside).

Faith is more than thinking something is true. Faith is thinking something is true to the extent that we act on it (W. T. Turkiser).

B. Communion Elements (6:56)

No one can doubt the connection between the actual flesh and blood of Christ offered on the cross and the representation of that death in bread and wine at the communion table. Luke records, "And he took bread, gave thanks and broke it, and gave it to them, saying, 'This is my body given for you; do this in remembrance of me.' In the same way, after the supper he took the cup, saying, 'This cup is the new covenant in my blood, which is poured out for you'" (Luke 22:19–20). The apostle John had probably experienced hundreds of communion services with believers down through the six decades between Pentecost and his death on Patmos.

But Jesus spoke these words to unbelieving crowds long before the institution of the Last Supper with the disciples or the celebration of communion by the early church. The bread and wine in the communion service are symbols of remembrance; the flesh and blood of chapter 6 are spiritual realities in our appropriation of the power of the cross. As Borchert writes, "That the evangelist may indeed have seen in the Supper a symbolic representation of the dying and rising son of God is quite likely. But the symbols in John always remained derivative representations of the great Passover event in Jesus. The symbols are not ends in themselves, nor are they nor can they be made powers in themselves. These elements can indeed symbolize the eternal and actual bread that came down from heaven (6:58), but they must never take the place of the living Lord, the one who was sent by God and who gave his flesh and blood for the life of the world (6:58)" (Borchert, p. 273).

C. The Twelve (6:67,70–71)

John mentioned the Twelve as a group here for the first time. Matthew did the same thing (Matt. 26:14), using the word as a title for the group, hence the NIV rendering of the capital "T." As an adjective, "the twelve disciples" offers a common designation throughout the Gospels. But the title appears only in Matthew 26, a variety of times in Mark (chaps. 4,9,10,11,14), Luke (chs. 8,9,18,22) and in John only here and in 20:24. If we had only the Gospel narratives to support the idea, we might conclude that the name was adopted by the disciples themselves. But in verse 70 of chapter 6 John recorded Jesus' use of *Twelve* as a formal title for the chosen disciples.

The New Testament offers four listings of the Twelve (Matt. 10:2–4; Mark 3:16–19; Luke 6:14–16; Acts 1:13). John is notably absent, again because his purpose focuses on the words of Jesus, not the general history of his life and ministry. The listings suggest three groupings of four, with Peter, Philip, and James the son of Alphaeus heading each group. There are also three groups of brothers among the Twelve: Peter and Andrew; James and John; James the son of Alphaeus and Judas the brother of James. One should not make too much of these observations, simply a recognition of God's calling and work in the lives of the men who surrounded Jesus.

VII. TEACHING OUTLINE

A. INTRODUCTION

1. Lead Story: World Hunger
2. Context: John offered us only a typical time reference in the broadest generalities ("sometime after this") to show that the feeding of the five thousand and the following sermon on the Bread of Life took place after the healing at the pool and prior to the Feast of Tabernacles. The content, not the chronology, is the key. The message of life through the Son continues with the metaphor of bread and the metaphor of water (ch. 7).
3. Transition: Again, the casual terminology of John at both the beginning of chapter 6 and the beginning of chapter 7: "some time after this" and "after this." Luke placed chronological markers throughout his Gospel and his record of the early church we call Acts. John wanted us to follow the theology of Jesus' words as he portrayed the Son of God, the Savior of the world.

B. COMMENTARY

1. Faith Is Expectant Obedience (6:1–15)
   a. People in need (6:1–6)
   b. Disciples in confusion (6:7–13)
   c. Jesus in hiding (6:14–15)
2. Faith Is Willing Trust (6:16–24)
   a. A lesson of authority for the disciples (6:16–21)
   b. A lesson of purpose for the crowd (6:22–24)
3. Faith Is Eternal Choice (6:25–33)
   a. Misunderstanding of God's plan (6:25–27)
   b. Explanation of salvation (6:28–29)
   c. Author of the Bread of Life (6:30–33)
4. Faith Is Mental Assent (6:34–51)
   a. Mental assent begins with election (6:34–37)
   b. Mental assent proceeds to security (6:38–40)
   c. Mental assent culminates in eternal life (6:41–51)
5. Faith Is Spiritual Appropriation (6:52–59)
   a. Spiritual appropriation provides initial life (6:52–55)
   b. Spiritual appropriation provides abiding life (6:56–57)
   c. Spiritual appropriation provides eternal life (6:58–59)
6. Faith Is Personal Commitment (6:60–71)
   a. Personal commitment comes through spiritual truth (6:60–63)
   b. Personal commitment comes through heavenly enabling (6:64–66)
   c. Personal commitment comes through individual choice (6:67–71)

C. CONCLUSION: THE GOSPEL TRAIN

VIII. ISSUES FOR DISCUSSION

1. How can we offer Christ everything we have in faith, no matter how little that might seem to us?
2. What kind of fears do we have today that could be minimized or even removed by recognizing Jesus' presence with us?
3. In what ways do we consistently eat the Bread of Life in order to live spiritually?
4. How firmly can we say with Peter, "We believe and know that you are the Holy One of God"?

John 7

Living Water

| Quote |

"*N*o sooner does the water of the Spirit come down upon a stubborn and rocky-hearted sinner, but he is made tender and pliable thereby."

B e n j a m i n   K e a c h

GEOGRAPHICAL PROFILE: GALILEE

- Part of the territory ruled by Herod Antipas, the northernmost region of Israel
- An area of rolling hills, large plains, and the famous Sea of Galilee
- Includes the towns of Cana, Capernaum, Nazareth, and the capitol, Tiberias
- Measures approximately fifty miles north to south and thirty miles east to west
- The name means *the ring*

IN A NUTSHELL

*M*an-made religion can never satisfy; only God provides living water. In this chapter we find the fresh message of Christ pitted against the traditional legalism of the Jewish leaders. The argument which ensued led to the first introduction of the Holy Spirit in John.

Living Water

I. INTRODUCTION

Molecules of Truth

A chemistry professor once started his lecture on molecules with the following poem:

> When Hydrogen "U" played Oxygen Tech,
> The game had just begun,
> When Hydrogen racked up two fast points,
> And Oxygen still had none.
> Then Oxygen scored a single goal,
> And thus it did remain,
> At Hydrogen 2 and Oxygen 1—
> Called because of rain.

This chapter is about water even though that theme occupies only three verses about two-thirds of the way through the chapter. John clearly built up to the words of the Lord on the last day of the feast and took us back with this metaphor to chapters 3 and 4 where water had already been discussed in its spiritual connotation. Yet the imagery is not some new covenant surprise; purification and spiritual washing had been a part of Jewish life for hundreds of years.

Furthermore, Old Testament prophets had predicted the significance of spiritual water in the future. Ezekiel declared, "I will sprinkle clean water on you, and you will be clean; I will cleanse you from all your impurities and from all your idols. I will give you a new heart and put a new spirit in you; I will remove from you your heart of stone and give you a heart of flesh. And I will put my spirit in you and move you to follow my decrees and be careful to keep my laws" (Ezek. 36:25–27).

The way Jesus used water in the Gospel of John demonstrates again his commitment to teaching in a way that could be understood by anyone. The most widely used of all solvents, water is essential for almost all plant and animal life. The word describes something as small as a tiny glass or even a droplet, and something as large as the Pacific Ocean. It exists in every human body and has given birth to a dozen idioms such as "above water" and "water under the bridge." It forms the defining adjective for pages of other terms in any major dictionary, everything from "water ballet" to "water witch."

But in chapter 7 of John, water takes on a whole new meaning as a reference to the Holy Spirit, an interpretation John did not leave to chance. The offer of Isaiah lives on: "Come, all you who are thirsty, come to the waters" (Isa. 55:1a).

II. COMMENTARY

> **MAIN IDEA:** *Living water is only available from the Messiah whom God sent to provide for our thirst.*

Living Water

A Brothers of the Messiah (7:1–13)

> **SUPPORTING IDEA:** *Time may be the most precious resource known to humankind. Like Jesus, we need to know how God is directing use of our time.*

7:1–5. The Feast of Tabernacles began on the fifteenth day of the seventh month, five days after Yom Kippur. It was one of the three main feasts of the Jews, symbolizing the protection of Israel in the wilderness (Lev. 23; Deut. 16). In this lengthy introduction of thirteen verses, we learn about the significance of the feast, the attitude of Jesus' brothers, and the reaction of the crowds. Public opposition was now in full swing and Jesus' life was constantly in danger.

John wasted no time in establishing the Lord's motive for staying in Galilee; the Jews in Judea wanted to kill him. Indeed, threats on the Lord's life dominate this chapter (vv. 1,13,19,25,30,32,44). Presumably the events of chapter 7 took place six months after chapter 6, since John referred to the Passover in 6:4 and now mentioned the Jewish Feast of Tabernacles. The record of chapter 7 begins before the feast and takes us to the last and greatest day. Borchert reminds us, "Tabernacles was a time of camping for Israel. Particularly in Jerusalem, visitors set up booths all over the city in remembrance of the years when Israel wandered in the wilderness. The festival originally lasted for seven days . . . but later an eighth summary day or Solemn assembly was added that brought together the reflections of Israel's history and hopes for Israel's future" (Borchert, p. 278).

Jesus' brothers (presumably half brothers all younger than he), still skeptical and perhaps even bitter about his popularity and notoriety, goaded him into making a public display of what he claimed to be. They were certainly right to argue, **No one who wants to become a public figure acts in secret.** But their motivation rested in their unbelief, as John indicated in verse 5. They described the pattern of secular politicians—a pattern Jesus urged his own disciples not to follow. Many disciples left Jesus at the end of chapter 6, and the scene reminds us of Joseph's jealous brothers tormented by his dreams of grandeur. The Feast of Tabernacles in Jerusalem was a media event, a photo op for any prophet seeking stardom.

Let us not rush too quickly over the word **brothers**. Westcott identifies these people as the sons of Joseph by a former marriage. The Roman Catholic view protects the perpetual virginity of Mary by referring to them as "cousins." Some interpreters do not even discuss this subject, assuming readers will choose the traditional evangelical view. Godet states it very succinctly: "We take the expression 'Jesus' brethren,' in the strict sense" (Godet, II, p. 54).

7:6–9. The issue at stake here is time (*kairos*). For Jesus' brothers, public display of political ambition was appropriate any time, but God's Messiah was on a strict schedule. Three times the Lord talked about time in this section. Clearly, the time had **not yet come**. There is human time and God's time; careless time and precious time; earthbound time and eternal time.

At this point in their lives, all of Jesus' brothers were still in **the world**, so they had nothing to fear from the enemies of Jesus. He had already condemned the world, so threats on his life were very real. He would go to the feast, but in his own timing and as a prophet, not a pilgrim.

Verse 8 contains a key word, though it does not appear in some manuscripts. The word is **yet**, indicating to his brothers that Jesus fully intended to visit the feast, but not according to the time frames they had set. Carson makes an interesting distinction between the use of *hora* used in 2:4 and *kairos*:

> The word *kairos*, found in vv. 6,8, unlike *chronos* but like *hora*, refers in this Gospel to a point of time, but unlike *hora* does not refer to Christ's "being lifted up," to his glorification by way of the cross. If that is the case, then unlike 2:4, Jesus is *not* saying that the time for unrestrained Messianic blessings has not yet dawned because the "time" of his glorification is not yet at hand (the final Passover was still more than six months away). Rather he is saying that the "time" for this going up to Jerusalem for this Feast of Tabernacles is not yet at hand.
>
> This interpretation is well-nigh necessitated by the final words of the verse: *For you any time (kairos) is right . . .* It is almost as if they are being excluded from divine sovereignty—not that God suspended his providential reign in their case, but that what they did was utterly without significance as far as God is concerned (Carson, pp. 307–08).

7:10–13. So Jesus went up to the feast **in secret**. As he moved among the crowds, their confusion must have been obvious. Some thought him a good man, others a deceiver. It would have been politically incorrect to offer a public opinion, so all these little discussions took place in private. When we read **Jews** at the end of verse 13, we should understand a reference to official authorities. Then as now, some religious groups consider it unacceptable to disagree with the official opinions of leadership. Morris reminds us that "the role of 'the crowd' throughout this chapter should not be overlooked. Except in chapter 12 there is nothing like it in this Gospel. The term denotes the uninformed majority, wanting to do the right thing but not sure what it was. They are distinguished from 'Jews' (which here must mean the religious leaders, for the crowds were Jews themselves), and also from the disciples of Jesus" (Morris, p. 402).

B Message of the Messiah (7:14–24)

SUPPORTING IDEA: *Important to the process of evangelization is the clear announcement of the gospel so that God's message is not misunderstood.*

7:14–15. Unlike the teaching of the rabbis, the message of Messiah comes from God himself. It was obvious Jesus had not attended official rabbinical schools, so where did he get such learning? Notice they did not ask Jesus directly but discussed this among themselves. Interesting that in just about a year in this very city others would refer to Jesus' disciples (Peter and John) as "unschooled ordinary men" (Acts 4:13). And this passage also evokes memories of Mark's words, "The people were amazed at his teaching, because he taught them as one who had authority, not as the teachers of the law" (Mark 1:22).

7:16–17. Although the question was not addressed to him, Jesus chose the opportunity to answer. This was only one of many occasions on which he would make this assertion: **My teaching is not my own. It comes from him who sent me.** Then comes a verse that tells us both how to know the truth and how to know God's will. God does not show us his will just to satisfy our curiosity; when we are prepared to do God's will, then in God's good time we will know it. Furthermore, only those prepared to do God's will are prepared to discern the truth of Jesus' words and the truth of Scripture as well. Jesus disavowed speaking for himself and deflected attention to the Father.

In *The Crises of the Christ*, G. Campbell Morgan points out the distinctive importance of verse 17.

> While that passage is generally quoted as declaring a philosophy of Christian discipleship, and while it has that application, it should never be forgotten that the first intention of the words is that of an answer to a question of the Jews, and is our Lord's account of His knowledge of the things that astonished His hearers. The Man Who perfectly does the will of God is the Man Who understands all mys-

teries; and is familiar with facts which ordinary men only understand by long effort and study. The secrets that lie hidden in Nature, fallen man with clouded intelligence must search after; but God's unfallen Man will read them upon the open page of Nature, discovering immediately the deepest philosophies of life (Morgan, pp. 104–05).

7:18. In chapter 1 Jesus called Nathanael "guileless" and now he applied that general principle to himself. In John's Gospel no one is **a man of truth** except God the Father and Jesus the Son (3:33; 8:26). Tenney states it well: "Spiritual understanding is not produced solely by learning facts or procedures, but rather it depends on obedience to know in truth" (Tenney, *EBC*, p. 84).

7:19. Man-made religion can never satisfy nor could anyone keep the law Moses gave. Why should their frustration at failure to keep the Mosaic Law turn them against the Bread of Life? The Law of Moses was clear in its position against murder, yet that is precisely what rested in their hearts during this conversation. In spite of all their bragging, their villainous hearts betrayed their own breaking of the law.

How differently we view people than God does. To us, a person four feet six inches tall standing beside a person six feet four inches tall demonstrates an enormous physical disparity. But put them both next to the Empire State Building and the difference becomes inconsequential. Jesus wanted his audience to stop comparing themselves with one another, or even with Moses, and to look to the righteousness of God.

7:20. Jesus' direct answer put an end to the private murmurings and opened a public dialogue. Apparently he touched a nerve with his reference to murderous hearts. Their response was, **You are demon-possessed** (8:48–52; 10:20–21). But notice we have changed from "the Jews" in verse 15 to **the crowd** in verse 20, so the guilt is more widespread than it was just minutes ago. Tenney, on the other hand, attributes the reaction of the crowd to bewilderment rather than guilt. Whatever the motive, they seemed hesitant to hurl the accusation.

Borchert picks up on the intent of the crowd: "It would be the equivalent of calling Jesus 'paranoid' today. Categorizing people is a time-honored way of refusing to take them seriously. It is crucial to note at this point that it was the Jewish people who were designated by the evangelist as the hostile name-callers. By the end of these Tabernacle chapters, however, the hostility rises to an exceedingly venomous level, and Jesus' death is virtually assured in the minds of the religious establishment" (Borchert, p. 284).

7:21–24. The message of Messiah, which comes from God himself, centers in truth and justice. Apparently the Lord brought up the healing of the lame man (ch. 5) on the Sabbath and told them again to stop worshiping the day and to worship the God who gave the day. The point of the law is to direct us to Christ (Gal. 3:19–25). Circumcision can be performed on the Sabbath because it is righteous, so Jesus, the Messiah, demonstrates the righteousness of his message by healing on the Sabbath.

But enough talk about Moses—circumcision came from Abraham. It had to be observed on the eighth day after birth, so occasionally it would fall on the Sabbath. Since this righteous act marked purification, why could not cleansing and healing be acceptable on the Sabbath? Godet paraphrases Jesus' point: "It is precisely *for this,* that is to say, with the design of teaching you not to judge as you are doing—when you are scandalized . . . at my Sabbath work—that Moses did not hesitate to impose the rite of circumcision upon you, while introducing into his law this conflict with the law of the Sabbath. Thereby, he has justified me in advance, by making all of you commit the transgression for which you are seeking to kill me" (Godet, p. 66).

Verse 24 of chapter 7 stands as a reminder for all humanity in all times and places. Human-designed religion lives in the constant morass of such error. The absence of faith creates attachment to icons and holy places. I heard about a sculptor who, on his death bed, was handed a marble crucifix as a gesture of comfort. He pushed it away, saying, "Alas, I made it."

Ⓒ Origin of the Messiah (7:25–36)

> **SUPPORTING IDEA:** *Many people reject Jesus and the claims of the gospel because they have erroneous ideas of who he is and what he offers.*

7:25–27. The religious authorities were trying to kill Jesus, but he spoke boldly and publicly without challenge. Is it possible, wondered the people, that the religious authorities have concluded he is the Messiah? Obviously not. Such thinking led many people into false conclusions about the origins of Messiah—a topic which left most in confusion. A twofold trap emerged from their misunderstanding. First, they determined they knew where Jesus came from (Nazareth), thereby denying the virgin birth. Second, they argued that no man would know the origin of Messiah, but the prophets spoke much of this with specific references to Bethlehem. As with many people today, ignorance of the facts about Jesus led them into further theological error.

Notice how John designated a specific group again—this time **some of the people of Jerusalem** instead of "the Jews" of verse 15 and "the crowd" of verse 20. The spotlight narrows from the broad pilgrims present at the feast to the locals who had made a regular practice of second-guessing their religious leaders. We should not infer that the Bethlehem reference of the Old Testament had been completely missed. The Herod-appointed scribes of Matthew 2 had no problem coming up with that name. But the spiritual blindness, especially in Jerusalem, had reached such levels that theological confusion about Jesus had clouded public thinking.

7:28–29. Once again Jesus answered rumors with direct proclamation. The origin of Messiah left most people in confusion, but that origin also linked him with God. In effect, Jesus' response to their confusion was three simple statements: (1) You know me in terms of my physical presence on earth; (2) but I really came from the Father and you do not know that because you do not know him; and (3) nevertheless, I know him because he sent me to earth.

So all this knowledge was no knowledge at all. John may have intended a deliberate irony in the way he recorded this passage. Since the Jews did not accept Jesus' divine mission, they did not accept the one who sent him.

7:30–32. Suddenly the bright side surfaces in our story because the origin of Messiah, properly understood, lifted some people to faith. Notice the sovereignty of God in John's careful description. They had every intent to **seize him** and presumably kill him, but **his time had not yet come.** Meanwhile, many in this crowd of so-called disciples actually did place their faith in him, concluding that they had seen enough. Surely even Messiah would not do more miraculous signs than they had seen Jesus do. He fulfilled Scripture; he gave eternal life to those who wished it; he healed the sick; and he mended broken hearts. Nevertheless, seeing still precedes believing, a violation of the faith principles of John's Gospel.

7:33–36. Only six months remained in Jesus' earthly pilgrimage—the period from the Feast of Tabernacles to the Feast of Passover. So he told the crowd that his invitation would be activated by the ascension. How interesting that in verse 34 he said, **You will look for me, but you will not find me; and where I am, you cannot come.** This is precisely the reverse message of John 14 where he told the disciples they knew where he was going and how to get there.

Again the Jews interpreted these words in earthly terms. Where would he go? To the Diaspora, Jews living outside of Palestine around the Mediterranean world? Or would he go and teach pagan Greeks?

All this seemed preposterous to Jews gathered for the Feast of Tabernacles, but that is precisely what happened in the early chapters of Acts. Paul sought out synagogue after synagogue across Asia Minor and Greece, proclaiming the gospel to Jews, Jewish proselytes, and pagan Gentiles.

Ⓓ Invitation of the Messiah (7:37–44)

SUPPORTING IDEA: *Amid discussions of his origin and departure, Jesus drove home the centerpiece of his mission—to provide living bread and living water for hungry and thirsty people.*

7:37–38. The invitation of Messiah is *received by believing.* We have come to the eighth day of the feast, the last and greatest day. Finally, as his brothers had urged more than a week earlier, Jesus "went public" with his message. This great water ceremony reminds us again of the link between water and the Holy Spirit in John 4, and quite possibly also John 3. Any thirsty people out there within the sound of Jesus' voice? Let them come and drink. And those who drink would have within themselves **streams of living water** falling from the inside out.

The surrounding context offered a dramatic backdrop for these brief but powerful words. The corporate mind had been focused on water for days. Hughes describes the scene:

> On the seventh day, the priest would circle the altar seven times in succession—as the people of Israel had encircled the walls of Jericho. When he came around for the sixth time, he'd be joined by another priest carrying the wine. They would ascend the ramp to the altar of holocaust where they were together to pour out the water and wine on the altar. When they were in place, there would come a pause as the priest raised up his pitcher. Always the crowd shouted for him to hold it higher and he would do so. It was considered to be the height of joy in a person's life if he could see the water being poured out onto the altar (Hughes, p. 139).

One cannot argue for certain whether Jesus' words were delivered on the seventh or the eighth day. Either could be called **the last and greatest day of the Feast.** Nor do we know what Scripture he had in mind in the citation of verse 38. Westcott argues, "The reference is not to any one isolated passage, but to the general tenor of such passages as Isa. lviii. 11; Zech. xiv. 8, taken in connexion with the original image (Exod. xvii. 6; Num. xx. 11)" (Westcott, p. 123).

7:39. Thank God for John the interpreter for surely we would have theology of all sorts flowing from the "streams of living water" in this passage. But John left no question about meaning because the doctrine of the Holy Spirit is one of his great themes. We find more detailed teaching on this theme in chapters 14–16, but the glorification of Jesus is another important message in this book. We see it repeated in 8:54; 11:4; 12:28; 13:31–32; and 14:13.

So the Spirit is the living water from within. This interpretation may help us with John 3:5 and 4:13–14. Note John's careful time delineations as well. The Spirit's coming at Pentecost was still future at this event, though John was writing decades later. Throughout the Old Testament, the Holy Spirit's descent upon servants of God was temporary, but soon believers would **receive** him. All this awaited until after the *glorification;* John uses the verb form for the first time here. As Tenney points out, "It has varied meanings in this Gospel. It may refer to establishing status or to enhancing a reputation (8:54; 12:28; 13:32; 14:13; 15:8; 16:14; 17:1,4,5,10; 21:19). In this particular context it refers to Jesus' death, which, despite all appearances, would be the entrance to glory for him (7:39; 11:4; 12:16,23; 13:31). The death and resurrection of Jesus would demonstrate the perfection of God's love and power through humiliation" (Tenney, *EBC*, p. 87).

7:40–44. Finally, we see the invitation of Messiah is divisive to unbelievers. How typical of the gospel. Invariably in Acts when the gospel is preached, some people believe, some hesitate, some scoff, and some want to kill the messenger. On this occasion, some believed a portion of what Jesus said; some believed but did nothing; some got lost in religious arguments; and some reacted in hostile indignation. How foolish to recognize that Messiah was prophesied to come from Bethlehem and yet not check the facts of Jesus' birth. Rejecting hearts are blinded still to the fact that Christ's origin was not Galilee but Bethlehem; indeed, it was not earth, but heaven.

John kept dropping in references to **the Prophet**, a device in line with his messianic emphasis. Yet there was still no clear connection in the people's minds between Moses' promise of a future prophet and the coming of this Messiah. One thing was clear—**the people were divided because of Jesus.**

E Rejection of the Messiah (7:45–52)

SUPPORTING IDEA: *The gospel is divisive. There are still many opinions on the true nature of Jesus. But one thing is clear: "No one ever spoke the way this man does."*

7:45–46. This chapter ends in an interesting way. John described conversations between the temple guards and the Pharisees. The officers who had witnessed all this and heard Jesus' words were impressed, more by his words than his works. But people who did not agree with the Pharisaic point of view were cursed.

7:47–49. The Pharisees questioned the guards with a series of rhetorical questions extending all the way to the end of the chapter. The word **rulers** probably refers to religious leaders other than Pharisees, perhaps the Sadducees and other members of the Sanhedrin. In this entire section, John set law against grace and faith as a means of relating to God. Certainly the mob knew the significance of the Old Testament. Morris explains their complaint: "It means that they did not know the Law in the way the Pharisees did. These students discern 613 commandments in the law, and they set themselves the task of earning their salvation by trying to keep them all. Even this was not the whole task, for they added the entire corpus of oral tradition concerning the law (which governed the interpretation of biblical passages). It was small wonder that ordinary pious people, like the crowd of pilgrims, simply gave up the task" (Morris, pp. 432–33).

The complaint divided the ignorant mob from the in-the-know religious leaders, indicating that only stupidity would lead anyone to believe in Jesus.

Certainly no Pharisee would ever do that. But was that really true? Apparently not.

7:50–53. Nicodemus asked whether Jewish law was being followed. But the blind Pharisees had no interest in law or in their colleague Nicodemus. It was a geographical issue. Jesus came from Galilee and no prophet would come from Galilee, so that was the end of the matter.

Let us not attribute more to Nicodemus than the text gives him. He did not defend Jesus nor cite any specific Old Testament text. He called for a more rational environment in which cooler heads could prevail. We see this behavior from another rabbi, Gamaliel, just about two years later (Acts 5:34–39). On the careless claim of the Pharisees about prophets in Galilee, Carson suggests a textual variation: "It is also possible that the original reading is not 'a prophet' but 'the prophet,' i.e., the prophet like Moses (cf. Notes on 6:14; 7:40): some of the earliest and best manuscripts support this reading, though admittedly the bulk of the textual attestation goes the other way" (Carson, p. 332).

> **MAIN IDEA REVIEW:** *Living water is only available from the Messiah whom God sent to provide for our thirst.*

III. CONCLUSION

Low Tide

In the nineteenth century Charles Haddon Spurgeon used to talk about "tides of spiritual blessing." He would describe the tide on the Thames River. When the tide was out, barges sat in the mud, but when the tide came in, they moved easily and readily. Then he would apply that familiar word picture to the spiritual status of people in churches, desperately in need of a spiritual high tide to move their boats out of the mud.

So it was with the Pharisees, and so it is with many deeply religious people today. Willing to place high priority and ritual in law, they are unwilling to recognize that Jesus is the Messiah sent from God. The water metaphor prevails throughout the chapter. The dry and brittle theology of the Pharisees needed the "streams of living water" offered by Jesus. But they refused to allow spiritual tides to approach their theological barges.

Anyone who has traveled in the mountainous part, of the United States can grasp the key metaphor of this chapter. The highways that run through the Rockies travel, for the most part, along rushing streams that dance over rocks and logs and anything else in their path. During heavy rains, or when the snow is melting, one can hardly carry on a conversation next to them because of the noise of the rushing water. This is symbolic of what Jesus taught in this exciting chapter.

PRINCIPLES

- God's timing was good enough for Jesus; it should be good enough for us.
- Knowing God's will depends upon knowing God's Word.
- Salvation begins by recognizing Jesus for who he is.

APPLICATIONS

- Stop judging by appearances.
- Drink deeply of Jesus and share the living water with others.
- If you are "divided" from other people, pray that it is because of the message of Jesus—not your own offensive behavior.

IV. LIFE APPLICATION

Obvious—But Wrong!

I once read about an assistant pastor who was leading a children's sermon in the regular worship service on Sunday morning. He wanted enthusiastic participation, so early in his remarks he asked the kids, "What is gray, has a bushy tail, and gathers nuts in the fall?" One five-year-old raised his hand and said, "I know the answer should be Jesus, but it sounds like a squirrel to me."

Perhaps to five-year-olds in a Sunday worship service, Jesus should be the answer to everything. The response seemed obvious, but it was wrong—a situation we see commonly in John 7.

Jesus' brothers assumed he would want fame and public recognition and therefore should head for Jerusalem to flaunt his stuff at the feast—but they were wrong.

It seemed obvious to the crowds at the feast that the mystery that surrounded Jesus suggested he was a deceiver of some kind—but they were wrong.

It seemed obvious to the Jewish religious leaders that no one could read their inner hearts and know their murderous intentions—but they were wrong.

The festal pilgrims saw that the authorities did not arrest the prophet they seemed to hate so much. They concluded that perhaps they had become believers as well—but they were wrong.

The Jewish leaders heard Jesus say he was going to some place where they could not find him. They assumed he would go teach Greeks—but they were wrong.

Jesus' enemies thought they knew him, his family, and his origins—but they were wrong.

It seemed obvious that Jesus' message must be false since only the ignorant mob took it seriously—but that was wrong.

Sincere belief in what appears to be obvious is no excuse for not searching for truth. Our belief system should rest on what God says.

V. PRAYER

Father, thank you for the living water Jesus has provided through the Holy Spirit. May we drink deeply and be able to refresh others with the overflow. Amen.

VI. DEEPER DISCOVERIES

A. Feast of Tabernacles (7:2)

The Jewish month of Tishri would not be unlike our December with great gladness and festivity occupying much of the month. It was preceded by the fast of atonement and followed on the tenth of the month by Yom Kippur, the day of atonement. Some place this particular feast that Jesus attended on the 11–18 of October A.D. 29 though we need not be bound by that chronology. The feast in John's Gospel is probably not the same as that referred to by Luke (Luke 9:51–53).

This joyous celebration was one of three required of every Jewish male who lived within twenty miles of Jerusalem. Thousands came from points much farther away than that. The temporary shelters were constructed so light came through. The roof had to be sufficiently open so the family could see stars at night. While many feasts, such as Passover, emphasized the past, the Feast of Tabernacles was futuristic (Zech. 14). Hughes tells us about the role of the *ethrog* in the festivities:

> At the heart of the celebration was a daily rite which we need to be aware of in order to understand John 7. Rabbinical literature tells us that each morning great multitudes gathered at the Temple of Herod, carrying a citrus fruit called an ethrog in their left hands. The ethrog was a reminder of the land to which God had brought them and of the bountiful blessings they had enjoyed. In their right hands they carried a lulab, which was a combination of three trees—a palm, a willow and a myrtle—emblematic of the stages of their ancestors' journey through the wilderness.
>
> Each morning the people would gather with the ethrog and the lulab. The crowds followed the priest who carried a golden pitcher to

the Pool of Siloam, chanting psalms and waving their lulabs in rhythm. As they approached the pool, the priest would dip his pitcher into the water and the people would say, "Therefore you will joyously draw water from the springs of salvation" (Isa. 12:3). The crowd then marched back to the temple, entering the Water Gate to the blast of the priest's trumpets. The priest who had led them circled the altar once, and with accompanying priests ascended to the platform, and poured out the water (Hughes, p. 137).

As our study in John continues, we will see chapters 8 and 9 also falling into the general context of the Feast of Tabernacles, though not quite as specifically as chapter 7. We talk a great deal in our day about contexualizing the gospel, by which we mean fitting our message into the lives of people so they can understand it in their cultural uniqueness. Every missionary learns this technique, and students in hundreds of intercultural ministries classes must master it as well. That is what we have in John 7—a contextualized message on living water set in the pattern of the great water festival.

B. Circumcision (7:22–23)

This practice was not unique to the Hebrews, although it was instituted with them by God as a sign of the covenant with Abraham (Gen. 17:12). Every male child was to be circumcised on the eighth day. In early days the ritual was performed by the father. The practice spread among many peoples, including Arabians, Moabites, Ammonites, Edomites, and even Egyptians. But it was never practiced by the pagan peoples in Babylonia, Assyria, Canaan, and Philistia. Jesus' point in this chapter emphasized that circumcision (even on the Sabbath) was a practice that went clear back to Abraham. However, it became part of the Mosaic code at Mt. Sinai (Exod. 12).

Apart from the issue of performing circumcision on the Sabbath, the rite itself became a major argument in the early church when Judaizing Christians argued for the necessity of circumcising Gentile believers.

VII. TEACHING OUTLINE

A. INTRODUCTION

1.   Lead Story: Molecules of Truth
2.   Context: Already in the first third of his book, John has entered the last six months of Jesus' ministry and will not, in his account, take us back to Galilee. The message on the living water will be followed in the next chapter by the message on the light of the world accompanied by similar arguments regarding origins and destinations of the Messiah.

3. Transition: The transition from chapter 6 is easily made with the simple words "after this" without any specific chronological reference. The transition to chapter 8, however, offers a major textual problem that we must address at the beginning of the next chapter.

B. COMMENTARY

1. Brothers of the Messiah (7:1–13)
   a. Debate in Galilee (7:1–9)
   b. Departure for the feast (7:10–13)
2. Message of the Messiah (7:14–24)
   a. Comes from God himself (7:14–19)
   b. Centers in truth and justice (7:20–24)
3. Origin of the Messiah (7:25–36)
   a. Leaves many in confusion (7:25–27)
   b. Links him with God (7:28–29)
   c. Lifts some to faith (7:30–36)
4. Invitation of the Messiah (7:37–44)
   a. Is received by believing (7:37–39)
   b. Is divisive to unbelievers (7:40–44)
5. Rejection of the Messiah (7:45–53)
   a. Proclaimed by the Pharisees (7:45–49)
   b. Challenged by Nicodemus (7:50–53)

C. CONCLUSION: OBVIOUS—BUT WRONG!

VIII. ISSUES FOR DISCUSSION

1. How can we understand the will of God so clearly that we know the times that he wants us to do certain things or to go certain places?
2. In what ways can we be people of truth who work for the God who sends us into the world?
3. How can we give the Holy Spirit such control in our lives that our inner living water will flow out to other people?

John 8

The Truth Shall Set You Free

"*Truth* is incontrovertible. Panic may resent it; ignorance may deride it; malice may distort; but there it is."

W i n s t o n   C h u r c h i l l

GEOGRAPHICAL PROFILE: MOUNT OF OLIVES

- Rises about one hundred feet over Jerusalem and gives an excellent view of the city which lies to the west
- Included the Garden of Gethsemane in an olive grove on its southwestern slope
- Place from which Jesus ascended into heaven (Acts 1)
- Both Jesus and David stood on this mountain, looked down on Jerusalem, and wept (2 Sam. 15:30; Luke 13:34)

PERSONAL PROFILE: ABRAHAM

- Spent his early years in the ancient city of Ur on the banks of the Euphrates River in Mesopotamia
- Migrated northwest along the fertile crescent to Haran, where he lived for a while on his way to Canaan
- Married his half-sister Sarah, daughter of their father Terah
- Called by God to be the father of the nation of Israel in a covenant which was renewed when Abraham was ninety-nine years old; Isaac was born a year later

IN A NUTSHELL

Darkness dwells in the world. But the light of Christ overcomes the world's darkness, centering in the truth which Jesus brought to the world. In this chapter Jesus proclaimed light and truth, based upon an act of forgiveness.

The Truth Shall Set You Free

I. INTRODUCTION

Climbing into the Wheelbarrow

*Y*ou may have heard the fascinating story of the French acrobat Blondin, whose spectacular feats in the mid-1800s captured global attention. In August of 1860 he crossed Niagara Falls on a tightrope 1,100 feet long strung 160 feet above the water. Then he pushed a wheelbarrow across. Ignoring protests from the Prince of Wales, he carried his agent on his back all the way across and then back again. Then he turned to the crowd and asked, "Do you believe I could do that with you?"

"Of course," responded a man. "I've just seen you do it."

"Well, hop on or hop in," said Blondin, "and I'll take you across."

The man had no intention of following through on his affirmation. The crowd had a good laugh from a display of words without faith. Actually, the man had faith, but faith alone does not save people, as we have already seen in chapters 2 and 6. When John referred to people as believers, he did not mean that they necessarily had trusted Christ in saving faith. In the chapter before us, the continuing discussion between Jesus and the Jews offers a contrast of truth and error, light and darkness, freedom and slavery, false discipleship and true discipleship. The word *truth* appears nine times, clearly the key word of the passage.

But before we reach that portion of the chapter we encounter the narrative on the adulterous woman, over which Bible scholars have argued for years. Its placement at the beginning of chapter 8 serves as a foundation for the rest of the chapter. John 7:53–8:11 records the beautiful story of a woman caught in adultery that illustrates the central dilemma of salvation: how justice and mercy can be harmonized without encouraging sin or condemning sinners.

In spite of the manuscript problem on this passage, the incident sounds very much like Jesus. Furthermore, it explains the Pharisees' peculiar statement in verse 41 and the whole discussion of morality and illegitimacy which seems to surface repeatedly throughout the chapter.

II. COMMENTARY

The Truth Shall Set You Free

MAIN IDEA: *As the light and the truth, Jesus offers grace and for-giveness to repentant sinners.*

A Truth and Forgiveness (8:1–11)

SUPPORTING IDEA: *We do not always act like forgiven people, but we should because none of us has the right to throw that first stone.*

8:1–6a. The earliest and most reliable manuscripts do not include John 7:53–8:11. Nevertheless, the NIV includes the entire segment—a wise choice, in my opinion. Borchert calls it "a text looking for a context" and refuses to deal with it at the beginning of chapter 8 since, in his view, "it disrupts the logic of the Johannine Tabernacles' argument" (Borchert, p. 369). Carson agrees that the narrative was probably not a part of John's Gospel (though Zane Hodges has argued its authenticity) but claims "there is little reason for doubting that the event here described occurred" (Carson, pp. 333–34). He suggests it belongs in the record of the last week but nevertheless deals with it here as I shall do.

The Pharisees posed a dilemma. If Jesus agreed to stone the woman, he would incur the distrust of the sinners he came to save as well as break Roman law. But a refusal to stone her would make him vulnerable to the accusation that he treated the Law of Moses lightly. It is a sad commentary on the culture of first-century Israel that they brought in the woman but no mention is made of the man. The sin of adultery and its handmaiden, divorce, represent almost the norm in modern America. But at least in our day we recognize mutuality of responsibility.

John left no doubt regarding the Pharisees' motivation: **They were using this question as a trap, in order to have a basis for accusing him.** So the chapter begins with public accusation, but it also goes on to talk about personal guilt. In one sense the Pharisees stood on solid ground with their appeal to the Law of Moses (Lev. 20:10; Deut. 22:22–24), but the law was not as clear as their accusation seems to imply. For example, her marital status would be a defining factor.

According to Carson,

> Stoning is the biblically prescribed punishment for a betrothed virgin who was sexually unfaithful to her fiancé, a punishment to be meted out to both sexual partners (Dt. 22:23–24). Elsewhere (Lv. 20:10; Dt. 22:22) death is prescribed for all unfaithful wives and their

lovers, but no mode (such as stoning) is laid down. In the Mishnah (*Sanhedrin,* 7:4), however, the two cases are sharply differentiated: the offense in the first instance is punishable by stoning (it is viewed as the more serious of the two), and the second by strangling. That would mean the woman in this passage was betrothed, not married. It is rather doubtful, however, that the distinction existed in Jesus' day (Carson, p. 335).

Whatever the particulars, the case indicated the intent of the Pharisees to trap Jesus with these charges with complete disregard for the woman in question. The real issue was the political motives of the accusers. Boice suggests that the entire thing was a set-up, what we would call today entrapment. In the rabbinical law, two or three witnesses had to observe the act of adultery in order for the death penalty to be enforced. Boice claims, "Under such circumstances it is almost self-evident that the rulers must have arranged the liaison somewhat as a trap, having stationed the witnesses in the room or at the keyhole. It was a situation quite similar to the use of private investigators and photographers in order to prove adultery today" (Boice, II, p. 315).

8:6b–8. Interpreters seem fascinated by Jesus' writing in the sand, certainly a reaction unexpected by the Pharisees. Why did Jesus do this? What did he write? One answer suffices for both questions: We do not know. It is useless to speculate, as some have done, that he wrote the names of other adulterers who were standing there among the group of accusers. We are bound to the text which tells us nothing more than that Jesus refused an immediate or reactionary response to the Pharisees' accusation. The centerpiece of this scene is the Lord's answer: **If any one of you is without sin, let him be the first to throw a stone at her.**

The writing in the sand was followed by the wisdom of the Son. This rubric is certainly valuable for judgmental Christians in our times. The perfect reply preserved both Jewish and Roman law while exposing the wickedness of the accusers. As Jesus began writing on the ground a second time, they had time to think about their own lives and God began to speak to those who were open to hear his voice. Again the accusers were brought face to face with the law they themselves had quoted. According to Deuteronomy 17:2–7, the witnesses of a crime who had reported it to the authorities would be the first to cast the stones.

8:9. What followed was the withdrawal of the sinners, one at a time, **the older ones first.** Did the older ones leave first because they had more time to accumulate sins of their own? Was it their maturity and sense of impending judgment that made them fleet of foot to escape this embarrassing predicament? Did they recognize that perhaps their sin was greater than the woman's and Jesus knew that full well? Again, the text does not tell us. But conscience must have played some role in this scene as the accusers left Jesus alone with the woman.

Imagine a stage play as you watch in silence—no dialogue, no music. The confident and critical Pharisees, moments ago pointing their fingers at the woman and at Jesus, now silently exit stage right or stage left without another word. Christians are not perfect—just forgiven. And because of the extent of God's forgiveness to us, we ought to be the least judgmental people in the world.

8:10–11. The first two scenes of the story described the charges and their response. Now we come to the verdict. With the accusers gone, there remained no condemnation. The Son of God refused to press the issue. Her sin was not just set aside; soon Jesus would pay the penalty for both the woman and her accusers.

James Boice tells the story of a man who sat in his office aware of his deep sin but unable to do anything about it. Boice ministered to him by using the illustration of a man walking along a street and splashed by a car in the dark. As he continued he came into the light of a street lamp and became aware of the stains on his clothing. Finally, the man decided he could not go on, turned around, and went home to put on clean clothes. At that point the young man in Boice's office responded by saying, "My problem is that I don't have any clean clothes."

Precisely. Chapter 8 tells about a woman who had no clean clothes—and about Pharisees who also had no clean clothes. She knew she did not; they thought they did. Jesus offered the clean clothes of forgiveness to all of them—and to us as well.

Jesus asked a rhetorical question and the woman answered it simply. Forgiveness rests upon the Lord's understanding. In this vignette we find recognition, repentance, regeneration, restitution, and reconciliation.

A second important lesson in these two verses is that forgiveness rests upon the Lord's grace. Remember the parable of the prodigal son in Luke 15? The father showed unconditional forgiveness and restoration when the son returned. Salvation does not come from suffering; it comes from grace—from the suffering and death of Jesus on our behalf.

Finally, we see that the verdict rests upon the Lord's forgiveness. Forgiveness demands a clean break with sin. In Matthew 9:2 we read, "Some men brought to him a paralytic, lying on a mat. When Jesus saw their faith, he said to the paralytic, 'Take heart, son, your sins are forgiven.'" In searching for a way to translate this, a missionary linguist working among the Guajira tribe in Colombia rendered the Lord's words, "I forgive you. Let's be friends again."

The same Jesus offers forgiveness today to sinners whose sins equal that of the woman or those of the Pharisees. And not only forgiveness for initial salvation but also for daily sins of anger, disobedience, envy, greed, and the judgmental character shown by the Pharisees which gave birth to this episode.

𝔹 Truth and Light (8:12–30)

SUPPORTING IDEA: *We find the light of truth in Jesus. In the midst of rejection and controversy, the message of this light can still lead people to put their faith in him.*

8:12. Here we find the second of seven "I Am" passages in John's Gospel. Like water (ch. 4) and bread (ch. 6), light is necessary for life. And the Lord wasted no time in explaining that spiritual light comes to those who willingly follow him. Since **light** is one of John's major themes, several assumptions arise from this verse. One is that the world needs light, something John has already told us in chapter 1. There are conditions for seeing and knowing the light—following Jesus. Finally, walking in the light can be permanent. The light of life can change a person so that he or she need never again walk in darkness.

Chapters five, six and seven of John's Gospel have picked up three major Old Testament wilderness reminders of how God dealt with his people: the comparison between manna and the bread of life in chapter 6; the comparison between water in the desert and the water of the Holy Spirit in chapter 7; and here in chapter 8 a comparison with the pillar of fire which led the people through the wilderness and Jesus, the light of the world.

The Feast of Tabernacles was also known as the Feast of Lights because of the many ceremonies that involved various kinds of lighting. From the earliest verses of the first chapter in this Gospel, John has been fascinated with the link between light and life. Here, however, we do not have a statement about everyone participating in the light, but the exclusion of all who do not follow the true light.

Some interpreters have suggested that Jesus may have drawn his illustration from the great candlestick (Menorah) which cast its light over the room in which he was teaching. Everyone there knew the Menorah would be extinguished after the feast. But Jesus indicated that his light would remain forever.

8:13–14. As we might suspect, Jesus was challenged by **the Pharisees.** They argued that his own self-defense was not admissible evidence. But of course it was, since he is the omniscient, impartial, and perfect Son of God. They misunderstood and misconstrued everything he told them. When he spoke of heaven, they thought of Nazareth. When he mentioned the Father, they impugned the legitimacy of his birth. When he spoke of home, they concluded he was planning suicide!

As in chapter 7, the issues of origin and destination prevail. And as in chapter 5, the question of who has authority to witness truth dominates the conversation. As Morris puts it: "In the present passage He has two points to make, the one that He is qualified to bear witness though His enemies are not, and the other that in any case His testimony is not unsupported. The Father bears witness of Him. Here Jesus is contrasting Himself with the Pharisees. He knows both His origin and destination, but they know neither. They are not in a position to comment on His witness. They are totally unaware of the great heavenly verities" (Morris, p. 440).

8:15–18. Throughout this Gospel the author emphasized words of Jesus that referred to his own deity. There was no question in John's theology that Jesus is God. This constant reference to the Father both in relationship and authentication forms a uniquely Johannine trait. In the eighteenth century, John Newton described the Light in these poetic terms:

> 'Round each habitation hovering, see the cloud and fire appear.
> For the glory and a covering, showing that the Lord is near;
> Thus deriving from their banner, light by night, and shade by day.
> Safe they feed upon the manna which He gives them when they
> pray.

8:19–21. Since Jesus had identified the Father as one of the witnesses to his message, the Pharisees asked, **Where is your father?** Notice the absence of the capital letter in their question. Jesus referred to heaven, while they pondered his earthly origin. But since they had rejected his message, they had no understanding of the Father. This theme runs throughout John's Gospel.

All this happened in a public place, at the temple where the offerings were received. But no one assailed Jesus because **his time had not yet come.** This important phrase appears seven times in John's Gospel. At the end of the passage Jesus issued a threat that must be proclaimed to all who reject Christ. In human law a clever attorney can create innocence out of guilt and let murderers and rapists go free. But there is no escape from the law of God, no universalism, no second-chance gospel in the message of the New Testament.

One inescapable truth jumps at us from these verses: the heresy that everyone will be saved some day denies the clear teaching of the Bible. There will be no escape for those who refuse the gospel—not in the first century and not today. Three times Jesus warned them, **you will die in your sins** (vv. 21,24). Borchert observes, "The use of the singular 'sin' here probably is a condemnation on their unwillingness to believe, but the repetition in the plural (sins) at 8:24 means that Jesus rendered his verdict on their evil actions as well" (Borchert, p. 299).

Verse 21 reminds us of 7:34,36. At that point his opponents pondered whether he would go live among the Gentiles and here they wondered about suicide. In the wider context, John referred to Jesus' glorification, including the cross, the empty tomb, and the ascension back to the Father.

8:22–24. In Exodus 3:14 God told Moses that he was being sent back to Egypt by "I AM." Jesus picked up on that phrase, making himself equal with the Father and emphasizing his deity. The Jewish leaders misunderstood the Lord's words and wondered about suicide. Like Nicodemus, their failure to comprehend earthly things left them unqualified to consider heavenly things. To **die in your sins** means to die with the burden of one's own sin and its penalty enforced by a righteous God (Rom. 6:23). Physical death separates the spirit from the body; spiritual death separates the spirit from God.

Jesus talked about hell here, although his listeners never comprehended that allusion. It is interesting that Americans believe in hell two to one over Europeans. But the percentage of people who believe in hell is much greater in this country than the percentage of people who think there is some possibility they will end up there. Human perception tells us that God made hell for Genghis Khan, Adolf Hitler, Idi Amin, and Pol Pot. Regular people who merely lie, cheat, and abuse their children cannot possibly be that bad. Somehow God will work out a plan to sneak them into heaven in spite of a lifetime of sin. This passage tells us that those who refuse the light will end up in eternal darkness and there is no escape.

Morris makes an excellent point regarding the kind of faith called for in this passage: "Basically faith is trust. But in our reaction against the view that faith means no more than a firm acceptance of certain intellectual propositions we must not go so far as to say that it is entirely a matter of personal relations. It is impossible to have the kind of faith that John envisages without having a certain high view of Christ. Unless we believe that He is more than man we can never trust Him with that faith that is saving faith" (Morris, p. 447).

8:25–30. Beginning with verse 13, the Pharisees uttered several distinct challenges to the Lord's claims:

- "Your testimony is not valid" (v. 13).
- "Where is your father?" (v. 19).
- "Will he kill himself?" (v. 22).
- "Who are you?" (v. 25).

In each case, their remarks called forth statements about the light. In verses 19–21 we learn about the origin of the light, in verses 22–24 about the destiny of the light, and now in verses 25–30 about the identity of the light.

These religious leaders asked a basic question of three simple words: **Who are you?** Jesus had already told them about the heavenly light, but they had no understanding of Jehovah as Father. And they certainly had not grasped that the cross would be the heart of the gospel by providing salvation, understanding, and attraction for believers. This section ends with a reference to the cross and a reminder that the world would know Jesus only after the sacrificial death. Then at least some would understand that all his words were the words of the Father.

The phrase **lifted up the Son of Man** refers to the way a body was placed on the cross and the cross elevated in public on a hill of execution. Often we pray that Jesus will be "lifted up," meaning we wish him to be exalted and glorified. But in John this terminology distinctly refers to the cross. Borchert reminds us, "The concept of 'lifted up' (*hypsoun*) in John is the way Jesus referred to the events involved in his glorification (8:28; cf. 3:14; 12:32–34), an expression used to identify his work on earth as the sacrificial lamb of God who died on the cross and was raised up in victory so that all who believe might have life (cf. the important combination in Isa 52:13 wherein *hypsoun* and *doxazein*, 'glorify,' both appear)" (Borchert, p. 300).

When we pray that Jesus will be **lifted up**, meaning "exalted" and "glorified," we must remember that has already happened at Calvary, where he achieved glorification through his death and following resurrection.

This section ends with the encouraging words, **Even as he spoke, many put their faith in him.** But also for believers, the light of Jesus wants to shine on the problems of life. We should take with us from this text more than just theology of Jesus as the light of the world or even as the Son of God. As God's children through faith in the Savior, we can say with Jesus, **The one who sent me is with me; he has not left me alone.**

Ⓒ Truth and Freedom (8:31–41)

> **SUPPORTING IDEA:** *True disciples keep Jesus' words. Because of this, the world hates them just as Jesus was hated by these people whose ill-placed faith he exposed.*

8:31–33. We have already learned that faith alone does not guarantee salvation (2:23–24; 6:64–66). Saving faith must center in Jesus himself, not just his miracles or some teaching about him. The remainder of this chapter tells us how truth will set us free from false faith, faith in inadequate but attractive objects that often clamor for our attention—relationships, religion, and righteousness. Verses 31–33 emphasize that true disciples are liberated from error.

Some of the Jews who **believed in him** claimed that their relationship with Abraham kept them from bondage. Abraham's descendents, they argued, had always been free (conveniently forgetting their bondage to Egypt, Assyria, Babylonia, Persia, Greece, and Rome). Since some of the Jews did believe, Jesus offered them more truth that could set them free. Now he talked to those "believers" and no longer to the Pharisees, though that dialogue rejoins the text in just a few more verses.

When banks train their clerks to spot counterfeit money, they spend little time dealing with the counterfeit itself and lots of time focused on the characteristics and designs of genuine currency. The Christian's handling of error should be like that. The more we know about God's truth, the easier it will be for us to spot untruth.

The first error attacked in this section is the belief that a relationship with some ancestral figure (in this case Abraham) guarantees a relationship with God. The gospel provides freedom from this kind of illusion.

Prominent in this section of the chapter is verse 32, which has become much loved and quoted. But our text does not talk about sociological or philosophical truth but the truth of the gospel.

8:34–38. In addition to freedom from error, true disciples are liberated from sin. What relationship does Jesus have with the Father, and what difference does that make in his authority to proclaim truth? People who sin—who are in an ongoing pattern of sinning—show that they are slaves to sin. Slaves are not sons and therefore not in God's family. Membership in Abraham's family—or Paul's, Peter's, Augustine's, Martin Luther's, John Calvin's, or John Wesley's—makes no difference whatsoever. An earthly family, despite the power of its patriarch, offers no sonship in a heavenly kingdom.

But Jesus, the Son from heaven, proclaims what he has seen **in the Father's presence.** This section ends with a fascinating assertion, aimed at the wider group of unbelievers rather than those who had just come to faith—**you do what you have heard from your father.** An optional reading appears in the margin of most translations: "Therefore do what you have heard from the Father." But the conversation that follows seems to support the rendering in the text. Jesus had not yet said who their father was, but one thing was already clear: they were not children of God or Abraham as they claimed.

8:39–41. Freedom from error, freedom from sin, and finally in this section John proclaimed that true disciples are liberated from unholy zeal. So the issue of origins continues. The crowds insisted that as Jews they were Abraham's children and therefore truth was their special contribution to the world. But Jesus told them since Abraham served God and since he (Jesus) was the Son of God, true children of Abraham should accept his message. But instead of accepting, they intended to kill this proclaimer of truth. Why? Because they behaved just like their father.

At this point we wish we could have audio aids for Bible interpretation—some way of hearing how these Jews responded. Perhaps the emphasis falls on the first word, "*we* are not illegitimate children." The implication and innuendo seem obvious—"like you are." Remember verse 19 where they asked him, "Where is your father?" In a small country like Israel, the rumors surrounding the virgin birth may have been known to many people, even in

Jerusalem. This stigma probably followed Jesus throughout his earthly ministry. On occasion, perhaps here, it became an issue of public debate.

A person cannot read John's Gospel and believe in universalism (the idea that God will eventually save everyone) or the universal fatherhood of God (the idea that all people are children of God in the spiritual sense). As Boice declares, "I do not know who first originated the popular phrase 'the universal fatherhood of God and the universal brotherhood of man,' but I suspect that it is a product of nineteenth-century liberalism. I know that it is not a proper expression of true Christianity. The phrase sounds good. It suggests that all men are really brothers despite their differences and that all worship the same God regardless of the different names they give to Him. But that is just not true, and both the Word of God and history refute it" (Boice, p. 369).

Truth and Lies (8:42–47)

> **SUPPORTING IDEA:** *Liars, murderers, terrorists, and all rebellious people reflect the attitude of Satan, even when they act in the name of religion.*

8:42–43. Jesus was speaking to religious leaders in these verses. In their ignorance they did not understand that true disciples love Jesus. Jesus continued to repeat himself and explain why their relationship to some father other than God had blinded them to the truth. They could not possibly be disciples of the true God. If they were, they would love his Son who was now speaking to them. They had some inherent disability to hear and understand what he was saying.

8:44–47. True disciples love Jesus, and true disciples resist Satan. Since we probably have only a capsule of the overall debate, we should assume that this discussion went on for hours. Jesus boldly proclaimed his relationship to the heavenly Father and they inferred his illegitimacy on earth. He indicated several times that they did not belong to Abraham but to some other father. Now he told them precisely who that was: **You belong to your father, the devil.**

Notice the connection between verses 43 and 44. In verse 43 Jesus asked, "Why is my language not clear to you?" Now in verse 44 he indicated that when Satan lies, **he speaks his native language.** Truth is the opposite of lying and the opposite of heresy. The only possible explanation for the inability of the religious leaders to understand Jesus was that they clung to Satan's lies so tightly that they could not climb out of the darkness and into the light that Jesus offered them.

Jesus' truth sails over the heads of some people who admit they have no interest in serving God, but they resist the suggestion that they are serving Satan. This text claims that those who reject Christ's truth and focus on serving themselves are deceived by Satan into believing they are children of God when they are not.

What makes a true disciple? He or she believes the truth of Jesus and obeys what God says. Why could not these skeptics in the audience hear God's truth? Because they did not belong to God. Believers have had a family transplant in the reverse way transplants are normally done. Rather than having a new family put into them, they have been put into a new family—removed from the family of Satan and placed into the family of God. John 8:47 explains why the Bible makes no sense to some people. Only those who have trusted Christ can grasp the truths of God's Word, believe them, and obey them.

E Truth and Reality (8:48–59)

SUPPORTING IDEA: *No religious appeal to Abraham can withstand honest exposure. Religious self-righteousness must be abandoned by any who would receive God's grace.*

8:48–51. Now the discussion turned ugly. Jesus' opponents had already questioned his proof and family connections; now they said what they had been thinking all along: **you are a Samaritan and demon-possessed.** Few insults could have carried more anger and bitterness in the first century. But Jesus ignored the name calling. He stuck to his basic theme of true discipleship by emphasizing that true disciples keep Jesus' words. The Lord emphasized truth and explained his relationship to the Father. In verse 51 the opening phrase (**I tell you the truth**) translates the two words *amen, amen* which appear in 127 verses of the New Testament.

Some interpreters emphasize the ethnic barriers John had already described in chapter 4. But the context deals not so much with religious practice as it does with rejection of Jesus. This may have been an intentional jab at his roots. We do not see the accusation of being a Samaritan anywhere else in the Bible, but demon-possession appears in John 7:20; 8:52 and 10:20 and in the synoptic Gospels as well (Matt. 9:34; 11:18; 12:24ff.; Mark 3:22ff.).

Let us not lose the message of eternal life in the difficult discussions of this chapter. John maintained this theme because he had heard Jesus speak of it so often. The Son does not glorify himself. The Father glorifies him. Those who trust the Son's word advance the Father's glory and **will never see death.**

8:52–53. The question of who would die and when and how and what would happen after death had occupied Jewish theology for centuries. Suddenly Jesus appeared, talking about life after death in almost casual terms and assuring hearers that acceptance of truth meant that true disciples would never die.

In verse 24 he had warned the religious leaders that they would die in their sins if they did not believe his message. He had been speaking about the Father's presence and returning there. But they saw only the earthly interpretation. Abraham died. The prophets died. Yet this strange Galilean promised a life with no death? Obviously, he must consider himself greater than Abraham and the prophets, an unthinkable arrogance which they diagnosed as demon possession. Do not miss the switch in the key question from "Who are you?" in verse 25 to **Who do you think you are?** in verse 53.

8:54–56. True disciples of Jesus are hated by the world. Jesus had been trying to tell them since the beginning of the discussion that he did not stand alone in witnessing the truth of his message. In fact, it was not his message at all but the message of the Father, the one they claimed as their God. Interpretations of these verses must recognize two different Greek verbs translated by the English word **know** in verse 55. These religious leaders did not know God by experience (*oidao*), but Jesus knew him by personal relationship (*ginosko*). Jesus came to tell them the truth about his relationship with the Father.

The reference to **my day** in verse 56 delineated Christ's birth and time on earth. Some interpreters have narrowed it to the crucifixion and/or resurrection, but such a scenario seems unwarranted here. Tenney connects an Old Testament promise to this statement, linking back to Genesis 12:3. "Although this interpretation is not founded on any specific statement of Scripture, it would mean that Abraham's personal experience at the sacrifice of Isaac could have been an object lesson to him of the coming incarnation, death, and resurrection of the promised Seed (see Gen. 22:1–18; Heb. 11:17–19)" (Tenney, *EBC*, pp. 98–99).

8:57–59. By this time the rejecting skeptics' patience had been bent to the breaking point. This young man (interesting they should say **not yet fifty years old**) had seen Abraham? Jesus' response provided the final blow. Once again he picked up a theme from the Old Testament: "God said to Moses, 'I AM WHO I AM. This is what you are to say to the Israelites: "I AM has sent me to you"'" (Exod. 3:14). In this chapter Jesus made himself equal with God, a cornerstone of biblical theology. How did they respond? **They picked up stones to stone him**, but Jesus slipped away **from the temple grounds.**

Borchert has a helpful paragraph on Jesus' claim to be one with the Father: "Extending the present into the past does not compute in most of our minds. It is a confusion to the way we think. But God does not fit into the teacups of our minds. More pertinent for our purposes, however, is the fact that Jesus claimed to be 'I AM' over against Abraham. That claim was a reminder of the claims for God in the Old Testament over against creation (cf. Ps. 90:2; Isa. 42:3–9) and of the self-designation for the comforting God of Isaiah (41:4; 43:3,13). The claim of Jesus, therefore, was clearly recognized from the

Jews' perspective to be a blasphemous statement they could not tolerate" (Borchert, p. 309).

> **MAIN IDEA REVIEW:** *As the light and the truth, Jesus offers grace and forgiveness to repentant sinners.*

III. CONCLUSION

Testimony in a Tent

I will never forget a ministry trip to southern Germany after my sophomore year in college. We conducted tent campaigns all over Bavaria, three services a day, including an evangelistic rally each evening. Sometimes we would stay in a town for a week, sometimes two weeks. In Hassloch we found our most productive ministry of the summer. For two weeks we proclaimed God's truth throughout the town and on the closing Sunday held a testimony rally.

My host for the two weeks, a quiet farmer, waited in a long line of local people whose testimonies for Christ lasted well over three hours that Sunday afternoon. When he approached the microphone he said quite simply, "You people know me. I have lived in this town all my life. You know that I have been a faithful member of our church and I've always believed that would take me to heaven and grant me favor with God. But last week I understood the gospel for the first time and I know that I can only go to heaven because Jesus died for me, and I trust his death to give me eternal life. So today I stand before you as a real Christian for the first time in my life."

The truth will set you free. This was true when Jesus first proclaimed those words, and it was true nearly fifty years ago in Germany. And the truth still sets people free today—free from faith in relationships, faith in religion, and faith in their own righteousness. But it will also set them free from faith in faith, an endless and fruitless search. Warm, fuzzy, religious feel-good nonsense abounds in our day commending faith in faith, a dead-end street. Faith must be placed precisely where Jesus described it in this chapter—in him, in his Father, and in his words. The object of faith, not the act of faith, makes the difference in eternal life.

PRINCIPLES

- Only those who spiritually appropriate light are recipients of its life.
- Forgiveness is God's promise that he will not remember our sin or use it against us.
- Faith for eternal life is also faith for contemporary living.

- The greatest need of humanity is the grace of God as revealed in Jesus Christ his Son.

APPLICATIONS

- Trust Christ for complete forgiveness from sin.
- Trust Christ for discipleship based on truth and light.
- Trust Christ for freedom from the struggles and bondage of a sinful world.
- Trust Christ for understanding and discernment of truth.

IV. LIFE APPLICATION

"Who's the Father?"

A huge billboard glared its message through the windshield of my car twice a day for years. I passed it going to and from my office located just east of downtown Dallas. The billboard rose high above Interstate 30 and contains a question and a phone number: "WHO'S THE FATHER? Call 1-800-DNA-EXAM."

What a commentary on our times! Children born out of wedlock, mothers wondering who among their sexual partners might have fathered a particular child. Now DNA will help us discover that, but it will hardly cure the moral rot of the culture. What the darkness of this world needs is the shining light of Jesus and a focus on the truth he brought to the world.

From the beginning of John 8 we learned that behavioral change is necessary because repentance demands a clean break with sin. Then Jesus went on to talk about light, truth, and freedom—popular words in our culture today. We have observed the principle that "forgiveness is God's promise that he will no longer remember our sin or use it against us"; but let us not forget that is also the model for our forgiveness of others.

The light of the world wants to shine on us: on those who need the light of the gospel for initial salvation; on those who need the light of wisdom for the confusing problems of life; on those who need an understanding of Scripture and the great themes of the Bible like the deity of Christ and eternal life. Jesus as the light of the world wants to brighten our world and enable us to reflect his brilliance.

In John 8 the question "Who's the Father?" takes on an entirely different and profound meaning. The religious leaders who argued with Jesus could not grasp who his father was. Throughout the Feast of Tabernacles as well as on other occasions, they emphasized their connection with Abraham and the Lord's questionable parentage. But Jesus made it clear that human parentage counts for nothing in eternal life. What matters is a relationship with the heavenly Father. This can come only through the truth that he brought.

V. PRAYER

Father, thank you that Jesus is the light of the world and that in a small way, we are also part of that light. Thank you for your truth and the opportunity we have to share it with others. Amen.

VI. DEEPER DISCOVERIES

A. The Adulterous Woman (7:53–8:11)

Casual Bible readers are stunned when they come to the end of John 7 and read in the NIV, "The earliest manuscripts and many other ancient witnesses do not have John 7:53–8:11." The RSV amplifies the issue a bit when it says, "The most ancient authorities omit 7:53–8.11; other ancient authorities add 7.53–8.11 either here or at the end of this gospel or after Luke 21.38, with variations of text."

How can this be? Can we trust a Bible in which people add and remove pieces from time to time? Boice offers a clear and simple paragraph of explanation:

> The difficulty, simply put, is that the majority of the earliest manuscripts of John do not contain these verses and, moreover, that some of the best manuscripts are of this number. The best evidence for the story is its presence in Codex Bezae, of the fifth or sixth century, now in the University Library at Cambridge, England. But it is not in the older Codices Sinaiticus or Vaticanus, nor in the Washington or Koridethi manuscripts. In fact, of the older manuscripts, eight omit it entirely, though two manuscripts leave a blank space where it would have come. And not until the Medieval manuscripts does it seem to have been included with any regularity. Some early manuscripts attach it at other places, such as at the end of the Gospel or after Luke 21:38 (Boice, II, p. 307).

So the problem is not textual authenticity but location. Few scholars want to throw this section out entirely, but more do not want it placed here. Borchert, in fact, refuses to deal with it in the order of the text and inserts an additional section at the end of his treatment of chapter 11, offering this explanation: "This little pericope is one of the great jewels of Christian Scripture. But as I indicated earlier, I have not set it in my commentary at the usual place where it appears in our English Bibles for several reasons. In the first place, it disrupts the logic of the Johannine Tabernacles argument. In the second place, from all that I can determine, it is hardly Johannine in style or form. In the third place, in the history of the transmission of our

New Testament documents, it is from my perspective a text looking for a context" (Boice, p. 369).

Primary scholarship favors this decision, but I prefer to treat the text where it appears without arguing one way or the other that it is distinctively Johannine in style and pattern. Certainly the story reflects Jesus' response to sin, especially among the helpless. One could argue that early manuscripts omit it because at the time they were written textual scribes might have feared an interpretation concluding that Jesus condoned adultery.

I agree with Boice when he says, "A good case can be made for its inclusion at this particular place in John's gospel. For one thing, without it the change of thoughts between verse 52 of chapter 7 and verse 12 of chapter 8 is abrupt and unnatural . . . for another thing, the introduction of a story at this point seems to fit the pattern that John has been using in these opening chapters" (Boice, p. 308).

In my view this narrative lays the foundation for the rest of chapter 8 and may even give us a clue to the Pharisees' statement in verse 41. If well-meaning interpreters and textual critics cannot agree to exclude it, nor agree where it should appear if we include it, it seems to me we should leave it exactly where it appears.

B. "I Am" Passages in John (8:12)

Some time after the incident with the woman taken in adultery—perhaps hours, perhaps weeks—Jesus announced the second of the seven "I Am" passages of this Gospel. We have already heard him say, "I am the bread of life" (ch. 6), and we will yet encounter "I am the gate" (ch. 10), "I am the good shepherd" (ch. 10), "I am the resurrection and the life" (ch. 11), "I am the way and the truth and the life" (ch. 14), and "I am the true vine" (ch. 15).

In the "Commentary" section I suggest that this reference, each time it was heard by the Jews, would evoke memories of Exodus 3 and assorted passages in Isaiah. Carson favors the Isaiah connection and, in the particular context of 8:24, emphasizes the meaning:

> For Jesus to apply such words to himself is tantamount to a claim to deity, once it is clear that the other potential meanings of *ego eimi* are contextually impossible. This does not mean that Jesus and Yahweh of the Old Testament are identified without reminder, since verse 28 (where this title next occurs) is immediately followed by verse 29, where Jesus again distinguishes himself from the Father (similarly 13:19–20). But this tension between unqualified statements affirming the full deity of the Word or of the Son, and those which distinguish the Word or the Son from the Father, are typical of the fourth Gospel and are present from the very first verse (Carson, p. 344).

Much has been written on the "I Am" sections of John, but we should not miss the "I Am" sections of this chapter. Though they are not linked with distinctive metaphor as the seven mentioned above, they still repeat Jesus' claims about himself. The key lies in verse 12, but the phraseology also appears in verses 14,16,18,23–24,28,58–59. Tenney sets the unique context in the public occasion of John 7 and 8: "The title became part of the liturgy of the Feast of Tabernacles, the time when this controversy recorded in John occurred. The phrase occurs in Jesus' response to the challenge of the high priest at his final hearing. When asked, 'Are you the Christ, the Son of the Blessed One?' Jesus replied, 'I am . . . and you will see the Son of Man sitting at the right hand of the Mighty One and coming on the clouds of heaven' (Mark 14:61–62). The violent reaction of the high priest in Mark 14:63 indicates that he regarded the use of the title as a blasphemous claim on Jesus' part to possess the quality of deity" (Tenney, p. 99).

C. Free (8:32)

The concept of freedom is found about forty times in the New Testament, based on various grammatical forms of the word *eleutheros* in Greek thought. The word denotes freedom from slavery and connotes the principle of freedom so precious in both Greek and Roman politics. Particularly important to the philosophical Greeks would be freedom of intellect. The Scripture almost always emphasizes freedom from sin or the bondage of man-made religious requirements. As Detzler observes, "Our spiritual freedom involves the Lord Jesus Christ. He Himself taught that when the Son makes people free, they are really free (John 8:36). This freedom is tied to belief in Him and reception of His truth (8:32). In fact, only the Lord can snap the chains of sin and set people free. Abraham Lincoln was known as 'the great emancipator,' but Jesus Christ is the greatest Emancipator" (Detzler, p. 170).

The theological hymnist, John Wesley, captured the concept well:

> Long my imprisoned spirit lay
> Fast bound in sin and nature's night;
> Thine eye defused a quick'ning ray,
> I woke, the dungeon flamed with light;
> My chains fell off, my heart was free;
> I rose, went forth, and followed Thee.

D. He Will Never See Death (8:51)

The words "he will never see death" in the NIV render seven Greek words which could literally be translated, "By no means will he taste of death unto the age." This same concept in slightly different form constitutes the closing phrase of the Gospel of Matthew—"to the very end of the age." No one disputes the meaning; whatever the translation, the concept of eternal life is inherent in this interesting phrase. As Borchert points out, "The expression *eis ton aiona* ('unto the ages') was a typical Greek adaptation used by Christians. The reason for its use is that the Greek language really had no direct way of saying 'forever.' This expression was thus the means writers in Greek used to import a linear time perspective of eternity into a cyclical-based view of repeating time" (Borchert, p. 308).

Doctrinally, John emphasized the eternality of life in Christ with the eternality of Christ himself. The significant difference is that all humans have a beginning point which Christ did not. But in terms of an ending point, believers are like their Lord; the only way to get life "unto the ages" is to come to him who had no beginning and no end.

VII. TEACHING OUTLINE

A. INTRODUCTION
1. Lead Story: Climbing into the Wheelbarrow
2. Context: Questions about the identity and origin of Jesus continue from chapter 7, broken only by the account of the forgiveness of the adulterous woman. Whether this took place within the same week or at a different occasion we cannot say for sure. I have intimated at various points in the "Commentary" section that the entirety of chapters 7 and 8 may have taken place during the Feast of Tabernacles. In any case, John developed at length Jesus' claims to deity and intimate connection with the God of the Old Testament.
3. Transition: As we have noted before, John is hardly obsessed with transitional phrases or the chronological notes that abound in Luke. Chapter 7 abruptly begins with the words, "after this," and chapter 9, "as he went along." Chapters 7 and 8 give two straight chapters of theological debate without a miracle, but the beginning of chapter 9 will bring us back again to the miracle-message method.

B. COMMENTARY
1. Truth and Forgiveness (8:1–11)
    a. The charges (8:1–6a)
    b. The response (8:6b–9)
    c. The verdict (8:10–11)
2. Truth and Light (8:12–30)
    a. Testimony of the light (8:12–18)
    b. Origin of the light (8:19–21)
    c. Destiny of the light (8:22–24)
    d. Identity of the light (8:25–30)

3. Truth and Freedom (8:31–41)
    a. Freedom from error (8:31–33)
    b. Freedom from sin (8:34–38)
    c. Freedom from unholy zeal (8:39–41)
4. Truth and Lies (8:42–47)
    a. True disciples love Jesus (8:42–43)
    b. True disciples resist Satan (8:44–46)
    c. True disciples belong to the Father (8:47)
5. Truth and Reality (8:48–59)
    a. Reality of Jesus' words (8:48–51)
    b. Reality of eternal life (8:52–53)
    c. Reality of the Father's glory (8:54–56)
    d. Reality of Jesus' eternality (8:57–59)

C. CONCLUSION: "WHO'S THE FATHER?"

VIII. ISSUES FOR DISCUSSION

1. How do you respond to the controversy surrounding John 7:53–8:11?
2. What does Jesus' statement in John 8:29, "I always do what pleases him," mean for our lives?
3. What marks of Satan can you see in our contemporary culture?

John 9

The Difference Between Light and Darkness

"*I*'d rather light a candle than curse the darkness."

J a m e s   K e l l e y

GEOGRAPHIC PROFILE: POOL OF SILOAM

- Located at the south of the Tyropoean Valley
- Built by King Hezekiah (2 Chr. 32:30)
- First explored in 1838 by Edward Robinson
- Its purpose was to bring water from the spring of Gihon into Jerusalem

John 9

I N   A   N U T S H E L L

*I*n this fifth major miracle of the Fourth Gospel, faith challenges fate and physical blindness is contrasted with spiritual blindness.

The Difference Between Light and Darkness

I. INTRODUCTION

Churches Settle Five-Hundred-Year-Old Debate

*I*t happened in Berlin on Reformation Day 1999. Representatives of the world's one billion Roman Catholics and 61.5 million Lutherans met to sign a joint declaration which, in the words of Associated Press correspondent Burt Herman, "put aside their differences over the way humanity achieves salvation." The agreement is the result of thirty years of consultation among theologians. The signing occurred exactly 482 years after Luther posted his theses on the door of the castle church in Wittenberg. World-class church historian Martin E. Marty observed that the two churches had been coming together more and more in recent decades. Cardinal Edward Idris Cassidy observed that "what we have tried to do in the dialogue has not been to pass judgment, neither in the Council of Trent nor Martin Luther."

At the heart of the agreement stands the following statement regarding salvation: "Together we confess: by grace alone, in faith in Christ's saving work and not because of any merit on our part, we are accepted by God and receive the Holy Spirit, who renews our hearts while equipping and calling us to good works."

No matter how these two faith groups interpret that paragraph, the statement itself could have been signed by John the Apostle. In fact, a reliance on faith alone as the means of salvation forms the centerpiece of John's Gospel. In this chapter we see that point illustrated in the contrast between a blind beggar and the high-profile religious leaders of Jesus' day. By the time the events of John 9 took place, there was increasing hostility to Jesus and his message. Blind beggars were a common sight in ancient Israel. God chose this one to demonstrate how fate and faith clash.

In this chapter the difference between light and darkness reflects the difference between fate and faith, between *kismet* and Christ, between Allah and the heavenly Father of the New Testament. As we approach the story, we do well to remember a paragraph from the Old Testament book of Ecclesiastes in which the writer paid tribute to faith. He was probably writing, as we would say today, "with tongue in cheek." But he pinpointed the thinking and perspective of people ensnared by the boundaries of expectation which cannot transcend the borders of the universe: "I have seen something else under the sun: The race is not to the swift or the battle to the strong, nor does food come to the wise or wealth to the brilliant or favor to the learned; but time and chance happen to them all. Moreover, no man knows when his hour will come: As fish are caught in a cruel net, or birds are taken in a snare, so men are trapped by evil times that fall unexpectedly upon them" (Eccl. 9:11–12).

II. COMMENTARY

The Difference Between Light and Darkness

MAIN IDEA: *Restoring sight to the blind was one of the miracles Jews expected to see in the Messiah. After chapter 8 in which Jesus claimed equality with the Father, John offered another miracle-message event, using the healing of a blind beggar to highlight the spiritual blindness of religion without Christ.*

A Purpose of the Miracle (9:1–12)

SUPPORTING IDEA: *For the second time Jesus announced that he was the light of the world and demonstrated physically and spiritually how dark life is without him.*

9:1–2. John wanted his readers to focus on the blindness of the man described in the first five verses. The disciples, wrapped in Old Testament legalism (Exod. 34:7), concluded there were only two possible explanations for the blindness: either his parents had sinned or the man had sinned. The disciples saw neither the man nor his parents but an opportunity for theological discussion. They displayed no compassion, only curiosity.

Many Bible students are amazed to discover that the Old Testament contains no story of the giving of sight to the blind. The only New Testament example outside the Gospels is the encounter between Ananias and Saul of Tarsus in Acts 9. But when we examine the ministry of Jesus, there are more instances of the healing of blind people than any other type of miracle (Matt. 9:27–31; 12:22ff.; 15:30ff.; 21:14; Mark 8:22–26; 10:46–52; Luke 7:21ff.).

9:3. John 8:12 forms a foundation by which we understand the events of chapter 9: "When Jesus spoke again to the people, he said, 'I am the light of the world. Whoever follows me will never walk in darkness, but will have the light of life.'" The light of life did not fix blame but offered grace, so Jesus rejected the alternatives of the disciples. In this man's life, hurting was the preparation for healing. Jesus' words to the disciples in chapter 11 offer insight: "This sickness will not end in death. No, it is for God's glory so that God's son may be glorified through it" (John 11:4).

Comparison of John 5 and 9 leads us to the conclusion that sin may result in sickness on some occasions, but we should never assume an essential connection. God can bring glory to himself through healing as in both of these accounts by John—or through not healing, as we learn later in the New Testament from the struggles of the apostle Paul. The focus is not on the comfort of the creature but the exaltation of the Creator.

9:4–5. The contrast between blindness and sight now moves to the contrast between night and day. Jesus was the sent one, and the disciples assisted him in his work. But this will soon end when night comes. Night probably refers to the difficult days of the passion week, particularly the cross. If we had only this text, we might conclude that the disciples could function in God's work only so long as Jesus was with them in the world; then all would be darkness.

Interpreters tiptoe around the possible meaning of these verses. The clue may lie in the hermeneutical principle of progressive revelation. The Lord had not yet explained the role of the Holy Spirit in illuminating their future ministry. At this point he focused their attention only on him, his divine mission, and their involvement during the short period of earthly ministry. Later in this Gospel he explained that light would shine again after the resurrection and the ascension as the Holy Spirit reproduced the light of the world through them.

Carson expresses it this way, "This does not mean that Jesus stops being the light of the world once he has ascended. It means, rather, that the light shines brightly while he lives out his human life up to the moment of his glorification. Throughout that period he is the light that exposes the world, judges the world, saves the world. Those who enjoy his light will be engulfed by darkness when he is taken away (12:35)" (Carson, p. 362).

Though we must take it as application, not interpretation, it is possible to see in these verses an emphasis on the urgency and brevity of our own time of ministry. Through the Holy Spirit the light now shines on us. Darkness will soon overwhelm the world when the Lord's people and the Holy Spirit are taken out of the world. So night is coming again as we are reminded in a familiar hymn written in 1854 by an eighteen-year-old Canadian girl, Annie Louise Walker. The hymn does not contain much gospel, but it focuses on the time limitations of service.

> Work for the night is coming, work through the morning hours;
> Work while the dew is sparkling; work 'mid springing flowers.
> Work when the day grows brighter, work in the glowing sun;
> Work for the night is coming, when man's work is done.

9:6–7. A strange thing happened as the blind man experienced healing by the Lord. We know Jesus did not need physical substance to work a miracle, so what was the point of the mud on the man's eyes? Some interpreters point out that the Jews believed clay and spittle had some medicinal value, but that would put the power in the instrument rather than the healer.

Others argue that clay often depicts creation in Scripture. But perhaps we can find here something as simple as a man who needed some physical symbol to encourage his faith, not unlike Gideon and his fleece. This healing was not remedial, since the man suffered congenital blindness. Verse 7 reminds us of the importance of obedience and also reflects the experience of the ten lepers (Luke 17). The clay did not create the healing; obedience to the word of Christ brought sight to this man.

Borchert compares the sending to Siloam with the healing of Naaman at the Jordan River (2 Kgs. 5):

> The implication in both stories seems to be that the healer demanded the man in need to obey the healer's instructions. As such the reader should not miss the close connection between obedience or effectual believing and experiencing the powerful work of God. Moreover, the name of the ancient pool was regarded as significant in this connection because the evangelist made a point of informing the reader of its meaning. According to John, the word 'Siloam' meant 'sent' (John 9:7). As such the pool's name is indicative both of Jesus' mission and his command to those who would receive his blessings and become identified as his followers (Borchert, p. 315).

9:8–12. What followed was reaction from the neighbors. Miracles were uncommon in Israel. Even his neighbors showed their amazement. Somehow this man born blind could see. His first step of faith was acceptance of the fact that his blindness had departed. He had no idea what had happened to him; he had no idea who had done it; he had no idea where Jesus had gone. The miracles of Christ work similarly in our day, whether physical or spiritual. He performed his miracles in accordance with acts of faith (not always on the part of the one healed) and in obedience to God's word. But the story goes on.

🅱 Perplexity of the Pharisees (9:13–34)

SUPPORTING IDEA: *As the Pharisees investigated the healing of the blind man, their motives became clear. Like modern evolutionists who reject a Creator, these religious leaders had already determined that Jesus could not have healed the man. They denied his personal testimony and threw him out.*

9:13–17. This portion of chapter 9 is dominated by three testimonies that reflect three attitudes toward Jesus. We begin with the first testimony of the man which reflects the prejudice of his accusers. The neighbors brought the man to the Pharisees. John raised the red flag when he pointed out in verse 14 that the day in which Jesus had made the mud and opened the man's eyes was a Sabbath. The neighbors were still confused, but the Pharisees offered their standard legalistic condemnation: anyone who did not keep the Sabbath could not heal. But if the healer were a sinner, how could he perform miracles?

The words and works of Jesus brought division. But this time when the Pharisees turned to the healed man, he had a different answer from his previous "I don't know." In his growing faith, he indicated that the healer must have been a prophet. Since John the Baptist was the first prophet these people had seen for about four hundred years, this was quite a statement of praise. A prophet? Roaming around Israel healing blind people? Impossible.

This Sabbath business had now been going on for several chapters. John had already said, "So, because Jesus was doing these things on the Sabbath, the Jews persecuted him" (5:16). John's earlier references to the Jews in general now focused more narrowly on the Pharisees. The Sadducees are never mentioned in this book and John was not concerned about the Sanhedrin. Historically, the Sanhedrin was the controlling body and it was dominated by Sadducees. This is the picture we get from Luke in Acts. But John, as we have said repeatedly, concerned himself very little with history and very much with theology.

The liberal Sadducees had watered down their theology. They were content with political posturing until Paul's preaching of the resurrection shook up their ranks. But the Pharisees were protectors of the righteousness of the law. No violator of the Sabbath could be permitted to carry about the reputation of healer while the Pharisees represented the moral minority of Israel.

But even they were a divided house as we know from the experience of Nicodemus and Joseph of Arimathea. So the man's neighbors, getting no help from their theologians, turned back to the man who uttered the first sign of a budding faith. Morris comments with typical warmth, "If this seems to us inadequate we must remember that the man had no way of knowing that Jesus was more. His contact with the Lord had been very brief. And for him 'prophet' was probably the highest place he could assign to a man of God. His answer puts Jesus in the highest place he knew" (Morris, p. 486).

9:18–23. From the first testimony of the man that unveiled the prejudice of some of the Pharisees, we move to the testimony of the parents and the pressure of religious legalism. Obviously the man could see; no one could doubt that. But they could doubt whether he had been born blind. The Pharisees asked the parents this question and got an affirmative answer. But the parents immediately tacked on their own caveat; they obviously did not want to discuss this business of healing. Earlier the man himself had said, "I don't know." Now the parents said, **We don't know.**

If this portion of chapter 9 ended at verse 21, we could see a normal parental reaction spoken in truth and frankness. But John wanted his readers to know there was a motivating fear—the pressure of excommunication. He also explained that already the Jews had decided that anyone who acknowledged that Jesus was the Christ would be put out of the synagogue. Many interpreters suggest that since we know Christians worshiped in synagogues in the Book of Acts, John must have been reading back into the text the rulings of a later day. But that may be attributing more to the text than John intended. Remember, he was not concerned with formal rulings of the Sanhedrin but the hostility of religious leaders.

I agree with Borchert: "From my perspective, therefore, the statement as contained in 9:22 would be reflective of the hostile context in the time of Jesus. After all, Jesus was indeed regarded as an enemy by the Jewish authorities" (Borchert, p. 320).

From our modern perspective we can hardly imagine the horror of excommunication in Jesus' time. Such a ban would curse these people forever from the religious life of their community. The defense of an unknown prophet, even one great enough to heal their blind son, hardly seemed worth such a risk. To avoid such punishment, the parents threw the burden of proof back on their son.

9:24–34. This portion of the chapter breaks clearly into three specific segments: the first testimony of the man, the testimony of the parents, and the second testimony of the man. The Pharisees' demands seemed simple enough—**give glory to God.** From Joshua 7:19 we know this demanded the truth. But it was also a deliberate attempt to divide Jesus from God, the precise unity the Lord attempted to build throughout chapter 8. The **we** of verse 24 is emphatic in the Greek; the Pharisees were stating their theological position on the matter.

In his growing faith, the man recited his simple testimony: **One thing I do know. I was blind but now I see!** But the questions persisted. The man's unwillingness to recant his story made him a victim of Pharisaic persecution not only in words (**they hurled insults at him**) but in the literal excommunication from the synagogue (**they threw him out**).

We find a simple logic in the words of this illiterate man. **God does not listen to sinners.** But since it was obvious that this man had healed his blindness, the man (whoever he was) had to be from God. But we also see some reason for the growing anger of the Pharisees. This man was a blind beggar—considered the dregs of first-century society. John portrayed him with something of an "in-your-face" attitude when he declared, **I have told you already and you did not listen.** Then he followed this up with, **Now that is remarkable! You don't know where he comes from, yet he opened my eyes.** The man did not understand all the theological implications of the event, but he kept a level head. His newly-found physical sight was rapidly joining forces with spiritual sight.

Carson notes, "His increasing boldness and sardonic wit stem from his most uncommon gift, common sense. What he finds *remarkable* is not his own belief, but the unbelief of the officials. Jesus has performed an astonishing miracle of healing, and they cannot decide *where he comes from* (which on the man's lips does not have metaphysical overtones) . . . It is always risky to identify spiritual power with divine power. But such theological niceties do not trouble the healed man. His spiritual instincts are good, even if his theological argumentation is not entirely convincing" (Carson, pp. 374–75).

Surely the Pharisees had not heard Jesus' dialogue with the disciples recorded at the beginning of the chapter. But they offered their own answer to the disciples' question in verse 34 when they said, **You were steeped in sin at birth; how dare you lecture us!**

So far in this chapter we have seen two kinds of blindness. The physical blindness of the man was treatable by the power of God's Son. But the Pharisees, unwilling to acknowledge their blindness, placed themselves beyond the realm of his healing power.

Priority of Faith (9:35–41)

SUPPORTING IDEA: *Mature faith in the Son of God does not come instantly or even easily. Like the blind man, we grow in our capacity to trust God with our lives and our problems.*

9:35–38. As the text unfolds, there seems to be no question that this man became a believer. The great Bible scholar B. F. Westcott claimed this was the first time Jesus offered himself as a personal object of faith. Let us not miss the fact that Jesus looked for the man rather than the other way around. How common our terminology when we talk about "finding God" or "finding Christ." But neither the Father nor the Son was ever lost. We are lost ones, and God finds us. As Jesus invited the man to believe, he moved from blindness to sight, from fate to faith, and from darkness to light.

Worship is the normal response of faith. Indeed, worship without faith is not worship at all. Chris Austin once wrote of this event, "The Jews cast him out of the temple, and the Lord of the temple found him." Up until now the man had not seen Jesus, so his question in verse 36 rested not in ignorance but great vulnerability and readiness to receive the truth. His faith response of verse 38 is one of the most beautiful statements of the New Testament—**Lord, I believe.** The words translated **sir** in verse 36 and **Lord** in verse 38 are exactly the same (*kurie*). But the NIV correctly renders the difference in the man's response after he knew who Jesus was.

Morris observes:

This is the climax for the man of a process that has been going on throughout the chapter. His insight into the Person of Jesus has been growing, and now this final revelation puts the coping stone on what has gone before. The man sees that Jesus is the one object of a right faith and accordingly puts his trust in him. This is the only place in this Gospel where anyone is said to worship Jesus. The verb occurs several times in chapter 4 of worshiping God, and it is found in the same sense in 12:20. It can be used of paying very high respect to men, but in John it is more natural to understand it of paying divine honors. The man has already recognized that Jesus came from God (v. 33). Now he goes a step further. He gives to Jesus that reverence that is appropriate to God (Morris, pp. 495–96).

9:39–41. Instead of faith in the Lord, the Pharisees demonstrated the futility of faith in one's self. John 9:39 is one of the most striking verses in the Bible. Jesus made himself the pivotal point of human destiny. Surely the verse emphasizes that spiritually blind people who recognize their malady will be given an opportunity to see. But those who are spiritually blind and deny it will never know the light. As Hughes points out, "Christ came to earth so that those who think they have spiritual insight may be shown to be blind, and those who do not suppose they have this spiritual insight may see. His whole argument centered around a person's sense of need. If someone felt no need, he would not see; but those who knew they were blind were the ones who could be made to see" (Hughes, p. 164).

The Pharisees asked what they thought was a rhetorical question: **Are we blind too?** The availability of light made them guilty of rejecting relief from their blindness. Every person who realizes his or her spiritual blindness becomes a candidate for seeing; those who refuse to recognize their spiritual blindness place themselves beyond help. We might paraphrase Jesus' final words like this: "If you would only admit your blindness, you would not be guilty of sin because I could forgive it; but because you claim your own self-righteousness, your guilt remains."

How many people enter church Sunday after Sunday thinking they must be good enough in God's eyes since they assess themselves as righteous. Yet they desperately need the light of God's truth to shine on their own wickedness so the light of the world can open their eyes and help them see his truth.

MAIN IDEA REVIEW: *Restoring sight to the blind was one of the miracles Jews expected to see in the Messiah. After chapter 8 in which Jesus claimed equality with the Father, John offered another miracle-message event, using the healing of a blind beggar to highlight the spiritual blindness of religion without Christ.*

III. CONCLUSION

Anonymous Theology

The hymn "My Faith Has Found a Resting Place" first appeared in *Songs of Joy and Gladness* back in 1891. The words are attributed to Lidi H. Edmunds. The hymn tune is an old Norwegian melody whose composer is unknown. Yet the strength of this hymn slowly moved it into popularity among Christians toward the end of the twentieth century. The text emphasizes the impact of this chapter of John with its focus on a simple yet growing faith and the object of that faith.

> My faith has founding a resting place—not in device nor creed;
> I trust the ever living One—His wounds for me shall plead.
> Enough for me that Jesus saves—this ends my fear and doubt;
> A sinful soul I come to Him—He'll never cast me out.
> My heart is leaning on the word—the written word of God;
> Salvation by my Savior's name—salvation through His blood.
> My great Physician heals the sick; the lost He came to save;
> For me His precious blood He shed; for me His life he gave.
> I need no other argument, I need no other plea;
> It is enough that Jesus died, and that He died for me.

Whatever its original name, the hymn tune is now known as "No Other Plea." It carries to our hearts and minds the great strength of the text which rests, perhaps, on 2 Timothy 1:12: "I know whom I have believed, and am convinced that he is able to guard what I have entrusted to him for that day." Of the theme of this hymn veteran church music leader Kenneth W. Osbeck writes:

> Saving faith is much more than a commitment to a creed, church, or a doctrinal system. It must be a commitment to a person—Jesus Christ. Doctrinal statements and creeds are important in defining and delineating truth, but they must never replace a personal relationship with "The Truth." We can get so caught up in our creedal statements, interpretations and arguments, or church traditions that we lose the sense of simple, child-like trust in Christ and his written Word. This was the concern of the Apostle Paul—"I am afraid that just as Eve was deceived by the serpent's cunning, your minds may somehow be led astray from your sincere and pure devotion to Christ" (2 Corinthians 11:3). Again and again we must take inventory of ourselves and determine what is the real foundation of our spiritual lives and the source of our resting place—Christ or merely a creed? (Osbeck, p. 188).

PRINCIPLES

- The first step of faith is to accept the fact of blindness.
- Faith grows as we exercise it.
- The Bible calls for informed faith, not blind faith.
- Genuine faith in Christ always leads to worship.

APPLICATIONS

- Obey whatever Jesus asks you to do.
- Become a walking candle lit by Jesus, the light of the world.
- Use your constant access to the light that dispels the darkness of this world.

IV. LIFE APPLICATION

Artist of Light

Visitors to a Thomas Kincaid gallery enter an oasis of peace in a world of chaos and perversity. Soft classical music plays in the background as one moves from room to room viewing the inspiring beauty of America's most-collected artist. The paintings portray simpler times of our world—cottages, hills, lakes, and churches—all with the strange and beautiful emphasis on light created by the unique use of colors in windows. Many of the pictures reflect scenes familiar to Christians with titles and even texts adopted from the Scriptures. Kincaid is a man of faith and family, a devoted husband and father of four. He believes art offers us a universal language to communicate the message of faith. He receives over two hundred letters a month from people who describe how his art has brought them joy and hope.

Recently we have decided to purchase one of Kincaid's paintings of light-houses for our own home. "Sea of Tranquility" reflects the surroundings of the west Florida coast where we live. But this painting also reminds us that there is a heavenly artist for whose message all of his children serve as light-houses in a dark world.

V. PRAYER

Father, thank you for the light that comes through Jesus, the light of the world. May we also be lights shining "like stars in the universe" as we hold out the word of life to others. Amen.

VI. DEEPER DISCOVERIES

A. Blindness (9:1)

The word *blind* (*tuphlos*) appears at least fifteen times in this chapter, more than in any other chapter in the New Testament and many more than in some entire New Testament books. Paul used some form of the word very rarely (Rom. 2:19; 2 Cor. 4:4) and Peter only once (2 Pet. 1:9). The noun and verb together appear only fifty-six times and frequently in the spiritual as well as the physical sense. Detzler tells us, "Though blindness today indicates a large degree of lost vision, in ancient times it usually referred to complete loss of sight. Aristotle indicated that blindness was a heredity disease in the Mediterranean basin. Sometimes blindness was inflicted by a conquering general on the vanquished. In all cases blindness was presumed to be incurable" (Detzler, p. 44).

B. Light (9:5)

As noted in an earlier study, the Greek word for "light" (*phos*) forms the foundation for many modern English words like *phosphorous* and *photograph*. The word appears seventy-three times in the New Testament, thirty-three times in John's writings and twenty-three times in this Gospel. The word was common in the ancient world. It was used generally to connote brightness, especially sunlight. Some philosophers like Aristotle regularly used it as figurative light, ethical understanding, and right thinking. In *The Republic,* Plato sees the right-living community illuminated by the light of a fire.

New Testament usage tends to be more spiritual (figurative) than literal. "Most often it is a metaphor referring to holiness, purity, or godliness. Jesus used the term in the Sermon on the Mount to describe his disciples and the holy standard of conduct that he expected them to model to the world (Mt 5:14–16; 6:23). In John's Gospel, however, Jesus himself is 'the light,' as stated in the Prologue (1:4–5) and in Jesus' own words (8:12; 9:5). In this case, the light is revelatory and reflects God's character or holiness; in other words, the *light* refers to God's revelation or disclosure of himself to the world in the incarnation (1:4–9)" (Blackaby, p. 24).

VII. TEACING OUTLINE

A. INTRODUCTION

1. Lead Story: Churches Settle Five-Hundred-Year-Old Debate
2. Context: The miracle-message method continues from chapter 6 as chapter 9 builds on a key verse in chapter 8 (v. 12). Like this blessed

beggar, we have access to the light that dispels darkness. Our fate also yields to the greater power of faith in the one who is the light of the world—and who has told us to become lights in our world as well.

3. Transition: As John arranged his material theologically, we find an easy and logical transition between the Lord's words at the end of chapter 8, "before Abraham was born, I am!" (v. 58) to the statement near the beginning of chapter 9, "While I am in the world, I am the light of the world" (v. 5). One blind beggar became the focal point of the world's endless conflict, the battle between sin and Christ. His hurting served as preparation for God's healing and his sorrow provided occasion for God's joy.

B. COMMENTARY

1. Purpose of the Miracle (9:1–12)
   a. Blindness of the man (9:1–5)
   b. Healing by the Lord (9:6–7)
   c. Reaction from the neighbors (9:8–12)
2. Perplexity of the Pharisees (9:13–34)
   a. First testimony of the man—prejudice (9:13–17)
   b. Testimony of the parents—pressure (9:18–23)
   c. Second testimony of the man—persecution (9:24–34)
3. Priority of Faith (9:35–41)
   a. Faith in the Lord (9:35–38)
   b. Faith in oneself (9:39–41)

C. CONCLUSION: ARTIST OF LIGHT

VIII. ISSUES FOR DISCUSSION

1. When people ask us who Jesus is and where they can find him, how well do we answer? What do we say?
2. What should Christian parents do when they discover their children want to place faith in Jesus? How can we prepare them for such a decision?
3. In what specific way does our faith lead us to worship?

John 10

The Good Shepherd

I. INTRODUCTION
An Ancient Youth Hymn

II. COMMENTARY
A verse-by-verse explanation of the chapter.

III. CONCLUSION
What Does It Cost?

An overview of the principles and applications from the chapter.

IV. LIFE APPLICATION
Working with a Safety Net

Melding the chapter to life.

V. PRAYER
Tying the chapter to life with God.

VI. DEEPER DISCOVERIES
Historical, geographical, and grammatical enrichment of the commentary.

VII. TEACHING OUTLINE
Suggested step-by-step group study of the chapter.

VIII. ISSUES FOR DISCUSSION
Zeroing the chapter in on daily life.

----| Q u o t e |----

"*All* kings are shepherds of the people."

Homer

GEOGRAPHICAL PROFILE: SOLOMON'S COLONNADE

- A porch on the east side of the temple that served as an ante-chamber to the Holy Place
- Dedicated by Solomon, along with the rest of the temple, in approximately 950 B.C.
- Rebuilt by Herod, with work beginning approximately 20 B.C. and not finishing until A.D. 64
- Solomon's Colonnade is mentioned in the New Testament in John 10:23; Acts 3:11; 5:12

GEOGRAPHICAL PROFILE: JORDAN RIVER

- The only large stream in Israel
- "Jordan" means "running down"
- Descending from four Syrian rivers, the Jordan River flows ten miles to the Sea of Galilee, which is as wide as six miles at points
- South of the Sea of Galilee the river covers a distance of only seventy miles, but because of its serpentine flow actually runs two hundred miles to the Dead Sea
- First mentioned in Numbers 35, the Jordan River makes numerous appearances throughout the Bible

IN A NUTSHELL

John's Gospel is all about salvation through a relationship with Jesus, and first-century hearers could certainly identify with a relational metaphor based on shepherds and sheep. Jesus explained that his disciples must follow him as sheep follow their shepherd.

The Good Shepherd

I. INTRODUCTION

An Ancient Youth Hymn

*W*e think of the modern youth movement as a post-World War II phenomenon, and, as we know it, that is essentially true. The concept of "teenagers" as a marketing model began in approximately 1941. Teens and "tweens" today (children 8–14) dominate a huge portion of the economy with their wants and needs. Most churches struggle to find new and effective ways to minister to Christians below the adult level.

But young people have always been with us, even though they may not have had their own sociological category. Some time between A.D. 202 and A.D. 220, Clement of Alexandria wrote a hymn text in Greek that we now know as "Shepherd of Eager Youth." The original title could literally be translated "tamer of steeds unbridled." It was apparently used as a hymn of Christian instruction for new converts. Commonly sung to an Italian hymn tune *Felice De Giardini* composed in the eighteenth century, the words pick up the metaphor Jesus uses in chapter 10 of John's Gospel.

> Shepherd of eager youth, guiding in love and truth through devious ways—Christ, our triumphant King, we come Thy name to sing; hither Thy children bring tributes of praise.

> Thou art our holy Lord, the all-subduing Word, healer of strife; Thou didst Thyself abase that from sin's deep disgrace Thou mightest save our race and give us life.

> Ever be near our side, our Shepherd and our Guide, our staff and song; Jesus, Thou Christ of God, by Thy enduring Word lead us where Thou has trod, make our faith strong.

Middle-aged and older adults familiar with hymnody know the tune and commonly sing it to the popular hymn, "Come Thou Almighty King." Osbeck picks up the relational theme of discipleship and focuses on the discipline necessary for sheep: "Christian nurturing of our children requires consistent discipline. Webster defines discipline as 'training, which corrects, strengthens, and perfects.' Discipline goes far beyond merely being punitive. Discipline and training have done their job only when they result in a changed character and a desire with self-control. Although there may be times when our youth may rebel and react against their early Christian training, they can never get completely away from it (Prov. 22:6)" (Osbeck, p. 81).

But shepherding is not just for children and young people. Early in the nineteenth century, Dorothy A. Thrupp wrote another hymn many of us have sung often, "Savior, Like a Shepherd Lead Us." Thrupp was a native and resident of London. She rarely signed her name to her hymn texts. When she did she often used a pseudonym. Osbeck tells us that even this familiar hymn "first appeared unsigned in her collection *Hymns for the Young,* in 1836" (Osbeck, p. 79).

> Savior, like a shepherd lead us; much we need Thy tender care;
> In Thy pleasant pastures feed us; for our use Thy folds prepare:
> Blessed Jesus, Blessed Jesus, Thou has bought us, Thine we are;
> Blessed Jesus, Blessed Jesus, Thou has bought us, Thine we are.

II. COMMENTARY

The Good Shepherd

MAIN IDEA: *John 10 is one of the most theological chapters in this Gospel, though often misunderstood. The Lord had entered an intense period of conflict and opposition to his ministry, as his enemies analyzed every word with the intention of punishment. He repeatedly alienated the Pharisees and yet drew his own flock closer to him with teaching sessions just like this one.*

A The Good Shepherd Offers Security (10:1–6)

SUPPORTING IDEA: *In contrast to those who steal and abuse the sheep, Jesus is a caring shepherd who takes care of the sheep.*

10:1–2. Beginning the chapter with his now famous **I tell you the truth** statement, Jesus changed the metaphor from blindness to sheep-stealing. We cannot tell whether the content of chapter 10 followed immediately on the discussion of chapter 9 or occurred on another occasion. Certainly the Lord intended his listeners to identify people of their day reflected in the metaphors of this parable.

The **sheep pen,** for example, represents neither heaven nor the church, but probably first-century Judaism. Verse 1 speaks of the thief invading the **sheep pen,** not the sheep. The "watchman," if we identify one specifically, may refer to John the Baptist, or perhaps even the Holy Spirit. Obviously, the **shepherd** is the Lord himself, and the **thief** and **robber** probably refers to the Pharisees against whom he had battled for several chapters.

Borchert describes the first-century pen of which John spoke: "The sheepfold was a place of security, not a place for intruders. Such a sheepfold would likely have been either a circular or square enclosure, probably constructed like a high stone fence or wall and perhaps topped with vines. The entrance would have been the only break in the wall, and once the sheep were safely inside at night, the watchman/guard (either a servant or a shepherd, usually an assistant) would lie down across the opening and serve both as the protector for the sheep and as a gate to the sheepfold. Unless an intruder was willing to confront the watchman, the only way into the sheepfold was to climb the wall (cf. 10:1)" (Borchert, p. 331).

Some interpreters place prophetic references on the various "figures of speech" as John calls them. But that is not necessary in light of the reality of the times in which Jesus spoke these words. This was a period of intense conflict in the life of our Lord. The Pharisees and their cohorts had committed themselves to exterminating this one whom they considered a "pesky prophet" from Nazareth. These first six verses emphasize security. In the ancient Middle East, one sheep pen held several flocks, so shepherd recognition was imperative. Only personal identification with a shepherd could make a sheep feel safe.

10:3. Verses 1 and 2 tell us that the shepherd knows his sheep, verse 3 that he calls them, and verses 4–6 that he leads them. Clearly the shepherd and the watchman cannot be the same since the watchman opened the door for the shepherd. But we should recognize the uniqueness of parables and not press every word for a specific meaning.

The active verbs seem important in this verse—**opens, listen, calls, leads.** John is quite specific about the intimacy between shepherd and sheep.

This shepherd does not just sound a call to the whole flock; he calls his sheep **by name.** This apostle John employed the same expression at the end of his third epistle when he told Gaius, "Friends here send their greetings. Greet the friends there by name" (3 John 14).

The emphasis on leading the sheep reminds us of Numbers 27 and the prayer of Moses for a successor "over this community to go out and come in before them, one who will lead them out and bring them in, so the Lord's people will not be like sheep without a shepherd" (Num. 27:16–17).

10:4–5. Not only do these sheep listen to the shepherd's voice, they **know his voice.** John seems to emphasize the point that they never leave the shepherd and never follow a stranger. Gariepy reminds us:

> The shepherd did not drive his sheep; he led them. Christ has gone the way before us. He has journeyed through life's thorn-grown wilderness. He knows life's dangers and perils. The Good Shepherd leads His sheep "beside the still waters." Otherwise a rushing current might sweep away the flock to destruction, or mask the sound of an approaching enemy. But he does not always lead us in pastures green or by waters still. Sometimes he leads us amid the tempests and down

into the deep ravines of life. But there is reassurance in the presence of the Good Shepherd (Gariepy, p. 212).

But who is this **stranger** whom the sheep avoid? We do not want to put any dogmatic assignments on the particulars of this parable, but one thing is clear—the **stranger** is anyone other than the shepherd they know. Strangers abound in our day in a variety of religions and cults as well as the secular domain. Shouting for sheep to follow is common practice, but the Lord's true sheep pay no attention because **they will never follow a stranger.**

10:6. As in many of Jesus' parables, people did not understand the metaphor, at least until he explained its various components which we find later in the chapter. But one thing seems clear in this first paragraph: the sheep were dependent on their shepherd, whom they knew and trusted. Furthermore, the shepherd took full responsibility for the sheep, even though thieves and robbers constantly tried to break into the sheep pen and steal them. In this verse John uses the Greek word *paroimia* (**figure of speech**), his preferred substitute for *parabole*. The first never appears in the synoptic Gospels and the second never occurs in John, although he used *paroimia* again in 16:25,29.

ⓑ The Good Shepherd Offers Shelter (10:7–13)

SUPPORTING IDEA: *The shepherd alone determines who may enter the fold. He guards the sheep, provides for them, and cares for them. This genuine shelter shows the difference between a true shepherd and a hired hand.*

10:7–8. Verse 7 begins just like verse 1 in the Greek text—*amen amen.* Before Jesus actually identified himself as the Good Shepherd, he described his activity at the sheep gate. We know from Luke 15 that a shepherd counts his sheep and from Psalm 23 how carefully he takes care of them. First-century listeners would have been certain to link this teaching with that familiar psalm.

Jesus did not merely explain the first paragraph of the chapter but actually expanded it. New features are added such as the "hired hand" (v. 12) and the adjective "good" (v. 11). **Thieves** we have seen earlier, but the "wolf" (v. 12) is a new character and the insertion of the teacher into the narrative in the first person—**I am the gate.**

Westcott expands the statement of verse 8: **all who ever came before me were thieves and robbers:** "They who 'came' who pretended to satisfy the national expectation inspired by the prophets, or to mould the national expectations after the Pharisaic type, who offered in any way that which was to be accepted as the end of the earlier dispensation, who made themselves 'doors' of approach to God (Matt. xxiii. 14), were essentially and continued to be inspired by selfishness, whether their designs were manifested by craft or by violence, and whether they were directed to gain or to dominion" (West-cott, p. 153).

We need to be careful with the words **before me**, since they could mean "came up to the gate" or "came ahead of me in time." The latter is preferred as indicated in Westcott's comment, but we must keep the cultural context well in mind. Jesus was not criticizing Moses and the prophets and certainly not John the Baptist. But the religious leaders who listened to Jesus' parables (notably the Pharisees) seem to be the direct target along with false messiahs who tried to entice the sheep.

10:9–10. In addition to guarding the sheep, the Good Shepherd provides for them—unlike thieves who **steal and kill and destroy.** Throwing aside the metaphor to reveal spiritual truth, Jesus told the sheep that he had come to give life so they might live it **to the full.** False shepherds intend to injure the sheep, but that is never the behavior of the true shepherd.

We need to watch carefully the flow between metaphor and spiritual reality here. In verse 9 Jesus is clearly talking about people as spiritual sheep, while verse 10 falls back into the metaphor at the beginning and then talks about spiritual life. The word **life** in verses 10 and 11 translates the Greek word *zoe,* which we have already discussed at some length. As we move into verse 11, we see the contrast built around this spiritual eternal life. The sheep may have it only because the Good Shepherd gives his own life to make this possible.

10:11. This verse provides the key to our passage and another one of the famous "I Am" statements of this Gospel. The good shepherd does not just lie across the opening of the pen to frighten away dangerous predators; if necessary he **lays down his life for the sheep.** Unlike the "worthless" shepherd of Zechariah 11:17, the **good shepherd** makes the supreme sacrifice.

The word *kalos* (**good**) emphasizes genuineness, value, and truth. This verse shows us how the **good shepherd** differs from other shepherds. They might risk their lives for the sheep as David did in fighting off lions and bears, but they would never intentionally die for the sheep as the good shepherd will do. This passage describes substitutionary atonement for sin, the supreme sacrifice of Calvary.

As Carson observes, "The shepherd does not die for his sheep to serve as an example, throwing himself off a cliff in a grotesque and futile display while bellowing, 'See how much I love you!' No, the assumption is that the sheep are in mortal danger; that in their defense the shepherd loses his life; and by his death they are saved. That, and that alone, is what makes him *the good shepherd*" (Carson, p. 386).

10:12–13. The good shepherd cares for the sheep in a way no hired hand could. We dare not equate the hired hand with the thieves and robbers described earlier. They are clearly evil; he suffers from poor motivation. Since the sheep do not belong to the hired hand, he will not risk his life to save them. He only wants his paycheck and will protect the sheep only when their enemies provide no threat to his own life and safety. Later in the New Testament Peter warned the elders of the church not to be like hired-hand shepherds who functioned with a mercenary attitude (1 Pet. 5:1–7).

◖ The Good Shepherd Offers Salvation (10:14–21)

SUPPORTING IDEA: *The good shepherd who sacrifices his life for the sheep also relates to them in trust and intimacy; he joins them with other flocks, and in the case of the good shepherd, he dies for the sheep.*

10:14–15. We see in this paragraph that the shepherd relates to the sheep in trust and intimacy. What a comparison! The good shepherd knows his sheep in the same way the Father knows the Son. Not only that, but the sheep know the shepherd in the same way the Son knows the Father. Notice how often the Lord talked about laying down his life for the sheep—five times in eight verses—a phraseology unique to John's Gospel. The third person statement of verse 11 has now become first person: **I lay down my life.**

Boice emphasizes the Lord's example for our own lives: "We will never be able to give our lives as Jesus gave His life for us—He died for us as our sin-bearer—nevertheless, there are other ways in which we can give our lives for others. We can give our time in order to help them. We can sacrifice things that we would rather do or rather have in order to serve and give to others. In other words, we must put others ahead of ourselves. Our primary desire must be for their spiritual well-being and comfort" (Boice, pp. 110–11).

10:16. But who are these **other sheep that are not of this sheep pen?** Most scholars believe this refers to non-Jews, the Gentile believers who would become a part of the Lord's people as the disciples preached the gospel in Acts. And in multiflock pens, it becomes all the more important for sheep to understand their master's voice. These various flocks, Jesus said, will be one because they follow one shepherd. This is a beautiful picture of the unification of genders and ethnic groupings through the Savior.

Jesus not only proclaimed additional sheep outside the scope of his hearers' thinking; he also said that he **must bring them** to the **one flock.** Through the centuries the English text has occasionally substituted the word *fold* for *flock*, thereby giving the verse a different orientation. There are many folds (pens) containing other sheep that must be reached. But when the spiritual unity of Christ's followers comes into correct perspective, there is only one flock—one body of Christ, with many denominations and affiliations.

10:17–18. The Lord emphasized that his death on the cross would not occur because earthly powers are stronger than the power of the heavenly Father. He would lay down his life willingly and at the time the Father required it. Substitutionary atonement is the heart of the gospel (Isa. 53:6), and that certainly focuses the Lord's words here. He would join the sheep from a variety of pens and he would die for all of them.

It is difficult to imagine that either Jesus or John intended to tell us that the Father loved the Son only because the Son willingly died for the sheep. Borchert emphasizes just the reverse and reads the text, "'Because [*dia touto*] the Father loves me, that is the reason [*hoti*, therefore] I lay down my life.' The model of the Father provided the model for the Son, which in turn should provide the model for the followers of Jesus (cf. 13:34; 15:12)" (Borchert, p. 336).

10:19–21. The more the Lord described himself, the more the Jews became angry and divided, resorting again to their charge of demon possession. Obviously the common people had not forgotten the healing of the blind man as verse 21 links chapter 10 with chapter 9.

Indeed, Morgan treats the chapters as almost one event, not an impossible approach:

> Here was the point in the ministry of Jesus, where, by an action, he opened the door of the new economy, and assumed authority over it. That poor blind beggar was barren of spiritual apprehension, Jesus opened his eyes, and by that act in the physical, led him professionally to the recognition of Who the Man was that had done it, so that he rendered worship to Him. He received that worship, and by that act opened the door of the new economy. The man now entered the new order through the Door; and from that moment he was into the true authority, the authority of the Shepherd Himself (Morgan, pp. 176–77).

Ⓓ The Good Shepherd Offers Signature (10:22–30)

SUPPORTING IDEA: *Christ's sheep can look to him for assurance, though the world around them is crumbling. And those sheep are recognizable because they believe in the Shepherd, they listen to the Shepherd, and they follow the Shepherd.*

10:22–24. For forty years I have signed official documents for three colleges and two seminaries. Often I write out the full name complete with middle initial, but in-house documents required only the initials KOG that I have signed thousands of time. Putting either my name or initials on a document indicates not only that I have read it but more likely that I have written it and am now officially and personally identifying myself with it. That is what these verses provide for the sheep—a signature, an identity by which people can know they belong to the one true shepherd.

Some time later, during the Feast of Dedication which we commemorate as Hanukkah, Jesus came to Jerusalem, still the target of the Pharisees and unbelieving Jews. At the invitation of the Jews to **tell us plainly** if he was really the Messiah, Jesus returned again to the metaphor of the shepherd and the sheep pen and emphasized the security for those sheep who belong to the true shepherd.

In these few verses John almost wrote like Luke with a seasonal notation, specific geographical reference, and identification of the surrounding crowd. The Feast of Dedication was also a Feast of Lights pointing to a time when Messiah would come to the temple and throw out all invaders, thereby reestablishing the kingdom. These grand visions persisted in the Israeli nation until the sack by the Romans in A.D. 70. The attack on Jesus claiming that he was demon possessed takes on greater impact when we recognize that "Johannine writings never mention any miracle of exorcism on Jesus' part but employ this language only to report the way his opponents described his utterances and behavior" (Tenney, *EBC*, p. 110).

10:25–26. Here is our key word again—**believe**—appearing in both verses and indicating that the first characteristic of true sheep is that they **believe** in the shepherd. Jesus made faith the cardinal issue separating unbelieving Jews from the true sheep. His miracles had been done publicly and in the Father's name, but unbelievers seemed unmoved by these divine acts **because you are not my sheep.** To be sure, one becomes a true sheep by placing faith in Jesus Christ for salvation. But once the Holy Spirit implants that nature in us, we respond to the Shepherd because that is what sheep do.

10:27. Though only thirteen words long in the English text, this verse identifies two more signatures of the sheep: they **listen** to the shepherd and then they **follow** the shepherd. This is not new information since we found it in verse 16, but repetition emphasizes importance. True sheep listen to the shepherd; false sheep pay no attention.

This segment of John's Gospel, particularly this portion of the chapter, overflows with basic doctrine. Consider the following list:

- *Union of Christ:* "my sheep"
- *Calling:* "listen to my voice"
- *Identification:* "I know them"
- *Sanctification:* "they follow me"
- *Grace:* "I give"
- *Security:* "eternal life"
- *Election:* "given them to me"
- *Omnipotence:* "greater than all"

10:28. Yet another signature of true sheep is that they receive eternal life from the Shepherd. Surely this is one of the strongest verses in the Bible emphasizing the believer's assurance of life in heaven. In one short verse Jesus stated it three ways: **I give them eternal life . . .they shall never perish . . . no one can snatch them out of my hand.** How did the old Swedish hymn writer put it? "More secure is no one ever than the loved ones of the Savior." Yet this security, this assurance that God will honor faith in the Good Shepherd should not be claimed apart from a balance of biblical responsibility. Borchert spells it out in clear terms:

> The perishing of true sheep was an unthinkable idea to early Christians. But contemporary Christians often wrestle with the question because they fail to perceive the logic of the biblical writers. Moreover, they often fail to read thoroughly texts like Hebrews 6. The biblical writers did not have such a superficial view of salvation that would consider walking down the aisle of a church and going through the waters of baptism to be a guarantee of salvation. Nor did the biblical writers have a superficial temporal view of salvation based on an inadequate understanding of John 3:3 and other passages. Instead, the biblical writers have no problem placing side by side texts concerning God's love, grace and covenant promises with God's stern warnings to the readers of the Scripture (Borchert, p. 339).

10:29–30. Sheep signatures, we now know, include belief in the Shepherd, listening to the Shepherd, following the Shepherd, receiving eternal life from the Shepherd, and now protection by the Shepherd's Father. This is not just the promise of a Galilean prophet whose miracles substantiated his claim to greatness. Throughout the entire narrative of John, Jesus repeatedly referred to the Father's power. Even if the unbelieving Jews doubted his ability and authority, they could never doubt the omnipotence of the Father.

But that is precisely the point of unbelief. Since they did not believe that this itinerant prophet, this carpenter from Nazareth, had any relationship with God, they did not see him as their shepherd. But his response was clear: **I and the Father are one.** Numerous verses in the Bible establish the deity of Jesus Christ, but few are as precise and pointed as this one.

Modern theologians argue that Jesus died a martyr's death because the people of his day misunderstood him. They argue that Jesus never claimed to be God and could have escaped death by denying this confusion. But the confusion is theirs. Jesus intended everyone who heard him speak to understand precisely that he made himself equal with God in every way—and that is why they killed him.

Nor can we miss the hint of election at the beginning of verse 29 when we read, **My Father, who has given them to me.** There can be no greater security, no safer shelter, no more sure salvation, and no more clear signature than this relationship to the God of the Bible through his Son the Good Shepherd. No wonder Paul could write, "Your life is now hidden with Christ in God" (Col. 3:3).

Lightner summarizes for us: "What security! The eternal presence of the Father and the Son guarantees the eternal security of the believer. The life which Christ gives is 'eternal.' Those possessing it shall 'never perish.' No one shall pluck the sheep from the Shepherd's hand. The irrevocable word of the Shepherd is, 'No one shall be able to snatch them out of the Father's hand'" (Lightner, p. 235).

Ⓔ The Good Shepherd Offers Safety (10:31–42)

SUPPORTING IDEA: *Instead of converting hypocritical hearts, this shepherd's promise ignited a new effort to stone Jesus. His enemies understood correctly his claims to be God, and they wanted him dead. Since the time of crucifixion had not yet come, he escaped their grasp and went to Perea on the east side of the Jordan River. There many more people heard his message and believed.*

10:31–33. Scarcely had Jesus proclaimed, "I and the Father are one" before the Jews **picked up stones to stone him.** Such blasphemy deserved death by stoning. How can anyone misunderstand a passage like this? They could hardly challenge the miracles or deny what so many people attested to be true. The issue was his nagging claim to deity. To put it another way, they nailed Jesus to the cross not for his works, but for his words.

As Boice explains, "Four important conclusions follow from this truth concerning Jesus' nature: (1) We have the knowledge of God in Him, for He is God; (2) we have forgiveness of sins in Him, for His death had infinite merit in atoning for sin; (3) we have victory over circumstances in Him, for he lived above circumstances; and (4) we have triumph over death in Him, for He rose from the dead and has promised to so raise all whom the Father has given to Him (John 6:39,40,44,54)" (Boice, p. 145).

10:34–36. Here we come to a section of this chapter more difficult to understand. Verse 34 quotes Psalm 82:6 in conjunction with Exodus 4:16 which says about Aaron, "He will speak to the people for you, and it will be as if he were your mouth and as if you were God to him." The word of God came to Moses, yet Moses was called (in metaphoric form) "God." If such could be said of Moses, how much more so the one who is really God sent into the world by the Father?

The Scripture cannot be broken was a strong tribute by the Son of God to the solidarity and inspiration of the Old Testament. Tenney cites other such illustrations in this Gospel (1:45; 2:22; 3:14–15; 5:39; 12:14–16; 13:18; 19:18,24,28,36) and says, "Whether all these other passages refer to Jesus' explicit statements or to the writer's explanation of his action, they presuppose a confidence in the authority and trustworthiness of Scripture that is in keeping with Jesus' attitude" (Tenney, *EBC*, p. 113).

10:37–39. Jesus reminded the Jews that they had a basic test for truth teaching: if people who claim to be God's Son do not do God's will, then their claims can be challenged. But the contrary should also prevail. If Jesus' behavior had been marked by the kind of righteousness and power that people associated with the God they had worshiped, why not believe his words and attribute his works to God? If they had done that, the unbelieving Jews would have understood that the Father was in the Son and the Son in the Father.

All this poured more fuel on an already raging fire. The more truth Jesus proclaimed, the less they believed him and the more they sought to kill him. Carson calls the relationship described here between the Son and the Father "mutual co-inherence—each is 'in' the other," and observes, "however precious such teaching might be to later believers, it was further evidence of blasphemy to those who first heard it" (Carson, p. 400).

10:40–42. Safety for the sheep rested not only in the courage and connections of the shepherd but also in the conversion of new sheep. John points out that Jesus went back to the east side of the Jordan (Perea) where John had baptized in the early days of his ministry. Not all the Jews were unbelievers. Not all followed the rejecting, murderous intentions of the Pharisees. Some people were impressed that though John the Baptist had never performed a miraculous sign, yet he had promised the Messiah would come. Now here he stood and they chose to be numbered among his sheep.

Are you a sheep? Do you hear the Shepherd's voice? Do you believe the Shepherd? Do you follow the Shepherd? This world affords no security or certainty. But the heavenly Shepherd promises that his sheep will live under his protection forever. Let the words of this key verse burn into your heart and fall often from your lips: "I give them eternal life, and they shall never perish; no one can snatch them out of my hand" (10:28).

> **MAIN IDEA REVIEW:** *John 10 is one of the most theological chapters in this Gospel, though often misunderstood. The Lord had entered an intense period of conflict and opposition to his ministry, as his enemies analyzed every word with the intention of punishment. He repeatedly alienated the Pharisees and yet drew his own flock closer to him with teaching sessions just like this one.*

III. CONCLUSION

What Does It Cost?

As we watch Jesus face death at the hands of his tormentors, we are reminded of how often he spoke to his disciples about the cost of discipleship. There is an old story about a brilliant violinist who performed with a major urban symphony. Presumably he served as concert master and occasional soloist. He was heard often and known well by classical music lovers in that city.

On one occasion one of his admirers chatted with him briefly at a benefit luncheon staged by the symphony society. After asking the usual questions about favorite composers, practice time, and guest conductors, the sponsor said to the violinist, "I'd give my life to play as well as you do." Without missing a beat the musician responded, "I did."

Life in Christ begins with regeneration, and the Gospel of John has a great deal to say about that. But throughout this Gospel as well as the synoptic Gospels, Jesus repeatedly called for followers who not only believed but followed through in obedience. Indeed, as New Testament theology develops, true faith can almost be equated with willing obedience.

As we read the Lord's description of himself as the Good Shepherd, we do well to examine our own lives in relationship to sheep, both "our own kind" and those of other flocks. How much do we speak to provide security for other sheep? How well do we serve so they may have shelter? How deeply do we sacrifice for their salvation? Such was the model of the good and perfect Shepherd.

PRINCIPLES

- Believers behave like sheep because that is what God has made them.
- The Good Shepherd has purchased our salvation with his blood and now offers shelter and security to all who follow him.
- Personal identification with the shepherd can make a sheep feel safe.
- Vicarious atonement is the heart of the gospel.

APPLICATIONS

- Understand Jesus' parables in the first-century context and do not try to assign some tricky meaning to every word.
- Trust your life to the Good Shepherd. No one can tear you away from his love.
- Learn and understand that the Father is in Christ and he is in the Father.

IV. LIFE APPLICATION

Working with a Safety Net

The Golden Gate Bridge was completed in 1937. At the time, it cost a mere seventy-seven million dollars and was built in two stages. During the first stage, work moved slowly and twenty-three men fell to their deaths because of treacherous conditions. Soon fear spread through the ranks and worked stopped. Somehow watching one's fellow employees plunge to their deaths in that vast and deep entrance to San Francisco Bay rendered many of the builders powerless to continue.

Then construction bosses began to think seriously about safety. A huge net was built below the bridge. It was the largest net ever built and cost a mere one hundred thousand dollars—a pittance in relationship to the cost of the bridge. Then the second phase of the bridge began, and ten more laborers fell from the bridge, each saved by the net. Slowly confidence returned. The workmen believed that even if they should fall, the safety net would save their lives. During the second phase of the work, construction moved along at a rate 25 percent faster than before.

Risk of danger brings people to public events. Football fans like to see and hear big hits; boxing fans cheer for a knockout or at least several knock downs; racing fans cheer for the winner but love to see a big crash. Surely it must be the sin nature in us that pays money to get excited by watching other people hurt one another or even die.

This chapter makes it clear that God has provided safety and security, shelter and salvation for those willing to be sheep, for those who believe and follow the shepherd. Never has there been such a small requirement for such great gain. Why would anyone work without a safety net for even another day?

V. PRAYER

Father, thank you for Jesus our Good Shepherd, who protects us, cares for us, and gives us eternal life. Amen.

VI. DEEPER DISCOVERIES

A. Shepherd (10:2,11)

Although this chapter is the only place in the Fourth Gospel that John uses *poimen*, such a reference would not have been surprising to Jesus' listeners. The word is grounded in the Greek Old Testament where *poimen* appears commonly to identify leaders of every kind, including the patriarchs, David, and Jehovah himself (Ps. 23). When the Messiah came, said the prophets, he would also be a shepherd (Ezek. 34:23).

Tasker reminds us, "In the Old Testament, the relationship between God and his people is often symbolized as that of a shepherd and his flock. The flock is always regarded as belonging to God though the care of it may be temporarily entrusted to others" (Tasker, p. 129).

John 10 connects directly with Ezekiel 34, where God denounced the false shepherds (i.e., false prophets) who led the sheep (the nation of Judah) astray (vv. 1–10). "For this is what the Sovereign LORD says: I myself will search for my sheep and look after them. As a shepherd looks after his scattered flock"

(vv. 11–12). "Finally, David will be the shepherd over God's people again (vv. 23–24). In using the shepherd/sheep imagery, Jesus was identifying Himself as the shepherd of Israel, just as the Lord had done in this OT passage—a clear statement that Jesus claimed to be deity" (Blackaby, p. 30).

B. Hanukkah (10:22)

First celebrated on December 25, 165 B.C., the Feast of Lights continued for eight days, commemorating the restoration of the temple after its desecration by Antiochus Epiphanes. Like its sister Feast of Tabernacles, this festival was filled with great pomp and joy. It was a bright spot in the winter season and in the winter of spiritual rejection portrayed in chapter 10 of John's Gospel.

Some interpreters dispute the unity of this chapter, suggesting that John intended a break at verse 22 to introduce a different occasion. But the unity of the content in the first twenty-one verses with verses 25 to 30 seems assured. Borchert faults the view on three counts:

> First, it tends to treat the evangelist as a pedantic newspaper reporter who has to signal a change in topics by a temporal designation. Second, it fails to understand the theological unity of this chapter: namely, the close connection between the shepherd's statements prior to 10:21 and those of 10:27 after the Dedication notation at 10:22. It likewise fails to account for the connection between the earlier image of the sheepfold as a place of security before 10:22 and the security statements in 10:28–29. Third, it also fails to recognize the similar pattern that can be seen in the later statement concerning the coming of Passover at the conclusion of the next chapter (11:55), the whole of which is clearly focused on hope in the midst of death. For all of these reasons as well as my thesis that chaps. 7–9 form a structurally definable unit on Tabernacles, I would insist that chap. 10 must be interpreted as a separate unit of profound theological significance (Borchert, p. 327).

C. You Are Gods (10:34)

Theologians have debated this text, some claiming that Jesus argued in rabbinic fashion what debaters call *ad hominen* (an argument centered in self), or that he was guilty of begging the question. It seems to me that an approach to the interpretation of the chapter centers in the phrase that drew our focus in the "Commentary" section—"Scripture cannot be broken." In both Greek and Hebrew understanding, not being broken refers to unity and the phrase itself argues that if Scripture says something, it must be true. The word *broken* is actually a common Greek word meaning "to loosen or unbind." We find it in John 7:23 where the NIV translates it as "broken."

The key appears in Matthew 5:17–18: "Do not think that I have come to abolish the Law or the Prophets; I have not come to abolish them but to fulfill them. I tell you the truth, until heaven and earth disappear, not the smallest letter, not the least stroke of a pen, will by any means disappear from the Law until everything is accomplished." In other words, once God has said something in the Old Testament, that Scripture cannot be kept from fulfillment. Jesus' appropriate reply centers in a consideration of the prophetic and typical character of the Old Testament judges of whom Psalm 82:6 speaks, and from a consideration of John's context and focus on Christ's role as judge (John 9:39).

In answer to his accusers, Jesus asserted his claim to deity, pointing out that the Father himself had foreshadowed the coming of the ultimate Judge who would judge righteously, shepherd his followers, and deliver them. He is, indeed, both God and man as Psalm 82 implies. Furthermore, this is not just some theological notion held by the ancients, but clearly written in Scripture that cannot be broken.

John did not intend here to prove deity to atheists or agnostics but to proclaim it as a statement of God's Word. This passage proclaims both law and gospel. The law reminded Jesus' opponents that they were rejecting not just his person and his works but the Word of God and should expect judgment. The Gospel asserted that the Scriptures promised the God-man would come and now he is here—believe.

VII. TEACHING OUTLINE

A. INTRODUCTION

1. Lead Story: An Ancient Youth Hymn
2. Context: Though it cannot be firmly stated, chapter 10 may be a continuation of the discussion of chapter 9, possibly held on the same occasion. But Johannine theology is greatly expanded in this chapter, with much information about Christ, salvation, and security, and building a bridge between the healing of the blind man and the raising of Lazarus in chapter 11.
3. Transition: John portrays Jesus as continuing his proclamation in the face of persecution. The death threats are real. But rather than hide, the Lord intensified the message by appearing at the Feast of Lights in the capital city. However, let us remember John's disenchantment with geographical niceties and chronological exactness. As chapter 11 opens we have no idea how much later it occurs, and we can only assume that the location may still be Perea.

B. COMMENTARY

1. The Good Shepherd Offers Security (10:1–6)
    a. The shepherd knows the sheep (10:1–2)
    b. The shepherd calls the sheep (10:3)
    c. The shepherd leads the sheep (10:4–6)
2. The Good Shepherd Offers Shelter (10:7–13)
    a. The shepherd guards them (10:7–8)
    b. The shepherd provides for them (10:9–10)
    c. The shepherd cares for them (10:11–13)
3. The Good Shepherd Offers Salvation (10:14–21)
    a. The shepherd trusts the sheep (10:14–15)
    b. The shepherd joins the sheep (10:16)
    c. The shepherd dies for the sheep (10:17–21)
4. The Good Shepherd Offers Signature (10:22–30)
    a. True sheep believe in the shepherd (10:22–26)
    b. True sheep listen to the shepherd (10:27a)
    c. True sheep follow the shepherd (10:27b)
    d. True sheep receive eternal life from the shepherd (10:28)
    e. True sheep are protected by the shepherd's father (10:29–30)
5. The Good Shepherd Offers Safety (10:31–42)
    a. Reason for the challenge: Jesus claimed to be God (10:31–33)
    b. Response to the challenge: both words and works support his claim (10:34–39)
    c. Relief from the challenge: many people chose to believe (10:40–42)

C. CONCLUSION: WORKING WITH A SAFETY NET

VIII. ISSUES FOR DISCUSSION

1. How well does the leadership of your church function in a shepherd role? What qualities of shepherding can be learned from chapter 10?
2. How do you work for the unity of Christ's total flock and the breakdown of artificial, cultural, and religious boundaries among believers?
3. Think of people you know who do not believe Jesus is God. How can you witness this biblical truth to them?

John 11

Friend of the Family

"*A* true friend is one in whom we have confidence and to whom we will listen."

K . A l v i n P i t t

GEOGRAPHICAL PROFILE: BETHANY

- Located on the east side of the Mount of Olives about two miles southeast of Jerusalem
- Often called the Judean home of Jesus
- Hometown of Mary, Martha, Lazarus, and Simon the Leper
- Located in the general area in which the ascension of Jesus took place

GEOGRAPHICAL PROFILE: EPHRAIM

- City north of Jerusalem named for the younger of Joseph's two sons
- Mentioned in 2 Samuel 13:23
- Most likely identified with the modern site of Et-Taiyabeh, a few miles northeast of Bethel

PERSONAL PROFILE: LAZARUS

- Brother of Mary and Martha, resident of Bethany
- Mentioned only here and in John 12
- Not to be confused with the beggar who died and went to Abraham's side (Luke 16)

PERSONAL PROFILE: MARY

- The name of at least five women in the New Testament
- This chapter introduces Mary of Bethany who is mentioned also in Luke 10:42 and John 12
- Commended for her personal worship

PERSONAL PROFILE: MARTHA

- Hosted Jesus in her home
- Grieved for her dead brother, Lazarus, along with her sister, Mary
- Proclaimed her faith in the resurrection (John 11:27)

PERSONAL PROFILE: THOMAS

- One of the original twelve disciples
- Mentioned three times in John's Gospel (John 11:16; 20:24; 21:2)
- Proclaimed the deity of Jesus after Jesus' second resurrection appearance to the disciples
- Tradition suggests Thomas later served as a missionary in Carthia, Persia, and India

PERSONAL PROFILE: CAIAPHAS

- Held the office of high priest from A.D. 18–36
- Son-in-law of Annas, who was appointed high priest in A.D. 7
- Presided over the second trial of Jesus (John 18:24)

John 11

 IN A NUTSHELL

We do not always understand what God is saying or what he is doing. And the most critical point of misunderstanding centers in what God has to say about life and death. Yet this very point separates Christianity from all other religions and exalts God above every pretender. If we miss his truth about life and death, we miss everything.

Friend of
the Family

I. INTRODUCTION

Life After Death

*O*n a difficult Sunday evening some twenty years ago, I found myself locked in bitter public debate with Madeline Murray O'Hare on a live television broadcast in Miami, Florida. The debate lasted for ninety minutes and was played by no rules other than those the two hostesses made up as we went along. In the original plan, we were to talk for about thirty minutes and then take calls. But the program director decided that the repartee was sufficient in itself and calls were not necessary. Before this decision, however, two or three calls did come in. One caller asked Mrs. O'Hare, "In the view of atheism, what happens when I die?"

You can imagine the response. Though I do not recall the exact words, Mrs. O'Hare indicated that death presented the absolute end of any existence and the caller need not pay any attention to Christian nonsense about life after death. You can also imagine my response, pushed in at some point where my adversary had to take a breath (the pattern for most of the evening). I affirmed the centrality of resurrection in the message of the gospel and the hope of eternal life with Christ so repeatedly promised in the Scripture. This is precisely the centerpiece of the chapter before us.

II. COMMENTARY

Friend of the Family

MAIN IDEA: *Many people have wondered why the synoptic Gospels ignore the story of Lazarus. After all, Jesus performed only three resurrections (other than the resurrection of Christ) mentioned in the Gospels: the widow's son in Luke 7; Jairus's daughter in Matthew 9, Mark 5, and Luke 8; and Lazarus here in John 11. The answer has to do with the purpose of the Gospel writers. This account by John centers precisely in Jesus' claim to be the Son of God.*

A Jesus Is Our Friend (11:1–16)

SUPPORTING IDEA: *We approach this familiar Gospel account from a different point of view, centering on Jesus rather than Lazarus, and noticing first that Jesus is our friend as he was a friend to the family of Lazarus.*

11:1–3. As we have studied the Gospel of John, we have seen how John chose to record at least seven miracles that prove that Jesus was the Christ, the Messiah, the Son of God. Seven miracles that produce faith in readers. In the first six, we have seen his power over the physical aspects of life, including the human body, the natural elements, time and space, and even food and drink. But in each case Jesus also demonstrated that his purposes went beyond the physical to the spiritual. Now the Lord revealed his power by reaching beyond this life and touching death and the afterlife—territory that belongs only to God.

Death is not a natural extension of life, though many psychologists and thanatologists argue that point today. Death is an enemy, created as a result of sin, and ultimately to be destroyed by God. The perfume-anointing described in verse 2 is further developed in Matthew 26 and Mark 14, although John mentions it just to identify the relationship among these two sisters, their brother, and Jesus. Sometimes the Lord's ways are hard to understand. Imagine the disciples listening to Jesus as he observed casually that the sickness would not end in death and then lingering around for a few more days before heading to Bethany.

Though he had not yet recorded the story of the foot-washing (chap. 13), John assumed his readers had heard it. Perhaps the story floated among early Christians in the first century. But once again, we see John's lack of concern with chronological order. And the message from Bethany immediately tipped the Lord's close relationship to this family: **Lord, the one you love is sick.** Here John used the common *phileo*, then switched to *agapao* in verse 5. Notice there was no request; among friends, requests are not always needed.

11:4–6. Even as we read this passage, we wonder about God being glorified through sickness, the strong point of verse 4. Of course, God was glorified through Jesus' resurrection, but he was also glorified through his death. Any crisis that brings glory to God is good. If God is glorified in illness, it is good, as difficult as this is for our human minds to grasp.

The Lord's words, **this sickness will not end in death,** show us how much more deeply he was thinking than the disciples. They could never have imagined that Lazarus' physical death would end and he would actually walk out of the grave after several days.

How was God glorified in this life-and-death event? Certainly through the resurrection, but also in the death. The faith and hope that Lazarus's death evoked in the sisters occupies a significant portion of this chapter.

It appears that the four days that passed between the death and the raising of Lazarus find their starting point just before the Lord left for Bethany. That allows two days after the original message for the intended delay, and two days for the trip.

But we ask, the trip from where? We simply do not know. The end of chapter 10 places Jesus and the disciples in Perea (Transjordan), and that may have been their location at the beginning of this chapter. Carson explains:

> This is why the "therefore" of v. 6 contributes to the flow of the argument. Lazarus' illness will not finally issue in death: it is for the glory of God (v. 4). This does not mean Jesus is indifferent to human suffering. Far from it: Jesus loves Martha, Mary, and Lazarus (v. 5). Indeed, it is in consequence of that love that he delays his departure by two days, waiting for the divine signal, the news of Lazarus' death, before he sets out on the four-day journey (v. 6), for this delay will make a substantial contribution to the strengthening of the faith of the Bethany family (Carson, p. 408).

11:7–10. The Lord and his disciples had probably been in Perea and had some distance to walk back to Bethany in the northeastern part of Judea. Death threats awaited there, and the disciples had serious reservations about the trip. Verses 9 and 10 represent the Lord's answer, though it does not seem to fit the context. Perhaps it was a proverb of the time, meaning duty is more important than haste. For Jews, the twelve hours of daylight would have been from 6:00 A.M. to 6:00 P.M., and perhaps Jesus emphasized that we have a full twelve hours, but no more. Each valuable hour should be used to glorify God.

Both Romans and Jews calculated time in twelve-hour blocks, and work was done during the daylight. The interesting expression **this world's light** obviously refers to sunlight, but John may have intended a veiled reference to working in the "Sonshine"—that time which the Father had allowed Jesus to be on earth. Ed Blum suggests, "In one sense he was speaking of walking (living) in physical light or darkness. In the spiritual realm when one lives by the will of God he is safe. Living in the realm of evil is dangerous. As long as He followed God's plan, no harm would come until the appointed time" (Blum, p. 313).

11:11–13. Jesus returned to the subject at hand and used a common New Testament euphemism for death—the word **sleep** (Matt. 9:24; 1 Cor. 11:30; 15:20; 1 Thess. 4:14). We see this again at the end of Acts 7 in the martyrdom of Stephen. According to Gangel, "*Sleep* is a common New Testament euphemism for death. It translates the Greek word (*ekoimethe*) from which we construct the English noun *cemetery*. A cemetery—supposedly fearsome and spooky—affords a Christian word of faith. Christians who die are not gone; they sleep temporarily until Jesus wakes them up. That sleep, of course, does not mean cessation of existence or awareness, because we learn later in Paul's writings that to be absent from the body is to be present with the Lord (2 Cor. 5:1–10)" (Gangel, pp. 111–12).

11:14–16. After having told them the sickness would not be unto death, Jesus then said clearly, **Lazarus is dead.** The disciples did not pick up on the word *sleep* and its connection with death. Not only that, but we learn the delay that allowed the death of his friend would work for the benefit of Jesus' disciples. They were on their way south to Bethany. This trip would take them through Jerusalem.

Thomas called Didymus offered the pessimistic cry of the martyr complex, **Let us also go, that we may die with him.** "What futility," they must have thought. "Lazarus is already dead; why put our own lives in jeopardy since we can't help him now." In the view of Thomas, all of them (certainly including Jesus) would be dead before this trip ended.

Thomas entered the narrative of John three times and in each case in a somewhat negative reference. The word **Didymus** means "twin" (not "doubter" as some have surmised), although we know nothing about his sibling. Indeed, the name **Thomas** is the Hebrew word for *twin*. One can almost hear the sign of futility, the complete ignorance of substitutionary atonement and resurrection victory.

Some interpreters make much of Thomas' loyalty on this occasion, and I yield that point. Let me cite Tenney's positive stance. He observes that Thomas along with the other disciples certainly understood their fate was questionable and their lives were in jeopardy, but "not withstanding this unhappy prospect, Thomas' loyalty is revealed by his readiness to share Jesus' peril. The skepticism that Thomas later evinced regarding the Resurrection was probably prompted by grief over Jesus' death rather than by disillusionment because of apparent failure" (Tenney, *EBC*, p. 116).

B Jesus Is Our Life (11:17–37)

> **SUPPORTING IDEA:** *With the Son of God, death never has the final word. Along with Lazarus's family, the Twelve learned that Jesus was more than their friend; he was their life.*

11:17–20. Their arrival in Bethany occurred at least four days later. In the cultural ostentation of Jewish funerals, the mourners, the spices, and the procession still lingered. This was a popular family in the small town of Bethany, so Lazarus's funeral was a major event. But none of the Lord's followers—not the disciples and not the sisters—yet understood how Jesus is our life, as he was to Martha.

In John we have seen the term **Jews** in negative reference used to refer to the Pharisees and assorted religious opponents of Jesus. Here it takes on the general ethnic designation. The adjective **many** may suggest some influence of Lazarus in the small community of Bethany.

The text of verse 20 literally tells us that Mary stayed seated in the house (*kathezesthai*). Borchert enlightens this interesting and more literal translation of our text:

> The custom was for the bereaved to remain seated in the house and for the guests to come and sit in silence and periodically support the grieving parties with sympathetic tears and moans. For me the experience of having observed modern wakes in the Middle East has left an unforgettable memory of what "sitting in the house,"crowded on benches in the heat of day and mourning for the dead, can mean. Moreover, one must not forget that it was the brother (the obvious wage-earner of that home) who had died. The loss was an intense one. Reading again Ruth 1:6–14 will provide some sense of the feelings that probably were present in that room (Borchert, p. 355).

11:21–24. Here we have one of the great conversations of the Bible. We already know the personalities of these women, so we are not surprised that Martha charged out to meet Jesus while Mary stayed at home. Her words to the Lord almost take the form of a mild rebuke: **if you had been here, my brother would not have died.** Yet she hinted at resurrection by adding, **God will give you whatever you ask.** Knowing her faith, Jesus responded, **Your brother will rise again** (the word "again" is not in the Greek text).

Martha recited the standard Old Testament view of the resurrection, not practicing the promises Jesus had taught so often. Surely she knew about the resurrection of the widow's son and Jairus's daughter, but somehow she never made the connection that the Lord could do the same for her brother.

Martha, Mary, and all these Jewish mourners responded in human fashion to death and sorrow, defeat and abandonment. According to their words, Jesus should have been there to prevent Lazarus's death. If he were really God, he would have prevented physical death because that is God's job. They treated death as the end of life, as the final defeat, a sign that God had deserted them. The presence of death meant the absence of God.

Martha could never have accepted the view of the Sadducees that denied the resurrection; she sided with the more conservative Pharisaic view that prevailed among the common people. Martha had no more hope than she had before Jesus arrived on the scene. But that was about to change—dramatically.

11:25–27. What follows is the wonderful promise almost every Christian has memorized—a passage used at Christian funerals for nearly two thousand years. It forms the key to the chapter, but what does it mean? Jesus said, **He who believes in me will live, even though he dies.** Does that mean spiritual life beyond the grave as many interpreters have suggested? The context seems to demand an emphasis on physical death and physical life—in other words, bodily resurrection. Verse 26 seems to indicate that whoever is still alive and believing at the time of the Lord's return will never die.

Martha did not grasp the entirety of this theology, but nevertheless placed her foothold of faith directly in Jesus' affirmation of his messiahship. She was not completely without faith. She still believed that Jesus was the Christ, the Son of God, and that he might still be able to do something, although she did not really know what. She understood only two categories of life: physical life on earth and some future life at a resurrection. In her mind, Lazarus had neither of those at the moment. She did not think there was anything Jesus could do about his death.

The key to the chapter and a foundation stone of the doctrine of resurrection and the afterlife appears in these beloved verses. This is another one of the Lord's seven "I Am" statements in this Gospel. Jesus said future resurrection was impossible without him. Martha (as well as Lazarus) had no hope without him in the picture. He also said that real life (life that extends beyond death) is possible only through him. A person attains it no other way. This life is both spiritual (**will live, even though he dies**) and eternal (**will never die**), and it comes only to those who believe in Jesus.

Martha's affirmation of Jesus in verse 27 fits directly into the Johannine pattern. She affirmed that Jesus is the Messiah and therefore the Son of God, and also that he was sent into the world by the Father—a fact he had been arguing in public for more than three years.

As Witmer explains:

> The title "Son of God" was first applied to Jesus by the angel Gabriel in his announcement to the Virgin Mary. Explaining that her conception would be by the Holy Spirit, he said that, "the holy one to be born will be called the Son of God" (Luke 1:35; cv. 32). John the Baptist, after witnessing the descent of the Holy Spirit on Jesus at his baptism by John, said, "I testify that this is the Son of God" (John 1:34). This was also the confession of Nathanael (1:49); of Martha, the sister of Lazarus and Mary (11:27); and of Peter, spokesman for the disciples (Matt. 16:15–16; c 14:33). When the earthquake occurred at Jesus' crucifixion, the centurion and soldiers who carried

out the execution "were terrified, and exclaimed, Surely he was the Son of God" (27:54; c Mark 15:39; Luke 23:47) (Witmer, p. 48).

It appears to the casual reader that Martha had climbed on board theologically and would no longer have any question about what Jesus could do. Yet a few minutes later she heard Jesus call for the removal of the stone and objected, "But, Lord . . . by this time there is a bad odor, for he has been there four days" (v. 39). So again Martha reminds us of ourselves—a willingness to verbally proclaim biblical truth without applying it in our lives.

Borchert reminds us that "the story thus serves as a significant warning even to evangelicals who may be able to mouth all the correct theological statements about Jesus but actually have failed to bring words and life together. It is not enough to make statements about Jesus. Indeed, if a person would make a statement akin to Martha's in some churches, the tendency would be to baptize such a person and to accept him or her into membership. But we must all be warned that verbal confessions and life commitments are not always partners with each other" (Borchert, p. 357).

11:28–32. Presumably, verse 28 contains an unrecorded invitation delivered personally at the request of Jesus, so Mary went outside the city with others following her, assuming she was headed for the tomb.

How interesting that her opening line was identical to Martha's, although she had not heard Martha speak and there seems to be no indication in the text that the women had discussed their reaction to the Lord. We have no idea where Mary met Jesus other than that he was at the same place and **had not yet entered the village.** We dare not miss John's notation that the Jews who had been with her in the house followed her. So Mary's conversation with Jesus was not, like Martha's, private. There are other differences. Martha engaged in theological debate; Mary **fell at his feet.** Martha expressed expectant faith ("God will give you whatever you ask"); Mary functioned at a more personal level.

11:33–37. Jesus **was deeply moved in spirit and troubled.** The Greek word for **deeply moved in spirit** is *embrimaomai*, used five times in the New Testament, always of Jesus (Matt. 9:30; Mark 1:43; 14:5; John 11:33,38). It probably suggests anger over sin and death which could cause such agony in Mary, Martha, and their friends in Bethany. The second word (**troubled**) translates *etaraxen*. It seems to emphasize agitation, again perhaps over the grief of the sisters.

Of the phrase **deeply moved in spirit** Carson writes, "It does not refer to the Holy Spirit, but it is roughly equivalent to 'in himself': his inward reaction was anger or outrage or indignation." And of the word **troubled,** "the same strong verb used in 12:27; 13:21. It is lexically inexcusable to reduce this emotional upset to the effects of empathy, grief, pain, or the like" (Carson, p.

415). When Jesus approached the tomb, he could no longer control himself and wept. John used a different word than the word he chose to describe the weeping of Mary and the Jews. Perhaps the intent was to show that Jesus' tears emerged for a different reason—not grief over Lazarus; he had that situation well in hand. Surely the same unbelief and theological ignorance that prompted his anger also produced his grief.

This response to the death of Lazarus on the part of Jesus is very contrary to the Greek idea of gods, but very much like the promised Messiah of the Old Testament (Isa. 53:3). The question of the group in verse 37 seems fair enough, but it has an obvious answer. Jesus could have kept this man from dying, but he chose not to for reasons he had already explained to the disciples earlier in the chapter.

C Jesus Is Our Power (11:38–44)

SUPPORTING IDEA: *Still emotionally tense, the Lord came to this cave-like tomb with a stone across the entrance. He was about to display his authority, and everyone would see it publicly and dramatically.*

11:38–40. The emotional intensity deepened as Jesus approached the tomb, **deeply moved**. The same word appears in verse 33. I have visited the Herod family tomb behind the modern King David Hotel in Jerusalem. This tomb is probably similar to the tombs of both Lazarus and Jesus. The tombstone was probably four or five feet in diameter and several inches thick. Since Martha had raised the protest, the response of verse 40 may be directed primarily at her, though it certainly established a general principle—one that we have repeatedly observed throughout this gospel: *Believing is seeing.*

We might also conclude that Jesus was speaking to the disciples, since to them he had said, "This sickness . . . is for God's glory so that God's Son may be glorified through it" (11:4). So to the sisters in their grief, the disciples in their bewilderment, and to all who seek faith for life at any age since this dramatic event, Jesus calls for faith first and sight later.

11:41–42. The power of Jesus is also seen in his prayer. These words must have been uttered audibly and publicly. The purpose of the prayer was to create faith in the hearts of those standing around the tomb of Lazarus wondering what would happen next. Here we get a glimpse into the relationship of the Trinity and particularly the Father-Son relationship within the Godhead that John dealt with so frequently in this Gospel.

All three of Jesus' prayers recorded in John call upon the Father to support the mission on which he had sent the son (11:41–42; 12:27–28; 17:1–26). Borchert points out: "Unlike the other prayers, however, this prayer focuses on thanksgiving and is not unlike the formula prayer in Ps. 118:21 (a psalm frequently cited by the NT writers). The prayer presupposes that Jesus knew the Father's will concerning Lazarus, and what he was about to do would not be merely for the sake of Lazarus but for those who would witness the incredible act that was to follow. The prayer thus was not primarily for his benefit, but it was aimed at bringing the observers into the group of believers (11:42)" (Borchert, p. 362).

What exactly did Jesus mean when he said to the Father, **I said this for the benefit of the people standing here?** This public gesture of looking up and speaking aloud was unnecessary, since the Father always hears the Son and responds. But Jesus' mission was to bring people to faith and John was mission-focused throughout this entire book. The unbelieving crowds of mourners heard Jesus' rhetorical question of verse 40, watched him, and heard him pray openly to the Father. We learn later that "many of the Jews who had come to visit Mary, and had seen what Jesus did, put their faith in him" (11:45).

Boice emphasizes how Jesus involved people not only in watching and hearing but in the miracle itself:

> Although it was Jesus alone who could bring the dead to life, he delighted to involve the bystanders in the miracle. First, they were told to move the stone. Then, after the miracle, they were told to unbind Lazarus. True, we cannot bring the dead to life. But we can bring the word of Christ to them. We can do preparatory work, and we can do work afterward. We can help to remove stones—stones of ignorance, error, prejudice and despair. After the miracle we can help the new Christian by unwinding the grave clothes of doubt, fear, introspection, and discouragement (Boice, p. 278).

11:43–44. Through this miracle we also see that Jesus is our power. How interesting that John should tell us Jesus called in a loud voice, for surely it was not necessary for that call to reach the ears of Lazarus. Perhaps he intended it for the crowd of mourners. No one present that day could possibly misunderstand what Jesus said or did.

This is one of the great dramatic scenes of the Bible, but we must be careful using the word "resurrection" to describe it. In one sense, Lazarus did experience resurrection because he came back from the dead. But New Testament "resurrection" refers to a return to life in a state of immortality so that one never dies again. That was the pattern of the resurrection of Jesus, of course, but not that of Lazarus who would die again. Yet the word "resuscitation" used by some commentators seems insufficient. Let us just recognize the limitations of resurrection performed in biblical times as over against that promised believers in a future day (1 Cor. 15; 1 Tim. 6:16).

The Greek verb rendered here **called in a loud voice** (*ekraugasen*) appears only nine times in the New Testament, eight of them in the Gospels.

No Hollywood depiction of this event could possibly capture the drama of what actually happened that day as Lazarus stumbled and staggered into the sun while wearing his grave clothes. Borchert describes what he looked like: "A long, narrow sheet was folded in half, and the body was inserted between the folded halves. Then the wrap was bound together, and the body was secured. The head was wrapped separately, which explains the note both in the Lazarus situation (11:44) and the separate head wrapping in the case of Jesus' grave clothes (20:6-7)" (Borchert, p. 362).

Ⓓ Jesus Is Our Substitute (11:45-57)

SUPPORTING IDEA: *Caiphas, an unlikely prophet indeed, prophesied that Jesus would die for sinners (v. 51). What a promise! What a hope! But only for those who know Jesus and trust in him.*

11:45-48. Many unbelieving Jewish religious leaders believed as a result of this dramatic miracle, but others complained to the Pharisees, who called a meeting of the Sanhedrin. Such religious upheaval could destroy the carefully protected *Pax Romana* and bring Roman armies thundering into Jerusalem. We dare not forget that happened in A.D. 70. Since John wrote this Gospel about A.D. 90, we find a fascinating irony about the way he stated their concerns.

Note there was no denial of the miracle but a clamor for some plan to cut losses and protect the religious hierarchy in the future. The faith of some was countered by the hostility of others as formal religious leaders put aside other differences to combine their opposition to this annoying prophet who opened the eyes of the blind and raised the dead.

Verse 47 contains the only mention of the Sanhedrin in this Gospel, but we find it mentioned frequently in Acts. Furthermore, this is the only place in the New Testament where we find the singular without an article, and Caiaphas seems to be just one of them, not the moderator. This leads us to conclude that this was a gathering of the council, not the formal Sanhedrin. As Morris points out:

> In convening it the chief priests apparently take the initiative. It is noteworthy that from this point on the Pharisees are not mentioned often and the opposition to Jesus is firmly in the hands of the chief priests. In all four Gospels the Pharisees are Jesus' principal opponents throughout His ministry, but in all four they are rarely mentioned in connection with the events associated with the Passion . . . It has always been the case that those whose minds are made up to oppose what Christ stands for will not be convinced by any amount of evidence. In this spirit these men recognize that the miracles have taken place, but find in this a reason for more whole-hearted

opposition, not for faith. In their hardness of heart they continue on their own chosen line and refuse to consider the evidence before their eyes (Morris, p. 565).

11:49–53. The arrogant Caiaphas made a prophecy far beyond his own understanding when he described the death of Jesus as an event in which one would die for many, particularly for the entire nation of Israel. We call this *substitutionary* (or vicarious) *atonement*. But Israel alone was not and is not the beneficiary. Jesus is our substitute as he is for all people. Unwittingly and in the providence of God, the high priest became a channel of divine revelation. Substitutionary atonement would reach beyond the Jewish nation to the "other sheep" of John 10 (Rom. 9–11).

Did Jewish law allow the murder of a person in order to benefit the state? Two possible answers emerge. First, as we know from the Book of Acts, the Sanhedrin or any of its tributaries held law and tradition in contempt when it suited their purposes. Obviously this was considered one of those emergency situations in which law made no difference. But also we have to look back to 2 Samuel 20 where another "troublemaker" was pursued and beheaded. But as John pointed out, the Caiaphas suggestion was a great deal more than that loathsome leader intended.

For centuries the hope of Israel rested not just on reclaiming the land and the temple, but on the return of **the scattered children of God.** Now, from his position on the mount of retrospect, John told his readers that Caiaphas prophesied the death of Jesus on Calvary for Jews, Gentiles, and the whole world to bring together the one flock that he had already described in chapter 10. The last week was upon them (12:1), and assassination efforts were well underway.

11:54. The public ministry had finished and Jesus isolated himself near the Judean desert, a safe haven for the fugitive he had become. We know little about the town of Ephraim, though it may be the Aphairema of First Maccabees 11:34. As Jesus told his disciples in 12:23, "The hour has come for the Son of Man to be glorified."

11:55–57. If one does not accept the suggestion that the unnamed feast of 5:1 refers to a Passover, this would be the third and last Passover of Jesus' public ministry, extending it for a period of just over two years. I have already argued, however, for a Passover recognition in 5:1, thereby extending Jesus' ministry over three years, possibly as long as three and one-half. The four Passovers mentioned by the Gospel of John include 2:13; 5:1; 6:4; and 11:55–12:1.

John noted that the visitors at the Passover **kept looking for Jesus,** presumably because of the resurrection of Lazarus. Tasker offers an interesting observation suggesting that the pilgrims "were eager to know where Jesus was, for they had the feeling that this particular Passover was likely to be memorable, if Jesus were present" (Tasker, p. 141). Conjecture, of course, but interesting. Those who thought that were certainly right, but just as certainly not in the way they expected.

Jesus is our friend, our life, our power, and our substitute. But how do we activate that now? Future hope such as that treasured by Martha is wonderful and very important, but how do we enact friendship with Jesus now? When we read a chapter like this and understand the behavior of Mary, Martha, and the disciples, how does our faith compare with theirs? The expectation of hope beyond the grave is not just some eschatological creed, but a life force that ought to engage our hearts and minds on a daily basis.

MAIN IDEA REVIEW: *Many people have wondered why the synoptic Gospels ignore the story of Lazarus. After all, Jesus performed only three resurrections (other than the resurrection of Christ) mentioned in the Gospels: the widow's son in Luke 7; Jairus's daughter in Matthew 9, Mark 5, and Luke 8; and Lazarus here in John 11. The answer has to do with the purpose of the Gospel writers. This account by John centers precisely in Jesus' claim to be the Son of God.*

III. CONCLUSION

He Took Our Poison

A story coming from the Kejave Medical Center in Kenya tells about a case involving an eight-year-old named Monica who broke her leg when falling into a pit. An older woman, Mama Njeri, happened along and climbed into the pit to help get Monica out. In the process, a dangerous black Mamba snake bit both Mama Njeri and Monica. Monica was taken to Kejave Medical Center and admitted. Mama Njeri went home, but never awoke from sleep.

The next day a perceptive missionary nurse explained Mama Njeri's death to Monica, telling her that the snake had bitten both of them, but all the snake's poison was expended on Mama Njeri; none was given to Monica. The nurse then explained that Jesus had taken the poison of Monica's sin so that she could have a new life. It was an easy choice for Monica. She then received Jesus as Savior and Lord on the spot (Swindoll, p. 541).

Jesus has taken all our poison. The poison of confusion which so clearly marked the disciples; the poison of sadness and hopelessness experienced by Mary and Martha; and the poison of the chief priests and Pharisees, who directed their murderous intent at Jesus. Caiaphas probably considered himself Jesus' worst enemy and most dangerous threat when he said the nation could be saved only if one man would die for the people. Jesus showed the way to true life by raising Lazarus and then a few weeks later, he led the way through his own death and resurrection. God used Lazarus to prove that he could take a person safely through death and back to life again. Now both Lazarus and Jesus call to us from the other side of the river, "Real life is over here."

How do we respond? Do we choose belief or unbelief? Do we put all our hope in the basket of this life, or can we invest in the real life to come? Do we see death as the end or just the beginning? A friend of the family shows us as he showed them how to move from death to life.

PRINCIPLES

- Jesus' actual presence is not essential for a miracle.
- The presence of death does not signal the absence of God.
- For Christians, physical death is not "real" death.
- Seeds may look dead, but for those who believe enough to plant them, they bring new life.

APPLICATIONS

- Believe God even when you cannot see him working.
- Recognize in Jesus God's understanding of real life.
- Shed tears for and with others who have lost loved ones.
- Let God remove the "grave clothes" of sin from your life and set you free.

IV. LIFE APPLICATION

Reduce Eye Strain

There it was right in front of me in a full-page advertisement. The bold print announced "Reduce Eye Strain." Right beneath it in large letters the marketing team had placed the words "Seeing Is Believing." And as if that were not enough, the large drawing occupying a full third of the space showed a man holding his open Bible and staring into it with a large eyepiece extended from a headband. This is apparently called MAGEYES—head-mounted, hands-free magnifiers whose dual lens prevents distortion!

The cushioned headband slips on and fits all sizes, the visor swings out of the way when not in use, and the MAGEYES motto shouts, "For all the world to see." John never saw a magnifying glass, but this ad would have made him sit up and take notice. He tried to get his readers to reduce eye strain and heart strain by recognizing that believing is seeing. But he would be in favor of any kind of dual lens that prevented theological distortion. Above all, he would love the motto of universal proclamation: "For all the world to see."

Both John and Jesus want us to take off our grave clothes and put on the MAGEYES of faith. They do not want us to live under the fear, sorrow, and deception of death. The assurance of eternal, spiritual life frees us to love God and live for him with utter abandonment, free of the worry, despair, and discouragement that bind those who do not know where they are headed.

One day the voice that called Lazarus and the power that raised Jesus from the tomb will bring us back from the dead (1 Thess. 4:16). And just as he will then call us out of our physical graves, he now calls us out of our spiritual graves to love him and serve him.

V. PRAYER

Father, thank you for our family friend who can weep with us when we grieve and still has the power to raise the dead. Amen.

VI. DEEPER DISCOVERIES

A. "Our Friend Lazarus Has Fallen Asleep" (11:11)

This exchange between Jesus and the disciples regarding Lazarus's condition helps us understand that only in early Christian theology (post-resurrection) does the concept of sleep take on the positive connotations of what it means to fall asleep in Jesus. The word *koimao* appears eighteen times in the New Testament in seven books: Matthew, Luke, John, Acts, 1 Corinthians, 1 Thessalonians, and 2 Peter. In fifteen of those eighteen appearances, the word offers a distinct euphemism—a figurative description of death. The other common New Testament word (*katheudo*) occurs sixteen times in the Gospels and four times in the Pauline epistles. Almost always it means literal death (with the single exception of Eph. 5:14).

We should note again that the noun form (*koimesis*) is found only in John 11:13. Actually, sleeping with one's fathers would be a common Old Testament designation, but that was never considered the kind of sleep out of which someone could be awakened a few days later. The disciples never quite picked up on Jesus' meaning, so he had to say to them, "Lazarus is dead."

But there is another potential problem here—the issue of soul sleep. Many people believe that dead people simply cease to exist. Since cremation was virtually unknown among early Christians, they would regularly see people (like Lazarus) in what appeared to be a state of sleep.

Tenney emphasizes how distinctly different Christian death is from what the Greeks understood:

The use of this verb as a metaphor for death appears in the Greek classics, in the HELLEX, in the vernacular of the papyri, and in the patristic writings. In the light of such passages as Luke 23:43—the promise to the dying thief, "I tell you the truth, today you will be with me in paradise"—and Paul's declaration of his longing to "depart and be with Christ, which is better by far" (Phil. 1:23), death for the child of God could hardly be an unconscious state. From Jesus' standpoint, Lazarus' death was comparable to a nap, which cut off consciousness of this world temporarily but did not mean a permanent severance (Tenney, *EBC*, p. 117).

B. "The Resurrection and the Life" (11:25–26)

These are certainly among the most important verses in the Bible. We memorize them and urge our children to grasp their meaning. Will people rise again "at the last day" as Martha believed? Indeed they will, but not in the sense or for the reason that she implied. The coming of Jesus brought a new order to things, and the old expectations have passed away because the Resurrection and Life himself walked the earth.

We cannot miss the close connection between life and faith in these verses. The Greek word here is *anastasis* and its verb form is *anhistemi*— words that literally mean "to stand up again." In the Septuagint the word describes Elijah bringing back the son of the widow at Zarephath (1 Kgs. 17) and also the physical acceptance of Enoch into heaven (Gen. 5:24). But *anastasis* is not a common word in this Gospel, occurring only in 5:29 and twice here. *Anhistemi* occurs only in 6:39–40,44,54 apart from this chapter.

Morris quotes Calvin: "First, He calls Himself the resurrection; for restoration from death to life precedes the state of life. But the whole human race is plunged in death. Therefore, no man will possess life unless he is first risen from the dead. Hence, Christ teaches that He is the beginning of life. Afterwards He adds that the continuity of life is also the work of His grace" (Morris, p. 550). Faith (*pistis*) and life (*zoe*) are common Johannine terms, and the New Testament links both of those concepts with resurrection.

What we see in this chapter is a small precursor of what John will show us toward the end of his book—the resurrection of Jesus Christ. It may be important for us to recognize once again that Lazarus did not gain immortality through this miracle. We have no idea how much longer he lived, but eventually he died. Of those who have participated in earth-bound humanity, only Jesus enjoys eternal immortality—a gift Lazarus will celebrate along with us some day. Paul made sure Timothy understood this distinction when he wrote of Jesus, "God, the blessed and only Ruler, the King of kings and Lord of lords, who alone is immortal and who lives in unapproachable light, whom no one has seen or can see. To him be honor and might forever. Amen" (1 Tim. 6:15).

C. "Scattered Children of God" (11:52)

Many interpreters have seen in this phrase only a reference to Jews of the first-century Diaspora, but the universality of John's Gospel certainly appeals for more than that. Verses 52–53 are John's hermeneutic on the Caiaphas comment. We should be sure by now that he will not waste the opportunity to get in another "whosoever."

According to Borchert, "However the Jews might have argued their case, the evangelist saw something quite different involved here. John sensed that God was at work in the words of the high priest, in spite of himself. If any human words in history could be described as an *ex cathedra statement* (words coming from the throne or 'seat' and representing the mind of God), it was these words of Caiaphas, who John indicated 'did not say this on his own' (11:51). It was for the evangelist a prophetic act, but it was laced with irony because Caiaphas did not realize the vast import of his own words" (Borchert, p. 365).

John had already talked about those who rejected Christ and those who believed in order "to become children of God—children born not of natural descent, nor of human decision or a husband's will, but born of God" (1:12–13). Now he tells us, as Acts will remind us and we will read repeatedly throughout the Pauline epistles, that these children will come from all over and will be gathered by God from every nation (Jas. 1:1; 1 Pet. 1:1–2).

VII. TEACHING OUTLINE

A. INTRODUCTION

1. Lead Story: Life After Death

2. Context: Spinning from the wonderful story of the Good Shepherd in chapter 10 and bouncing from the healing of the blind man in chapter 9, John came to one of his big narratives—the resurrection of Lazarus. How could he keep from shouting when he wrote verses 25–26 or from smiling when he recited Jesus' words, "Did I not tell you that if you believed, you would see the glory of God?" (11:40). There are dark days ahead but John is not quite ready to go there. In fact, he is still climbing the mountain that will take us all the way through chapter 17. Then he will take us down the mountain and across the Kidron Valley.

3. Transition: The end of chapter 11 serves as a launching ramp for chapter 12. It prepares us for the anointing about which John will

next write. The two references to the Passover in 11:55 link distinctly to the first verse of chapter 12.

B. COMMENTARY

1. Jesus Is Our Friend (11:1–16)
   a. As he was to the family of Lazarus (11:1–6)
   b. As he was to the disciples (11:7–16)
2. Jesus Is Our Life (11:17–37)
   a. As he was to Martha (11:17–27)
   b. As he was to Mary (11:28–37)
3. Jesus Is Our Power (11:38–44)
   a. As seen in his authority (11:38–40)
   b. As seen in his prayer (11:41–42)
   c. As seen in his miracle (11:43–44)
4. Jesus Is Our Substitute (11:45–57)
   a. As he was for Israel (11:45–50)
   b. As he is for all people (11:51–57)

C. CONCLUSION: REDUCE EYE STRAIN

VIII. ISSUES FOR DISCUSSION

1. Consider your friendship with Jesus. Do you identify more with Martha or with Mary?
2. Explain substitutionary atonement in your own words.
3. If you have not done so previously, memorize John 11:25–26.

John 12

God's Grand Entrance

I. INTRODUCTION
The Crises of the Christ

II. COMMENTARY
A verse-by-verse explanation of the chapter.

III. CONCLUSION
An Impressive Appearance

An overview of the principles and applications from the chapter.

IV. LIFE APPLICATION
Art Critics

Melding the chapter to life.

V. PRAYER
Tying the chapter to life with God.

VI. DEEPER DISCOVERIES
Historical, geographical, and grammatical enrichment of the commentary.

VII. TEACHING OUTLINE
Suggested step-by-step group study of the chapter.

VIII. ISSUES FOR DISCUSSION
Zeroing the chapter in on daily life.

Quote

"All glory, laud, and honor to Thee, Redeemer, King, to whom the lips of children make sweet hosannas ring: Thou art the King of Israel, Thou David's royal son, who in the Lord's name cometh, the King and Blessed One!"

Theodolph of Orleans

PERSONAL PROFILE: JUDAS ISCARIOT

- Iscariot is commonly thought to mean "a man of Kerioth"
- Treasurer of the disciples
- Betrayer of Jesus
- Committed suicide in remorse after Jesus was captured
- Always mentioned last among the apostles

John 12

IN A NUTSHELL

*J*ohn 12:1 tells us we have come to the last week of the Lord's life before the cross. John has spent nearly half of his Gospel narrative on events of that crisis-filled week, and we now enter the passion story. Through the chapter we will see our Lord facing several crises—crises of values, confrontation, timing, and faith.

God's Grand Entrance

I. INTRODUCTION

The Crises of the Christ

Published in 1903, G. Campbell Morgan's book, *The Crises of the Christ,* stands as a classic handbook on Christology a century later. He covers events from Jesus' birth to his ascension, emphasizing the effects of the Lord's ministry on all who put their trust in him.

We find several of those crises in this chapter. The last two paragraphs of chapter 11 introduce chapter 12, and we have already learned that the public ministry has ended (11:54). Jesus and the disciples have settled down in the small village of Ephraim. John marked the epics of Christ's life by Passovers so he mentioned another one here and emphasized the hostility against the Lord. Jesus was now a public enemy, a hunted man, and the chief priests and Pharisees put out an order for his arrest.

II. COMMENTARY

God's Grand Entrance

> **MAIN IDEA:** *Amid the swirl of relationships in this chapter, we learn that the central crisis is one of faith. John has called us to faith in the prophets, faith in the Father, and faith in the message of Jesus.*

A Crisis of Values (12:1–11)

> **SUPPORTING IDEA:** *John began with the account of Mary anointing Jesus' feet with expensive perfume. As she offered this generous gift, Judas spoke his first recorded words in the Gospels: "Why wasn't this perfume sold and the money given to the poor?" (v. 5). At issue here was a contrast of values. Judas spoke not out of concern for the poor but as a tight-fisted treasurer of the disciples.*

12:1–3. Mary's prophetic act regarding Christ's death and burial has already been mentioned in 11:2. Here we learn that her behavior was not a donation but an investment, rather like the famous story "The Gift of the Magi." John tells us that **the house was filled with the fragrance of the perfume.** Of course. It remained in Mary's hair throughout the day. This was an act of worship also recorded in Matthew 26 and Mark 14, but certainly not the same event as the record in Luke 7, though some of the patterns are similar.

Some people struggle with the comment in both Matthew and Mark that the dinner was held in the house of Simon the Leper, but that problem dissolves when we read carefully the text, noting that the location of the dinner was not specified. In fact, the phraseology **a dinner was given** tends to make us think it was in some home in Bethany other than that of Mary, Martha, and Lazarus.

The **expensive perfume** is identified as approximately half a liter and it was pure (*pistikos*), a word not found elsewhere in the Gospels. Morris describes the event in context: "The use of unguents was very common in the first century especially on festive occasions. But the oil was normally poured on the head. The peculiar thing about this anointing was that Mary poured it on the feet of the Lord. This is probably to be taken as an act of utter humility. Mary is taking the lowliest possible place . . . The act is all the more striking in that a Jewish lady never unbound her hair in public" (Morris, pp. 576–77).

12:4–6. How altruistic Judas seems in this statement—a year's wages was an enormous amount of money to be used in what seemed like a frivolous way. Soon he would sell Jesus for 120 denarii, just scarcely half the 300 denarii reflected in a year's wages. Assuming Judas was linking the value of the perfume with the money that could have been given to the poor, we might assume a modern equivalent value of something in the neighborhood of ten thousand dollars. If that figure is even close, we get some understanding of the sacrifice involved as Mary may have used her entire life savings for this anointing.

John developed a biography of Judas throughout this book, and he wanted his readers to understand the motive behind the intervention—greed and robbery, not concern for the poor. This is the only place in the four Gospels where Judas shows himself, but John had been building the evidence already which, when complete, would look something like this:

- He was a devil (6:70–71).
- He was an outwardly moral person (12:5).
- He was a selfish thief (12:6).
- He was a hypocrite (13:18).
- He was the son of perdition (17:12).

12:7–8. Some interpreters find the grammar of this text difficult, pondering what Jesus meant when he said, **it was intended that she should save this perfume for the day of my burial.** Obviously she had not saved it for that specific day, but within the boundaries of the last week the inevitable "hour" had come. Certainly no one else in the room besides Jesus understood that he referred to the cross, so Mary (like Caiaphas in chap. 11) projected more truth than she knew.

A loose paraphrase capturing Jesus' intended meaning might go like this: "Leave her alone. In God's great plan, suffering and death for sin has already begun and this woman shows her love for me at a time when I am already headed for the tomb. As for the poor, taking care of them is a good and biblical act of righteousness and you should do it. However, you'll have ample opportunity to demonstrate that concern; I'll be gone within a week."

12:9–11. Notice how easily theology and politics merge. Rather than being a hero or a medical phenomenon, Lazarus had become a threat to unbelievers because of his life and witness. The evidence of Christ's truth was inescapable and indestructible. Many people believed in Jesus because of Lazarus. But not the religious leaders, whose anger and hatred increased in spite of the undeniable evidence of bodily resurrection. Once again, John seems to use the term **Jews** without any negative connotation. We have to assume that the faith identified at the end of verse 11 is genuine saving faith. The expression **going over to Jesus** assumes a conscious decision to leave the views and behavior of the chief priests and identify themselves with the Lord.

B Crisis of Confrontation (12:12–19)

SUPPORTING IDEA: *Quickly the crisis of values gave way to a crisis of confrontation, the first truly public presentation of the Messiah to Israel. Jesus initiated the event, probably to stir good people to action, to fulfill Scripture, and to offer himself as the Passover lamb.*

12:12–13. This was indeed an "hour of decision" for the crowd. In this event, recorded also in Matthew 21, Mark 11, and Luke 19, Jesus allowed himself to be recognized as **the King of Israel**. The word **hosanna** means "save now," likely a plea for action against the authority of Rome. The first confrontation was a confrontation of choice. The blessing of verse 13 comes from Psalm 118:25,26 and John's later citation in verse 15 from Zechariah 9:9.

Josephus estimated the Passover crowd at 2,700,000, suggesting they would have been driving over a quarter of a million lambs into Jerusalem for this Passover feast. The palm branch had become a national symbol during the time of the Maccabees, and the nationalism and liberation of this occasion would certainly fit the scene.

Carson sums it up: "The crowds do not simply pronounce a blessing in the name of the Lord on the one who comes, but pronounce a blessing on the one who comes in the name of the Lord. The next line shows that this is the way the crowd understands their own words: *blessed is the king of Israel* is not a quotation from Psalm 118, but messianic identification of 'he who comes in the name of the Lord'" (Carson, p. 432).

12:14–15. The synoptic Gospels make a great deal more of the donkey than does John, and herein we see his purpose and focus once again. As to the quote from Zechariah 9:9, we should not be thrown off balance by the fact that it is not an exact citation. The phrase **Daughter of Zion** is a personification of Jerusalem, and in a broader sense the nation of Israel. The general spirit of the coming of the gentle king certainly captures the essence of the Zechariah passage. Lewis remarks, "The Zechariah prophecy, though known to be messianic, linked Messiahship to peaceful and non-political ideals, and Jesus only chose to make such a public 'statement' when His rejection by the Jewish rulers was irreversible and His death very near" (Lewis, p. 169).

The key to much of this type of New Testament text is the phrase that appears at the end of verse 14—**as it is written.** Everything about Jesus' life and ministry fulfilled Old Testament promises. This triumphal-entry event forced people to make a decision, fulfilled what the Bible promised, and offered the Passover Lamb—the only lamb in the city that day riding on a ceremonial donkey.

12:16. The disciples still had not grasped Christ's nature and work, even as long as they had been with him. Writing many years after these events, John admitted that only after the glorification of Jesus (probably a reference to both resurrection and ascension) did they really grasp what had happened to them. Indeed, we find them trying to recreate this kind of event in Acts 1 when they asked, "Lord, are you at this time going to restore the kingdom to Israel?" (Acts 1:6). Like the disciples, our faith may have slow formation, but it should lead us to rock-solid commitment.

The inscription on the fly leaf of a Bible found in a tin box under the cornerstone of Wellesley College reads, "This building is humbly dedicated to our heavenly Father with the hope and prayer that He will always be first in everything in the institution—that His Word may be faithfully taught here, and that He will use it as a means of leading precious souls to the Lord Jesus Christ." Whether that mission still guides the leaders of Wellesley is another matter. What we do know is that it should serve as the lodestar for every evangelical church, college, and mission board.

12:17–19. The confrontation and misunderstanding led to hostility. Actually, we find nothing new here. The common people, still affected by the Lazarus event, came out to see Jesus. The religious leaders rejected him with increasing malice. Their exaggeration makes us wish they had spoken the truth, but public miracles do not always produce personal faith.

John once again applied a touch of irony in reciting the last phrase of our passage: **Look how the whole world has gone after him!** Again like Caiaphas, we see a prophecy unintended by the prophet. Surely John wanted his readers to grasp his use of the word *kosmos* to include many beyond the numerous pilgrims crowding Jerusalem for the Passover feast. For him the word describes lost and blind people on a planet in rebellion against its Maker. And if we wonder how far John was willing to push his point, do not go away—Gentiles were right outside the door.

Ⓒ Crisis of Timing (12:20–36)

SUPPORTING IDEA: *Once again our Lord raised the issue of the hour. But this time, it had come; the time of death had arrived. How should we pray in crisis, when our souls are troubled? Look at verse 28: "Father, glorify your name." The dying son of man "will draw all men" to himself (v. 32). The true gospel knows no boundaries of race, color, or culture.*

12:20–22. Some interpreters have speculated that Philip may have been a Greek since he had a Greek name, but that cannot be confirmed. Furthermore, we are not surprised that some Greeks came to worship at the Passover. As they approached Philip, he chose to contact Andrew; and they came to the Lord together. Not until we open the Book of Acts do we really grasp the significance of how Gentile salvation will glorify Jesus and fulfill God's plan. But at various places in the Gospels we find the foundations of this grand plan of the evangel for all nations, and this is one of them. Did Jesus interview the Greeks? We do not know, because the mention of Gentile visitors provoked the announcement of verse 23.

12:23–24. Up to now **the hour** has always been coming, but now it **has come**. Rejection by the Jews coupled with interest by Gentiles evoked the parable of the seed. Only when the kernel of wheat dies does new life come, and that is what will happen to Jesus. Like seed, he will be planted in the ground; and like that seed, he will give birth to a glorious new plant. Indeed, it will produce not only a plant but **many seeds**.

12:25–26. Not only does this principle of dying and rising apply to Christ; it becomes a whole mindset for his followers. As Tasker observes:

> The grain of wheat must fall into the ground and die that it may produce fruit. Even so, eternal life for the many comes through the sacrifice of the One. And the same providential law is applicable to each individual believer. He must disown the imperious authority of his selfish ego, if he is to live the life of an integrated person; he must abandon ruthlessly a self-centered existence lived in conformity to the standards of the world, if the higher element in him is to be preserved unto life eternal. This he cannot do by himself. He must have an example to follow. Jesus is that example. By looking to Him, a life of service to Him is made possible; and that life of service constitutes the "dying in order to live" which is the theme of Jesus' teaching in this passage (Tasker, p. 148).

The word **life** is mentioned three times in verse 25. But the first two translate *psuche* and the third *zoe,* an obvious difference referring to life in this world (physical) and life eternal. But what does verse 25 mean? Presumably this call to obedience is predicated on the demonstration that Christ would do anything the Father asked. Those who wanted to follow him (whether disciples or inquiring Greeks) had to follow that same pattern.

12:27–29. Along with the time of dying, there is also a time for judgment. We see the emotional trauma in Jesus' heart as he pondered the cross, refused to retreat, and asked that God would be glorified through his death. Then, for the third time in Scripture (first the baptism, then the transfiguration), the heavenly Father spoke **from heaven** with a promise to do precisely what Jesus has asked.

Interpretations differ on what the crowd heard. Jesus' prayer had already been answered, since the Father had already **glorified** his name. How? Surely the immediate reference aims at the life and work of Jesus up to that point and the immediate projection at the death, resurrection, and ascension. But we do not stretch the text to see the sweeping hand of God's glorification going all the way back to creation and all the way forward through the ages to the gathering of the church.

Westcott says, "This glorification was not a mere repetition but a corresponding manifestation of the Father's glory. Glorification during the limited, earthly ministry to Israel was followed by a glorification answering to the proclamation of the universal Gospel to the world" (Westcott, p. 182).

12:30–33. Jesus told them plainly that judgment (*krisis*) was coming, and deliverance from that judgment was faith in his work on the cross. Once again the reference to Jesus being **lifted up** centers not on exaltation but death. The cross forms the centerpiece of the gospel. And verse 33 shows us that John had no intention of drawing his readers' focus anywhere else. Here we must go a bit further in our understanding of verse 32: **But I, when I am lifted up from the earth, will draw all men to myself.** Certainly the Lord had no intention that we should read into this text the idea that everyone would be saved because we know only believers find eternal life.

Morris takes this view on the subject: "We must take the expression accordingly to mean that all those who are to be drawn will be drawn. That is to say, Christ is not affirming that the whole world would be saved. He is affirming that all who are to be saved will be saved in this way. And he is speaking of a universal rather than a narrowly nationalistic religion. The death of Christ would mean the end of particularism. By virtue of that death 'all men' and not the Jews alone would be drawn. And they would be drawn only by virtue of that death" (Morris, pp. 598–99).

12:34. This business of being lifted up did not fit with the first-century idea of the Messiah who **will remain forever.** How does this "Son of Man" prophecy fit in with our religion? Jesus favorite name for himself threw the crowd into consternation. How could a dead prophet throw out the Romans and restore the kingdom? Indeed, though the title occurs sixty-nine times in the Synoptics and twelve times in John, they could not grasp the connection. They asked, **Who is this "Son of Man"?** Intellectual and religious confusion had set in.

12:35–36. John's key word *life* in just a few verses now changes to **light**— hardly a new concept since John introduced it early in the first chapter. He expected his readers would understand that Jesus was talking about himself as the light of the world. But the immediate crowds on that day still struggled. Surely the disciples would have remembered the moments immediately following their receipt of the news about Lazarus's death. On that occasion Jesus told them "a man who walks by day will not stumble, for he sees by this world's light" (11:9).

Again, he warned that the light would soon be gone, but individual torches can be lit from the original flame and go on burning in the darkness, even when that flame is withdrawn.

Morris notes an interesting grammatical switch in this text. The words **put your trust in** at the beginning of verse 36 appear in the present tense, emphasizing continuous belief but **become** late in the verse occurs in the aorist, pointing "to a once-for-all becoming sons of light. While faith is an activity to be practiced without ceasing, one does not become a son of light by degrees. One passes decisively out of death into life (5:24)" (Morris, p. 601).

How do we pray when our souls are troubled and crisis threatens to crush our lives? Surely the appeal of the Lord to glorify the Father offers an example for us.

D Crisis of Faith (12:37–50)

> **SUPPORTING IDEA:** *John called us to faith in the prophets, faith in the Father, and faith in the message of Jesus. As we have noted repeatedly, faith leading to eternal life is the central focus of this Gospel.*

12:37–41. After dealing with life and death, chapter 12 of John ends on a note of faith, with the first reference to faith in the prophets. Notice the phases of unbelief in this section. In verse 37, **they . . . would not believe**; in verse 39, **they could not believe**; and in verse 42, **they would not confess their faith.** This unbelief, John tells us, fulfilled Isaiah's prophecy (Isa. 53:1). They had denied for so long that God closed their eyes and hearts. This is another citation from Isaiah—Isaiah 6:10. Whether or not Isaiah knew it at the time, John assures us he saw the glory of Messiah Jesus and spoke about him often in his writings.

As we read verse 40, we are reminded of God's dealings with Pharaoh centuries before. Indeed, Isaiah himself begged God to show his merciful side to the people to whom he sent his prophet (Isa. 63:15–19). But how can we understand the human responsibility of those whose eyes had been blinded and whose hearts had been deadened by God himself? Carson has an interesting observation on this question:

> If a superficial reading finds this harsh, manipulative, even robotic, four things must constantly be borne in mind: (1) God's sovereignty in these matters is *never* pitted against human responsibility (cf. notes on v. 38); (2) God's judicial hardening is not presented as the capricious manipulation of an arbitrary potentate cursing morally neutral or even morally pure beings, but as a holy condemnation of a guilty people who are condemned to do and be what they themselves have chosen; (3) God's sovereignty in these matters can also be a cause for hope, for if he is not *sovereign* in these areas there is little point in petitioning him for help, while if he is sovereign the anguished pleas of the prophet (Is. 63:15–19)—and of believers throughout the history of the church—makes sense; (4) God's sovereign hardening of the people in Isaiah's day, his commissioning of Isaiah to apparently fruitless ministry, is a stage in God's "strange work" (Is. 28:21–22) that brings God's ultimate redemptive purposes to pass. Paul argues rather similarly in Romans 9:22–33 (Carson, pp. 448–49).

12:42–46. The second element of faith in this section is faith in the Father. How sad that even those leaders who wanted to trust in Jesus felt they could not—a fear not unlike that of many people today. Even those who escaped the divine blinding insisted on being at best "closet Christians" not for fear of their lives, but because **they loved praise from men more than praise from God.**

How are we to take the effectiveness of their faith? Westcott says, "This complete intellectual faith (so to speak) is really the climate of unbelief. The conviction found no expression in life . . . the belief only lacked confession, but this defect was fatal" (Westcott, pp. 185–86). I disagree with Tenney, especially in the light of the three verses which follow in which John seems to indicate that Jesus equated the frightened faith of the leaders with the genuine faith of salvation. This would also be a great representation of the remnant idea—God preserving a small number of trusting people even in the midst of great public opposition.

In verses 44 to 46, Jesus offered a mini-resumé, emphasizing again that he was God, light, and the Savior. Did these people at the feast come to see the Lord Most High? They needed only to look and listen to the message of his Son. No one must remain in darkness, for the **light** has come to dispel it. As Boice points out, "When the Lord Jesus Christ came into the world and shone as God's light, he exposed the darkness of the world as no one had ever done previously. And of course, those who had a vested interest in things as they were hated him for exposing their darkness and eventually had him crucified" (Boice, p. 389).

12:47–50. What will be the basis for judgment of the final day? That is the issue as this chapter comes to a close with a focus on faith. The answer, centers not in the person of the Lord Jesus; he came into the world to save it, not to judge it. The focus of judgment will be the actual Word of God. God's words through Jesus as well as through the prophets and other biblical writers form the final authority for obedience. They are the message of faith. God will ultimately judge people by how they received and responded to what the Bible says. This is not a common invitation in John 12, but a command to turn away from darkness to light and from death to life.

> **MAIN IDEA REVIEW:** *Amid the swirl of relationships in this chapter, we learn that the central crisis is one of faith. John has called us to faith in the prophets, faith in the Father, and faith in the message of Jesus. Faith leads to eternal life—and that is what this Gospel is all about.*

III. CONCLUSION

An Impressive Appearance

Grand entrances are a part of life and have been for almost all recorded history. During the fifteen years we lived in Dallas, we went often to the Morton-Myerson Symphony Hall for performances by the orchestra or other visiting groups. The protocol had become ritual. After the orchestra is seated, the concert master enters amid great applause and goes through the tuning process. That achieved, he takes his seat (with a minor flourish) and a hush settles over the house for just a moment. Then from the wings the conductor emerges to greater applause, smiles at the audience as he mounts the platform and the concert begins. Pretty tame stuff by standards of the Oscar or Emmy shows, but nevertheless intended to impress.

We have no exact record of how the Jews expected the Messiah to appear, but a baby in a manger and a prophet on a donkey did not seem to measure up to what they thought God might produce. Yet that was precisely the point of both entrances as God introduced his Son with dignity, gentleness, and humility.

That day so carefully recorded in all four Gospels presented a distinct "hour of decision" for the multitudes in Jerusalem at the Passover. The first sixteen verses described the entrance; the next twenty verses described the debate; and the last fourteen verses indicated the response. The vast majority of people missed their hour of decision or used it to decide against trusting the Messiah when he presented himself. Yet how many still acknowledge his coming today. Indeed, just through one radio broadcast—Billy Graham's "Hour of Decision"—certainly millions have come to faith in Christ.

I am told that at the funeral for Winston Churchill a bugler played "Taps" in the echoing chambers of St. Paul's church. As those mournful notes signaled the passing of one of the world's great leaders, people could ponder again the power of death. But as the last notes of taps faded out through the chambers of the building, that same bugler surprised the mourners by beginning reveille. From the silence of his coffin, Churchill still signaled that death is the gateway to life.

That is John's message as well, and we shall see it unfolding with even greater impact in the chapters before us.

PRINCIPLES

- The secret of witness is first to be with Jesus, then to be like him.
- Only the seed willing to die can live and grow.
- The birth, life, and death of Jesus are prophesied in the Old Testament.
- Faith in Jesus is faith in God.

APPLICATIONS

- Care about the poor, but not for selfish motives.
- "Put your trust in the light while you have it."
- Learn how to pray when your soul is troubled.
- Remember that our choice is simple—faith or judgment.

IV. LIFE APPLICATION

Art Critics

There is an old story about tourists wandering through a European art museum casually making critical comments about some of the paintings they disliked or did not understand. Finally, one of the attendants, unable to put up with their discourteous behavior any longer, responded, "The paintings in this museum are not on trial; only the spectators are."

So it is with the Word of God. For two thousand years religious leaders and atheists, wealthy and poor, brilliant and ignorant, have critiqued God's Word, but in the final analysis as John so aptly said, "It will judge us all."

V. PRAYER

Father, thank you for this warm record of Mary's personal worship and the public presentation of our Lord's kingship. Deliver us from the fear of the non-confessing leaders. May we live our lives in the brightness of your light through Jesus. Amen.

VI. DEEPER DISCOVERIES

A. Hating Life (12:25)

This verse centers in the New Testament truth that faith culminates in obedience—a willingness to do anything God asks. People who love their lives to the exclusion of loving God, who set up an idolatry of possessions and personality, will hurl themselves toward an eternity without God.

True believers, on the other hand, hate their own lives. This distinction is a bit more difficult to grasp. It is based upon a Hebrew way of thinking that emphasizes priority rather than forcing a choice of either loving or hating. A person who minimizes the importance of life in this world denies himself and carries the cross (Mark 8:34–35). I like the way Morris puts it: "John means us to understand that loving life is a self-defeating process. It destroys the very life it seeks to retain . . . The man who loves his life is destroying it right now. [Hating] points to the attitude that sets no store by this life in itself. The man whose priorities are right has such an attitude of love for the things of God that it makes all interest in the affairs of this life appear by comparison as hatred" (Morris, pp. 593–94).

B. "Father, Glorify Your Name!" (12:28)

This concept of glory that appears also in verse 41 will come to our attention again in chapter 17, since it is a strong description of the pre-incarnate and post-incarnate Christ. The noun (*doxa*) is used 19 times in John's Gospel, 36 times in other Johannine writings, and a total of 166 times in the New Testament. When applied strictly to the glory of God, it appears some 280 times in the Septuagint.

In the teaching of Jesus, the ultimate concern is the glorification of the Father, though he later prayed to be glorified with the glory he had experienced earlier (John 17:1–4). Glory originates with the Father and shines through the Son upon believers. We will also eventually share the glory of God in heaven (Rom. 8:17–18,21). In fact, glory is part of our everyday lives. In answering its initial question, "What is the chief end of man?" the Westminster Shorter Catechism replies, "To glorify God and to enjoy him forever."

"The glory of the Lord refers to His nature and holiness as manifested to His creatures, humans and angels, both of whom can share in that glory. Even in the incarnation, Jesus shared in the Father's glory and especially manifested His grace and truth (Jn 1:14; see 17:5). The greatest manifestation of God's glory happened at the cross (Jn 13:31–32; the related verb *doxazo* [glorify] is used here), for here God's greatest work occurred. We praise God when we give Him glory, acknowledging that He is of greatest importance to us. Thus, *doxa* may often mean praise. John 12 contains a word play with these two meanings" (Blackaby, p. 38).

C. Prince of This World (12:31)

The judgment narrative hangs heavily over this chapter with this strong segment in verses 30–33 and the emphasis of the last paragraph (vv. 47–50). No one doubts that the reference is to Satan, since we see it again in 14:30 and 16:11 (as well as 2 Cor. 4:4; Eph. 2:2; 6:12). The word for prince is *archon* commonly translated "ruler," though the translation "prince" certainly does the job. The cross represents the defeat of Satan, although it appears to many as his victory.

VII. TEACHING OUTLINE

A. INTRODUCTION

1. Lead Story: The Crises of the Christ
2. Context: We now enter the last week of the life of Christ. John purposefully gives nearly half his book to thirty-three and one-half years and the other half to one week.
3. Transition: The Passover citations carry us through this chapter quite comfortably and, one assumes, with definitive literary intent. In 11:55 John tells us "it was almost time for the Jewish Passover." As chapter 12 opens, we learn it is "six days before the Passover." And at the beginning of chapter 13 we read, "it was just before the Passover Feast." We have noted that John is considerably less interested in chronology than other Bible writers, but here he seemed to make a special point of how he would emphasize the last week of Jesus' life.

B. COMMENTARY

1. Crisis of Values (12:1–11)
    a. Human values (12:1–3)
    b. Economic values (12:4–8)
    c. Political values (12:9–11)
2. Crisis of Confrontation (12:12–19)
    a. Misunderstanding (12:12–16)
    b. Hostility (12:17–19)

3. Crisis of Timing (12:20–36)
    a. Time for dying (12:20–26)
    b. Time for judgment (12:27–34)
    c. Time for trust (12:35–36)
4. Crisis of Faith (12:37–50)
    a. Faith in the prophets (12:37–41)
    b. Faith in the Father (12:42–46)
    c. Faith in the message (12:47–50)

C. CONCLUSION: ART CRITICS

VIII. ISSUES FOR DISCUSSION

1. In what ways do you sincerely help the poor?
2. How do you put into practice the Lord's words telling us we need to hate our lives in this world so we can keep them for eternal life?
3. How do we avoid the problems of the Jewish leaders who would not confess their faith because they were afraid of public consequences?

John 13

Loving to the Limit

"*I* think that love is the only spiritual power that can overcome the self-centeredness that is inherent in being alive. Love is the thing that makes life possible or, indeed, tolerable."

Arnold Toynbee

John 13

IN A NUTSHELL

*T*he last part of John 13:1 could be translated "to the limit," but the NIV captures well the intent of John's words—Jesus loved his disciples to "the full extent." Two of this Gospel's key words appear twice in the first verse of this chapter. "Love" is one of John's central themes, and "world" appears 185 times in the New Testament, 105 of them in John's writings.

Loving to the Limit

I. INTRODUCTION

Who Can Pay?

*I*n his helpful commentary that I have cited repeatedly in this study, James M. Boice tells a story which he heard from the popular evangelist, Harry Ironside. I have paraphrased it for our purposes here. It comes from the reign of Czar Nicholas I of Russia who had assigned a young soldier to a military border fortress and put him in charge of money to pay the soldiers.

As the story unfolds, the young man gambled away all his own money and a significant amount of government funds. One day he heard an official was coming to inspect the books, and he knew he was in serious trouble. He totaled the amount he owed and wrote on the page for examination in large letters, "A GREAT DEBT; WHO CAN PAY?" He could not face the terrible dishonor the next day held, so he determined to kill himself at midnight.

Nicholas had acquired the habit of putting on the uniform of a common soldier in visiting his troops. He did this that night, particularly looking for the young friend he had appointed. He came to the barracks shortly before midnight and saw the light on and the door open. He found the young officer asleep, looked at the books, and read the note. In Ironside's words, "Moved by generous impulse, the Czar leaned over, picked up the pen that had fallen from the hand of the sleeping officer, wrote just one word, and tiptoed out."

The man slept well past midnight, suddenly jerked awake, and reached for his revolver. As he did so, he caught sight of the note—"A GREAT DEBT; WHO CAN PAY?"—and under it he saw the one word that had not been there before: "Nicholas." He rushed to the files to find the signature of the Czar and compared it with the signature on his note. It was genuine. He said to himself, "The Czar has been here tonight and knows all my guilt; yet he has undertaken to pay my debt; I need not die."

II. COMMENTARY

Loving to the Limit

MAIN IDEA: *Like us, the disciples lived in a society that had rebelled against God. Like us, they learned more quickly from modeling and demonstration than by being told what was right. So on that final night before his death, Jesus exemplified love, explained it, and then exhorted his disciples to follow his example. How patient he was with Judas, how humble with these proud disciples! In contrast, Peter acted too "spiritual" to allow the Lord to wash his feet, but not too spiritual to command the Son of God!*

A Love Exemplified (13:1–5)

SUPPORTING IDEA: *Jesus had demonstrated his love throughout the Gospels and especially in the Gospel of John. Now we see his love in his patience with Judas and his service to the disciples.*

13:1. We have talked often about key words in John's Gospel. The thirteenth chapter opens with three of them appearing in the first verse. **The time had come**, and Jesus would soon leave **this world**. The word *kosmos* appears 185 times in the New Testament; 8 times in Matthew; 3 times in Mark, 3 in Luke; but 78 in the Gospel of John. And if we add John's epistles and Revelation, 105 of the 185 New Testament uses come from John's pen. The other two key words are **time** and **love**. We take our title from the latter part of this verse where **full extent** translates the Greek word *eistelos* that means "to the limit."

Some interpreters have noted a change in John's vocabulary beginning with this chapter. The *life* and *light* words that dominated the first half of the Gospel appear in some form a total of 82 times in chapters 1 through 12. But in chapters 13 to 17, *life* words occur only six times and *light* words not at all. The key word for the next five chapters will be *agape* (love).

13:2. Judas typifies a society in rebellion against God, but the Lord's treatment also demonstrates God's grace and compassion with that society. Though the disciples never grasped Judas' true nature until after the betrayal in the garden, Jesus knew it from the beginning. Yet he gave Judas every opportunity to turn from his wicked ways, repent, and follow his Lord.

John pulled no punches in his description of the betrayer and his evil master. In a few more verses (v. 27) we read that "Satan entered into him." But even at the beginning of the meal the concept of betrayal had already been thrown (*ballo*) into Judas's mind. There is some grammatical argument over the text, but the plain intent indicates a willing perpetrator whose assassination plot originated with supernatural sources.

13:3–5. Verse 3 reminds us that Jesus was the omnipotent God. Rather than zapping Judas immediately, he allowed the full scenario to play out as the errant disciple made choice after choice leading to his ultimate suicide.

Some interpreters take these words symbolically, making the water equal to the Word, the towel demonstrating righteousness, and so forth. That hardly seems necessary in light of the culture of the first century. Luke 22 tells us about this event of physical humbling in light of the arrogant attitude still maintained by the disciples after the night of the crucifixion. An old proverb says, "Actions speak louder than words," and the Lord's willingness to wash the feet of his disciples, even Judas's, reflects servant leadership at its best.

People who are familiar with first-century culture will immediately recognize how socially inappropriate this behavior was. Never in Jewish, Greek, or Roman society would a superior wash the feet of inferiors. As Carson observes, "The reluctance of Jesus' disciples to volunteer for such a task is, to say the least, culturally understandable; their shock at his volunteering is not merely the result of being shame-faced, it is their response to finding their sense of the fitness of things shattered. But here Jesus reverses normal roles. His act of humility is as unnecessary as it is stunning, and is simultaneously a display of love (v. 1), a symbol of saving cleansing (vv. 6–9), and a model of Christian conduct (vv. 12–17)" (Carson, pp. 462–63).

In the brilliant *kenosis* passage of Philippians 2, we read about the condescension of Christ "who, being in very nature God, did not consider equality with God something to be grasped, but made himself nothing, taking the very nature of a servant, being made in human likeness" (Phil. 2:6–7). The Philippians passage speaks about the human nature of the Savior, but here we see it in action.

𝔹 Love Explained (13:6–11)

> **SUPPORTING IDEA:** *Love is not an emotion as much as it is an attitude, an attitude that results in action.*

13:6–7. Little discussions with Peter fill the synoptic Gospels, and John enjoys recording them as well. Shocked by the cultural reversal as he literally looked down at his Lord, Peter said in effect, "What's going on here?" And Jesus replied, "You have no idea, but some day you will." Presumably Jesus began the foot-washing with Peter, so he was the first to be shocked. Tasker picks up on the meaning of the moment: "Peter resists the attempt of Jesus to wash his feet, precisely because he failed to associate what his Master was doing with His death, but regarded it merely as an act which any slave might perform before a banquet. In making this protest Peter was in fact displaying the pride of unredeemed men and women, who are so confident of their ability to save themselves that they instinctively resist the suggestion that they need divine cleansing" (Tasker, p. 155).

13:8–9. Peter was too humble to have his feet washed but not too humble to command the Lord. As soon as Jesus emphasized that this symbolic act united the disciple with the Lord in some significant way, Peter took the full plunge. Let us not miss the practical theology of these verses. There is no place in the body of Christ for those who have not been cleansed by the Lord. Washing in this symbolic context cannot refer to baptism, but the atoning cleansing of sin.

13:10–11. Here we have a beautiful picture of forgiveness and one of the most important theological texts of the New Testament. How often does a person need to be saved? Once? Every time he or she sins? Just before death to make sure? These verses tell us that a person who has been completely cleansed once will only require regular washings after that.

The first verb (*louo*) appears in the perfect tense, indicating completed action, obviously union with the Lord through salvation. The second (*nipto*), rendered **wash**, means precisely the kind of rinsing Jesus demonstrated on this occasion. A full bathing depicts initial regeneration; the repeated washings symbolize forgiveness of ongoing sinful behavior.

This is not the only interpretation of the text. "Roman Catholics sometimes have interpreted verse 10 to mean that after infant baptism only penance is needed. A preferable interpretation emphasizes that after salvation all one needs is confession of sins, the continual application of Jesus' death to cleanse one's daily sins" (Blum, p. 320). Here are a few sample "one-liners" on this key text:

> "He who is bathed needs, so to speak, only to remove the stains contracted in the walk of life; just as the guest, after the bath, needs only to have the dust washed from his feet when he reaches the house of his host" (Westcott, pp. 191–92).

> "Individuals who have been cleansed by Christ's atoning work will doubtless need to have subsequent sins washed away, but the fundamental cleansing can never be repeated" (Carson, p. 465).

> "Those who are Christ's are totally justified men and women, but they do need constant cleansing from their repeated defilement by sin in order that the fellowship they have with the Father and with the Son might not be broken" (Boice, IV, p. 32).

ⓒ Love Exhorted (13:12–17)

SUPPORTING IDEA: *Perhaps there exists no act more menial than washing another's feet, but nothing is beneath a disciple. Did the Savior intend to initiate an ordinance here? Some believe the command to wash the feet of others must be taken literally. But Jesus called us to acts of humble service for other Christians and, as Harry Ironside used to say, "When washing each other's feet, we should be careful of the temperature of the water."*

13:12–14. The washing not only demonstrated humility and servanthood to the disciples but also laid an experiential foundation for the teaching of verse 10. When the foot-washing ended, Jesus taught an important lesson about the relationship of believers—**you also should wash one another's feet.**

As Mother Teresa has shown us, perhaps more than anyone else in the twentieth century, if our teacher and Lord does not hesitate to wash our feet, how can we fail to wash one another's feet? Certainly there can be no harm in the literal practice of foot-washing, but the symbolism of first-century behavior seems more appropriately replicated in the way we serve people in a variety of ways.

Incidentally, the only other reference to foot-washing appears in 1 Timothy 5:10, so we have scant evidence that the New Testament church actually practiced this as a regular ordinance.

Jesus emphasized the words **Teacher and Lord** in contrast with the way they had behaved toward him. The Lord reminded them that he washed their feet as their leader. Morris says, "Jesus proceeds to endorse this way of speaking. He commends the disciples, for these expressions point to his true position. But precisely because of this there are implications. His repetition of 'the Lord and the teacher' (a reversed order may be significant) emphasizes his dignity. This exalted Person has washed their feet. They ought, therefore, to wash one another's feet" (Morris, p. 620).

13:15–17. Throughout the New Testament we learn the importance of example, never more so than when Jesus refers to himself. But here we are not focused on some great spiritual reality or doctrinal truth; the passage deals with how we treat other people. As Francis Schaeffer often observed, love is the ultimate mark of the Christian. Since Jesus loved his disciples and loves us in the same way, we need to do for others what he has done for us.

In verse 16 we find John's only use of the word *apostolos*, the common New Testament word for "apostle," here translated as **messenger.** Interesting that no church office or spiritual gift comes to view here. The context remains one of foot-washing as an example of how Christians treat one another. If we would be Christ's messengers in any capacity, we must behave toward others the way he behaved toward his disciples.

We receive God's joy by acting on the principles of conduct that Jesus taught. First we ought to pray, "Lord, wash me"; then we need to pray, "Lord, help me wash others." And let us not forget that the word **blessed** can also be translated "happy." We can be happy as Christians by acting on the principles of these verses, conducting our lives in such a way that we forgive, serve, and love the brothers and sisters in Christ. When we avoid criticism, complaining, and conflict, harmony and unity gain strength in the body.

Hughes calls this kind of behavior, "'people of the towel': When Jesus said, 'Do you know what I have done to you?' he might have added, 'and do you know who you are, as heirs to the towel?' The power, the impetus, and the grace to wash one another's feet is proportionate to how we see ourselves. Our Lord saw Himself as King of kings, and He washed their feet. Recovery of a consciousness that we serve Christ the King will also compel us to service" (Hughes, p. 38).

D Love Exchanged (13:18–30)

SUPPORTING IDEA: *Jesus knew precisely what to expect from his friends. Of the original Twelve he chose, all would turn away in his time of greatest crisis. One would betray him for money (v. 21) and one would deny him publicly (v. 38).*

13:18. We must see the remainder of chapter 13 in the light of the first seventeen verses which showed Jesus' intimacy with his friends. When we remember verse 14, "now that I, your Lord and Teacher, have washed your feet, you also should wash one another's feet," we can link it with the key verse of the second part of the chapter: "all men will know that you are my disciples, if you love one another" (v. 35).

Verse 18 stands in stark contrast to the verse immediately preceding it. Jesus had just said, "now that you know these things, you will be blessed if you do them" (v. 17). Now he changed the mood dramatically with a frightening caveat: **I am not referring to all of you.** One of the Twelve was not among the **chosen.** Of him Jesus quoted Psalm 41:9: "Even my close friend, whom I trusted, he who shared my bread, has lifted up his heel against me." This fulfilled prophecy showed the messianic deity of the Savior.

The words **lifted up his heel** suggest the kick of a mule, a phrase that reminds me of something that happened to our family some years ago. I was speaking at a Bible conference in Canada. During the week we went on a group trail ride. When we returned and dismounted, our five-year-old daughter wanted to give her horse a pat on the back. As she approached it from the rear, the horse kicked her, knocking her backward in an explosion of fears and tears. She was just bruised a bit, but she learned at a very early age never to approach a horse or mule from the rear. That shocking kick describes what Judas did, and Jesus predicted it without labeling the betrayer.

13:19–20. The fact of fulfilled prophecy takes center stage again in verse 19. Jesus not only quoted a prophetic psalm but immediately offered a prophecy himself—a prophecy intended to produce greater faith. He claimed equality with God (**I am He**) on the basis that one of their group would betray him. They knew it ahead of time and should have remembered at that moment that the Son of God predicted it. Then he went on to tell them that they represented him so closely that anyone who accepted a person who came in Jesus' name with Jesus' message accepted the presence of Jesus himself.

Carson says, "This verse powerfully ties the disciples to Jesus, and therefore serves as a foil for the failure of Judas Iscariot. The mission of Jesus is here assigned the highest theological significance, the most absolutely binding authority—the authority of God himself. Failure to close with Christ is failure to know God. And because his disciples re-present him to the world, their mission, their ministry, takes on precisely the same absolute significance" (Carson, p. 471).

13:21. This was not an easy conversation. In this verse John reminded us of two different occasions in chapter 11. First, the Lord wanted to be sure the disciples grasped the meaning of the quote from Psalm 41:9 so he said plainly, **one of you is going to betray me.** Second, we find here the same word that we have seen in 11:33 and 12:27, translated **troubled** in each case. Once again, **I tell you the truth** translates the familiar *amen, amen.*

13:22–26. The disciples' ignorance indicated how easy it was for Judas to disguise his motives and his purpose. Peter had to ask John to request further identification. Even when the Lord specifically said, **It is the one to whom I will give this piece of bread,** the disciples still had no idea what was going on.

It is helpful here to look at a similar account of the same event in Matthew's Gospel: "They were very sad and began to say to him one after the other, 'Surely not I, Lord?' Jesus replied, 'The one who has dipped his hand into the bowl with me will betray me. The Son of Man will go just as it is written about him. But woe to that man who betrays the Son of Man! It would be better for him if he had not been born.' Then Judas, the one who would betray him, said, 'Surely not I, Rabbi?' Jesus answered, 'Yes, it is you'" (Matt. 26:22–25).

The comparison of Matthew with the John passage might suggest that only Judas heard the answer, but it is certainly clear that the disciple band trusted their treasurer and had no idea what would happen. We cannot identify Christ's elect by outward appearance. Even a person who seems to be close to the Lord may be lost.

Did Jesus' offer of the bread constitute a last opportunity for Judas to repent? Some argue that point. Blum writes, "Giving the morsel to Judas was an uncaught sign of recognition to John, but it was also the Lord's final extension of grace to Judas. Hosts giving a morsel of bread to a guest was a sign of friendship. How ironic that Jesus' act of friendship to Judas signaled Judas' betrayal of friendship" (Blum, p. 321).

13:27–30. Here we find the only mention of **Satan** in John's Gospel. We must remember that John wrote this account many years later, so he casually described Judas' departure, having already told us in 12:6 that Judas was a thief who helped himself to the treasury.

As far as the disciples knew, Judas was a follower of Jesus, as strong in his commitment as any of them. That is one reason why Jesus warned in Matthew 13 that we should be careful about trying to point out the difference between the wheat and the weeds.

As Judas exchanged Christ's tenderness for the terror of that awful night, love's appeal became hate's dynamic: **and it was night.** Our chapter began in the evening. John wanted us to know that the sun had long gone and the Son would soon be gone as well. Judas had begun, and now continued, as Eugene O'Neill once put it, "a long day's journey into night."

E Love Extended (13:31–38)

> **SUPPORTING IDEA:** *God glories in what we often see as tragedy. Five times in verses 31–32 John recorded Jesus' use of the words "glorify" and "glorified" as he directed the disciples' thinking toward the cross.*

13:31–32. Once Judas had left, his evil presence removed from the room, the Lord could speak to the remaining eleven about his glorification. We sing, "In the Cross of Christ I Glory." This hymn may have its foundation in these verses. The horror of Roman execution glorified the Son of God and glorified the Father. Having been glorified, the Father glorified the Son with resurrection and ascension. That is why Jesus could pray in chapter 17, "Father, the time has come. Glorify your Son, that your Son may glorify you" (17:1).

Once again the Lord identified himself as **the Son of Man.** According to Westcott, "This title . . . is the key to the interpretation of the passage. The words are spoken of as a relation of 'the Son of Man' to 'God,' and not of that of 'the Son' to 'the Father'" (Westcott, p. 196). The phrase appears twelve times in John's Gospel and this is the last (1:51; 3:13–14; 5:27; 6:27,53,62; 8:28; 9:35; 12:23,34; 13:31).

We have already studied the significance of glory (*doxa*) in its various forms. In these verses John seemed to multiply its use deliberately. Tenney reminds us, "In this concept the Cross and the Resurrection are united as phases of a single redemptive event by which the purpose of God is completed and his righteousness vindicated" (Tenney, *EBC*, p. 141).

13:33–35. The words **where I am going, you cannot come** offer the only saying in John that appears three times with the same wording (7:33; 8:21). Imagine the confusion of the disciples at this point. They did not have the luxury of knowing the opening verses of chapter 14. They could only ponder what the Lord meant until he continued his teaching with further explanation.

Love extended leads to discipleship and denial and perhaps even to death. But the sacrifice itself should not be the focus for the disciples, but the motive behind it. These verses lay a strong groundwork for John's three epistles. This is a new commandment and a new object. Not just "love God" or "love me," but **love one another.**

In 1 John this theme of loving one another appears in 2:9–10; 3:11–18; 4:7–12,19–21; and 5:1–3. It was not only a new commandment and a new object, but a new mode (**as I have loved you**) and, perhaps most difficult and shocking of all, a new judge. Verse 35 can be identified as the key verse of this chapter. God allows the world to judge whether people are truly Jesus' disciples by the way they behave toward one another. Sadly, the church has not done very well on this point. Perhaps this accounts for some of the struggles the gospel has had for almost two thousand years.

In the 1960s when Christian folk music was becoming popular, we often sang a song that repeated the phrase, "and they'll know we are Christians by our love." Not by the size of our buildings. Not by the frequency of our attendance. Not by the multiplicity of religious duties we observe. Not by the ostentation of our public worship. As Morgan puts it, "The measure in which Christian people fail in love to each other is the measure in which the world does not believe in them, or their Christianity. It is the final test of discipleship, according to Jesus" (Morgan, p. 241).

13:36–38. When Jesus stopped to take a breath, Peter jumped in with a question he could no longer contain: **Lord, where are you going?** Jesus told him and the other disciples that they would follow, but not now. We know, of course, the place was heaven and the explanation would come in chapter 14. But Peter persisted. Not satisfied to come later, he wanted to go with Jesus now, even though he had no idea where. To make his point he appealed, **I will lay down my life for you.**

We find it difficult to imagine that Peter could have been prepared for the Lord's response. A chilling announcement of his denial not once, not twice, but three times must have hit him in the face like a stinging snowball. And all four Gospels record this announcement (Matt. 26; Mark 14; Luke 22). In John's account, Peter did not say another word until chapter 18. And here is this chilling prophecy introduced with the classic formula, **I tell you the truth** (*amen, amen*).

The end of chapter 13 and most of chapter 14 record questions and difficulties raised by individual disciples as Jesus explained in detail the cross and the home in heaven. We understand the sadness of that upper room and the broken hearts of the Lord's followers, so we are not surprised to find chapter 14 opening with the words, "Do not let your hearts be troubled."

MAIN IDEA REVIEW: *Like us, the disciples lived in a society that had rebelled against God. Like us, they learned more quickly from modeling and demonstration than by being told what was right. So on that final night before his death, Jesus exemplified love, explained it, and then exhorted his disciples to follow his example. How patient he was with Judas, how humble with these proud disciples! In contrast, Peter acted too "spiritual" to allow the Lord to wash his feet, but not too spiritual to command the Son of God!*

III. CONCLUSION

How to React When Your Friends Let You Down

Before the retirement and death of Charles Schultz, each year the football season began with Charlie Brown charging the football while Lucy held it. Each year he believed this time she would keep it there until he kicked it. But each year she yanked the ball away at the last second and Charlie fell on his backside, once more let down by his friend. We must learn to cope with such disappointment in life. Those whom we trust will sometimes fail us. Often this failure occurs when we least expect it.

How can we love one another to the full extent? How can we express that love adequately in both word and deed? How do we react when our friends let us down? Let us recognize the vast difference between Peter's denial and Judas's betrayal. With Judas it was deliberate; with Peter it was accidental. Judas displayed meanness; Peter showed weakness. Judas committed the act of an unbeliever; Peter committed the act of a believer.

But that still does not answer our question. How should we react when friends let us down? How did Jesus react? Imagine what he could have said to Judas and Peter. Imagine what he could have done to them with his miracle-working power. But, to both of them he showed an attitude of patience, honor, dignity, forgiveness, and love. That is how we should react when friends let us down, because that is the only way we can be like Jesus.

PRINCIPLES

- We cannot identify God's elect; anyone can look like a disciple.
- Constant cleansing is a requirement and a necessity for every Christian.
- Jesus was in charge of the schedule leading to the cross.
- Christians glorify God by loving one another.

APPLICATIONS

- Understand what true love is and how it works.
- Consider ways to put into practice the Christlike behavior of loving to the full extent.
- Believe, value, and practice verse 17: "Now that you know these things, you will be blessed if you do them."

IV. LIFE APPLICATION

Expulsive Power

When a new love enters our hearts, it can drive out old and stagnant feelings, even attraction for things that would do us harm. One writer called this kind of love "the expulsive power of a new affection."

Imagine for a moment a young child playing with something extremely dangerous, perhaps a knife from the kitchen. One way to solve that crisis would be to approach the child and try to grab the knife. Perhaps another would be to command the child to place the knife on the table or the floor.

But using the expulsive power of a new affection, one might offer the child an attractive toy, a delicious piece of candy, or a shiny coin to attract immediate attention and then exchange the coin for the knife.

God's love is like that in our hearts. We only love one another because of the way Jesus loved us. But when we do what he commands, others will notice that we are his disciples, cleansed and changed by the expulsive power of a new affection.

V. PRAYER

Father, thank you for all your grace in our lives, for our bath, for our regular foot-washing, and for the glorious reality of your love in our hearts. Amen.

VI. DEEPER DISCOVERIES

A. Teacher (13:13–14)

How interesting that Jesus would refer to himself by the name he had so often heard his disciples use, a word so familiar in our modern vocabulary—*Teacher*. The word appears fifty-nine times in the New Testament, eight of those times in John's Gospel. It translates the Greek word *didaskalos* that commonly refers to Jesus in its Gospel uses but never points to the Lord outside the Gospels.

The common usage would not always take the definite article and the capitalized first letter. In Jesus a common word referring to instructors becomes a title. We saw it in 11:28 when Mary went to call Martha and said, "the teacher is here."

This term is the equivalent of *rabbi*, a title which disciples applied to John the Baptist as well as Jesus.

B. Satan Entered into Him (13:27)

In the prologue to Job, Satan roamed the earth and reported to heaven on the behavior of God's human subjects. The picture is one of ancient Persia where officers known as "the king's eyes" circulated around the kingdom and reported to the imperial court.

The word *satan* means "adversary," someone getting in the way or standing as opposition. By the end of the Exile, the Jews recognized it as a name rather than just a word and dropped the definite article. This should be a word of great interest in our day, alive as it is with interest in the supernatural. Angels and demons are everywhere in modern entertainment, but we seem no closer to understanding the nature of the fallen archangel.

Lightner provides helpful information on Satan's origin: "We usually think of the biblical account of the sin of Adam and Eve in the garden, but when we look more carefully we see that it was not really the first sin after all. Our parents were not the first intelligent creatures to violate the law and character of God. In Genesis 3 we are told of one called the serpent who was already God's enemy, and who tempted the first humans to eat of the forbidden fruit, thereby disobeying God's clear command not to eat of it" (Lightner, p. 212).

As Satan used the serpent in the Garden of Eden, now he used Judas—and in both instances, he worked in rebellion against God's plan for the world.

C. A New Commandment (13:34)

Only here in this Gospel did the Lord use the term *new* (*kainos*). John used it in 19:41 to describe Jesus' tomb. But how is this commandment about loving one another actually new? Obviously the Mosaic Law already included this (Lev. 19:18), but here we find a whole new motivation and the emphasis falls on group behavior rather than the relationship between neighbors. Dods says, "It was 'new,' because the love of Christ's friends for Christ's sake was a new thing in the world." Morris adds, "The new thing appears to be the mutual affection that Christians have for one another on account of Christ's great love for them" (Morris, p. 633).

Carson helps us grasp its importance: "The new command is simple enough for a toddler to memorize and appreciate, profound enough that the most mature believers are repeatedly embarrassed at how poorly they comprehend it and put it into practice . . . with a standard like this, no thoughtful believer can ever say, this side of the Parousia, 'I am perfectly keeping the basic stipulation of the new covenant' (Carson, p. 484).

VII. TEACHING OUTLINE

A. INTRODUCTION
1. Lead Story: Who Can Pay?
2. Context: The upper room narrative has begun and will continue through the end of chapter 17. A betrayal has been set into motion and there is no turning back either for Jesus or Judas.
3. Transition: Springing from the last verse of John 12 and its reference to a command that leads to eternal life, John launched his pre-crucifixion narrative which flows like a seamless garment for the next several chapters.

B. COMMENTARY
1. Love Exemplified (13:1–5)
   a. In patience with Judas (13:1–3)
   b. In service to disciples (13:4–5)
2. Love Explained (13:6–11)
   a. As the washing of feet (13:6–9)
   b. As the bathing of the whole person (13:10–11)
3. Love Exhorted (13:12–17)
   a. By Jesus' teaching (13:12–14)
   b. By Jesus' model (13:15–17)
4. Love Exchanged (13:18–30)
   a. For betrayal (13:18–21)
   b. For exclusion (13:22–30)
5. Love Extended (13:31–38)
   a. Through disciples (13:31–35)
   b. Through betrayal (13:36–38)

C. CONCLUSION: EXPULSIVE POWER

VIII. ISSUES FOR DISCUSSION

1. In what ways does the Lord continually "wash our feet" to keep us clean?
2. In what ways can we wash the feet of others?
3. If you are teaching or preaching John 13:35, how will you explain what kinds of things unsaved people will see Christians doing which could identify them as Christ's disciples?

John 14

One Way to the Father

Q u o t e

"*T*he world has forgotten, in its concern with Left and Right, that there is an Above and Below."

G l e n   D r a k e

PERSONAL PROFILE: JUDAS

- One of six people in the New Testament with this name
- An apostle of Jesus often called "Judas son of James" (Luke 6:16)
- Also identified as "not Iscariot"

John 14

IN A NUTSHELL

*T*he danger with troubled people is not that they will believe nothing, but that they will believe anything! To avert such loss of truth and certainty in his disciples, Jesus turned their minds to the Father. He offered the personal touch of a heaven where the Father lives, personally prepared by the Son, and containing enough room for all who follow him.

One Way to the Father

I. INTRODUCTION

Final Call

Nobel Prize-winning author William Saroyan lay dying from cancer in May of 1981. He picked up the phone next to his hospital bed and called the Associated Press. Getting a reporter on the line, he said, "Everybody has to die, but I always believed an exception would be made in my case. Now what?" Indeed—"now what?"

Scripture tells us it is appointed unto humans once to die and there are no exceptions. All Jesus' talk about his own death, and this mysterious discussion about going some place where the disciples could not come (13:33–37) had left the disciples in a state of confusion and perhaps even terror. Our own cynical world contains many troubled people with deep questions about death and the afterlife. We have learned from the success of cults and false religions in the world that troubled people are gullible.

So now it became necessary for Jesus to break into their frightened hearts and tell them precisely where he was going and why. The key word in our study is "Father," which appears twenty-two times in chapter 14 and thirteen times in these first fourteen verses.

II. COMMENTARY

One Way to the Father

> **MAIN IDEA:** *This chapter teaches an exclusive gospel. No universalism (the hope that everyone will someday be in heaven), but a narrow way—salvation through Jesus alone. Philip wanted tangible evidence, the privilege of seeing the Father (v. 8). But that is precisely what he had seen for three and one-half years; anyone who has seen Jesus has seen the Father.*

A Heaven—the Father's House (14:1–4)

> **SUPPORTING IDEA:** *The thought of death troubles human beings and always has. Jesus had spoken to the disciples about his death (13:33,36), and they were troubled. Now he said to them in essence, "Stop worrying."*

14:1. Troubled people need peace and affirmation. The problems of the disciples were as real as our problems. In fact, it is probably fair to say that most Christians are realists. From Scripture they recognize the reality of sin, the reality of evil in the world, the reality of deliverance from sin, and the reality of ultimate eternal life.

These disciples, good Jews, had already trusted in God and now Jesus asked them to trust in him. They had watched him feed five thousand people and bring Lazarus back from the dead, but now they must trust him not just for food or miracles, but with their lives.

Some question exists about the grammatical nature of the verbs rendered **trust** in this verse. The NIV offers the preferred translation with the verbs appearing in what Greek scholars would call an imperative/imperative pattern. Rather than saying, "You have trusted in God so now trust in me," or some similar phrase, both sections of the sentence offer a command.

14:2. Let us acknowledge at the beginning of this chapter that this portion of Scripture is not about huge buildings in heaven but about space. Lots of songs have been written to proclaim "mansions over the hilltop," but Jesus simply told his disciples, "There's room in heaven for you."

But he also wanted to indicate that he would go ahead of them to do specific work—the preparation of heaven (14:2b). The New Testament teaches us we are pilgrims and wanderers in this world. We may own homes, and some of them may be huge and beautiful. But we do not belong here because we are not primarily citizens of this world. In heaven we will be where we really belong because Jesus has gone ahead to prepare a place for us.

Paul Tournier once suggested that a place of one's own has been the basic desire of every heart since Eden. Let us not think of this preparation as the Lord's return to his carpentry skills, pounding two-by-fours in a housing project for believers. It surely describes his death, resurrection, ascension, and princely role at the Father's right hand.

The promise "I will come back" (v. 3) has been variously understood by interpreters. But in the context of death, ascension, and heaven, it seems difficult to arrive at any conclusion other than the second coming of Jesus. As to the **Father's house**, I agree with Carson: "The simplest explanation is best: my Father's house refers to heaven, and in heaven are many rooms, many dwelling-places. The point is not the lavishness of each apartment, but the fact that such ample provision has been made, that there is more than enough space for every one of Jesus' disciples to join him in his Father's home. Besides, have they not just been encouraged to trust him (v. 1), and always found strong reason to do so? Can they not therefore be assured that if heaven were other than what he has described, he would have told them?" (Carson, p. 489).

14:3–4. Forget the mansions; what this passage talks about is the personal touch of the Savior. Count the times he says **I** or **me** in these two short verses, and you will come up with five. He wanted the disciples to trust him personally. It was not just preparation of a place in focus here, but the personal return of Jesus to take his own to heaven. This passage does not speak about levels of reward or big buildings in heaven. It promises the second coming of Jesus Christ. Did they really know the way? They should have known; it has been obvious in this book since chapter 3.

The setting of these verses centers on promise and peace. Jesus would take care of his disciples by making sure they could be with him in the Father's presence. By this point in his ministry, they were expected to **know the way to the place where I am going.** Of the coming and going in this passage Westcott writes, "This departure is itself the condition of the return: separation, the cessation of the present circumstances of fellowship, was the first step toward complete union" (Westcott, p. 201).

🅱 Jesus—the Father's Reflection (14:5–11)

SUPPORTING IDEA: *Some Christians struggle with the exclusivism of the gospel, but Scripture allows us no other choice. God offers no variety of ways leading to heaven—only Jesus Christ.*

14:5–7. Thomas was an honest follower though always the skeptic, so he was the first to ask, **Lord, we don't know where you are going, so how can we know the way?** Jesus' response is the key verse of the passage, memorized by Christians all around the globe. Jesus is the way—reconciliation; Jesus is the truth—illumination; Jesus is the life—regeneration. This is the exclusive gospel. The New Testament knows nothing of universalism—the idea that God will find some way to save everybody. What could be clearer than Jesus' words in verse 6, **No one comes to the Father except through me.**

Why did the disciples need all this talk about trusting Jesus? Why do we need it? Because like them, we do not know Jesus well enough; so we struggle to understand the Father. Repeatedly Jesus emphasized the link between the heavenly Father and the Son, but right up to the end the disciples did not get it—and we struggle with the concept as well.

This is one of those places at which we would like to have audio aids for the Bible. What was Thomas's tone of voice when he said this? Is he still the skeptic? The pessimist? The negative thinker? It would appear so, but we admire his openness and vulnerability. The impact of Jesus' answer echoes through the centuries to the present hour. He embodies the way to God, the truth about God, and the life in God. And if the disciples really knew him as they should, they would understand the inseparability between the Father and the Son.

This announcement in John 14:6 prepares the way for the author of Hebrews to write, "We have confidence to enter the Most Holy Place by the blood of Jesus, by a new and living way opened for us through the curtain, that is, his body" (Heb. 10:19–20).

14:8–11. Philip either did not understand his Old Testament well or he failed to link the Father and the Son. Or perhaps he was born in Missouri, the "show me" state. If Jesus could produce physical evidence of the Father, Philip claimed the disciples would finally be satisfied.

We must remember Jesus' response. There is no difference between the Father and the Son; they are both God—equally powerful. Here again we find the theme "believing is seeing" that surfaced so clearly in 11:40. Notice Jesus' emphasis on both **words** and **work** in verse 10. Jesus' words reflected his deity much more than his work did. The disciples had been fascinated by his work, but they had not listened carefully enough to his words. Almost in frustration, the Lord said, **at least believe on the evidence of the miracles themselves.**

What is God like? I once heard a sermon on this topic. The pastor talked on and on about God being like flowers, sunsets, the cry of a newborn baby, the beauty of a clear blue sky. Certainly, all those are part of God's natural revelation and therefore reflect him. But he never got to the bottom line: God is like Jesus Christ.

In actuality, Philip's confusion is typical of the disciples throughout the first four books of the New Testament. The depth of theology in these discussions overwhelmed the disciples, probably until the coming of the Holy Spirit at Pentecost. Even Christians today who hold the entire Bible and enjoy the illuminating power of the Holy Spirit struggle with the doctrine of the Trinity and oneness of the Father and the Son.

Tenney's point is instructive: "Furthermore, if a personality must be employed to represent God, that personality cannot be less than God and do him justice, nor can it be so far above humanity that it cannot communicate God perfectly to men. For this reason John says that 'the only Son, who is at the Father's side, has made him known' (John 1:18). The way Jesus made known the character and reality of the Father was by his words and works. The truth of God filled Jesus' words; the power of God produced his works" (Tenney, *EBC*, p. 145).

◉ Faith—the Father's Glory (14:12–14)

SUPPORTING IDEA: *Our ministry for Christ begins with faith, follows through by imitating the perfect model, and then through the Holy Spirit spreads out around the world.*

14:12. This is one of the most interesting verses in the Bible. Interpreters have pondered what Jesus meant by telling his disciples that they would do greater things than he, the Son of God, had done. But perhaps the best way to understand the verse is to take it literally, exactly as Jesus said it. Jesus' earthly ministry was limited in time and space. He served the Father for three and one-half years and never outside the boundaries of Palestine. The disciples, on the other hand, as Acts clearly attests, carried out ministry that was greater geographically, in terms of numbers of people reached and long-lasting effect.

We find a leadership principle here as well. All parents should be able to say to their children; all pastors should be able to say to their staffs; all leaders should be able to say to their followers: "You have the potential to do greater things than I have done." To empower and develop followers whose ministry exceeds the impact of their mentors is to follow the model of Jesus.

14:13. In this verse we find one of the great prayer promises of the Bible that focuses first on the purpose of prayer. Jesus answers prayer in order to bring glory to the Father. Our praying, therefore, ought to be directed toward that goal and end. But we have to pause at the dramatic implications of words like **whatever you ask** and "ask me for anything" (v.14).

Perhaps a word of caution is in order here. No theology should be built from a single verse or even a handful of verses in the Bible. The Bible contains huge blocks of information on prayer, and this is one of them. Jesus had already taught the disciples much about prayer, and here we have only a final reminder, not everything that applies to the subject. Nevertheless, this promise of prayer we cannot ignore. In fact, what we see here is a New Testament formula of asking in the name of Jesus, something new to the disciples though they would hear it again before Jesus finished his teaching.

Notice the similarity between this teaching and chapter 16: "In that day you will no longer ask me anything. I tell you the truth, my Father will give you whatever you ask in my name. Until now you have not asked for anything in my name. Ask and you will receive, and your joy will be complete" (John 16:23–24).

14:14. Obviously, just saying "in Jesus' name" creates no magic potion for prayer. The culture in which these words were spoken took names very seriously, so much so that they equated one's name with the character, spirit, and power of that person. That is why the Jews never spoke the name of Yahweh.

Imagine a child playing in the middle of the street when her father arrives home from work. When he scolds her and calls her back to the yard immediately, she says, "Mommy told me I could play in the street; I'm out here in mommy's name." A ridiculous illustration, but it points out how often Christians do strange things and then claim they are behaving "in Jesus' name." Since Jesus' name is always connected in some way with our prayers even if we do not speak those words, if we cannot ask in his name we should not ask at all.

Tasker reminds us that Jesus, "departure to the Father, so far from ending his influence on earth, will mean its continuance under wider conditions and with the results rendered possible by the power of effective prayer" (Tasker, p. 166).

D The Holy Spirit—the Father's Counselor (14:15–24)

SUPPORTING IDEA: *Although the Holy Spirit's activity is best demonstrated in Acts, perhaps no book of the Bible contains more theology of the Holy Spirit (what theologians call "pneumatology") than John 14–16.*

14:15–18. How do people know that they are Christians? How do you and I gain confidence that we are born again by the regenerating power of God's Holy Spirit? The world cannot know because the world cannot accept the Holy Spirit. But the disciples were told that the Holy Spirit **lives with you and will be in you.** Pentecost was still in their future, so at the present time the Holy Spirit was constantly with them. But after Pentecost, he would actually be in them and in every other believer since that day. Consequently, they were identifiable (as we are) as God's children, not orphans.

What did Jesus mean by the promise at the end of verse 18: **I will come to you?** Some interpreters suggest this refers to the resurrection while others see another promise of the second coming. But in the context of these verses, it surely means the coming of the Holy Spirit at Pentecost. Jesus lives in us through the person and power of the Holy Spirit.

The Holy Spirit lives in us to identify his children. The doctrine of the indwelling Holy Spirit does not rest completely on this passage, but verse 17 is of great significance. Of this important verse Gromacki writes:

> First, the spirit was dwelling "with" the apostles in the Gospel era. In Greek the words "with you" literally mean "beside you." In that sense, the Holy Spirit had a companion ministry to the apostles. He was beside them, but not inside them.
>
> Second, Christ predicted that the Spirit would be in them. After the death, resurrection, and ascension of Christ, the same Spirit who was beside them would be inside them. Christ also changed verbal tenses to show the difference in the two relationships of the Spirit to the apostles. The verb *menei* ("dwells") is in the present tense, whereas the verb *estai* ("will be") is in the future tense (Gromacki, p. 136).

Not only that, but this indwelling will be endless—the new Counselor will **be with you forever.** No orphans in the family of God, no abandoned people with no place to turn. The Holy Spirit will be a constant presence of Jesus with all believers.

14:19–21. How well we remember the song that states, "Because he lives I can face tomorrow; because he lives all fears are gone." Perhaps the idea for the lyrics had its birth in John 14:19. When did the disciples (later called the apostles) realize that Jesus was in the Father and that they dwelt in him? Did they have to wait for the second coming for that? Of course not. The reference to **that day** must refer to the coming of the Holy Spirit at Pentecost. That frightened, hesitant group of believers huddled in an upper room knew the power of the Holy Spirit broke forth upon them because it literally blasted them around the city, around the country and around their world.

But notice again the emphasis on behavior. A person does not show that the Holy Spirit lives in him by bizarre behavior or belief, but by knowing and obeying the commands of the Lord Jesus. How desperately we need balance in the church. Making too much of the doctrine of the Holy Spirit leads to mysticism; making too little of him leads to legalism. Only the balance can lead to unity. How like sinful human beings to divide the church over the Holy Spirit, sent by God to unite us.

As we might expect, interpreters have debated the meaning of the words **on that day**, although the context seems to point to the resurrection. As Morris puts it, "When he is risen and when the Spirit is come, then they will know the truth of his relationship to the Father, and they will know that he dwells in them and they in him" (Morris, p. 652).

14:22–24. The Holy Spirit lives actively in us all the time; we do not need to pray for him to come to a certain meeting, or a certain occasion, or at a certain time. He is not some kind of theological or spiritual helicopter looking for a place to land.

The disciples always wanted to know why Jesus treated them differently than he did the world, and we find that question again in verse 22. But the answer is always the same. Jesus reveals himself to people he knows will respond to him and obey his teaching. The key word of these three verses is **obey** or perhaps even the phrase **obey my teaching**. Again the Lord linked himself with the Father and indicated that the Father and the Son through the Spirit take up residence in the lives of believers.

Judas is also mentioned in Luke 6 and Acts 1 but only here does he speak. Likely he is the same person as the Thaddaeus of Matthew 10:3 and Mark 3:18. His interruption, like those of Thomas and Philip, reminds us not only that the disciples were confused about all this doctrine, but also that they felt comfortable enough in the presence of the Lord to interrupt him with questions. But what is the answer to his question? Quite simply, love. The obedient children of the Father receive the Holy Spirit who will manifest (**show**) Jesus to them, although his true nature will still be hidden from the world.

E Peace—the Father's Gift (14:25–31)

SUPPORTING IDEA: *Jesus reminded the disciples of truth and peace, and he strengthened their faith. Peace of mind and spirit is essential to all of us, especially in an age of stress and confusion.*

14:25–27. The Holy Spirit reminds us of truth that Jesus taught. In the case of the disciples, it was an immediate application to their spiritual memories. In our case, it is assistance in understanding and applying the Word of God. In their lives and ours, constant awareness of the Spirit's presence is a daily practicality.

But Jesus also promised peace. Verse 27 reminds us of the early verses of this chapter: **Peace I leave with you; my peace I give you . . . Do not let your hearts be troubled and do not be afraid.** Let us remember that these were troubled, frightened disciples. They needed assurance of peace. But they were not peculiar in that need. Peace of spirit and mind is an essential part of a healthy home, a healthy workplace, and a healthy life. But only those who have peace *with* God can have the peace *of* God.

As Hughes expresses it, "To the unregenerate mind, the mysteries of God's purpose in life remain barred. But to the believer, the indwelling Spirit gives comprehension and comfort. He brings before our troubled hearts the Word of God and applies its comfort. Words can never adequately convey the comfort of the Holy Spirit, but I have seen it, as I have stood in a hospital room with those whose lives are literally falling apart, and have witnessed the Holy Spirit bringing to their remembrance the promises of the Word" (Hughes, p. 57).

14:28–29. Here it is again—that constant nagging reminder to the disciples that Jesus would leave them. But this time he actually told them they should be **glad.** And when the Lord said, **the Father is greater than I,** he did not imply any denial of deity. Jesus was going back to heaven to take his appropriate role as our advocate by the Father's throne. But he would not leave his people alone on earth, so he sent the Holy Spirit to live the life of Jesus in the disciples and in us.

The Holy Spirit teaches us by strengthening our faith to trust the Father. We have no competence in ourselves for Christian living, parenting, teaching, or leading. Second Corinthians 3 could not be clearer: "Such confidence as this is ours through Christ before God. Not that we are competent in ourselves to claim anything for ourselves, but our competence comes from God. He has made us competent as ministers of a new covenant—not of the letter but of the Spirit; for the letter kills, but the Spirit gives life" (2 Cor. 3:4–6).

We wonder about the conditional past tense in the middle of verse 28—**if you loved me.** According to Carson, "now he goes over to the offensive, however mildly: their failure to understand, their failure to trust him, is also a failure of love. If they truly loved him (and the clear implication is that they do not), they would be glad that he's going to the Father" (Carson, p. 506).

14:30–31. The Holy Spirit also strengthens our faith to witness to the world. Jesus told the disciples, **the world must learn that I love the Father and that I do exactly what my Father has commanded me.** Would not it be wonderful if we could say exactly the same thing about our lives? Imagine a Christian father asked by a little child, "Daddy, why do we give money to missionaries?" and the dad responds, "Sweetheart, it's because the world must learn that we love the Father and we do exactly what the Father has commanded." Perhaps a mother who has forgiven a child for the fifth or sixth time in the same day is asked why she is so patient and loving and she can reply the same way. That is what it means to have another Counselor in our lives.

The last phrase, **Come now; let us leave,** indicates that the upper room portion of the Lord's teaching was finished. They probably walked out into the garden, and chapter 15 continues in that outdoor setting.

This dynamic passage ought to leave us with several crucial questions. How do we practice the presence of the Holy Spirit in our lives? How do we guard against sinning in ways that offend the Holy Spirit such as quenching or grieving him? How do we flesh out the kind of demonstration the world must see to know that Jesus is alive and living in us through the Holy Spirit?

Two phrases in our text reach for our attention before we leave this section. First, Jesus' comment about **the prince of this world** is an obvious reference to Satan, although this Gospel does not mention the temptation of Jesus so prominent in the synoptic Gospels (Matt. 4:1–11; Mark 1:12–13; Luke 4:1–13). Tenney says, "Jesus did not fear Satan because Satan had no claim on him. There was nothing in Jesus' character or action that could be used against him. Satan had no valid accusation that could be used as leverage to divert Jesus from the will of his Father. His obedience had been perfect, and he intended to complete the Father's purpose irrespective of what it might cost him" (Tenney, *EBC*, p. 149).

Second, we pause for a moment at the closing words of the chapter, **Come now; let us leave.** John 18:1 says, "When he had finished praying, Jesus left with his disciples and crossed the Kidron Valley." We wonder about the geography at the end of chapter 14. Some interpreters suggest that Jesus and his disciples left the room at the end of chapter 14 and that chapters 15–17 describe discussions along the way with the prayer somewhere in route. Others find cause for textual dislocation and rearrangement of the text.

Perhaps the best approach indicates that they began to leave at the end of chapter 14 but did not actually get away until the beginning of chapter 18. Morris observes, "Anyone who has tried to get a group of a dozen or so to leave a particular place at a particular time will appreciate that it usually takes more than one brief exhortation to accomplish this. There is nothing at all unlikely in an interval between the uttering of the words and the departure of the group. And if an interval, then there is no reason why Jesus should not have continued to speak during it" (Morris, p. 661).

> **MAIN IDEA REVIEW:** *This chapter teaches an exclusive gospel. No universalism (the hope that everyone will someday be in heaven), but a narrow way—salvation through Jesus alone. Philip wanted tangible evidence, the privilege of seeing the Father (v. 8). But that is precisely what he had seen for three and one-half years; anyone who has seen Jesus has seen the Father.*

III. CONCLUSION

Honk If You Love Jesus

Although I do not put bumper stickers on my own car, I like to read them. And I like to hear stories about some of the bumper stickers we have grown accustomed to seeing. For example, I heard about stalled traffic on the Santa Ana Freeway in southern California, a common occurrence. The freeway was in total gridlock and nothing moved. But one driver incessantly and obnoxiously leaned on his horn as if somehow the noise would clear the whole freeway.

Finally, the driver in front of him went back in anger, screaming at the noisy horn blower. Much to his chagrin, he received the response, "I wasn't blowing my horn to get you to move; your bumper sticker says, 'Honk if you love Jesus.'"

This passage reminds us that the presence of the Holy Spirit is not demonstrated by bombastic honking but by behavioral holiness. Let us remember that John now writes about the last week in Jesus' earthly ministry in chapters 12–21 of this Gospel. No other Gospel writer goes into such great detail about Jesus' final week of teaching to the disciples. The first fourteen verses of this chapter focus on the Father, and chapters 14–16 deal with the Holy Spirit.

This was new truth for these disciples. They had not previously heard about another Counselor, the *paraclete* who would stand by their side from the time of the ascension to the time of the Lord's return.

PRINCIPLES

- Once again John's Gospel reminds us that believing is seeing.
- Faith is important for anyone who would do greater things than Jesus did.

- Jesus' promises about prayer and the Holy Spirit are just as true today as they were when these disciples first heard them.

APPLICATIONS

- Do not let your heart be troubled; believe that Jesus is in the Father and the Father is in him.
- Trust the Holy Spirit to be your counselor and teacher.
- Expect God's peace to calm your heart in troubled times.

IV. LIFE APPLICATION

I Have a Dream

Along with Franklin Roosevelt's "we have nothing to fear but fear itself" speech, and Kennedy's "ask not what your country can do for you" inaugural address, the words of Martin Luther King, Jr. offered on the steps of the Lincoln Memorial in May of 1957 represent one of the greatest speeches of the twentieth century. One does not have to agree with King's politics or theology to recognize the brilliance in the speech and its impact over the past forty years.

At one point King quoted a piece of verse by James Weldon Johnson, first published in 1917:

> God of our weary years, God of our silent tears,
> Thou who hast brought us thus far on the way;
> Thou who hast by Thy might, led us into the light,
> Keep us forever in Thy path, we pray.
> Lest our feet stray from the places, our God, where we met Thee,
> Lest our hearts, drunk with the wine of the world, we forget
>   Thee.
> Shadowed beneath Thy hand, may we forever stand,
> True to our God, true to our native land.

Dr. King's dreams of racial harmony have not been fully realized, although most would agree great progress has been made. But the dreams Jesus offered to his disciples that night have been largely fulfilled. He did go back to the Father; he is preparing space for all believers; the Holy Spirit has come to live in Christians and, for those who will accept it, Jesus has offered peace to the world. Now we wait for the final part of the dream, "I am going away and I am coming back to you" (v. 28).

This glorious chapter ends on a high note of testimony. Jesus affirmed his purpose to glorify the Father, and his words might well become ours: "the world must learn that I love the Father and that I do exactly what my Father has commanded me" (v. 31). What a testimony! Make that your goal as you serve the Lord.

V. PRAYER

Father, we thank you for the comfort and promises of John 14. May this chapter live in our hearts and lives, and may we share its truth and encouragement with others. Amen.

VI. DEEPER DISCOVERIES

A. The Way (14:6)

The common Greek word is *hodos* that appears 102 times in the New Testament. John used it to warn people that they should prepare for the *way* of the Lord (Matt. 3:3); the Pharisees told Jesus that he taught the *way* of God in accordance with the truth (Matt. 22:16); the Book of Hebrews talks about coming to God by a new and living *way* (Heb. 10:20); and Peter writes about the *way* of truth (2 Pet. 2:2). None of these passages, however, carry the drama of the word as it appears here in John 14.

In Acts, the Christian movement takes on the title "the Way." Luke likes to use it in reference to the early Christians. According to Marshall, the term designates "the true way of worshipping and serving God, for the Christians believe that the God of their Jewish ancestors was being rightly worshipped by them. Their understanding of true religion was based on the Old Testament, which they regarded as laying down the essentials of Christian faith and practice. The church was claiming, in fact, that the Old Testament was a Christian book" (Marshall, pp. 377–78).

John 14:6, however, indicates that our concept of "the way," along with our understanding of the gospel in general, dare not focus on a movement or a religious point of view. Our understanding of faith centers in a person, and that is exactly what Jesus says in this text.

B. Counselor (14:16,26)

The word *Counselor* translates the Greek word *parakletos* that means "someone who stands beside someone else." It could be an advisor, an attorney, or an intercessor of some kind. In our text it emphasizes the Holy Spirit's function in representing God to believers and encouraging them. The adjective *another* reminds us that their primary counselor was Jesus and that the Holy Spirit would take his place on earth. Some interpreters emphasize the legal aspect of the term. In its classical Greek setting, that certainly is true. But in our understanding, lawyers do not always comfort and they rarely teach, yet both aspects are strongly emphasized in this passage.

Jesus is never directly called a *paraklete* in this Gospel, but John did use exactly that reference in 1 John 2:1: "My dear children, I write this to you so that you will not sin. But if anybody does sin, we have one who speaks to the Father in our defense—Jesus Christ, the Righteous One."

Walls and Anders pick up on the metaphor: "The advocate speaks with extraordinary authority before the judge, however, because his defense for us is that he, the defense attorney, has already paid any price the judge could impose. The willingness of the judge to forgo judgment is not based on the life of the one on trial (us), but rather on the merits of Jesus' sacrifice. Jesus sacrificed his life in our place. He paid the price for our sin with his death. He is our atoning sacrifice (sacrifice that pays the price and allows forgiveness)" (Walls and Anders, p. 160).

In light of the use of the word *paraklete,* we can understand the tribute the early church paid to Barnabas when they nicknamed him *huios parakleseos,* "the son of consolation" or "the son of encouragement." New Testament usage is deeper than the legal ramifications of the word itself. Gromacki uses the title *helper* and says, "Christ was a personal Comforter and Encourager to the Twelve; thus the Holy Spirit would also be a personal helper. Christ contrasted Himself with another person, not with an impersonal influence or thing" (Gromacki, p. 5).

C. The Father Is Greater Than I (14:28)

One of the most difficult arguments to maintain in the Christian faith is the doctrine of the Trinity. Verses like this, which seem to challenge the equality of a triune Godhead, must be dealt with and carefully explained. One possibility here is a contrast between the eternal nature of Christ and his incarnate state.

According to Morris, "The incarnation involved the acceptance of a certain subordination as is insisted throughout the New Testament . . . He is talking about the departure of the human Jesus from this earth to be with the Father" (Morris, pp. 658–59). Doubtless that is sound since Jesus took that position throughout this Gospel.

Carson, however, offers a different twist: "Although the interpretation of v. 28 advanced here turns on the distinction between the Father in his glory and the Son in his incarnation, nevertheless this verse also attests to the pattern of functional subordination of the Son to the Father . . . the Father is God sending and commanding, the Son is God sent and obedient" (Carson, p. 508).

D. The Prince of This World (14:30)

A significant dimension to Satan's temptation of Jesus in the wilderness focused on his power to deliver the kingdoms of the world, something of a shortcut to Christ's ultimate destiny. We should know in the Gospel accounts of that temptation that Jesus denied Satan's ability to control the world for he is "the prince of this world," a phrase John uses in 12:31 and 16:11 as well as here. Add to such references passages like 2 Corinthians 4:4 and Ephesians 2:2, and we see something of the cosmic dimensions of Satan's influence.

Perhaps a practical note on this theology brings a caution against confronting such power by ourselves. Lightner warns, "As previously discussed, each believer has three enemies—the devil, the world, and the flesh. The way of victory, however, is not deliverance or escape from these enemies in this life but constant opposition to them in the power of the Spirit of God. Christians are to 'stand' against Satan, to 'resist' him, to 'love not the world' (KJV), and not to let sin reign in their mortal bodies (Eph. 6:14; James 4:7; 1 John 2:15; Rom. 6:12)" (Lightner, p. 158).

VII. TEACHING OUTLINE

A. INTRODUCTION

1. Lead Story: Final Call
2. Context: The upper room discourse that began in chapter 12 continues throughout chapter 14. As we noted in the "Commentary" section, it may actually carry through the end of chapter 17, although we cannot know for sure where chapters 15–17 were spoken. In any case, John provided six chapters of final teaching during the last week of the Lord's life, and three on the final night before the crucifixion.
3. Transition: John 14 links with chapter 13 in the way that a healing salve is placed on a cut. Judas would betray and Peter would deny, but Jesus exhorted the disciples, "Do not let your hearts be troubled." The chapter began on a high note and kept climbing as the disciples learned that "the world must learn that I love the Father and that I do exactly what my Father has commanded me." Only then are the disciples ready for permission to leave.

B. COMMENTARY

1. Heaven—the Father's House (14:1–4)
   a. The peace of heaven (14:1–2a)
   b. The preparation of heaven (14:2b)
   c. The promise of heaven (14:3–4)
2. Jesus—the Father's Reflection (14:5–11)
   a. Knowing the Father (14:5–7)
   b. Showing the Father (14:8–11)

3. Faith—the Father's Glory (14:12–14)
   a. The purpose of prayer (14:12–13)
   b. The promise of prayer (14:14)
4. The Holy Spirit—the Father's Counselor (14:15–24)
   a. He identifies the children (14:15–18)
   b. He unites the family (14:19–21)
   c. He fosters obedience (14:22–24)
5. Peace—the Father's Gift (14:25–31)
   a. Peace for comfort (14:25–27)
   b. Peace for confidence (14:28–31)

C. CONCLUSION: I HAVE A DREAM

VIII. ISSUES FOR DISCUSSION

1. How important is our expectation of a place in heaven?
2. How should we understand verses 13 and 14 in the light of the way we pray today?
3. Explain the doctrine of the Trinity and why it is important in Christian theology.

John 15

Requirements for a Fruitful Life

"*What* does love look like? It has the hands to help others. It has the feet to hasten to the poor and needy. It has eyes to see misery and want. It has the ears to hear the sighs and sorrows of men. That is what love looks like."

Augustine

John 15

IN A NUTSHELL

In the Old Testament, God spoke of the vine as a symbol of Israel (Ps. 80:8; Isa. 5:1–2,7; Jer. 2:21). In John 15 Jesus expanded the analogy. As the fulfillment of the Lord's purpose for Israel, the great Son of David identified himself as the vine and his followers as branches. If you like to look for key words in Bible study, note the eleven occurrences of "remain" in 15:4–10.

Requirements for a Fruitful Life

I. INTRODUCTION

No More Slaves

*W*e are all on a mission, all sent by our Lord and empowered by the Holy Spirit to carry out that mission. In the eighteenth century, many American Quakers were affluent, conservative slave holders, totally oblivious to the horror and anti-biblical nature of that role. A young Quaker, John Woolman, set a lifetime goal—to rid his beloved Society of Friends of this terrible practice. Woolman lived to the age of fifty-two and spent nearly all his adult years in his efforts to extinguish slavery among his Christian friends. By 1770, nearly one hundred years before the Civil War, no Quakers held slaves.

This chapter of John does not deal with social justice, but it does teach righteousness and the kind of social virtues that result from the indwelling Holy Spirit. John 14 has already talked to us about practicing the presence of the Holy Spirit. As the Lord's teaching continued, quite possibly out in the garden now, he emphasized how we can avoid inclusion in the ranks of those who sin regularly. The key words are *abide* and *fruit,* the latter used eight times.

An understanding of the purpose of the New Testament is crucial to the understanding of the metaphors and warnings of this chapter. Almost every book in the New Testament was written to professing believers. Even though their content was controlled by the guiding hand of the Holy Spirit, biblical authors could not discern the spiritual condition of those who would read their writings. Among the vast number of people receiving and reading this Gospel, there would have been those who had no experience of regeneration. John had more than half a century to observe the behavior of people who claimed to be Christians before he wrote this chapter.

II. COMMENTARY

Requirements for a Fruitful Life

MAIN IDEA: *This chapter emphasizes two great truths—our personal relationship with the Lord and our divinely appointed mission to go and bear fruit—fruit that will last.*

🅐 Abiding in the Lord (15:1–8)

SUPPORTING IDEA: *The allegory or parable of the vine, spoken to the disciples in a serious context, offers a word picture of the life of Christians.*

15:1. Though this section of our study is only two paragraphs, it is impossible to separate the components of the analogy that our Lord put forth. They appear as contrasting couplets throughout the passage. First we have the vine and the branches. This was imagery that every Jew would understand. In the Old Testament the vine appeared regularly as a symbol of Israel (Ps. 80:8–10; Isa. 5:1–2,7; Jer. 2:21). The Father owns the garden, Jesus is the vine, and his followers are the branches.

Christ and not the church is the true vine. Branches placed anywhere else are false branches. The word for **gardener** is *georgos*, the common word for *farmer,* a role retained by the Father himself. The vine with which these disciples would have been familiar was Israel, described in some detail in Psalm 80. There the psalmist prayed, "Return to us, O God Almighty! Look down from heaven and see! Watch over this vine, the root your right hand has planted, the son you have raised up for yourself" (Ps. 80:14–15).

15:2. Three types of believers are named or inferred in this first part of the chapter: those who bear no fruit, those who bear some fruit and, later in verse 5, those who bear much fruit. The fruit-bearing branches, it would appear from the text of this verse, represent true believers. But to whom does the text refer when it says, **he cuts off every branch in me that bears no fruit?**

This passage is capable of dangerous interpretation, especially when the idea of fruit-bearing centers in evangelism. Some people teach that those who do not win others to Christ will themselves be snatched out of the vine. Such an idea is alien to the teaching of the New Testament. Perhaps Galatians 5:22–23 helps us here: "But the fruit of the Spirit is love, joy, peace, patience, kindness, goodness, faithfulness, gentleness and self-control. Against such things there is no law."

Viewing the removed branches as unregenerate professing Christians is not the only possible way of handling the text. Westcott says, "Even the unfruitful branches are true branches," but then he chokes on the later reference to being thrown away and notes, "It is not perhaps necessary to attempt to determine the mode of this removal" (Westcott, p. 217). Perhaps it is best not to force every reference in this parable any more than any other but to focus on the pruning.

Boice escapes the difficulty of interpretation by translating **cuts off** (*airo*) as "lifts up," certainly one of its meanings. He argues, "This translation makes better sense of the passage in every way, and in addition it is much better theology. First, the emphasis of this opening section of the parable is, quite rightly, upon the care of the vine by the Father. It would be strange, granting this emphasis, if the first thing mentioned is the carrying away of unproductive branches. But it is not at all strange to emphasize that the vinedresser first lifts the branches up so that they may be better exposed to the sun and so the fruit will develop properly" (Boice, IV, p. 228).

15:3. The disciples, however, needed neither cutting off nor trimming clean (a nice handling of the Greek word by the NIV) because they had already been cleansed by the Lord's word. One thing is clear at the outset of the chapter: this is not a passage on salvation, a topic John covered in earlier chapters. Here he dealt with requirements for a fruitful life on the part of believers.

15:4. Another key here is the word **remain** (abide) which appears no fewer than eleven times in the passage. It seems to suggest an effortless resting in the Lord, confident in the promised union between the vine and the true branches.

Furthermore, John used the word *remain* forty times in his Gospel and twenty-seven more times in his epistles. In the context of this passage, it seems to emphasize an ongoing faith and loving obedience to the Father and the Son that results in fruit. The fruit in this passage seems to focus on spirit-generated behavior of Christians, though again this is not the only interpretation. Many sermons have been preached on emphasizing fruit as other people who have been influenced by the gospel.

This is new covenant thinking. The disciples and all believers since them must give up the idea that true Christianity emphasizes memberships and associations rather than life in Christ through the Spirit. True believers, demonstrating the fruit of the Spirit because the Spirit of God lives in them, are pruned so their fruit will increase.

15:5. Here we have the key verse of the passage, although it only expands what we have already learned on the first paragraph. Gromacki writes, "Christ identified Himself as the true Vine, the believers as the branches, and God the Father as the vine dresser (John 15:1,5). The fruit of the vine is Christlikeness. Although the Holy Spirit is not called a vine, He is a producer of fruit. The analogy could refer to a grapevine or to a fruit-bearing tree" (Gromacki, p. 57).

Let us go back to the Galatians passage and see how this teaching of John 15 links closely to what Jesus has already said in John 14 about the Holy Spirit: "Those who belong to Christ Jesus have crucified the sinful nature with its passions and desires. Since we live by the Spirit, let us keep in step with the Spirit. Let us not become conceited, provoking and envying each other" (Gal. 5:24–26). In my view, John 15 is not a passage on evangelism and the **fruit** does not describe new believers. This passage probably deals with discipleship and **fruit** describes godly behavior.

15:6. Verse 6 narrows other possible interpretations of verse 2. We struggle a bit with the words, "he cuts off." But **thrown away and withers** takes it further than we want to go in any reference to people who may have been true believers at one time. Certainly the words **thrown into the fire and burned** could never refer to those who were at one time true believers.

Blum treats this carefully and wisely:

> These words have been interpreted in at least three ways: (1) the "burned" branches are Christians who have lost their salvation. (But this contradicts many passages, e.g., 3:16,36; 5:24; 10:28–29; Rom. 8:1.) (2) the 'burned' branches represent Christians who will lose rewards but not salvation at the judgment seat of Christ (1 Cor. 3:15). (But Jesus spoke here of *dead* branches; such a branch "is thrown away and withers.") (3) the "burned" branches refer to professing Christians who, like Judas, are not genuinely saved and therefore are judged. Like a dead branch, a person without Christ is spiritually dead and therefore will be punished in eternal fire (cf. Matt. 25:46) (Blum, p. 325).

15:7–8. The focus of this passage is on the positive side (the branches remaining) and the Lord put aside all reference to branches that are removed. He also indicated that fruit-bearing is to the Father's glory and that those who bear **much fruit** demonstrate their relationship to Christ.

The distinctive factor here links an effective prayer life with fruit-bearing. Carson sums it up: "In short, Christians must remember that the fruit that issues out of their obedient faith-union with Christ lies at the heart of how Jesus brings glory to his Father. Those who are contemplating the claims of the gospel, like John's readers, must reckon with the fact that failure to honour the Son is failure to honour God (5:23)" (Carson, p. 518).

But John also talked here about complications in the application. Even when we understand the metaphor and grasp the analogy, we struggle with how best to make this work in our own lives. Let us understand Jesus' words: You are already clean; you must remain in me; your fruit glorifies God. Even in this temporary life, some things remain. The abiding realities of this passage include answered prayer, the Father's glory, and Jesus' affirmation of discipleship.

B Affection in the Body (15:9–17)

SUPPORTING IDEA: *What issue results from remaining in Christ? Joy, and a lasting friendship with Jesus. Up to this point in Scripture, only Abraham had been called God's friend; but now the circle widened and the Lord invited eleven disciples in. Notice again the emphasis on love. Described in an earlier chapter as a testimony to the world (13:35), love now becomes an absolute command for believers, the chief fruit of the Spirit (Gal. 5:22–23), and the essential quality for all ministry.*

15:9–10. Here we enter one of the great love passages of the New Testament. Six times in the next eleven verses the disciples will be told to love one another.

Once again, Jesus placed himself between the Father and the disciples. The Father loves first; then the Son reflects that love; and we, his people, remain in his love. Remaining in the Lord's love also requires obedience and brings joy.

If we thought that abiding in the vine-like branches constitutes some mystical relationship, we learn immediately that it centers on obedience—a theme that John has emphasized before. And when we obey Christ's commands, we follow his example with the Father.

15:11. A new word enters the chapter as the Lord told the disciples he wanted them to experience the joy he had already found in obedience. Morris observes, "It is an inspiring thought that Jesus calls his followers into *joy*. The Christian life is not some shallow, insipid following of a traditional pattern. It is a life characterized by 'unexhausted (and inexhaustible) power for fresh creation'" (Morris, p. 674).

15:12–14. Not only do the friends of Jesus remain in his love; they must also obey his commands. These three verses represent a power-packed passage of the New Testament.

John never forgot these words. They appear in various forms throughout his three epistles, particularly the first. John 15:13 is one of the most dramatic verses of the New Testament: **Greater love has no one than this, that he lay down his life for his friends.** But we sometimes forget verse 14 that links friendship with obedience to the command to love. Sometimes Christians get so busy figuring out how they should be loving God that they forget to love one another. In fact, a constant and genuine love for one another would be one way to show love for God. We do well at this point in the Gospel of John to remember Romans 5:8: "But God demonstrates his own love for us in this: While we were still sinners, Christ died for us."

When we study the imperatives of the four Gospels, we see that Jesus left many commands for his disciples and for us. But this one seems to take precedence over all the others. The central command has nothing to do with doctrine, church size, or the order of worship. It could not be more simple to understand or more difficult to carry out: **Love each other as I have loved you.** Tenney comments, "Unity instead of rivalry, trust instead of suspicion, obedience instead of self-assertion must rule the disciples' common labors. The measure of their love for one another is that of his love for them . . . which would be further demonstrated by his forthcoming sacrifice" (Tenney, *EBC*, p. 153).

15:15. The disciples were Jesus' **servants**, but he wanted to elevate their status to **friends**. But we must not forget that servant (*doulos*) was a positive Old Testament concept. The word *friend* may have shocked the disciples, since in the Bible only Abraham is called God's friend (Jas. 2:23). It is interesting, too, that Jesus linked this friendship with his teaching. These disciples had become Jesus' friends because of what he had shared with them about the Father's truth.

We need to remember, particularly in this day of easy language about relationships with God, that the friendship of this passage is not reciprocal. Jesus may call the disciples his **friends,** but they still address him as *Lord* and *Master.* In fact, that is the pattern of the entire Bible. As Carson points out, "Neither God nor Jesus is ever referred to in Scripture as the 'friend' of anyone. Of course, this does not mean that either God or Jesus is an *'unfriend':* if one measures friendship strictly on the basis of who loves most, guilty sinners can find no better and truer friend than in the God and Father of our Lord Jesus Christ, and in the Son whom He has sent. But mutual, reciprocal friendship of the modern variety is not in view, and cannot be without demeaning God" (Carson, p. 522).

15:16–17. Verse 16 reminds us again that we do not find God; he finds us. The linking of answered prayer with spiritual fruit in one's life comes at us in Scripture over and over again. The connection with the Galatians passage is important since the first and foremost fruit of the Spirit is love. Lest the disciples misconstrue the nature of the central command, verse 17 repeats it one more time.

In the context of love, this mission for the Master goes on and goes out. These abiding, fruit-bearing, loving branches—Christian believers who obey the Father and the Son—are candidates for answered prayer as these men learned in the following years. Here, the reference to fruit can possibly be stretched to the concept of new converts, although we dare not dismiss the idea of living out the spiritual fruit of Galatians 5 in a lasting way.

Some New Testament scholars believe that verse 17 launches the next section of the chapter rather than closing this one. Loving each other is central to bearing fruit of any kind and will be a significant defense against the onslaught of an evil world.

C Antagonism in the World (15:18–27)

SUPPORTING IDEA: *The world hates Christians because of their link with the Lord. We could say that persecution comes because of separation (Christians are not a part of the world; they belong to the Savior), and proclamation (Christians, like their Lord, speak the truth about sin).*

15:18–19. Once again, the concept of God's sovereignty leaps from the text. We were all once in the world, but those who belong to Jesus have been chosen by him out of the world. The hatred the world shows Christians is nothing more or less than a reflection of the hatred it shows Jesus himself. Believers have a different nature than "worldlings." John 17 offers a detailed commentary on this, and the epistles of Paul develop it into a full-blown theology of two natures. Such a comparison should not lead us to pride. Jesus reminded the disciples that they had a special nature because he chose them out of the world and allowed the Holy Spirit to minister through them.

In this passage the present tense of the last verb (**hates**) indicates that this should be an expected and normal state of being—a Christian lifestyle. John used the word **world** five times in two verses, emphasizing the disharmony between those whose citizenship is in another country but who live on this planet.

15:20–21. The quotation in verse 20 comes from 13:16 and indicates the reason for the world's antagonism: Jesus' disciples are inseparably connected with their Master. When John wrote these words, the persecution under the Roman emperor Tacitus had already begun. In this chapter we have grown accustomed to seeing the word *love*, but now we see a new word—*hate*, which appears seven times in verses 18–25. All of us have cause at one time or another to lean heavily on John 15:21: **They will treat you this way because of my name, for they do not know the One who sent me.**

Two other factors surface. We have seen that the world hates believers because they have a different nature. In verse 20, we note the world's hatred because of our association with Christ. Verse 20 tells us the hatred stems from the world's ignorance of the truth. This leads us into the next section where the Lord indicated this antagonism is also caused by proclamation.

15:22–23. The second reason for worldly antagonism is the resentment at Jesus' person and message. When people are brought face to face with the gospel message and refuse it to continue in their sin, they bring upon themselves the guilt and consequences of their sin. This is strong language, especially in view of the brief statement of verse 23. The phrase **be guilty of sin** "implies that the sin in question remains like a personal possession with the person who commits it. It is not something that can be over and done with" (Morris, p. 681).

The truth of the gospel convicts. When people are brought face to face with the ugliness of sin in their lives, they tend to fall back on the solution of killing the messenger. It is not difficult to picture a motorist rushing home from work, delighted that the traffic allows him greater freedom on this particular day. He takes advantage of it by driving ten or fifteen miles over the speed limit. Pulled over in a radar check, he becomes angry not at himself for speeding but at the officer for pulling him over and writing a ticket for one hundred dollars.

In today's world of relative truth, relative ethics, and relative morality, we assume people will try to get away with anything they can and will justify their behavior when they do get caught. What we cannot tolerate in our sophisticated sinning is the carelessness of people who get caught. And since we are a society of victims—none of us responsible for our own behavior—we must find someone else to blame: our parents, the repressive culture, poverty, that pushy policeman, perhaps even God.

15:24–25. Here we add a fourth reason for the world's hatred—conviction by the gospel. At the end of the passage Jesus redirected the disciples' thinking to the miracles they had seen. He argued that if he had never proclaimed the Father's message, never done any miracles, he could have gotten along just fine in the world. Once they understood that a messianic prophet was among them, they fulfilled Psalms 35:19 and 69:4 by rejecting both the Son and the Father.

So condemnation came because of Jesus' presence, his proclamation, and his **miracles.** Jesus repeatedly asked anyone who would listen to place faith in him and his message, not just in the miracles. The point here is that they had rejected him, his message, and his miracles. Carson says, "Religious interests that pursue signs may be suspicious (4:48), and faith based on sight is intrinsically inferior (20:29); even so, it is infinitely better than no faith, and the signs and works of Jesus make legitimate claim on faith (4:34; 5:36; 9:32–33; 10:38). Rejection of Jesus' words (v. 22) and works (v. 24) is thus the rejection of the clearest light, the fullest revelation; and therefore incurs the most central, deep-stained guilt" (Carson, p. 526).

15:26–27. These two verses form a bridge into chapter 16. The Counselor, whom we met in 14:16,26, will come from the Father and his chief work will be to proclaim the message of Jesus. We talk a great deal about spiritual gifts—a concept appearing in four major passages of the New Testament (Rom. 12; 1 Cor. 12; Eph. 4; 1 Pet. 4). A spiritual gift is a special order of grace that enables Christians to serve God effectively. Spiritual gifts come to us through the agency of the Holy Spirit who acts sovereignly in determining who gets what gift. He also provides the power for the exercise of these gifts.

We see that the Counselor is far more than just a defense attorney; he energizes us for the work he calls us to do. And part of that work reminds us that the Holy Spirit testifies to the world through witnesses like the disciples—and like us.

This verse ought to take away any casual carelessness we have about our role in God's plan for the world. How easy it would be to assume that God sends the Holy Spirit to descend upon whomever he wishes and to zap that person into regeneration. But we know that faith comes by hearing and hearing by the Word of God. Jesus reminds the disciples, **you also must testify.**

> **MAIN IDEA REVIEW:** *This chapter emphasizes two great truths—our personal relationship with the Lord and our divinely appointed mission to go and bear fruit—fruit that will last.*

III. CONCLUSION

Two Horses Wide

The distance between the rails on a standard U.S. railroad gauge is four feet, eight and one-half inches—a strange number. Why was it used? The New World copied a British model, a pattern that has characterized much of our life for over two hundred years. Then why did the English build railroads four feet, eight and one-half inches apart? The first rail lines in Great Britain were built by people who had built the pre-railroad tramways. They used the same tools and measures they had used for building wagons. Therefore, the rails ended up with the exact same spacing between them as the wagon wheels.

But why were wagon wheels four feet, eight and one-half inches apart? Because this corresponded to the wheel ruts in their ancient roads, and it simply did not make any sense to change the width and thereby damage the wagons. Apparently they had not yet learned that "wider is better!"

In this crucial historic quest, we keep digging to find out how the wheel ruts in their ancient roads got to be four feet, eight and one-half inches wide. We learn that the roads in ancient Britain were built by the Roman legions. Those ruts that determined the space of rails on modern trains were first created by Roman war chariots. They were designed exactly wide enough to accommodate the back ends of two war horses!

John 15 is a chapter about standards and measurements. But it does not ask us to go back and compare ourselves with the first-century church that struggled through the Roman Empire when those war chariots rampaged over the Mediterranean world and as far as Europe, Asia, and the British Isles. It tells us we must make the comparison with the vine and keep the connection so the relationship will never be severed. And the standard is not four feet, eight and one-half inches but the life, message, and commands of our Lord Jesus Christ.

John 15:1–25 was dropped into the middle of strategic teaching in this Gospel about the Holy Spirit. This probably accounts for the constant relational emphasis of these verses and helps us understand the meaning of *fruit*. What seems clear is that Christians must arrange their lives to make this abiding possible so love and joy can abound even in the face of the world's hatred.

PRINCIPLES

- No branch can bear fruit by itself.
- Greater love has no one than this, that he lay down his life for his friends.
- No servant is greater than his master.
- Jesus said, "If they persecuted me, they will persecute you also."

APPLICATIONS

- Remain in Christ and his word to be fruitful.
- Love other Christians faithfully and fervently.
- Do not be surprised by the world's antagonism.

IV. LIFE APPLICATION

The Discipled Minority

By the year 2001, a minority majority will exist in 226 U.S. counties. California reached a state-wide minority majority in 2000 and Texas will get there by 2010. In less than one life span, Americans who belong to racial and ethnic minority groups—Blacks, Asians, Native Americans, and Hispanics—will outnumber non-Hispanic whites and attain a majority about the year 2050.

Minority strongholds like New Mexico, Hawaii, and the aforementioned counties show us the vanguard of a demographic shift that will transform politics and business over the next fifty years. The specific rapidly-growing areas will be few and far between; we will have some areas in which whites will be a minority and others in which each of the traditional minorities will represent small and foreign-looking groups.

If we plot this on a map, we see a vast half-moon of Hispanic and black populations across the whole southern third of the United States, while huge northern blocks, including some entire states, remain almost exclusively white. More than ever before in North American history, everyone will get a chance to feel what it is like to be a member of a minority group.

In this section of the Fourth Gospel, Jesus attempted to explain to his disciples how they would no longer be majority Jews in their own homeland of Israel, but would become spiritual resident aliens, pilgrims, and strangers on planet earth. To endure the world's hatred and still offer necessary witness, they had no choice but constant abiding in the vine.

Upon concluding his teaching about the vine and the branches and what that would mean in terms of a minority relationship to surrounding culture, Jesus returned to what he had been saying in the upper room. He referred again to the coming Counselor, the Helper who would make it possible for believers to function as a spiritual minority group.

V. PRAYER

Father, thank you that we can abide in you and in your Son Jesus. Please keep us tightly connected so the sap of your love can flow freely into our lives, and through our lives into the lives of others. Amen.

VI. DEEPER DISCOVERIES

A. Friends (15:13–15)

Know anyone who lives in Philadelphia? Ever had an experience with a philanthropist? The first root of both of these words (*phil*) comes from the

Greek word *philos,* describing the love of a friend. Greek literature used the word to describe followers of a political leader, clients of a wealthy man, or even legal assistants. The Romans personalized the word a bit more, using it to refer to relatives and those connected to the family.

Philos appears twenty-nine times in the New Testament, of which more than half appear in the writings of Luke. In almost every case Luke uses the term exactly the way we would use it today (e.g., 11:5–8; 14:12; 15:16). It emphasizes a special relationship we can have with a person who knows us well, has been one of us, and yet has the power to solve our problems and relieve our distress.

The concept of the divine friend forms one of Gariepy's *100 Portraits of Christ:* "If the worth of a friend is determined by that person's love, its quality and consistency, and bringing the best out of us, our reasoning leads us to realize that the greatest Friend we have is the One who loved us with an infinite love and enables us to become the best that we can be. Jesus gave the supreme test of friendship when he said, 'Greater love has no one than this, that one lay down his life for his friends' (John 15:13). Our Lord's sacrifice on Calvary is the greatest act of love ever demonstrated on our behalf. By his salvation and power he lifts life to its highest heights as he enhances, enriches, and ennobles the life we yield to him" (Gariepy, pp. 139–40).

B. Fruit That Will Last (15:16)

The Greek word for *fruit* (*karpos*) appears sixty-six times in the New Testament. It generally refers to the harvest of the earth, trees, bushes, flocks, and herds. Jesus cursed the fig tree when it did not bring forth fruit (Mark 11:13–14,20–21), and *communion* is called the "fruit of the vine" in Matthew 26:29. The analogy moves further when Elizabeth spoke of Jesus as the "fruit" of Mary's womb (Luke 1:42, KJV) and Peter called him the "fruit" of David's line (Acts 2:30, NKJV).

The first introduction to fruit as spiritual character appears in Matthew 7 in the Sermon on the Mount where we read that "every good tree bears good fruit, but a bad tree bears bad fruit. A good tree cannot bear bad fruit, and a bad tree cannot bear good fruit. Every tree that does not bear good fruit is cut down and thrown into the fire. Thus, by their fruit you will recognize them" (Matt. 7:17–20).

Perhaps John 15 builds on that sermon which would have been familiar to the disciples. Whether the fruit refers to godly characters or others won to Christ, the principle is still the same—Christians produce a lifestyle glorifying to God as long as they remain in the vine. Hughes sums it up: "While the love of Christ is unnatural to us, it is still possible. The potential for the *agape* love which our Lord commands exists within the relationship of abiding in Him. As we as branches abide in the Vine, we will relate in right fashion to the other branches. We will sacrifice for each other. We will foster a deep mutuality, and we will promote one another until we all feel like kings" (Hughes, p. 78).

C. Chosen (15:19)

The sovereignty of God in selecting individuals for salvation rises off the pages of this Gospel like steam from blacktop highways baked in the sun, then showered by rain. The English word *choose* translates the Greek word *eklegomai,* meaning "to select someone or something out by speaking." The verb occurs twenty-one times in the New Testament and the noun (*choice*) about thirty times. Detzler identifies four truths which "need to be seen, if one is to understand election: God is eternally just; a man is responsible to obey God's call; evangelism is essential to Christian living; faith supersedes logic" (Detzler, p. 71).

The *Westminster Confession of Faith* describes the doctrine of election in the following words: "All those whom God hath predestined unto life . . . He is pleased, in His appointed and accepted time, effectually to call by His Word and Spirit."

D. They Would Not Be Guilty (15:22)

We would miss the meaning of this verse if we thought that God would not hold first-century peoples responsible for their own destiny if Jesus had never come and proclaimed the gospel. The issue centers in the result of unbelief and rejection. Carson says, "By coming and speaking to them Jesus incited the most central and controlling of sins: rejection of God's gracious revelation, rebellion against God, decisive preference for darkness rather than light" (Carson, p. 526).

VII. TEACHING OUTLINE

A. INTRODUCTION

1. Lead Story: No More Slaves
2. Context: John 15 represents a continuation of the Lord's teaching on the night of his death. As they strolled through a garden, he explained the significance of abiding in him and how the Counselor sent from heaven testifies to a hateful world about Christ through miracles, witnesses, and persecution.
3. Transition: Remember that John 15 has been dropped into the middle of a strategic teaching about the Holy Spirit. This probably accounts for the constant relational emphasis of these verses and helps us understand the meaning of *fruit.* Christians must arrange or rear-

range their lives to make room for abiding in Christ, or his will can never be realized.

B. COMMENTARY
1. Abiding in the Lord (15:1–8)
    a. Components of the analogy (15:1–4)
    b. Complications in the analogy (15:5–8)
2. Affection in the Body (15:9–17)
    a. Friends of Jesus remain in his love (15: 9–11)
    b. Friends of Jesus obey his commands (15:12–14)
    c. Friends of Jesus love one another (15:15–17)
3. Antagonism in the World (15:18–27)
    a. Caused by separation (15:18–19)
    b. Caused by association (15:20–21)
    c. Caused by proclamation (15:22–25)
    d. Caused by testimony (15:26–27)

C. CONCLUSION: THE DISCIPLED MINISTRY

VIII. ISSUES FOR DISCUSSION

1. Name some specific things we can do to abide in Christ.
2. How do we relate to Christ differently as his friends than we would as his servants?
3. Give some examples of the world's hatred of Christians.

John 16

When Jesus Speaks

Quote

"*All* I have seen teaches me to trust the Creator for all I have not seen."

Ralph Waldo Emerson

John 16

IN A NUTSHELL

This is the last chapter of Jesus' teaching to the disciples in this Gospel. He had already mentioned the Holy Spirit twice, and now he explained in detail how the Holy Spirit would teach and lead the disciples. In addition, he reminded them how important it was that they listen to him because when Jesus spoke, important things happened in the lives of those who heard.

When Jesus Speaks

I. INTRODUCTION

How's That Again?

The Los Angeles Times recently printed a sampling of signs from around the world that attempted to communicate in English. Here are just a few examples.

In a hotel elevator in Paris: "Please leave your values at the front desk."

In a hotel in Zurich: "Because of the impropriety of entertaining guests of the opposite sex in the bedrooms, it is suggested that the lobby be used for this purpose."

On the door of a Moscow inn: "If this is your first visit to Russia, you are welcome to it."

In a Soviet newspaper: "There will be a Moscow exhibition of arts by 15,000 Soviet Republic painters and sculptors. These were executed over the past two years."

In a Bucharest hotel lobby: "The lift is being fixed for the next day. During that time we regret that you will be unbearable."

Communication can be a tricky thing, and not only when language translation is involved. We often think of communication as *word* exchange, but in fact, it is *meaning* exchange—two or more people sharing ideas and understanding what is *meant*, not just what is *said*.

In John 16 Jesus reviewed for the disciples many of the promises and challenges he had already put before them. In this chapter communication words abound—words like *told, remember, warned, asks, said, speak, mean*. And if that were not enough, we have communication expressions such as "now you are speaking clearly" and "without figures of speech" (v. 29).

Along with the disciples, we can learn much in these verses about what happens when Jesus speaks to us. Verse 20 seems to be the key: "I tell you the truth, you will weep and mourn while the world rejoices. You will grieve, but your grief will turn to joy."

II. COMMENTARY

When Jesus Speaks

MAIN IDEA: *The Holy Spirit is not some supernatural "influence" hovering in the clouds above. He comes to us, and through us he carries out his ministry to the world. He is a significant part of the communication process when Jesus speaks.*

🅰 Confusion Turns to Truth (16:1–16)

SUPPORTING IDEA: *Persecution comes to those who faithfully stand up for Christ. The Book of Acts barely gets underway as two of these disciples (Peter and John) are arrested for their proclamation of the resurrection (Acts 4:1–3). So the promise of the Spirit also warns that those who are filled with the Spirit will suffer for their faith.*

16:1–4. These verses prophesy the conditions that the church endured in varying degrees from Pentecost to A.D. 313. Obviously, the early years of persecution were made more difficult by the absence of the Lord, and he made that point in these verses. The purpose of the Lord's teaching was to counteract the temptation these men would face to **go astray** as they faced two major types of persecution.

The first was excommunication: **they will put you out of the synagogue.** Peter and John were arrested at the temple; Paul, Barnabas, and Silas were thrown out of numerous synagogues; Martin Luther was exiled from the Roman Catholic church. These verses spin directly from John 15:18–20 where the Lord had predicted persecution because of hatred by the world.

The second dimension is murder: **anyone who kills you will think he is offering a service to God.** From Stephen to the thousands of modern martyrs, witnesses for Jesus have always faced the possibility of death. Like the Pharisees and Sadduccees who pursued Christians in the New Testament, people today still persecute followers of Jesus for religious reasons. In fact, there were more martyrs for the Christian faith in the twentieth century than all previous centuries put together.

Hughes quotes Bonhoeffer's challenge from 1937 during Hitler's rise in Germany: "Suffering . . . is the badge of true discipleship. The disciple is not above his Master . . . Luther reckoned suffering among the marks of the true church . . . Discipleship means allegiance to the suffering Christ, and it is therefore not at all surprising that Christians should be called upon to suffer" (cited in Hughes, p. 83).

The practical application of these warnings is in verse 4. These disciples would experience persecution in a matter of weeks, certainly months. And the Lord wanted them to recall this quiet night of teaching when chaos later broke out on the streets of Jerusalem. Some have puzzled over the sentence, **I did not tell you this at the first because I was with you,** especially in view of the prediction of persecution in Matthew 10:17,21,28. But this was personal instruction linked with the role of the Holy Spirit, something absent from Matthew 10.

16:5–7. The Lord told the disciples he was leaving them and going back to the Father. This caused them deep sorrow. But in fact, the glass was half-full rather than half-empty. If Jesus did not leave, the Counselor could not come, and he had important work to do in the world. Jesus did not say why the Holy Spirit could not come until he went away, but we understand from the New Testament that the Son's return to glory was a condition for sending the Holy Spirit to work in the world.

But that is our perspective. We dare not let our understanding, derived from the text of the entire New Testament, detract from the fear and confusion the disciples must have felt on this dreary night.

Imagine a mother of two children whose husband has been away on business. She must go to the airport to pick him up. She informs the children that they will be alone at home for three or four hours while she makes this lengthy trip across the city. They do not want her to leave; they fear what might happen to them; they want to go with her. But for a variety of reasons she must go alone. She assures them that all will be better for the family when she returns with their father, whom they have missed. The anticipation and reluctance of those children can be magnified many times by the sadness of the disciples on this occasion.

16:8. Many evangelistic sermons have been preached with three points prominently displayed—sin, righteousness, and judgment. We will look at these words in the following verses, but here we want to concentrate on the central verb **convict** that translates the Greek word *elegcho*. What did Jesus mean when he said the Holy Spirit **will convict the world of guilt?** Translations have handled the word differently, choosing English words like *reprove* or *convince*. In the Septuagint, we see the word primarily focused on correction (Job 5:17; Ps. 141:5; Prov. 3:11–12).

Since the New Testament speaks often of the Holy Spirit's work in the lives of believers, we find it a little more difficult to understand what the Spirit does in the world (*kosmos*). We must not miss the important words "to you" at the end of verse 7. The Holy Spirit does not float around the cosmos like Casper the friendly ghost, spreading general feelings of conviction. The New Testament makes it plain that conviction and awareness of sin come through the hearing of Scripture. Godet emphasizes the Holy Spirit's work "through the agency of the disciples" and says, "The discourse of St. Peter at Pentecost and its results are the best commentary on this promise" (Godet, II, p. 309).

The reference to *world*, as we have seen repeatedly in this Gospel, centers in the unbelieving society which will be challenged and shaken in its devotion to sin by the power of the Word and the Spirit working through God's people. John centered on the Spirit's work to unbelievers in verses 8–11 and then switched to his work in believers in verses 12–15.

16:9. The last part of verse 9 offers the key to this section. The work of the Holy Spirit in the lives of Christians convicts unsaved people because their message radiates Christ. Unbelief is the condemning sin that closes the door to heaven and opens the door to hell. People do not go to hell because they smoke, drink, or curse but because they reject faith in Christ. Furthermore, this sin characterizes every unregenerate person. God is not looking for perfect people but people who are willing to accept atonement that he has already provided.

16:10. The Holy Spirit also convicts the world **in regard to righteousness.** This element of the message is connected to the ascension which completed the glorification process and therefore proved the righteousness of Christ (Pss. 17:1,15; 24:1–4). It is not that the world does not believe in righteousness; unbelievers and believers alike magnify the work of people like Albert Schweitzer and Mother Teresa. But the world only believes in *relative* righteousness, and Christ's righteousness is *absolute*.

These chapters tell us how the Counselor, the Spirit of truth, can produce God's righteous fruit in our lives that is patterned after the life and righteousness of Jesus himself. People do not see their need for Christ and do not believe in him (v. 9) because they have a confused view of righteousness unformed by the truth. Justification is a central issue in salvation, and it has everything to do with righteousness. God declares believers righteous on the basis of the death of Christ who paid the penalty for sin.

16:11. Here is where so much preaching on this passage goes awry. A discussion of sin and righteousness seems to lead almost automatically to a warning about judgment for those who reject Christ. But the word **because** that appears after each of these key words indicates that the Lord was not talking about "judgment to come" as he did in 12:31–32. The final judgment of this world and Satan was accomplished at Calvary. That great enemy of truth is now living on borrowed time. Judgment will come, but the focus here is on an awareness that the prince of this world **now stands condemned.**

16:12–13. Verse 12 is a good example of progressive revelation—the principle that God does not dump all truth at one time and expect us to remember it but teaches us truths as we need to know them. The Bible itself is the greatest example of this as we read God's progressive unfolding of the plan of salvation from Genesis to Revelation. Does the phrase **more than you can now bear** mean the disciples were not able to understand everything or that they could not accomplish necessary ministry without the Holy Spirit's help? We should probably conclude that both were true. But when the Counselor comes, it will be a different situation. He will teach God's truth to believers.

Some people see this passage relating only to the revelatory work of the Spirit in the lives of those who wrote the New Testament. Certainly that is in view, but there is a broader emphasis here on illumination as well as revelation—the Spirit of God enabling us to understand what others have written about God's truth. How often Jesus told anyone who would listen that he had no personal agenda, no particular message of his own. He had been sent by the Father and would proclaim only the Father's truth. Now he said exactly the same thing about the Holy Spirit.

All truth is God's truth and it comes to us through creation, through the person of Jesus, and through the Scriptures. Tenney tells us that "'guide' implies leadership toward a person who is interested in travelling on the right path, but who needs help in finding it . . . The believer may not have progressed far along the way of truth, but is desirous of going on in the right direction, and needs the good offices of the Spirit to conduct him on his way" (Tenney, p. 235).

16:14–15. When truth is communicated and believed, it brings glory to God. More specifically, the Holy Spirit, the Counselor, will glorify the Son of God by telling Christians even more about God's truth than Jesus had time to do during his brief years on earth. These verses are fulfilled repeatedly when people in our day read the writings of Paul or Peter and know more about Jesus because the Holy Spirit first revealed it and now explains it.

16:16. Finally, the Lord emphasized the purpose of truth by reminding the disciples one more time that he was leaving. This verse serves as a connection between the early part of chapter 16 and the remainder that deals with the disciples' reaction to Jesus' departure. The phrase **you will see me** appears again in verses 17–19 and reminds us of 14:18: "I will not leave you as orphans; I will come to you."

Bible scholars argue whether this refers to the second coming, the arrival of the Counselor, or the return of Jesus from the dead after the resurrection. It seems that the context best fits a post-resurrection appearance, although other interpretations are possible. But the meaning was not clear to the disciples.

B Grief Turns to Joy (16:17–24)

> **SUPPORTING IDEA:** *Grief turns to joy when believers understand the Lord, actualize the hope of seeing him again, and ask in his name. The result is not just grief followed by joy but the actual transforming of grief into joy.*

16:17–18. Now we find the disciples more confused than ever, still not able to grasp the Lord's words and unable to activate the command, "Do not let your hearts be troubled" (14:1).

John wasted no time getting into the flow of the problem. Both these verses contain the question, **What does he mean?** The disciples asked that question more than twice, since verse 18 tells us, **they kept asking.** Their conclusion? **We don't understand what he is saying.**

The word *communicate* does not appear in this passage. But we have already seen communication as a theme of the entire chapter. It contains a flurry of words related to the communication process. In the second half of the chapter, the word *ask* shows up ten times; *said* appears six times; *tell* four times; and *mean* three times. And we do not want to focus only on the historical setting of the disciples. What happened to them when Jesus spoke can also happen to us.

16:19–20. Jesus had just repeated what he told the disciples in verse 16, and he acknowledged that he understood their confusion. There would be a time of sadness and grieving, but there was also a promise: **your grief will turn to joy.** Confusion turns to truth and grief turns to joy when we understand what Jesus has said.

But all this takes us back to the time frame. When is this **little while?** Jesus had not linked the **little while** with his return to the Father, but the disciples made that connection in verse 17. The issue for us is this: did they misunderstand or was that his intent? Since the entire context of John 14:1–16:33 centers in the Lord's departure and the coming of the Holy Spirit, we are directed to that time frame to understand the meaning of **a little while.**

From the crucifixion to the resurrection, all Jesus' disciples (not only the eleven) would weep and mourn. They needed to understand that he would see them again personally, and then after his ascension the Counselor would come.

16:21–22. Their grief would also turn to joy because they would see him again. We cannot be sure that the Lord intended any kind of time frame in the choice of this analogy. But the pain of labor, however long it may seem, is normally a little while. Because of the confusion brought on by grief, Jesus kept repeating himself—another key to communication that we now call "the principle of successive rehearsals." The grief turning to joy was not like a sorrow followed by joy—for example, illness. In that case, the absence of the cause of the grief brings about the joy. Not so with the birth of a baby. When pregnancy culminates in delivery, the cause of pain becomes the cause of joy.

16:23–24. Finally, we learn that grief can turn to joy because we ask in his name. Verse 23 contains two different words rendered by the English word **ask.** The first might be translated "inquire," and the second, "request." These two words are not the same in meaning. To inquire means to ask for information. To request normally relates to soliciting favor or help in need. Although Jesus would teach his disciples after the resurrection, the high intensity of this session would cease.

The obvious need was to get rid of the grief—genuine sorrow at the Lord's departure that elated the world and crushed the disciples' dreams. Think about the couple on the road to Emmaus described by Luke. When Jesus approached them, "They stood still, their faces downcast" (Luke 24:17). They were headed home convinced that all the messianic promises had come to naught.

Asking in Jesus' name was introduced in chapter 14. "In Jesus' name, Amen" is no magical or mystical formula. When we pray in Jesus' name, it connects us to him by faith, it honors him as God, and proclaims his lordship in our lives.

As Hughes points out, "Praying in Christ's name means coming only in his merit, not our own. Christ's full name is Lord Jesus Christ, which means Jehovah, Saviour, God's anointed. It is this name whose merit we must humbly pray. We cannot think that somehow God will hear us because of our virtue. We come by virtue of his merit. Poverty of spirit is the basis on which we approach God, and our on-going poverty is the crown of blessing. If we learn this, if we come to God in poverty of spirit, we can expect our prayers to be answered" (Hughes, II, pp. 102–03).

Ⓒ Doubt Turns to Faith (16:25–30)

SUPPORTING IDEA: *During the forty days between his resurrection and ascension, Jesus taught his disciples that the Father loved them and the Son claimed them. We also need those important lessons.*

16:25–26. Ahead for these eleven men lay forty days of serious teaching that would take place between the resurrection and the ascension. During that time their doubt turned to faith—a faith that turned into zeal at Pentecost. In the life of any believer, doubt turns to faith because the Father loves us.

Some interpreters have suggested that Jesus deliberately created ambiguity because there were so many things about the crucifixion and resurrection that the disciples could not grasp. But if we adopt a communication model for this passage, it appears that the Lord spoke as clearly as he could at this point. Now he promised that he would speak plainly about the Father—probably a reference to those forty days of teaching. Jesus is the intercessor for all believers at the right hand of God the Father. But here he talked about prayer—going directly to the Father's throne.

This is a stunning passage. We know what the New Testament says about not needing any earthly mediator to reach the Father. Now the Lord said, **I am not saying that I will ask the Father on your behalf.** Those who have bonded with Jesus Christ through salvation, who have the presence and power of the Holy Spirit in their lives, who show the fruit of the Spirit because of their branch-like attachment to the vine—these people are accepted by the Father.

16:27–28. The origin of Jesus—such a controversial subject in chapter 8—now begins to break through to the disciples. In verses 27–28,30, the text asserts that Jesus came from the Father. Tenney's emphasis on the use of three different prepositions is worth reproducing here:

> It is unlikely that the prepositions (*para, ek,* and *apo*) were used interchangeably, since John differentiated the uses here and since he was not generally averse to repetition. The variation may be attributed fairly to design. The first preposition carries the idea of authority,

sometimes with the connotation of commission. It was employed in the Prologue (1:6) where John the Baptist's commission was stated. The second preposition implied source, "from within." It carried the idea of nature, for He who came out from the Father revealed the Father's nature to the world. The third expression was the disciples' word, which meant separation. Jesus had been in the company of the Father and now was separated from Him. In the lowest sense it implied pre-existence, which the disciples had acknowledged (Tenney, p. 241).

Verse 28 contains no fewer than four major doctrines, all a part of Christology: origin, incarnation, crucifixion, and ascension—all stated in one sentence.

16:29–30. Doubt can also turn to faith because the Spirit illumines us. These disciples had the right answer. But Jesus had just finished telling them he was speaking figuratively and would have to do so until the little while had passed. But they claimed to understand everything, to recognize his omniscience. They said they believed he came from God. This was the last week Jesus would spend with these disciples before the crucifixion. They had been listening to him teach and watching him work for three and one-half years. Now suddenly they claimed they had reached the conclusion that he came from God.

Of course, naiveté still clouded their thinking. They did not yet have the Spirit's illumination. The difference between not understanding and understanding the Bible comes not from years of seminary training, but from the presence and teaching ministry of the Holy Spirit.

D Fear Turns to Peace (16:31–33)

SUPPORTING IDEA: *Jesus punctured deceptive self-assurance with a penetrating question to remind the disciples that they would soon scatter and leave him. But his peace would abide with them in their grief and confusion.*

16:31. The marginal note at the beginning of this verse suggests even more strongly Jesus' response. It makes the exclamation a question: "Do you now believe?" Obviously they did not, and they were hampered by a deceptive self-assurance.

Picture a child picking up a heavy bowl from the dinner table in an effort to please Mom by carrying it to the kitchen. Mom says, "I think you'd better leave that for me; it's very heavy." But the child already has the bowl a few inches off the table. As she turns and takes a step or two, the bowl crashes to the floor.

Not everyone takes this verse in a negative tone. Tenney says, "The reply of Jesus was pathetic. . . . He was still unsure of their faith as he was when, after Peter's confession he said: 'Did I not choose you the twelve, and one of you is a devil?' (6:70)" (Tenney, p. 242.) But Godet accepts Jesus' words as commendation and even triumph: "Here is for Jesus a moment of unutterable sweetness; He has been recognized and understood—He Jesus—by these eleven Galileans. This is for Him enough; His work is for the moment ended; the Holy Spirit will finish by glorifying Him in them, and through them in mankind. There remains nothing further for Him but to close the conversation and give thanks" (Godet, p. 321).

Part of serious Bible study is thinking through options and letting God's Spirit direct you to a conclusion. Given the content of verse 32, it seems to me that Godet is unwarranted in his optimism.

16:32. These disciples had lived most of the past three years in self-confidence. Several times this had come out verbally, particularly in the pronouncements of Peter. But harder times were ahead. At the cross they would leave their Master, and after the cross they would be scattered. But after that traumatic little while, their fear would turn to peace because they would learn how to trust the Father.

Did they believe at this moment? John delayed his own testimony until he was inside the empty tomb, and even then with some reservation. "Finally the other disciple, who had reached the tomb first, also went inside. He saw and believed. (They still did not understand from Scripture that Jesus had to rise from the dead)" (John 20:8–9).

16:33. Inner peace is conditional; it can come only through Jesus. The world offers only trouble that need not plague Jesus' followers. We belong to the one who overcame the world. Fear turns to peace when we learn how to apply Jesus' victory in our lives.

For the final time Jesus said, **I have told you these things.** His intent for the whole evening drew to a climax in peace. Trouble in the world? Certainly. **But take heart! I have overcome the world.**

> **MAIN IDEA REVIEW:** *The Holy Spirit is not some supernatural "influence" hovering in the clouds above. He comes to us, and through us he carries out his ministry to the world. He is a significant part of the communication process when Jesus speaks.*

III. CONCLUSION

Ben's Little Book

Rebecca Rupp tells us that young Ben Franklin composed a master list of twelve resolutions that would guide his life. He kept track of his performance in a small book in which he entered a black mark every day for each resolution broken. Franklin had intended to reuse the little book, eventually erasing all the black marks as his performance improved. It did not. So many black marks appeared on top of black marks that the little book developed holes. He had to resort to keeping his records on a piece of ivory, from which the accumulated black marks could be erased with a wet sponge.

All of us are horrible spiritual failures. The Bible calls us to cast ourselves upon God's grace and to place our faith in Jesus. Failure will turn to success and faith will turn to sight when Jesus returns. Meanwhile, we cling to John 16:33 and delight that the Holy Spirit works these wonders in our hearts.

This is a great chapter for Christians, especially those who serve God as parents, pastors, or teachers. We struggle to understand passages of the Bible and then explain them to other people. Jesus has sent the Counselor to handle the Word of truth carefully so that we may grasp and receive truth, joy, faith, and peace when Jesus speaks.

PRINCIPLES

- The Spirit brings conviction to the world, and we are his instruments.
- Sin reigns because of unbelief, the ultimate sin that closes the door to heaven.
- Righteousness comes only through the risen Son who shares his righteousness with all who believe in him.

APPLICATIONS

- Understand that the struggles we face in the world come because of our relationship with Jesus.
- Let the Spirit of truth guide you into all truth.
- Know that Jesus alone can turn your grief to joy.
- Trust the Lord for peace in a troubling world.

IV. LIFE APPLICATION

Persecuted Christians

I wrote the first draft of this chapter just days after the annual observance of Persecuted Christians Sunday. The words of Jesus were not just for his immediate disciples to whom they were spoken, but for hundreds of thousands of modern believers who still struggle with grief, fear, and perhaps even doubt. Robbery, kidnapping, rape, and murder are common practice in many parts of the world where Christians live as an oppressed minority. Jesus speaks to them through this chapter.

Communication is meaning exchange, not a word exchange. How often the disciples had problems with that distinction. They heard Jesus' words clearly, but they failed to grasp the meaning behind the message.

John 16 introduces no significant new themes other than the details about the Holy Spirit's ministry in the world. John presented a graphic picture of the way the disciples would feel after Jesus left them and before the Counselor came. We learned at the beginning of chapter 14 that the disciples were troubled people, and we also know the troubling confusion of our own day.

So we read passages like this and we listen for the voice of Jesus through the Holy Spirit. Like our struggling brothers and sisters around the world, we hear him say, "I have told you these things, so that in me you may have peace. In this world you will have trouble. But take heart! I have overcome the world."

V. PRAYER

Father, thank you for the peace that Jesus gives, and thank you for the Holy Spirit, who guides us into truth and brings glory to you through us. Amen.

VI. DEEPER DISCOVERIES

Sin, Righteousness, and Judgment (16:11)

Correctly handling this text has challenged interpreters for years and will likely continue to do so for years to come. From another time and place we accept wisdom from one who has already gained the portals to dwell with the immortals. In *The Crises of the Christ*, Morgan offers a great paragraph springing from this passage:

> The first work of the Spirit with fallen man is that of producing conviction concerning sin, righteousness, and judgment. All these subjects are dealt with, however, from the centre of Christ and His work. Sin is shown to consist in the rejection of the Saviour; righteousness is declared to be possible through the fact of His ascension; and judgment is pronounced against all rebellion, "because the prince of this world hath been judged." The initial work of grace, therefore, is that of bringing the sinner to a consciousness of the truth concerning these vital matters. At this point human responsibility commences. If man refuses to yield to the truth understood, he remains outside the sphere of salvation. If, on the other hand, he responds to conviction by submission to Christ, and trust in Him, then the Spirit performs the stupendous miracle of regeneration. By communicating to the man "dead through trespasses and sins" the life of Christ, He quickens his spirit. This act of God restores man to his own true balance and proportion, lifting to the throne of his personality the spirit so long neglected, and dethroning the flesh so long

having occupied the place of power. More than this, the Spirit of God enters now into a perpetual partnership with the spirit of man, and thus initiates the life of power and of victory (Morgan, p. 376).

VII. TEACHING OUTLINE

A. INTRODUCTION

1. Lead Story: How's That Again?
2. Context: John 14–17 flows like a seamless garment of final instruction and prayer. The break between chapters 15 and 16 is inconsequential as the Lord's teaching continues on the subject of the Counselor.
3. Transition: The transition comes at the end of the chapter where Jesus announced his victory over the world and then, as chapter 17 opens, began his high priestly prayer.

B. COMMENTARY

1. Confusion Turns to Truth (16:1–16)
    a. Because Jesus warned us (16:1–4)
    b. Because Jesus ascended (16:5–11)
    c. Because Jesus sent the Spirit (16:12–16)
2. Grief Turns to Joy (16:17–24)
    a. Because we understand him (16:17–20)
    b. Because we see him again (16:21–22)
    c. Because we ask in his name (16:23–24)
3. Doubt Turns to Faith (16:25–30)
    a. Because the Father loves us (16:25–27)
    b. Because the Son claims us (16:28)
    c. Because the Spirit illumines us (16:29–30)
4. Fear Turns to Peace (16:31–33)
    a. Because we learn to trust the Father (16:31–32)
    b. Because we learn to apply the Son's victory (16:33)

C. CONCLUSION: PERSECUTED CHRISTIANS

VIII. ISSUES FOR DISCUSSION

1. Think of some ways the Holy Spirit guides you into all truth.
2. In what ways does the Holy Spirit use Christians to convict the world of sin, righteousness, and judgment?
3. How can your church minister more effectively to persecuted Christians around the world?

John 17

The Lord's Prayer

"*P*rayer is the soul's sincere desire,

unuttered or expressed."

James Montgomery

John 17

IN A NUTSHELL

*T*he real "Lord's Prayer" is not found in the synoptic Gospels but here in the seventeenth chapter of John's Gospel. It is offered from the wide and loving expanse of the Lord's heart. The prayer focuses on a series of relationships that provide a beautiful picture of how God expects his people to live.

The Lord's Prayer

I. INTRODUCTION

A Mother's Prayer

*A*s a child I recall lying in bed at night, listening to my mother praying aloud in the next room. Along with the prayers I could also hear at times the curses and anger of my atheistic father, who tried to interrupt her communication with God. I always felt on those occasions that I should not be able to listen, since prayer is a private and sacred domain one ought to maintain in secret. It does not seem right to be able to listen to your mother praying, especially when she is praying for you.

Yet that is precisely the type of experience every Christian can have when reading the seventeenth chapter of John's Gospel. Here, of course, it is not a mother but the Son of God praying aloud, praying *for the record.* And not only for the benefit of disciples who may have been within earshot but for every reader of the New Testament right up to the present time.

The Lord was just hours from the cross. A final evening of instruction began in the upper room at mealtime, and Jesus had explained to his disciples all the matters recorded in chapters 13–16 of this Gospel. Foremost among the themes of the evening had been an emphasis on the coming of the Holy Spirit and the continuing relationship the disciples would have with their Lord, even though he would be in heaven while they would extend his work on earth.

These five chapters of John are a golden repository of truth to which Christians have come for guidance and blessing for almost two thousand years. The capstone of the unit lies before us now as we listen to what one member of the Trinity says to another about what it is like to live "in the world." In this moment of grief as well as triumph, our Lord turned his eyes from earth to heaven and asked the God of the universe to heed his petitions on the authority of his relationship to his Father.

II. COMMENTARY

The Lord's Prayer

> **MAIN IDEA:** *One of Jesus' current ministries in heaven is to pray for us, and we may sometimes wonder what he says. Certainly there would be some difference between his current advocacy and what we find in this chapter, but John provided some general clues about matters that concern the Lord about the life of believers on earth.*

▲ Relationship of the Father to the Son (17:1–5)

> **SUPPORTING IDEA:** *Jesus, the model "finisher," asked the Father twice to have his glory returned (vv. 1,5). Right at the beginning of this prayer we learn that the Father's glory is the foundational purpose in praying.*

17:1. We have talked often in these studies about John's key words. In this chapter the words *they, them,* or *those* appear no fewer than nineteen times. These pronouns generally refer either to the world or to the disciples. The prayer begins by establishing the Sonship of our Lord. In the Old Testament, God was the Almighty One, the Sovereign, but rarely the Father. But this new covenant truth appears frequently in the Gospel of John.

There was no question that God loved his people and cared for them through the ages, but approachability was another matter. The pattern was fixed—God appeared through the priest and the high priest, who were confined to a certain place and time. But now earth had become the visited planet, and God moved among people in the person of his Son. No longer would there be a veil, but a family relationship between God the Father and his children—a relationship exemplified by Jesus the Son.

Verse 1 shows us how specifically Jesus prayed. It begins with a petition: **Glorify your Son, that your Son may glorify you.** Throughout the entire prayer Christ made only two requests for himself, and we find both of these in this first section of the chapter. G. Campbell Morgan observes, "The deepest passion of the heart of Jesus was not the saving of men, but the glory of God; and then the saving of men, because that is for the glory of God" (Morgan, p. 270).

17:2. In the Father-Son relationship of this passage, we also see the sovereignty of our Lord: **authority over all people.** This is the same word (*exousian*) found in the Great Commission when Matthew recorded Jesus' words about having received all authority from the Father. We do not often use the word *glorification,* but the New Testament applies it to Jesus in order to describe a fuller manifestation of his true nature that would become more acute at the time of the resurrection and ascension.

We should note that the Lord did not request power. Jesus did not take on sovereignty and omnipotence after the ascension. These eternal qualities he possessed then and he still possesses today as a member of the eternal Godhead. The result of this **authority over all people** and the major purpose of its exercise by the Son centers in eternal life for those designated to receive it. The entire prayer keys to this central idea of eternal life, since that is the result of the glorification of Christ in the lives of people. The Father gives Christ believers. This fact is emphasized no fewer than seven times in this chapter (vv. 2,6,9,11–12,24).

17:3. We also see here the salvation of our Lord in what has become a major New Testament text on the theology of redemption. What is eternal life? Knowing the only true God and Jesus Christ whom he sent. John recalled these words (which he probably overheard) in his first epistle: "And this is the testimony: God has given us eternal life, and this life is in his Son. He who has the Son has life; he who does not have the Son of God does not have life" (1 John 5:11–12).

For hundreds of years people have tried to know God without coming through the only door or walking the narrow way. But the Bible offers no access to the Father except through the Son. Any theology of God that leaves out Jesus Christ borders on idolatry (1 John 5:20–21).

Christ's definition of eternal life is important because it differs from the current concept of endless existence. The word **know** in verse 3 is *ginosko*, emphasizing an experiential relationship rather than just necessary information. The verb also appears here in the present tense, suggesting a continuing personal experience and contact with both the Father and the Son. Tenney writes, "However fully man lives in the world, he ultimately reaches the point where nothing is new because he has reached human limits. Only the knowledge of God can give enduring satisfaction, because God alone is eternal. Contact with God will provide the fullest experience, and the experience of God's eternal being will be eternal life" (Tenney, pp. 245–46).

17:4–5. The fourth segment of this first paragraph teaches us about the status of our Lord. Jesus' earthly ministry had now finished. Indeed, he would announce that from the cross. Here again we have the second petition, identical to the first—Jesus' only request of the Father regarding himself. He wanted to return home to claim again his status as the prince of heaven. Jesus had always been "about his Father's business." Now that earthly business was drawing to a close.

This was not some work Jesus constructed for himself but the completion of obedience to God's plan. Soon he would reassume the independent exercise of his divine attributes. "The hour," which he had so frequently said had not yet come, had now arrived.

We dare not miss the practical application of this paragraph while relishing the splendor of its theology. Jesus set a model for finishing tasks God gives us to do. Think of pastors leaving churches before their work is finished. Think of missionaries returning from the field before God's actual release. Think of the many times you and I have started some task for the Lord with great enthusiasm only to abandon it—unfinished—in the busyness of our lives.

But what specifically is the **glory** spoken of in this passage? Dods emphasizes that it is a **glory** "not of position only, but of character—a glory which disposed and prepared him to sympathize with suffering and to give himself to the actual needs of men" (Dods, vol. 2, p. 253). The humiliation of death in humanity is, for the Lord, glorification. What we would consider the end of life, Jesus considered return to the reality of eternal life. Christian praying depends on Jesus' relationship to the Father. Through him we have access to the Almighty God of the universe—a fact established by his own words in this prayer.

Ⓑ Relationship of the Son to Believers (17:6–12)

> **SUPPORTING IDEA:** *Believers are described as those who have obedience, faith, and knowledge. Yet the Lord felt a need to pray for two more gifts of God's grace for us: Protection in the world and unity among ourselves.*

17:6–7. The theology of this high priestly prayer continues. Now the crescendo of plural pronouns bounces off the walls of our text with a penetrating, sometimes even confusing echo. The rich theology of the prayer also escalates. Perhaps we can best approach the paragraph by asking two questions: What does Christ do for believers? And what should be our response?

We start the answer to the first question with the word *proclamation*. The disciples heard about God and his plan from the Son. Most sons probably reflect their fathers, perhaps in facial features, height, hair color, personality, and sometimes even worldview. Jesus specifically identified his task in the world as one of revelation to a select group of people chosen by the Father.

The verb **revealed** is the Greek word *phaneroe,* which appears forty-nine times in the New Testament, almost half from the pen of John. Jesus referred to the incarnation here. John is the unchallenged New Testament exegete of the truth that God took human form to communicate with the world. The first act of the Son in drawing disciples unto himself in the vibrant relationship of new life was to tell them and show them what the Father is like. Believers are gifts from the Father to the Son. All people belong to the Father by creation, but those who trust in the Son and relate to him by faith become God's children by redemption.

17:8. By this time in the Gospel of John, we know that Jesus spoke only what his Father had told him. He can describe his own teaching ministry by saying, **I gave them the words you gave me.** Hardly a surprising close to a ministry that had always been described by Jesus as originating with the Father in heaven.

In this verse the Lord also talked about edification. When Paul stayed three years with the Ephesians declaring God's truth, he followed the example of Jesus who did the same thing with these disciples (Acts 20:17–21). Here we encounter John's interesting contrast of the Greek terms for *word* and *words*. There must have been an obvious intent on John's part to distinguish between *word* and *words* with a special focus on the singular to emphasize the unity of the message.

17:9–10. The Lord also spoke of intercession. Verse 9 contains the curious phrase, **I am not praying for the world.** We should not infer here that the Lord never prayed for the world. This particular prayer focuses on those believers **you have given me** and emphasizes again the reality of the Bible's teaching on election. I believe in election and free will because I think the Bible teaches both. The fact that I cannot harmonize them in my finite human mind does not trouble me.

The switch to the present tense is an important notification of the Lord's on-going ministry. One paraphrase of this verse says, "And all of them, since they are mine, belong to you; and you have given them back to me with everything else of yours, and so they are my glory!" (v. 10, TLB). What a stunning reality! Faltering, failing, sinning human beings represent the glory of the holy Son of God!

17:11. Jesus brought before the Father the fact that his people would be staying in the world after he left. The word **world** occurs eighteen times in this prayer. This is a strong testimony to the importance of the context of our life and ministry. The address **Holy Father** is unique here in the New Testament. The NIV Study Bible says, "The name suggests both remoteness and nearness; God is both awe-inspiring and loving."

But what did Jesus mean by **the name you gave me?** F. F. Bruce observes, "The name of God in the OT denotes not only his character (as in verse 6 above), but also his power . . . By the Father's power, imparted to Jesus, Jesus himself had guarded them as a treasure entrusted to him by the Father, and now he gives account of this stewardship" (Bruce, p. 332).

The prayer for unity appears again in verse 21, and we will deal with it there. Suffice it to say here that the text talks about the spiritual unity of the body rather than any kind of organizational or structural relationship.

17:12. In this verse Jesus spoke of protection. The disciple band was still intact with one exception: Judas fulfilled the Scripture by his treason.

But we asked two questions earlier, and the second centers in how believers then and now respond to what the Lord does for them. In virtually every case, Jesus included that in his prayer. When he offered proclamation, the disciples responded with obedience; when he offered edification, the disciples grew in knowledge until he could say to the Father, "Now they know that everything you have given me comes from you" (v. 7). When he offered intercession, they responded in faith; and when He offered protection, they responded in unity. How the church of today could benefit by focusing on John 17:11: "So that they may be one as we are one."

The keeping ministry of believers is the act of a Holy God in contrast with a sinful world. Of all those who are genuine disciples, **none has been**

lost. Only Judas who never had a relationship in the first place was not **kept . . . by that name you gave me.** The play on cognate words in the original text is most striking: "Not one perished but the son of perishing."

C Relationship of Believers to the World (17:13–19)

> **SUPPORTING IDEA:** *In these verses Jesus used several prepositional phrases in requesting that the Father watch over Christ's people who must stay in the world though they are not of the world. He wanted us as his followers to be kept from evil so we can be witnesses to the world.*

17:13. Monasticism, the cloistering of people into private compounds where they have no contact with outside society, is a human invention, not a godly design. Jesus had been **in the world,** and now his disciples would remain **in the world.** They were learning about the Father so they could handle being in the world and still enjoy **the full measure of my joy within them.**

This section of the prayer contains some of the most difficult and negative aspects of the continuing life of believers on earth. But it begins by expressing the reality of joy in their lives. If the disciples heard this part of the prayer (and many scholars believe they listened to the entire prayer), they may have remembered the words of the Lord spoken earlier that evening: "I have told you this so that my joy may be in you and that your joy may be complete" (15:11).

Godet picks up on the word **say** (*laleo*) and suggests that the Lord actually told us he was speaking these words aloud "in the presence of His disciples, before leaving them, [so] that He may associate them in the joy which He Himself enjoys. This joy is that which is inspired in Him by the certainty of the protection with which the Father shelters Him at all times, a certainty to become theirs" (Godet, II, p. 335).

17:14. Twice Jesus uttered these exact words, the first instance in the middle of verse 14 and the other at the beginning of verse 16: **not of the world.** The antipathy between the Word of God and the world of humanity takes center stage in this verse. He had already told the disciples about the world's hatred (15:18–21), and now he reminded the Father of the antagonism they would face in the world.

Language like this reminds us of the Hans Christian Anderson story about the ugly duckling whose appearance and behavior was obnoxious to pond-bound ducks among whom it spent the early part of its life. The persecution and pain it endured from others in its limited environment made life miserable until it finally realized its nature was not that of a duck but a swan.

Since swans were unwelcome creatures in duckland, one day it flapped its wings and flew away. In closing the story, Anderson tells us, "Before it knew how all this happened, it found itself in a great garden, where the trees smelled sweet and bent their long green branches down to the channel that wound past. Oh, here it was so beautiful, such a gladness of spring!" Eventually Christians too will go to the land where others possessing the same nature of Christ will gather in joy. But for now, it is clear from our Lord's prayer that we had better learn to live and minister in the duckland of this world.

17:15–17. How is it possible to be "in the world" and yet not **of the world?** These verses answer that question. Whatever the biblical doctrine of separation might mean, it certainly does not mean isolation. In the early Middle Ages when the world began to corrupt the purity of the church, some saw monasticism as the only solution. It was apparent to them that one could maintain purity of life and a clear relationship to God only by hiding from the world behind ten-foot walls. Some believers even became lone hermits living in the hills until communal monasticism became more popular.

One could never derive such a view from John 17. Jesus prayed not for removal from the world but for an awareness of its evils so they could be avoided. The danger is not the general presence of evil but **the evil one.** The New Testament indicates that the world is in the ultimate control of the prince of the power of the air who does battle against the living God by affecting the lives of his people. The antidote is sanctification. The Greek word for **sanctify** is *hagiazo*, which means "to set apart for God's use." As Bruce points out:

> This involves their consecration for the task now entrusted to them; it involves further their inward purification and endowment with all the spiritual resources necessary for carrying out that task. This purification and endowment are the work of the Spirit, but here Jesus declares the instrument of that work to be "the truth"—the truth embodied in the Father's "word" which Jesus had given to the disciples as he himself had received it from the Father (vv. 8,14). The very message which they are to proclaim in his name will exercise its sanctifying effect on them: that message is the continuation of his message, just as their mission in the world is the extension of his mission (Bruce, p. 334).

17:18–19. From the very first days of Christianity, true believers have practiced separation by infiltration. The Father sent the Son into the world and now the Son was sending the believers into the world. Here the Lord introduced the word *sanctify* in different verb forms. In effect, he said, "Lead these disciples to an act of dedication as I have dedicated myself to your work. Then as they live their lives for you, Father, they will ultimately enjoy the fixed and final dedication you bestow upon them."

In the midst of modern conveniences and sophisticated technology, the church finds it more and more difficult to live in the world without being of the world. We find it increasingly tricky to escape the snares of the evil one and the enchanting attractions of our own flesh and the world around us. Calvin once put it this way: "As the wantonness of our flesh ever itches to dare more than God commands, let us learn that our zeal will turn out badly whenever we dare to undertake anything beyond God's Word."

John probably remembered these words of our Lord when he wrote his epistle some years later. To all believers everywhere he issued a ringing admonition: "Do not love the world or anything in the world. If anyone loves the world, the love of the Father is not in him" (1 John 2:15). Worldliness is more an attitude than an act; it has to do not so much with what we do as why we do it.

Perhaps the contrast to separation by *isolation* is separation by *infiltration*. The disciples were able to go **into the world** because they were not of the world. Some interpreters suggest that the reason Jesus said "I am not praying for the world" in verse 9 was because the battle plan which he would suggest in his prayer just a few minutes later would be the ministry of his disciples in the world: "In order that I may reach the world, I am not for the moment praying for the world, but for those through whom I am going to reach the world."

D Relationship of Believers to the Father (17:20–26)

SUPPORTING IDEA: *Mentioned earlier, this fourth relationship now becomes the main theme. Unity in the church is to be patterned after the unity of the triune Godhead so the world can see how believers dwell in the Lord and he in the Father.*

17:20–21. If we had any doubt that this prayer applies to believers today, it is erased by verse 20. The heart of this final paragraph of the chapter focuses on unity—the ultimate demonstration of God's work through his people in the world. We learn here that body unity is patterned after divine unity. The absolute oneness of the Father and the Son will now be spiritually transferred to believers for a specific purpose—spiritual unity.

The union of the church is not patterned after some earthly organization or any well-meaning intentions of humanity. God joins our spirits through the Holy Spirit because Jesus' blood is "thicker than water" and thicker than human bonds.

Some interpreters consider this verse to be a pivotal point separating those words specifically related to the disciples from words now spoken to the universal church. Certainly the implication of the verse goes beyond its actual words.

Perhaps there is no verse in all of Scripture which has been more frequently quoted to support ecclesiastical church union than John 17:21. However, the emphasis of the prayer centers in spiritual unity, not organizational unity. It must be understood in the light of John 10:30, "I and my Father are one." If we are to understand the unity of the church, we must first understand unity between the Son and the Father.

17:22. Christian unity is facilitated by **glory**, first given to Christ and then in turn to the disciples. **Glory** (*doxa*) in this context is not an absolute attribute of God but a relative possession that can be reassigned to believers. Some interpreters see heaven here, but there would be no point in such a futuristic view with respect to the mission statement of verse 23: "to let the world know that you sent me." Peter wrote that the divine nature was already in us as a result of regeneration, so we already have a measure of the glory of Jesus himself.

A former ministry companion of mine, now in the ultimate glory of heaven, once wrote, "Child of God, don't you know only you share the glow. It's a light from within, when the blood covers sin. It's the wonderful glory of God."

17:23. We also learn in this passage that body unity is a witness to the world. Like a set of matched mixing bowls, we are the smaller one that fits into Christ who fits into the Father. Purpose? **To let the world know that you sent me.** Mixing bowls may provide too mundane a metaphor here, but Jesus' teaching about the vine and the branches in chapter 15 is affirmed by this prayer of chapter 17.

The unity of believers calls forth a recognition of God's hand by observers in the world even while the church is on earth. Just a few hours before this prayer, Jesus told the disciples, "By this all men will know that you are my disciples, if you love one another" (13:35).

17:24. Furthermore, body unity will be complete only in heaven. If the disciples listened to this prayer (which I believe they did), they may have remembered Jesus' teaching from chapter 14 as he promised them they would eventually arrive at the place where he was going. He wanted them to see him there. They had seen him scorned and hated on earth. Soon they would see him killed and buried. But they had never seen the splendor of heaven and his role as the Son of the Father.

We see just a touch of humanity in this verse. Just as we invite our friends home to show them how hard we have worked to make it attractive and comfortable, so Jesus looked forward to the time when all his people would be in his Father's house.

What a reminder that our Lord was always a pilgrim and stranger on earth. Now he prayed for guests to visit his eternal home. Notice also that heaven is heaven because of the presence of the Savior, not because of any other physical or material accoutrements.

The glory of verse 24 seems different than what we saw in verse 22. Here believers observe it but do not partake in it personally, so we focus now on an attribute of deity. The glory and splendor that belong to Christ in heaven are a gift from his Father. This gift was motivated by love that the Father had before the foundation of the world. Before Adam, the Father loved the Son. This love will continue throughout all eternity so that believers may see its effects in the heavenly position afforded the Messiah.

17:25–26. Again we find the contrast between the world and disciples we saw in verses 9,14,16. The words **Righteous Father** in reference to God appear only here in the New Testament. They appeal to the justice of God. The world will be excluded from final glory because it has rejected the only means of grace. But the disciples, and all believers, live life with a divine viewpoint because they have known the incarnate God.

The exegesis of the Father that occupied Christ's ministry is both complete and continuous. Complete in the sense that the incarnation demonstrated what God was like to those who would listen. Continuous in that it will go on as long as the world lasts. The impact of the latter part of the verse suggests that the very person of Christ lives in us. Through that inseparable union, we are recipients of divine love. The church of Jesus Christ dare not let the pagan society preempt its keynote theme of love. The love of God in the Son and consequently in the church marks Christians and enables them to reflect and communicate God's love.

As White expressed it, "The situation, then, is perilous; the world antagonistic and unbelieving; the future dark for Master and men: all this is accepted without resentment, without fear. Jesus goes forward; his men, soon to be scattered and shaken, will also in time go forward, imbued with the Spirit, united in loyalty, sure of God's love in Christ, with a gleam of glory in their hearts, and aware of the unfailing presence of the living Christ among them. In them, and upon us, the Lord's own prayer is being constantly fulfilled" (White, p. 132).

MAIN IDEA REVIEW: *One of Jesus' current ministries in heaven is to pray for us, and we may sometimes wonder what he says. Certainly there would be some difference between his current advocacy and what we find in this chapter, but John provided some general clues about matters that concern the Lord about the life of believers on earth.*

III. CONCLUSION

The Orphan Lamb

As the final words of Jesus' prayer trail off at the end of this chapter, we sense something of the hush the disciples must have felt in hearing these sacred moments in Dolby surround-sound. We are *in* the world, but not *of* the world, so that we may be a witness *to* the world. And because we are Christ's, we are God's. Our security rests on the possession of the new nature in the Son and not on anything we do for ourselves.

I am reminded of the touching story of an orphan lamb that a shepherd attempted to keep alive by putting it with a ewe whose own lamb had died. But the ewe rejected the foreigner and would not feed the offspring of another. In desperation, the shepherd skinned the dead lamb and laced its fleece over the starving orphan. Immediately upon recognizing the infant as her own, the ewe exercised the role of mother, giving new life to the orphan. Because of what the dead lamb had been to the mother, the stranger who deserved nothing was adopted and made a member of the family with all appropriate privileges.

God sees Christ's blood on us and because of that substitutionary atonement, we are loved by the righteous Father through the Son. What a spectacular display John has recorded for our encouragement and understanding.

Was this prayer of Jesus ever answered? To that question we would note from the Gospel of John that the Father always hears and answers the Son (8:28–29; 11:42). But let us look at the specifics.

The request concerning the disciples was certainly answered. These men went on to become the pillars of the early church. Not one of them defected, not one of them denied the faith, not one of them deserted the Lord.

And the request concerning all believers is still reaping a harvest today. Every day people are born again. Through faith and obedience to God's Word, they are conformed to the image of Christ. Every true believer is a living, breathing witness to the fact that God answers prayer, especially this remarkable prayer of the Lord Jesus. John Knox had this chapter read every day in the weeks just before his death. Perhaps we should not wait for death or its immediate threat to take seriously what our Lord prays for us.

PRINCIPLES

- Our relationship to Jesus is the foundation for a biblical view of prayer.
- Living in the world does not mean being part of the world.
- For Christians, infiltration is a better strategy than isolation.
- Unity and harmony in the church serve as a witness to the world.

APPLICATIONS

- Learn to be a finishing Christian, especially in family and ministry projects.
- Trust God's protection for your spiritual and physical life.
- Fulfill God's will for the church by working to keep its unity.

IV. LIFE APPLICATION

Praying or Wishing?

Archeologist Dr. Jim Strange from the University of South Florida (Tampa) visited a Buddhist temple in Tibet. As he watched the flow of people come and go, he noticed a group of teenagers gathered at the temple. They were dressed like American teenagers from the 1980s, and he thought it peculiar that they would light incense and bow in the traditional manner. So he asked his guide, "What are they praying for?" The guide responded, "They're not praying. They're wishing for money, good relationships, and success."

When a person bows before a temple with lighted incense and intently "wishes," that is praying, even though it may be mistakenly aimed. Many modern people in a plethora of languages and cultures pray for money and success. But the "good relationships" angle is interesting. In a very real sense, that was part of the essence of Jesus' prayer. And he was not "wishing" either but devoutly committing himself to the Father for a return to heaven and the ongoing empowerment of his disciples.

We learn a great deal about prayer from this chapter but perhaps even more about relationships. A relationship to the Father and the Son is primary, but our relationships with other believers in the world get significant attention in this high-priestly prayer. We can activate this chapter in our lives by praying in the pattern of Jesus. But perhaps even more important is for the modern church to allow the Spirit of God to activate his love through us to other believers.

The result of Christian unity on earth is a radiance of the love of the Father and Son in us. I remember an old chorus from the days of my youth:

May Christ be seen in me, O Lord.
Hear thou my earnest plea.
O take me, fill me, use me, Lord,
'Til Christ be seen in me.

V. PRAYER

Father, thank you that Jesus prays for us. Help us to show the world how we can relate to other believers and show them your love. Amen.

VI. DEEPER DISCOVERIES

A. "The Time Has Come" (17:1)

In the first record of his public ministry (John 2), Jesus announced to his mother that whatever expectations she might have as a result of his involvement at the wedding feast would not be satisfactory since his hour had not yet come. Numerous times over the years of ministry with his disciples, he repeated that phrase, "My time has not yet come" (2:4; 7:6,30; 8:20). But returning to Jerusalem after a brief visit to the home of Lazarus, he announced that the hour had arrived (12:23). Surely the phrase refers broadly to the total glorification of the Son of God. This included his death, resurrection, and ascension to his pre-incarnate position with the Father.

Some Greek words even look like English words and this is one of them—*hora* (hour). John used it twenty-six times in this Gospel and twelve more times in his epistles and Revelation. That accounts for more than one-third of the 106 appearances of the word in the New Testament. "The Greek word *hora* seldom if ever refers to a period of sixty minutes in the NT. Even 'one hour' in Revelation (17:12; 18:10,17,19) should be understood as an idiom meaning *quickly* or *suddenly*. In John's Gospel a special use of *hour* occurs several times and refers to Jesus' death, though his exaltation and glory is often in view also. . . . The appointed moment for his death on our behalf was set in eternity past and could not have been changed by anyone, no matter how powerful" (Blackaby, p. 47).

B. "Doomed to Destruction" (17:12)

The obvious reference was to Judas in a fate already mentioned earlier in this book (6:70–71). A literal translation would be "son of destruction," though the NIV meaning is certainly clear. The CEV uses "the one who had to be lost" and the NEB "the man who must be lost," while the Jerusalem Bible (JB) selects "the one who chose to be lost." The word *destruction* is frequently used in the New Testament as the final fate of those without God (Matt. 7:13; Rom. 9:22; 1 Tim. 6:9).

It is interesting to see how Bible translators struggle with a phrase like this. According to Newman and Nida, "In English the form *lost* fits very well into this type of context, but in other languages a literal rendering may be misleading, since it might suggest that in some way or other Jesus had lost sight of Judas. A more appropriate equivalent in some languages is 'has gone astray' or 'has suffered ruin.' Accordingly, the phrase 'the man who was bound to be lost' may be rendered 'the man who would certainly go astray' or 'the man for whom there was nothing else but to suffer ruin'" (Newman and Nida, p. 537).

C. Church Unity (17:21)

The unity among believers centers in the blending of personalities in the triune Godhead in spite of their various functions. Although the concept of the Trinity is difficult to understand even for mature theologians, all evangelicals accept the distinction of three persons. The fact that these persons can be separate and yet relate together in beautiful love and harmony sets the pattern that Christ had in view in this verse.

Some interpreters would argue that the emphasis of the chapter could only refer to individuals and does not take into account the church, since the word *ekklesia* does not appear in the chapter and the church had not yet come into existence. But we must remember that our Lord was praying in the presence of the men who would form the nucleus of the new body. He had already talked to them about what the church would be and how it would function. His commands and teachings became the code for the Jerusalem church in Acts. It seems reasonable to accept the assumption that this prayer of unity for the disciples also included the unity of the church.

This emphasis appears in verses 11,21–23 and depends on John 10:30. Applying this prayer for unity to the church does not argue for ecclesiastical connections but to personal relationships among members of the body. It does not negate denominations or other kinds of church distinctions, but those things are secondary to the union among members in the body.

D. Sanctification (17:17,19)

Although we might expect to find the imperative verb *sanctify* in the present tense, it does not appear that way in this verse. Instead, the aorist indicates that the sanctification in view here is an event rather than a process. From the Old Testament point of view, this kind of consecration was a ritual act conducted externally. In the New Testament, however, it takes on spiritual value and, in effect, represents a request to the Father to give the disciples a complete devotion to God and to his work in the world.

But Christ prayed not only for the end but also the means. The purity of will and life that he desired comes to the point of commitment through impartation of his Holy Word. As Westcott puts it, "The 'truth' is not only a power within him by which he is moved; it is an atmosphere in which he lives. The end of the Truth is not wisdom, which is partial, but holiness, which is universal" (Westcott, p. 245).

VII. TEACHING OUTLINE

A. INTRODUCTION

1. Lead Story: A Mother's Prayer
2. Context: We have no idea where this prayer was offered. But we assume from what references John gives us that it occurred somewhere between the upper room and the Mount of Olives. The time context is the final night before the crucifixion.

3. Transition: There is hardly any disconnection between chapters 16 and 17 as John introduced the prayer by saying, "after Jesus said this." The genuine break appears at the end of chapter 17, or more properly at the beginning of chapter 18 where there is clear movement to another section of the Gospel.

B. COMMENTARY

1. Relationship of the Father to the Son (17:1–5)
   - a. Sonship of our Lord (17:1)
   - b. Sovereignty of our Lord (17:2)
   - c. Salvation of our Lord (17:3)
   - d. Status of our Lord (17:4–5)
2. Relationship of the Son to Believers (17:6–12)
   - a. They obeyed your word (17:6)
   - b. They accepted your word (17:7–8)
   - c. They belong to you (17:9–10)
   - d. They are still in the world (17:11–12)
3. Relationship of Believers to the World (17:13–19)
   - a. In the world (17:13)
   - b. Not of the world (17:14)
   - c. From the evil world (17:15–17)
   - d. Into the world (17:18–19)
4. Relationship of Believers to the Father (17:20–26)
   - a. Body unity is patterned after divine unity (17:20–22)
   - b. Body unity is a witness to the world (17:23)
   - c. Body unity will be complete in heaven (17:24)
   - d. Body unity results in a life of love (17:25–26)

C. CONCLUSION: PRAYING OR WISHING?

VIII. ISSUES FOR DISCUSSION

1. What practical lessons for your own prayer life can you take from this chapter?
2. Name some ways your congregation reflects the unity Jesus prayed for in this chapter.
3. How does the modern world see the love of God in Christian believers?

John 18

Four Witnesses— Four Decisions

"*H*ateful to me as are the gates of hell, is he who, hiding one thing in his heart, utters another."

H o m e r

GEOGRAPHICAL PROFILE: KIDRON VALLEY

- A brook running north and south on the east side of ancient Jerusalem
- Separated the temple area from the Mount of Olives
- The site of the Garden of Gethsemane is thought to be just west of the Kidron Valley on the way to Bethany

PERSONAL PROFILE: ANNAS

- Served as high priest from A.D. 6 to 15
- He also had four sons and a son-in-law who served, including Caiaphas from A.D. 18 to 36
- Even when he was not actively the high priest, he served as the "godfather" of religious operations in Jerusalem

PERSONAL PROFILE: PILATE

- Appointed governor by the Emperor Tiberias in A.D. 26 and held the post for ten years
- Experienced difficult relationships with the Jewish population in Palestine
- Finally deposed in A.D. 36 by Vitellius, governor of Syria, and sent to Rome

PERSONAL PROFILE: BARABBAS

- Terrorist guilty of murder and revolution
- A notorious prisoner who was part of a revolutionary gang
- Convicted of rebellion against Rome
- Some believe his name indicates that his father may have been a rabbi

John 18

I N   A   N U T S H E L L

In April, about the time Jesus crossed from Jerusalem to Gethsemane, the Kidron became a roaring stream running south into the Valley of Hinnom. At Passover season it was often red with lamb's blood—a striking divide between the city and the wealthy mountain gardens to the east. To an olive grove in one of those gardens Jesus retired with his disciples, awaiting the arrest that would signal the events of the dark night. Four people occupy John's report in chapter 18—four people who saw Christ the night before his crucifixion and were forced to some decision about him.

Four Witnesses—
Four Decisions

I. INTRODUCTION

Facing Death at Columbine

*O*n Thursday, May 27, 1999, Daryl Scott, father of two victims of the Columbine High School shooting in Littleton, Colorado, testified before the subcommittee on crime of the House Judiciary Committee of the United States House of Representatives. This event took place at 2:00 P.M. at 2141 Rayburn House Office Building.

Scott talked about his loss and how amazed he was in the days following the tragedy that people pointed fingers at all kinds of groups trying to fix blame—the NRA, a permissive school atmosphere, insufficient government funding for school safety, and a host of other culprits. But Scott believed the attitudes that gave birth to the Columbine massacre rested in the vacuum of the school itself long before the tragedy occurred. He saw the raw secularism of much contemporary public education as a breeding ground for the kind of chaos that took the life of his daughter. And he wrote a poem commemorating the event:

> Your laws ignore our deepest needs, your words are empty air.
> You've stripped away our heritage; you've outlawed simple prayer.
> Now gunshots fill our classrooms and our precious children die.
> You seek for answers everywhere, and ask the question "Why?"
> You regulate restrictive laws through legislative greed,
> And yet you fail to understand that God is what we need.

Mr. Scott went on that day to tell the members of the subcommittee, "We do not need more religion. We do not need more gaudy television evangelists spewing out verbal religious garbage. We do not need more million-dollar church buildings built while people with basic needs are being ignored. We *do* need a change of heart and a humble acknowledgement that this nation was founded on the principle of simple trust in God."

Tragedies like Columbine force us to face the reality of death and the fact that a person's death may come at the hands of friends. So it is with Jesus in this chapter. He was denied by Peter and betrayed by Judas, forced to the only remaining line of defense and comfort, the heavenly Father.

II. COMMENTARY

Four Witnesses—Four Decisions

MAIN IDEA: *East of the city of Jerusalem one can see the Mount of Olives on which were located many elaborate gardens. To this place, at this time, Jesus took his disciples for the betrayal and arrest that would lead to the cross.*

A Malchus: Impressions in a Garden (18:1–11)

SUPPORTING IDEA: *The first witness of the events of this chapter was Malchus, servant of the high priest. A curious bystander during earlier events, he became actively involved when Peter swung his sword with good courage and poor aim. The Bible records no response by Malchus, but one can imagine some interesting explanations to Mrs. Malchus later that day. Jesus healed the ear and told the disciples to stop their violent behavior.*

18:1–3. As he told his story, John wanted us to see that Jesus hid from no one. The availability of the fugitive became obvious, since we learn that Jesus had visited this garden often with his disciples. Certainly Judas would have known it well.

In the fulfillment of prophecy and surely the clear anticipation by Jesus, Judas brought quite an entourage—certainly no fewer than two hundred soldiers (the word **detachment** is *speira*) and the "big wigs" from among the chief priests and Pharisees. Picture them entering that quiet sanctuary with their **torches, lanterns and weapons.**

One wonders at this strange group that went out to meet Jesus. At first it looked like the usual religious antagonists and their uniformed guard. But the phrase **a detachment of soldiers** added a Roman group to this advance party in the garden. Bruce reminds us, "The fact that Roman troops were there as well as temple police implies that the Jewish authorities had already approached the military command, probably indicating that they expected armed resistance to the officers. That it was the Jewish authorities and not the Romans who took the initiative is shown by the fact that, after the arrest, the Jewish authorities were allowed to take Jesus into their custody. When Judas is described as 'taking' the cohort and the police to the place, all that is meant is that he acted as their guide" (Bruce, p. 340).

18:4–9. John also wanted us to see that Jesus controlled this night. His response to the events was different than the reaction of the guards. Notice Judas came **with them,** electing almost total allegiance to those who could make him richer. We can hardly imagine what caused the guards to draw back and fall down. A miracle? The repetition of that familiar **I am** closely linked to the Lord God of the Old Testament? Parallel passages in the other Gospels (Matt. 26:36–46; Mark 14:32–42; Luke 22:39–46) do not help us much. This mob of armed officials displayed greater fear than the victim they were looking for.

Twice Jesus asked the same question; twice he received the same answer. He surrendered himself and released the Eleven. John's commentary reviewed 6:39, again fulfilling the prophecy that Jesus would lose none of those true believers whom the Father had given him. Throughout this Gospel we see reminders that Jesus died for us, what theologians call substitutionary (vicarious) atonement (1:29; 3:14–16; 10:11,15–18; 12:32; 17:19).

In verse 9 John offered another of his famous hermeneutical helps. He told us how Jesus requested the release of the disciples and then emphasized that this happened because of the prophecy of John 6:39. Surely it would have been easy to take Jesus' words purely in the physical realm. After all, he was the one they sought; let the other disciples escape. But not John. He saw the clear spiritual connection. Bruce puts it this way:

> But in Jesus thus stepping to the front and shielding the disciples by exposing himself, John sees a picture of the whole sacrifice and substitution of Christ. This figure of his Master moving forward to meet the swords and staves of the party remains indelibly stamped upon his mind as the symbol of Christ's whole relation to his people. That night in Gethsemane was to them all the hour and power of darkness; and in every subsequent hour of darkness John and the rest see the same divine figure stepping to the front, shielding them and taking upon himself all the responsibility. It is thus Christ would have us think of him—as our friend and protector, watchful over our interests, alive to all that threatens our persons, interposing between us in every hostile event (Bruce, pp. 268–69).

18:10–11. Peter displayed admirable courage and loyalty but poor aim. He was a fisherman, not a swordsman. John did not record the healing of the ear, a detail reported by Luke. John's only reference to Jesus' final prayer came at the end of verse 11. We read more detail in Matthew 26, Mark 14, and Luke 22.

Why did John not include more garden narrative as the other Gospels did? The answer seems to lie in his purpose—to focus on the words of Jesus, thereby showing him as the Son of God rather than detailing history of his life incident by incident. The last phrase of this section is important for us, since the rhetorical question gives the motive for Jesus' behavior on this occasion. The Father has given a cup of suffering and death. The Son, in obedience and subjection, will drink it.

Ⓑ Peter: Denial by a Fire (18:12–18,25–27)

> **SUPPORTING IDEA:** *The second person who dominates this chapter is Peter, who was warming himself at the fire built by Jesus' enemies. The predicted denial now took shape as this confused and frightened disciple offered the wrong answers for the wrong reasons.*

18:12–14. We will bypass these three verses at this point since John introduces Annas and Caiaphas, focusing on Annas in verses 19–24. But we can stop long enough to note that the garden contingent did not take Jesus to the high priest but to Annas, father-in-law of the high priest. This gave John one more opportunity to remind his readers of Caiaphas's famous prophetic announcement of substitutionary atonement back in 11:49–50.

18:15–16. In John's narrative it becomes necessary to pick up two different segments of text to understand Peter's role on this fateful night. John first showed us how his friend was at the wrong place at the wrong time. The military and religious intruders had dismissed the eleven disciples, as Jesus asked. But Peter and **another disciple** followed their Lord and his captors. Almost every reputable scholar agrees this second disciple was John himself. His family had ties to the priesthood through Salome and Elizabeth. His influence allowed both men into the courtyard.

18:17–18. The **girl at the door** asked what appears to be a rhetorical question, calling for a simple negative response. Peter took the bait and joined the crowd around the fire (*anthrakian*), probably made of charcoal. John told the story straight: **Peter also was standing with them.** Having followed too far behind, he now joined a group of the Lord's enemies. Leon Morris puts it well: "This was the last place where one might expect to find one of Jesus' followers" (Morris, p. 759).

18:25–27. Once again we do a bit of juggling in the text to get the Peter segment all together. Notice how the first two questions were rhetorical, "Surely you are not another of his disciples?" And the third got more personal, **Didn't I see you with him in the olive grove?**

We have already seen this in verse 17, but here it is again. Warming himself at an alien fire, Peter heard the same kind of question and he gave the exact same answer. But the heat increased (someone has said that Peter's ministry career could be summarized in three stages—at the fire, under fire, and on fire). This time a relative of the servant whom Peter had wounded got too specific for comfort: **Didn't I see you with him in the olive grove?**

For the third time Peter denied Christ, and the prophetic rooster began to crow (13:38). One legend that grew up around this event indicates that wherever Peter went for years after this night, people would make the sound of a rooster to harass and humiliate him.

Theologians and interpreters argue for endless pages about how many rooster crowings the Bible records. The prediction is quoted in all four Gospels (Matt. 26:34,75; Mark 14:30,72; Luke 22:34,61; John 13:38). From the available information, some have suggested three denials before one crowing of the rooster, but a variety of other numbers have been put forth as well. We should not get caught up in that kind of banter, since the gist of the incident indicates a threefold betrayal before **a rooster began to crow.**

No serious scholar believes that God miraculously manipulated this rooster to crow at this particular time. This is a general time notation for early morning, similar to our common observation, "getting up with the chickens." Before the night was over, before the roosters began their morning announcements, Peter denied Jesus three times.

ⓒ Annas: Questions in an Apartment (18:19–24)

SUPPORTING IDEA: *No longer high priest himself, this powerful man still controlled Jerusalem politics through his son-in-law, Caiaphas. Any Jew of that day knew about the bazaars of Annas where sacrifices were sold for twenty times the honest price.*

18:19–21. While Peter stood by the fire, Jesus was taken to Annas, the godfather and power behind the high priestly throne. His residence was close to the wall on the south side of Jerusalem. He had served as high priest from A.D. 6 to 15, and then in predominant nepotism watched four sons and a son-in-law (Caiaphas) hold the office. John remembered one good point about Caiaphas: he predicted the substitutionary atonement of Jesus (11:49–50).

In verses 19–24, Jesus asked two key questions while being questioned himself. Although John does not mention blasphemy in this paragraph, Annas tried to establish subversion and revolution on the part of Jesus. But Jesus emphasized the openness of his ministry and asked, **Why question me?**

There was a good bit of switching from house to house as Annas sent Jesus to Caiaphas and Caiaphas then sent him to Pilate. Interpreters find a bit of a curiosity regarding the number of bindings, although that is not the central point of the passage from John's viewpoint. Godet tries to clear it up: "Jesus had undoubtedly been unbound during the examination; after this scene, Annas causes him to be bound again, in order to send him to the house of Caiaphas. Probably he was unbound a second time during the session of the Sanhedrin. This explains why in Matthew xxvii. 2 and Mark xv.1, he is bound anew at the time of leading him away to Pilate" (Godet, p. 362).

18:22–24. What a lesson these verses contain. Christianity is not a secret sect or a covert cult. Jewish law prohibited self-incrimination (a precursor to the Fifth Amendment). If Annas wanted to find out what Jesus had been teaching, hundreds of people could verify his message. For his defense, Jesus received a blow on the face. Whether this was ordered by Annas or not we do not know. The Lord called for the appropriate application of Jewish law (calling defense witnesses first), and asked the second question, **Why did you strike me?**

John carried the narrative no further at this point, but showed us that Annas sent Jesus to his son-in-law Caiaphas, who would have occupied another office in the same building.

Pilate: Confrontation in a Palace (18:28–40)

SUPPORTING IDEA: *Pilate entered the saga ready to play the role that has kept his name notorious for almost two thousand years. This weak man learned that he confronted a king and that he had an opportunity to defend truth rather than protect the fragile political peace of Israel. But he failed, caving in to the screaming crowds stirred up by agents of the high priest.*

18:28–32. By now it was approximately 7:00 or 8:00 in the morning. John was about to introduce the longest trial narrative in the Gospels. It began with the charges. Jesus had already been charged with blasphemy (Mark 14:60–64), but on this occasion his enemies offered no charges against him. Instead, we have one of the classic lines of the New Testament: **If he were not a criminal . . . we would not have handed him over to you.**

Pilate had no intention of meddling in Jewish religious affairs, though we should hardly consider him a gentle fellow. On five occasions Pilate slaughtered Jews, earning such a violent reputation in Jerusalem that the emperor Tiberias finally yanked him back to Rome. The New Testament identifies seven different charges against Christ.

1. He threatens to destroy the temple (Matt. 26:61).
2. He is an evildoer (John 18:30).
3. He perverts the nation (Luke 23:2).
4. He has forbidden the Jews to pay taxes (Luke 23:2).
5. He is a revolutionary agitator (Luke 23:2)
6. He makes himself king (Luke 23:2).
7. He claims to be the Son of God (John 19:7).

All this happened early Friday morning, with the beginning of the Passover less than twelve hours away. But Pilate could not get a Roman handle on the charges. It must have been a confusing situation. And this dialogue regarding who should carry out the execution seems like political buck-passing between the Romans and the Jews until we read John's comment in verse 32: **This happened so that the words Jesus had spoken indicating the kind of death he was going to die would be fulfilled.** Had the Jews taken him, he would have been stoned. But repeatedly he had talked about being lifted up to die—an exclusively Roman execution.

Where did this discussion take place? Some have suggested in Herod's palace, a magnificent building with three towers located north of Caiaphas's palace. Another suggestion is the Tower of Antonia at the northwest corner of the temple, a fortress that Herod the Great had used as his headquarters before his own palace was built.

18:33–37. The incredulous Pilate could not imagine this broken and beaten man before him was **the king of the Jews.** But Jesus would not give him the satisfaction of claiming or disclaiming such an office. All this turned Pilate's disdain for the Jews up another notch in verse 35. He characterized this entire trial as petty religious bickering among these Jews whom he was authorized to control.

Verses 36–37 offer poignant truth from the lips of the Lord. All earthly kingdoms find their source with sinful humanity, but Jesus' **kingdom is not of this world.** It needs no human defense. Jesus was not referring to the ultimate millennial kingdom; his spiritual kingdom of truth represents the lordship of the King over the lives of his people. Who forms this kingdom? **Everyone on the side of truth listens to me,** said Jesus.

Once again Jesus set truth as the dividing standard for right and wrong. But if truth was all he cared about, he posed no threat to Rome. Pilate would have to weasel out of this situation in some other way.

18:38–40. In effect, Pilate declared Jesus innocent: **I find no basis for a charge against him.** Nevertheless, to appease the Jews, he let them select a prisoner of choice for release at the Passover. He seemed to be saying, "Let's be done with all this foolishness. You don't seem to care much for this king of the Jews fellow, but you certainly don't want Barabbas back out on the streets, so let's make that choice and get on with life."

But one should never underestimate the popularity of a folk hero, even a guerrilla who had participated in a rebellion against Rome. Pilate got caught in his own trap.

In this chapter we see intelligent and religious people warped by hate, much like the Nazis and neo-Nazis perverted the minds of their followers. We also see a fascinating play on the name Bar-Abbas, which means "son of the father." One son of a father was released, and the other, Son of the Father, went to death row.

As we look at these four characters, we may ask ourselves where we find a personal likeness. Do we see ourselves in Malchus, an innocent bystander watching the proceedings? Like Peter, who denied the Savior and warmed himself at the enemies' fire? Like Annas, who illegally put Jesus on trial? Or like Pilate, confused and wanting to be rid of religious hassles as quickly as possible?

One thing is clear from these four witnesses and their four decisions: there is no place to hide when it comes to Jesus. We either decide for him or against him.

MAIN IDEA REVIEW: *East of the city of Jerusalem one can see the Mount of Olives on which were located many elaborate gardens. To this place, at this time, Jesus took his disciples for the betrayal and arrest that would lead to the cross.*

III. CONCLUSION

The Son of the Father

One day a poor Scottish farmer by the name of Fleming was working in his bog trying to make a living for his family when he heard a cry for help from a nearby bog. He dropped his tools and ran to find a terrified boy, mired to the waist in black muck. Farmer Fleming saved the lad from what would have been a slow and terrifying death.

The next day a fancy carriage pulled up to the Scotsman's farm. Out stepped an elegantly dressed nobleman who introduced himself as the father of the boy whom Fleming had saved. "I want to repay you," said the nobleman. "You saved my son's life."

Fleming waved off the offer and declined payment. At that time his own son came to the door and was noticed immediately by the nobleman. "Is that your son?" he asked. Fleming affirmed that he was. The nobleman said, "I'll make you a deal. Let me take him and get him a good education. If the lad is anything like his father, he'll grow to be a man you can be proud of."

And that is just what happened. Farmer Fleming's son graduated from Saint Mary's Hospital Medical School in London and went on to become known throughout the world as the celebrated Sir Alexander Fleming, the discoverer of penicillin.

Years later, the nobleman's same son was stricken with pneumonia. To save his life, doctors treated him with penicillin. That nobleman was Lord Randolph Churchill, and his son who had been saved from the bog by Farmer Fleming was Sir Winston Churchill.

Throughout this Gospel Jesus emphasized his relationship with the Father, and we see him making his way to the cross—the first step in glorification. It must have been apparent to his disciples that he was mired in the bog, unsavable and without a chance of fulfilling the messianic dreams they had treasured for three and one-half years. But in spite of betrayal, denial, and an illegal trial, the Son of the Father will arise victorious.

PRINCIPLES

- Jesus was in control of all events related to his death and resurrection.
- Jesus does not need us to defend him in any way.
- Christians should never expect a completely fair trial in the courts of this world.

APPLICATIONS

- Never be caught warming yourself at the fire of Jesus' enemies.
- Show that you are committed to truth by obeying Jesus' words.
- Remember that all the events surrounding the death of Christ were prophesied in the Old Testament.

IV. LIFE APPLICATION

"Dr. Williams Is Upstairs"

A doctor who had devoted his life to helping the underprivileged lived over a liquor store in the poor section of a large city. In front of the store was a small sign reading "DR. WILLIAMS IS UPSTAIRS." Patients knew the place by the big neon sign, and they were directed to the location by the small sign at the bottom of the stairway.

When the doctor died, he had no relatives and left no money for his burial. He had never asked payment from his patients, so friends scraped together enough money to bury him. But they had insufficient funds for a tombstone. For a time it appeared that his grave would be unmarked, and then someone came up with a great idea. They took the old sign from the front of the liquor store and nailed it to a post over his grave. There it remained as an appropriate epitaph: "DR. WILLIAMS IS UPSTAIRS."

In this chapter Jesus was rapidly moving "upstairs." In spite of the confusion of the disciples and the interference of people like Annas, Caiaphas, and Pilate, the plan of the Father unfolded in his perfect timing. Jesus heads for the cross, the empty tomb, and the ascension.

In this chapter four people had opportunity to respond to the Lord correctly—five if we count Caiaphas. Yet there is no record that any but Peter changed from a negative lifestyle to a positive commitment to the Son of God. Everyone who reads this record stands in the same position as these witnesses. We have the opportunity to see Jesus through John's words. He calls us to respond to what he has written—to believe and obey.

V. PRAYER

Father, thank you for bringing your Son through the agonies of these final days to the place of glory and honor in heaven where we will see him some day. Amen.

VI. DEEPER DISCOVERIES

A. I Am (18:5)

Throughout our study we have drawn attention to this reappearing phrase *ego eimi* used numerous times throughout the Gospel. Here it has a surprising effect on this interesting and varied group of people who came to capture Jesus in the garden. We lose something of the impact when we read "I am he," though John clearly intended us to sense the impact of that statement when he told us that upon hearing it they "drew back and fell to the ground."

As Bruce puts it, "In an appropriate setting *ego eimi* is more than that; it is a word of power, the equivalent of the God of Israel's self-identifying affirmation 'I Am He.' On the lips of Jesus it has already had something approaching this force in the Gospel of John (cf. 8:24,28); and that it has this force here is plain from the retreat and prostration of those addressed" (Bruce, p. 341).

This expression is used only eleven times in the New Testament, and nine of them appear in this Gospel. We saw it in 4:26 when Jesus identified himself to the woman at the well in Samaria. And in 13:19 as well as other places. Most evangelical scholars agree that Jesus intended to identify himself with Jehovah of the Old Testament and therefore to firmly establish his deity.

I have repeatedly emphasized that Jesus controlled every event throughout this dramatic chapter. His response in the garden is a good example of this. Hughes notes, "Jesus' answer was one of his last uses of the power by which he calmed the seas, stilled the winds, and healed the sick. The cohort didn't arrest Jesus—he arrested them. His words were a gracious warning that they were in over their heads. Christ was not caught on the wheel of history. Rather, he is the axis of history" (Hughes, pp. 129–30).

B. Pontius Pilate (18:29)

There is an old story about a group of Sunday school children who were asked to draw pictures of the Christmas story. Some drew the shepherds, others drew angels, and many drew the traditional manger scene. But one boy drew a picture of an airplane in which the teacher could make out four people. When asked about the drawing, the boy indicated it was a picture of the "flight to Egypt" with Joseph, Mary, and Jesus. "But," the teacher asked, "who is the fourth person in the airplane?" To which the boy responded, "That's Pontius—the pilot."

Actually, we do not know a great deal more about Pilate than that boy. But Pilate was such a prominent figure in first-century Israel that John introduced him by referring to "the palace of the Roman governor" (v. 28). During this time Galilee was still under the control of Herod Antipas, the murderer of John the Baptist, but Archelaus, the former tetrarch of Judea had been deposed and even banished. Affairs in Jerusalem were administered as part of the Roman province of Syria, controlled by procurators with headquarters in Caesarea. Pilate was the sixth of such governors and stayed in office for about ten years. Many interpreters believe that the occasion of chapters 18 and 19 occurred during a visit by Pilate from Caesarea to Jerusalem for the Passover feast.

One could hardly say that Pilate was *famous,* since *infamous* would be a better word. John need not worry that his readers would not remember the cruelty of this man. Edersheim tells us that earlier governors had been guilty of "grievous fiscal oppressions," but in general they respected the religious surroundings of Jerusalem.

As Edersheim puts it:

> The exactions, and the reckless disregard of all Jewish feelings and interests, might have been characterised as reaching the extreme limit, if worse had not followed when Pontius Pilate succeeded the procuratorship. Venality, violence, robbery, persecutions, wanton malicious insults, judicial murders without even the formality of a legal process, and cruelty—such are the charges brought against his administration. If former governors had, to some extent, respected the religious scruples of the Jews, Pilate set them purposely at defiance; and this not only once, but again and again, in Jerusalem, in Galilee, and even in Samaria, until the Emperor himself interposed (Edersheim, I, p. 262).

VII. TEACHING OUTLINE

A. INTRODUCTION

1. Lead Story: Facing Death at Columbine
2. Context: Jesus was now in an olive grove on the east side of the Kidron Valley, having crossed the brook after the Lord's prayer in John 17. This is generally thought of as the Garden of Gethsemane, although that name is not actually mentioned in this chapter.

3. Transition: John hits us with a staccato delivery of the betrayal, arrest, denial, and trial in this chapter and without break will continue with the trial before Pilate into chapter 19.

B. COMMENTARY

1. Malchus: Impressions in a Garden (18:1–11)
    a. Availability of the fugitive (18:1–3)
    b. Reaction of the guards (18:4–9)
    c. Healing of the ear (18:10–11)
2. Peter: Denial by a Fire (18:12–18,25–27)
    a. The wrong place at the wrong time (18:12–16,18)
    b. The wrong answer for the wrong reasons (18:17,25–27)
3. Annas: Questions in an Apartment (18:19–24)
    a. "Why question me?" (18:19–21)
    b. "Why did you strike me?" (18:22–24)
4. Pilate: Confrontation in a Palace (18:28–40)
    a. The charges (18:28–32)
    b. The claim (18:33–37)
    c. The choice (18:38–40)

C. CONCLUSION: "DR. WILLIAMS IS UPSTAIRS"

VIII. ISSUES FOR DISCUSSION

1. Can you think of any way that Christians today could deny Jesus?
2. Why would the Father allow Jesus to go through so much humiliation and pain even before the cross?
3. What are the implications in our world of Jesus' words, "Everyone on the side of truth listens to me"?

John 19

Behold the Man!

"Blessed Cross! Blessed Sepulchre! Blessed, rather, be the Man that there was put to shame for me!"

J o h n   B u n y a n

GEOGRAPHICAL PROFILE: GABBATHA

- An Aramaic word meaning "height" or "ridge"
- The judgment seat used by Pilate in sentencing Jesus
- Possibly a part of the Castle of Antonia

GEOGRAPHICAL PROFILE: GOLGOTHA

- A Greek word taken from the Aramaic word for *skull*
- The Latin equivalent is *Calvarius* or Calvary
- Possibly so named because it has the appearance of a skull or because it was a place of execution
- Its actual location is a matter of dispute

PERSONAL PROFILE: MARY WIFE OF CLOPAS

- Possibly the mother of James and Joses
- Counted among Jesus' disciples in Galilee (Luke 8:2–3)
- Mentioned also by Matthew (27:56) and Mark (15:40)
- Witnessed Jesus' burial (Mark 15:47) and came to the tomb (Mark 16:8)

PERSONAL PROFILE: MARY OF MAGDALA

- Woman from whom Jesus cast out seven demons (Mark 16:9, Luke 8:2)
- A devoted disciple from a town on the southwest coast of the Sea of Galilee
- Stood at the cross and then followed Jesus' body to the grave (Matt. 27:61)
- First person to learn of the resurrection (Matt. 28:1–8; Mark 16:9; Luke 24:1,10)

- A wealthy man and member of the Sanhedrin (Matt. 27:57; Mark 15:43)
- A God-fearer looking for the kingdom of heaven (Mark 15:43; Luke 23:50)
- A secret disciple because of fear (John 19:38)
- Gave his own new tomb for Jesus' burial

John 19

I N   A   N U T S H E L L

*L*ike most Roman officials of his day, Pilate functioned according to a single political mandate: protect the Pax Romana. The potential for riot in Jerusalem would have frightened even a courageous governor. Throughout his confrontation with Jesus, Pilate must have known that he was not the one in control. Jesus spoke when he wanted to and remained silent when he wished.

Behold the Man!

I. INTRODUCTION

Costly Carelessness

In May of 1999 the United States Postal Service printed one hundred million stamps with a picture of the Grand Canyon and the words "Grand Canyon—Colorado" marked on the stamp. A slight error, just another little blip in the federal budget—this one costing about $500,000. Somebody figured if the Colorado River runs through the Grand Canyon, it must be in Colorado!Throughout John 18 and 19 we see a careless handling of justice. Sloppy religious leadership by Annas and Caiaphas was followed by sloppy political leadership by Pilate. Legal authorities have pointed out how many laws were broken during these proceedings. Yet through it all, God worked to provide the ultimate and only sacrifice for our salvation. His exactness magnified the carelessness of the human agents involved.

But we dare never be careless about the cross. Sometimes this violent and dreadful form of Roman execution is celebrated by Christians in light-hearted ways that minimize its terror. Certainly it is no sin to wear a variety of jewelry and other knick knacks that remind us Jesus died for us, but we dare not let any of that detract from the horror of Calvary.

II. COMMENTARY

Behold the Man!

> **MAIN IDEA:** *This chapter reminds us again that we participate in both the cross and the empty tomb. God's spirit "baptizes" all believers into Christ's death and resurrection. Awareness of that fact can help us live holy lives today.*

A Sinful Sentence (19:1–16)

> **SUPPORTING IDEA:** *Ultimately, Pilate gave in to the bottom-line argument: "If you let this man go, you are no friend of Caesar" (v. 12). For this pagan politician, career survival loomed more important than truth, or even life, and so "Pilate handed him over to them to be crucified" (v. 16).*

19:1–3. In typical Roman fashion the process began with the humiliation of the prisoner. We are familiar with the flogging, the crown of thorns, and the mockery of the soldiers. Cruelty has always been a major hallmark of sin in the world, and the Romans had honed it to a fine art.

It seems apparent that Pilate never intended crucifixion and expected to beat Jesus and release him. Carson argues convincingly that this was likely a *fustigatio*, the least severe flogging on the Roman menu: "The chronology of Luke and John is correct. But this means that Jesus received a second scourging, the wretched *verberatio*, after the sentence of crucifixion was passed. This would hasten the death, and the nearness of the special Sabbath of that week provided the officials with some pressure to ensure that the agony of crucifixion, which could go on for days, would not be permitted to run on too long (JN. 19:31-33). This also explains why he was too weak to carry his own cross very far" (Carson, pp. 597-98).

19:4-7. After the humiliation of the prisoner, the law required a formal presentation, and Pilate did the honors. The text seems quite clear that Pilate found no legal basis for arresting and holding Jesus, much less physically punishing him. Perhaps he thought the bloody sight of a beaten countryman would move the Jews to pity. But as he uttered the words **Here is the man!** (*ecce homo*), the mob became even more violent in their clamoring for crucifixion. The Jews had no authority to crucify, so Pilate seemed to mock them when he told them to take the crucifixion process into their own hands.

Of all the possible charges bouncing around that day, John settled on the one we find in verse 7, a choice completely in line with his purpose for this Gospel and the only correct charge on the list (John 10:34-38). In this maneuver the Jews attempted to invoke the law of blasphemy as the basis for their claims that Jesus must die (see Lev. 24:16).

19:8-11. Finding no success in any of his attempts to end this religious and cultural nonsense, Pilate returned to another interrogation of the prisoner. He was already afraid of this volatile situation, and now his fear increased. He tried to get some information out of Jesus that would help him arrive at a mutually satisfactory conclusion.

But, we can ask ourselves, what did Pilate fear? Quite possibly this quiet prophet who, for reasons unknown to the governor, had evoked such emotional response from the mobs outside the palace. He also feared the mobs lest they break the sacred *Pax Romana*. Ultimately, however, all Roman governors feared Caesar, and the Jews knew that very well. In a moment the Jews would go to the mat: "If you let this man go, you are no friend of Caesar" (v. 12). But we dare not rush to verse 12 since verse 11 may be the key to this first section: **You would have no power over me if it were not given to you from above.**

We do not know why Jesus interacted with Pilate in chapter 18 but now refused to respond at all. The Gospels mention Jesus' silence at various points during the trial (Matt. 26:63; 27:14; Mark 14:60; 15:5; Luke 23:9). As much as the silence infuriated Pilate, immersed as he was in his own importance, most scholars see it as a clear fulfillment of Isaiah 53:7.

Suddenly Jesus spoke again when Pilate emphasized his own power. His answer proclaimed that a Roman governorship was nothing in the eyes of Almighty God (Rom. 13:1). Of this key statement Carson writes:

> Typical of Biblical compatablism, even the worst evil cannot escape the outer boundaries of God's sovereignty—yet God's sovereignty never mitigates the responsibility and guilt of moral agents who operate under divine sovereignty, while their voluntary decisions and their evil rebellion never render God utterly contingent (e.g., Gen. 19:20; Isa. 5:10ff.; Acts 4:27–28). Especially in writing of events that lead up to the cross, New Testament writers are bound to see the hand of God bringing all things to their dramatic purpose . . . no matter how vile the secondary causalities may be; for the alternatives are unthinkable. If God merely outwits his enemies, if evil sets both the agenda and the pace, then the mission of the Son to die for fallen sinners is reduced to a mere after-thought; if God's sovereignty capsizes all human responsibility, then it is hard to see why the mission of the Son should be undertaken at all, since in that case there are no sins for the Lamb of God to take away (Carson, pp. 600–01).

19:12–13. Suddenly we learn this governor did have a sense of justice and conscience, but they were no match for screaming mobs. The deciding factor here had nothing to do with the law or religion—it was purely political. The phrase that changed Pilate's mind was not connected in anyway to any of the charges against Jesus: **If you let this man go, you are no friend of Caesar.** This was no small threat on the part of the Jewish mobs.

As Tenney puts it:

> The phrase "a friend of Caesar" was more than a casual allusion to Roman patriotism. It usually denoted a supporter or associate of the emperor, a member of the important inner circle. The cry was a veiled threat: if Pilate exonerated Jesus, the high priest would report to Rome that Pilate had refused to bring a rival pretender to justice and was perhaps plotting to establish a new political alliance of his own. Tiberias, the reigning emperor, was notoriously bitter and suspicious of rivals. If such a report were sent to him, he would instantly end Pilate's political career and probably his life, too (Tenney, *EBC*, p. 178).

19:14–16. John gave us detailed information on the time and place Pilate actually **handed him over to them to be crucified.** Backed into a corner of fear and confusion, bewildered by this articulate prophet, and frightened by the threat of some kind of political report to Rome, Pilate caved in. In their misguided zeal the Jews were already out of control. In saying **we have no king but Caesar,** the chief priests denied all authority of Herod and even took Caesar's power beyond what the Romans would claim. Caesar was never called king by the Romans (at least up to this point), but the Greek word *basileus* seems to serve well in this context.

As Bruce puts it, "Their status and privileges depended on their collaboration with the imperial power. But normally they would not have been so rash as to say so outright and thus scandalize true Jewish patriots even more than they already did: they were goaded into saying so by Pilate's insistence that Jesus was their king" (Bruce, p. 365).

Let us be careful about the words **to them** in verse 16. In the context of previous verses, it sounds as though Jesus was being handed over to the Jews. But we already know they had no authority to carry out the death sentence. In light of verse 16b, however, we grasp that John intended us to see the soldiers in the pronoun **them.**

B Cruel Crucifixion (19:17–27)

SUPPORTING IDEA: *John gave a detailed account of the crucifixion. Pilate's sign was written in the language of the Jews (Aramaic), the language of the Roman Empire (Latin), and the language of culture and commerce (Greek). Only John among the apostles remained close as the Savior died. In looking back on that day, the beloved disciple remembered the tender instructions given by Jesus about his mother (vv. 26–27).*

19:17–18. We know too well the narrative of our Lord's crucifixion between two thieves. Scholars still argue about the day and even more about the place—but there is no question about the fact. Unlike the Synoptic Gospels, John had little to say about the pain and agony of Roman crucifixion. He focused on other accompanying information more in line with his purpose. John's passion account vested in his eyewitness understanding that the one who hung on the cross was the Messiah of Israel, the Prophet of God predicted in the Old Testament.

In line with the theme of fulfilled prophecy, John emphasized what some other Gospel writers omitted—the division of clothes, the casting of lots for the garment, the offering of wine, the breaking of the legs of the thieves, and the piercing of Jesus' side with a Roman spear. And he told us repeatedly that these events specifically fulfilled Scripture.

Jesus placement between two thieves was a position probably intended to disgrace the Lord. But even the position of the cross fulfilled prophecy, since Isaiah had said, "[He] was numbered with the transgressors. For he bore the sin of many, and made intercession for the transgressors" (Isa. 53:12).

The scene leading up to the actual crucifixion would have been common in any part of the Roman Empire. Hughes has summarized it well:

> Jesus was placed in the center of a quaternion, a company of four Roman soldiers. The crossbeam or patibulum of the cross was placed on his torn shoulders like an oar. This weighed over 100 pounds. As Christ stumbled along the route to Calvary, an officer preceded him carrying a placard describing Jesus' crime. It read, "Jesus the Nazarene, the King of the Jews." Customarily, a man about to be crucified was led to the site of his execution by the longest route possible, so that everyone might see that "crime does not pay" and also to give opportunity to anyone who might speak up in his defense. So it was that Christ trod the Via Dolorosa so weakened, finally, that a bystander had to be drafted to carry the cross the rest of the way.
>
> At the place of the execution, Christ was laid upon the patibulum. Spikes were driven through his hands or wrists and the crossbar was hoisted into place. His legs were nailed, leaving only enough flex in the knees so that he could begin the horrible up-and-down motion necessary for breathing. The medical assessments of the written misery provide a terrible picture (Hughes, p. 147).

19:19–22. The cross penetrates all of life and slashes through cultural and linguistic barriers. What was Pilate's intention with this memorable sign that only John tells us was written in three languages? In Westcott's view, "The Roman governor found expression to the last for the bitterness which had been called out in him by the opposition of the Jews . . . The incidents which have been related before explain perfectly why the title is written, and how the heathen governor completed the unwilling testimony of the Jewish priest (11:49f.)" (Westcott, p. 274).

19:23–24. Soldiers gambled for Jesus' clothes as no fewer than twenty Old Testament prophesies were fulfilled within the twenty-four-hour period at the time of the crucifixion. What seemed to be whimsical potpourri by the soldiers John wanted us to understand occurred as a direct fulfillment of Psalm 22:18. But the one verse John cited leaves behind a context worth reviewing as we consider this horrible crucifixion scene: "I am poured out like water, and all my bones are out of joint. My heart has turned to wax; it has melted away within me. My strength is dried up like a potsherd, and my tongue sticks to the roof of my mouth; you lay me in the dust of death. Dogs have surrounded me; a band of evil men has encircled me, they have pierced my hands and my feet. I can count all my bones; people stare and gloat over me. They divide my garments among them and cast lots for my clothing" (Ps. 22:14–18).

With his emphasis on biblical fulfillment, John intended us to see even this common division of an executed man's clothing as a detail of interest to God. It was of such interest to God that he had foretold it in the Old Testament Scriptures. In the words of Tasker, "It is as the great High Priest offering the perfect sacrifice that Jesus is dying; and it is stated in the Jewish law that the robe of the priest's ephod shall be of woven work and so constructed that it be not rent (Ex. 28:31–32)" (Tasker, p. 210).

19:25–27. When taken as a harmony, the four Gospels do not seem entirely clear on how many women were at the cross. For those wanting to pursue this matter in detail, Carson has an excellent analysis of the NIV punctuation that indicates four. Most scholars understand this passage as a commitment of Mary, Jesus' mother, to John, since Joseph was probably already dead by this point and Jesus knew that none of his half-brothers had yet made a commitment to his mission. Perhaps at that point Mary might have remembered Simeon's prophecy: "This child is destined to cause the falling and rising of many in Israel, and to be a sign that will be spoken against, so that the thoughts of many hearts will be revealed. And a sword will pierce your own soul too" (Luke 2:34–35).

But the commitment was mutual, and some interpreters have understood this as a theological statement beyond the boundaries of uniting the two people perhaps most loved by Jesus on earth. As Boice points out:

> It is customary in Catholic theology to see this word as a commending of John, and through him all Christ's disciples, to the patronage of Mary. For example, Bishop Fulton J. Sheen remarks, "When our Lord spoke of John, he did not refer to him as John for then he would have been only the son of Zebedee. Rather, in him all humanity was commended to Mary, who became the mother of men, not by metaphor, or figure of speech, but by pangs of birth." Actually, the opposite was the case. Jesus did not commend John to Mary, but Mary to John. The real meaning of this episode is that Jesus was caring for his mother and thus fulfilling the Old Testament commandment to "honor thy father and thy mother" (Exod. 20:12) (Boice, V, p. 212).

Though this is the first of the "seven last words" recorded by John, it is in fact a third in the recognized series. It may be useful for us to identify them here in the order they were uttered:
1. "Father, forgive them, for they do not know not what they are doing" (Luke 23:34).
2. "I tell you the truth, today you will be with me in paradise" (Luke 23:43).
3. "Dear woman, here is your son" . . . "Here is your mother" (John 19:26–27).

4. "My God, my God, why have you forsaken me?" (Mark 15:34).
5. "I am thirsty" (John 19:28).
6. "It is finished" (John 19:30).
7. "Father, into your hands I commit my spirit" (Luke 23:46).

Ⓒ Dramatic Death (19:28–37)

SUPPORTING IDEA: *God's holiness and justice made the cross an absolute necessity. Events at the crucifixion happened as they did so "the scripture might be fulfilled" (v. 24). No fewer than twenty Old Testament prophecies were fulfilled within twenty-four hours at the time of our Lord's death. Some have speculated that the Lord meditated on Psalm 22 while on the cross, an idea perhaps suggested by the traditional "seven last words."*

19:28–29. The phrase **knowing that all was now completed** has given scholars pause for centuries. Since Jesus had not yet died, the atonement was not completed and beyond that lay the resurrection and ascension.

Carson observes that "Jesus' knowledge *that all was now completed* is the awareness that all the steps that brought him to this point of pain and impending death were in the design of his heavenly Father, and death itself was imminent" (Carson, p. 619). The cry **I am thirsty** probably refers to Psalm 69:21, a psalm that has already been cited twice in this Gospel (2:17; 15:25).

Westcott has this observation: "The incident loses its full significance unless it be regarded as one element in the foreshadowed course of the Passion. Nor is there any difficulty in the phrase 'are not finished' as preceding it. The 'thirst' was already felt and the feeling included the confession of it. The fulfillment of the Scripture (it need scarcely be added) was not the object which the Lord had in view in uttering the word, but there was a necessary correspondence between His acts and the divine foreshadowing of them" (Westcott, p. 277).

Wine vinegar would contract the throat muscles and keep the victim from shrieking in pain. This liquid is not to be confused with the "wine mixed with myrrh" of Mark 15:23. We should not read any compassion into this act, since the bitterness would prolong pain by extending the life of the victim.

19:30. Of greatest consequence in John's narrative is this phrase, **It is finished**, an idea which occurs for the second time in three verses. Surely this refers to the suffering and earthly life of Jesus, but also the task of bringing salvation to the human race. We should remember the prayer John uttered earlier, "I have brought you glory on earth by completing the work you gave me to do" (17:4). The words **it is finished** translate *tetelestai* that appears in the perfect tense. Even the grammar of the text signifies the full completion of Jesus' work.

Tenney observes, "The expression may be interpreted in various ways: as a cry of relief, because suffering is ending; as a cry of anguish, because his ministry has ended in failure; or as a shout of victory, because the purpose of God has triumphed in his death. The last of these seems to be the author's intent. He makes it the final report of Jesus to the Father, who will now exalt him to glory" (Tenney, *EBC*, p. 184).

As John has told us repeatedly, and as we have emphasized in the pages of this commentary, the significance of Christ's death on the cross centers in substitutionary atonement—his death on our behalf. God's holiness and justice made the cross an absolute necessity. James Denney has written a masterful work titled *The Death of Christ*. A few sentences are helpful here.

> The Son of Man *must* be lifted up if He is to save those who believe. The corn of wheat *must* fall into the ground and die if it is not to abide alone. Not much, indeed, is said to explain this. The various ends secured by Christ's death—the advantage of the flock for which as the Good Shepherd He lays down His life (x.11), the eternal life of those who believe in Him (iii.14f.), the rallying 'round Him as a centre of the scattered children of God, so that He becomes the head of a new humanity (xi.52): these, no doubt, are all dependent upon it somehow; but how, the evangelist is at no pains to tell. But we do no violence to his thought when we put this and that in the Gospel together in order to discern what he does not explicitly say. Everything, we have seen, comes from the love of God; the death of Christ is to be construed in harmony with this, not in any antagonism to it . . . Nor are we left without sufficiently clear hints as to the necessity which determine the gift. In the passage just referred to (iii.16), we see that apart from it men are lost; they perish, instead of having eternal life (Denney, pp. 266–67).

19:31–33. The Romans hastened death by breaking the legs of victims so they would no longer be able to support their bodies. Consequently, the victims' lungs collapsed and they died from suffocation. At Calvary, the soldiers carried out this procedure with both thieves, but Jesus **was already dead.**

Crucifixion brought death to its victims through shock, suffocation, or both. At the beginning victims would brace their feet on the platform and push upward, enabling the lungs to function just a bit. In typical Roman cruelty, the legs would be broken when the soldiers had finished their execution games and asphyxiation would take place almost instantly. But John tells us that did not happen with Jesus.

According to Tasker:

> The occurrence of the death of Jesus earlier than the authorities had expected made it unnecessary for the soldiers to hasten the end by breaking his legs so that the body might be removed and buried before sunset, when the new day began, which was not only a

Sabbath but the Passover Sabbath. There was thus no violation of the Jewish law that the body of a condemned man must not hang all night upon a tree (Dt. xxi.23). The evangelist is also careful to note that another law, relating to sacrifice, was also fulfilled. This stated that no bone of the sacrificial lamb should be broken (Ex. xii.46). The sacrifice of the true Passover Lamb is thus shown to have been complete both in the perfection of its own inner self-offering and in its external details (Tasker, p. 212).

19:34. Perhaps to make sure Jesus was dead, one of the soldiers slashed his side with a spear, causing a flow of blood and water that removed any doubt since, had he still been alive, only blood would have flowed out. Countless pages have been written on this verse and multiple medical explanations offered. But John's point seems simple. The word had become flesh, genuine flesh that could bleed and die. Many people have argued that John intended some theological symbolism by emphasizing blood and water. It seems to me he was focusing on the reality of the death Jesus died.

Consider these words from the great G. Campbell Morgan in his classic work *The Crises of the Christ*: "By the way of that Cross, and by that way alone, God may be just, that is, true to Himself in nature; and justify the sinner, that is, place man into the position of one for whom sin is made not to be, and who is therefore clear from guilt . . . Thus we have foregathered on the outer margin of that deep sea of sorrow through which the God-man wrought with God, though for a while in separation from the consciousness of his presence, a redemption which meets all difficulties, and solves all problems, and opens the kingdom of heaven to all believers" (Morgan, p. 267).

19:35–37. Scholars suggest that John may have been the only disciple eyewitness at the cross and therefore referred to himself in verse 35. This language is common to the Johannine epistles. He wanted his readers to know that he was there, and he wanted his readers to know that the cross, like virtually everything else in Christ's earthly ministry, fulfilled Scripture (in this case, Exod. 12:46; Num. 9:12; Ps. 34:20).

How well I remember spending Sunday evenings as a child in the beautiful Broadway Baptist Church of Paterson, New Jersey. Every Sunday evening at a certain point in the service, the house lights would dim and then disappear and a beautiful lighted cross at the front would shine brightly as we rose to sing,

> Jesus, keep me near the cross, there a precious fountain
> Free to all, a healing stream flows from Calvary's mountain.

The words, of course, are Fanny Crosby's. She wrote this particular poem to fit a tune composed by William H. Doane. Doane was twelve years younger than Fanny Crosby, but they died in the same year—1915. If memory serves me, we sang only the verse cited above, and perhaps the chorus, "In the cross, in the cross be my glory ever; 'til my raptured soul shall find rest beyond the river."

We have noted that John's mission statement appears in 20:30–31, but note the similarity here in 19:35: **He knows that he tells the truth, and he testifies so that you also may believe.** John emphasized that the decision not to break the legs of Christ but to pierce him with a Roman spear fulfilled two prophecies—the one we noted above and the second in Zechariah 12:10.

Bruce makes this pointed observation:

> Since the king is God's representative, the treatment he receives is reckoned by God as meted out to himself; hence the divine oracle runs (in the NEB rendering of Zech. 12:10, which does justice to both pronouns at once): "They shall look on me, on him whom they have pierced." But John recognizes the fulfillment of the oracle in no merely symbolical piercing, but in the literal piercing of the side of him who endured a real passion, historical and not simply dramatic, as "the King of the Jews." The oracles of Zech. 9–14 have profoundly influenced all four passion narratives in the NT, but nowhere more impressibly than here (Bruce, p. 378).

🄳 Beloved Burial (19:38–42)

SUPPORTING IDEA: *Jesus' burial was handled by Nicodemus and Joseph of Arimathea—two prominent men who were friends of Jesus, and probably secret believers. The price had been paid. The suffering was over. Satan had been defeated at the cross, but full victory awaited God's power at the open tomb.*

19:38–39. Joseph of Arimathea and Nicodemus—intimate disciples or secret believers? We may never know this side of heaven, but John seemed to imply in verse 38 that Joseph had placed his faith in Jesus and had become a disciple. John probably assumed we would remember the record of Jesus' discussion with Nicodemus from chapter 3.

As a member of the Sanhedrin, Joseph would have had some legitimate access to Pilate's ear. Though his act drew the attention of all four Gospel writers, it would have earned Joseph nothing but contempt from his fellow members of the religious elite.

Although Joseph gets press in all four Gospels, Nicodemus is mentioned only by John. His seventy pounds of spices would have been wrapped with the sheets around the body. Morris observes, "It is not without its interest that, whereas the disciples who had openly followed Jesus ran away at the end, the effect of the death of Jesus on these two secret disciples was exactly the opposite. Now, when they had nothing at all to gain by affirming their connection with Jesus, they came right out into the open" (Morris, p. 26).

19:40–42. In this brief and tightly wrapped paragraph about the burial, John provided the basic facts, although the site is still disputed to the present time. From John's record we have no doubt that Jesus died; we have no doubt these men intended the most caring, perhaps even elaborate burial; and we have no doubt that when John wrote these words, he could hardly wait to plunge into the next section of his Gospel.

Matthew's Gospel (27:59–60) tells us "Joseph took the body, wrapped it in a clean linen cloth, and placed it in his own new tomb." Why did John belabor the point that Jesus was buried in **a new tomb, in which no one had ever been laid?** Carson claims, "From the perspective of the Jewish authorities, this was doubtless less offensive than burying a crucified sinner in an occupied tomb . . . but the Evangelist's concern is unlikely to have been to mollify their scruples. More likely his purpose is to prepare for chap. 20: if on the third day the tomb is empty, only one body had disappeared, and only one person could have been resurrected" (Carson, pp. 630–31).

> **MAIN IDEA REVIEW:** *This chapter reminds us again that we participate in both the cross and the empty tomb. God's spirit "baptizes" all believers into Christ's death and resurrection. Awareness of that fact can help us live holy lives today.*

III. CONCLUSION

Marco Polo and the Kublai Kahn

His name is most often shouted by children playing games in a swimming pool, but Marco Polo is a character of no small significance in the history of Asia. His exploits were celebrated in a television mini-series aired by NBC in May of 1982 and titled simply *Marco Polo*. The second episode offered a scene in which the great Kublai Kahn fingered a gold cross that was brought to the Orient by Nicolo Polo. He slowly looked up at his European visitors and said, "Yours is the only religion which has transformed an instrument of death into a symbol of glory and power."

A symbol of glory and power indeed! Philip Bliss spoke for all of us when, still a young man, he wrote both the words and the music to one of the most theologically sound and biblically triumphant hymns sung by Christians over the past century.

> Man of sorrows! What a name
> For the Son of God who came

Ruined sinners to reclaim!
Hallelujah, what a Savior!
Bearing shame and scoffing rude,
In my place condemned He stood—
Sealed my pardon with His blood:
Hallelujah, what a Savior!

Guilty, vile, and helpless we,
Spotless Lamb of God was He;
Full atonement! Can it be?
Hallelujah, what a Savior!
Lifted up was He to die,
"It is finished," was His cry;
Now in heaven exalted high:
Hallelujah, what a Savior!

When He comes our glorious king
All his ransomed home to bring,
Then anew this song we'll sing:
Hallelujah, what a Savior!

PRINCIPLES

- Organized religion has often stood against truth, but never more than on the day of the crucifixion.
- Secular authorities may not fear us, but God can certainly make them fear him.
- The death of Jesus Christ on our behalf, along with his resurrection for our justification, is the centerpiece of the gospel.

APPLICATIONS

- Never treat the cross lightly or with disrespect.
- Take your stand on Scripture and fulfilled prophecy.
- When you are tempted to be a secret disciple, remember Joseph and Nicodemus.

IV. LIFE APPLICATION

"Daughter of Her Son"

In 1499 St. Peter's Cathedral in Rome admitted a magnificent work of art which stands there still. Sculpted from the fine white marble of the Carrara quarries, Michelangelo's world-renowned Pietà was crafted when he was under the age of twenty-five. Like many Renaissance works, it shows Mary not with the baby in the familiar Madonna and child pattern, but as a broken-hearted mother holding the body of the crucified Christ. Such artworks are called Pietàs, taken from the Italian word for *pity*. In a wonderful book called *The Handel's Messiah Family Advent Reader,* Payne and Lenzo pick up the theological significance of Michelangelo's work.

> Some of those who saw the Pietà for the first time complained that Mary's beautiful face looked too young. She looked younger than the son that she holds. Whether Michelangelo meant it or not, others have found a special meaning in Mary's young face. It is the meaning, too, of the body she holds so tenderly in her lap. This meaning of the Pietà is explained best by a line from poet Alighieri Dante. In his poem *Paradiso,* he addresses Mary as "virgin mother, daughter of your son." That is the mystery of Mary's son. The human baby she held in her arms is her creator and father. He existed before the dawn of the universe. Every human face is young compared to him. And because he is God, his death was not a meaningless death. The sorrow of the Pietà was turned to joy for Mary and for all of humanity when her son rose from His grave, conquering death for us all (Payne and Lenzo, pp. 44–45).

V. PRAYER

Father, thank you for the cross. Thank you for the day that Jesus bore our sins at Calvary and paid the penalty, enabling us to have eternal life as a free gift of your grace. Amen.

VI. DEEPER DISCOVERIES

A. "The One Who Handed Me Over" (19:11)

The word *paradidomi* is used of Judas in 18:2,5 and of the Jews in 18:30,35. In 19:16 the word is applied to Pilate. The NIV typically (and correctly) translates the expression by the English words "handed over." But commentators are not completely agreed on the person or persons Jesus intended to identify when he said to Pilate, "The one who handed me over to you is guilty of a greater sin."

Without question the most common nominee is Caiaphas since he, not Judas, actually delivered Jesus to Pilate. Carson says, "On the whole, it seems best to fasten on Caiaphas, since he not only took an active if not determinative part in the plot against Jesus (11:49–53) and, as high priest presiding over the Sanhedrin, he took a leading part in formulating the charges against

Jesus (cf. Mark14:61–64), charges of which John demonstrates his thorough awareness. The critical point, however, is this: whether the person *guilty of a greater sin* refers to Judas or Caiaphas, the distinguishing feature in that sin is its initiative, the active role of handing Jesus over" (Carson, p. 601).

Religious wars have been fought for centuries over the question, "Who killed Jesus?" Some blame the Jews, others the Romans—and those are two of four answers the New Testament provides. The other two, however, point to humanity in general and to God himself. Since every human participated in the sin nature whose penalty Jesus paid on the cross, we are all equally guilty in making his death necessary. But Peter Lewis emphasizes the cross as a gracious gift of God.

> For the cross is not simply or even primarily the result of the malice of men, but it is the work of God. Secretly, unsearchably, but nonetheless certainly, God's mastering love moved behind the malice of men. They did their worst—but in their worst God did his best. Out of different motives, all of them bad, Judas, Caiaphas, Pilate, and the soldiers all united to accomplish God's unutterably good will.
>
> It is a fundamental and repeated doctrine of the New Testament that we have in the death of Christ not merely the hand of men, but principally the hand of God. Christ's death was neither an accident, nor even a martyrdom, but a sacrifice (Lewis, p. 293).

B. The Day of the Crucifixion (19:14)

When John wrote at the end of this Gospel about the world not having "room for the books that would be written" (21:25), he could have been talking about arguments concerning the day of the crucifixion. Traditionally "Good Friday" holds the overwhelming portion of both popular and scholarly choice. It fits the apparent chronology of Luke 23 and gains the support of a huge percentage of scholars. In that scheme Jesus ate the Passover with his disciples on Thursday Nisan the fourteenth, followed by the Passover and crucifixion on Nisan the fifteenth, Sabbath on Nisan the sixteenth, and the resurrection on Nisan the seventeenth.

This view, despite its commonality, is not without its problems. For one thing, it forces the time element of Christ's stay in the tomb and gives no comfortable answer to the "nights" of Matthew 12:40. Furthermore, Christ, our Passover Lamb, was slain after the Passover has already been eaten (1 Cor. 5:7).

Some have argued for a Thursday crucifixion in order to solve some of the problems identified above. Certainly there is an attractiveness to allowing more time for the events described in the four Gospels. The Thursday view is expounded by Boice, who begins his chronology with his discussion of the triumphal entry. He identifies in some detail the problem mentioned above and arrives at the following conclusion:

> The solution is simply that two Sabbaths were involved in this last week of Christ's earthly ministry. One was the regular weekly Sabbath, which always fell on Saturday. The second was an extra Passover Sabbath which, in this particular week must have come on Friday. I should point out, in case it was not entirely self-evident, that the Passover Sabbath always came on the fifteenth on the month of Nisan and would therefore naturally fall on different days of the week in different years. It was, however, always observed as a Sabbath. In this reconstruction Jesus would have been crucified on Thursday and would have been raised from the dead sometime before dawn on Sunday morning (Boice, III, p. 320).

Some scholars have even put forth arguments for a Wednesday crucifixion. This view rests in the contention that the word *Sabbath* in the chronology of the passion week does not always mean *Saturday* but can mean a feast Sabbath. Leviticus 23:39 talks about the fifteenth day of the month that would not always fall on a Saturday, as Boice has argued.

In Mark 16:1 the verb *bought* is present tense and indicates that the women purchased their spices after the Sabbath. A. T. Robertson and others interpret that as a reference to some time after sundown, but one could claim that "two Sabbaths" are likely in the passion week. With this kind of scenario, the chronology would look very different with the crucifixion on Wednesday, Nisan the fourteenth, The Feast Sabbath (Passover) on Thursday the fifteenth, the preparation of the spices on Friday, the sixteenth, a rest over the Sabbath on the seventeenth, and the visit to the tomb on Nisan the eighteenth. Proponents of this view, however, have to place the resurrection some time after 6:00 P.M. on Saturday, although Jesus was not seen until Sunday morning.

The attractiveness of this view offers a full three days and three nights, and it fits the typology of the Passover Lamb. But one still has to contend with Luke 24:21, the weight of scholarship indicated earlier, and the fact that almost all scholars frown upon the concept of a Saturday evening resurrection.

Essentially this is a fair though greatly abbreviated version of three views. The concept of the "Preparation" (*paraskeuo*) plays a big role in the interpretation, since John introduced it in verse 14 and again in verse 31. But we should notice that it is not specifically the preparation for the Passover but the preparation for the Sabbath of Passover week that it is in view.

I write as one who has held to each of the views at some point over the last four decades but finds himself acquiescing to the cogent arguments supporting the traditional view. I conclude with a brief summary by Bruce: "As John has recorded the place explicitly, so now he notes the time, 'it was Passover eve' he says—or, since *paraskeuo* acquired in Jewish Greek the special sense of 'Sabbath eve,' i.e., Friday, we might render his words, 'it was Friday of Passover week.' Since on this occasion Passover fell on a Sabbath, it was Friday which ever way we take it" (Bruce, p. 364).

C. Fulfilled Prophecy (19:24,36)

Twice in our study of this chapter I have referred to the fact that over twenty prophecies were fulfilled during the trial and crucifixion of Jesus. Since this is a major point in the way John presented his case, it seems useful here to identify those prophecies with a reference to the Old Testament text and the New Testament fulfillment.

Old Testament Prophecies		New Testament Fulfillment
Psalms 41:9; 109:4	Betrayal by Judas	Mark 14:10
Zechariah 11:12	Sold for thirty pieces of silver	Matthew 26:15
Zechariah 11:13	Blood money used to buy a field	Matthew 27:6–7
Psalm 27:12	Accused by false witnesses	Matthew 26:60
Isaiah 53:7	Silent during the trial	Matthew 26:62–63
Psalm 22:7	Scorned and mocked	Mark 14:65
Psalm 69:21	Given vinegar to drink	John 19:29
Psalm 22:16	Pierced in his hands and feet	John 20:27
Zechariah 12:10	Pierced in his side	John 19:34
Isaiah 53:12	Crucified with sinners	Matthew 27:39
Psalm 69:4	Hated by his accusers	John 15:24–25
Psalm 22:8	His relationship to the Father derided	Matthew 27:41–43
Isaiah 53:4–5	Suffered for humanity	Matthew 8:16–17
Psalm 34:20	No bones broken	John 19:33
Isaiah 53:9	Buried with the rich	John 19:41
Psalm 16:10	Rose from the dead	Matthew 28:7
Psalm 68:18	Ascended back to heaven	Acts 1:9
Psalm 109:8	Judas' office taken by another	Acts 1:21–26

VII. TEACHING OUTLINE

A. INTRODUCTION

1. Lead Story: Costly Carelessness
2. Context: The narrative of John 18–19 holds together like the seamless garment for which the soldiers gambled at the cross. We should remember through the entire second half of this Gospel that John was dealing with just the last week of Christ's life.
3. Transition: John has been making his way to chapter 20 for almost the entirety of this book. In between his introduction of the Messiah in chapter 1 and the final appearance of the disciples in chapter 21, he has been preparing his readers for the ultimate miracle—resurrection.

B. COMMENTARY

1. Sinful Sentence (19:1–16)
   a. Humiliation of the prisoner (19:1–3)
   b. Presentation of the prisoner (19:4–7)
   c. Interrogation of the prisoner (19:8–11)
   d. Condemnation of the prisoner (19:12–16)
2. Cruel Crucifixion (19:17–27)
   a. Between two thieves (19:17–18)
   b. Under a Roman sign (19:19–24)
   c. In front of loved ones (19:25–27)
3. Dramatic Death (19:28–37)
   a. Fulfilling the Father's will (19:28–30)
   b. Fulfilling the Father's word (19:31–37)
4. Beloved Burial (19:38–42)
   a. The undertaker (19:38)
   b. The embalmer (19:39–40)
   c. The tomb (19:41–42)

C. CONCLUSION: "DAUGHTER OF HER SON"

VIII. ISSUES FOR DISCUSSION

1. Discuss the power of God over secular authorities on the basis of verse 11.
2. In your view, why did John keep referring to fulfilled Scripture in this chapter?
3. What can we learn about courage to stand up for Jesus from the experience of Nicodemus and Joseph of Arimathea?

John 20

Sights of Super Sunday

"*The* resurrection of Jesus Christ is absolutely the best attested fact in ancient history."

Horace Bushnell

John 20

IN A NUTSHELL

This chapter records Jesus' appearances immediately after his resurrection. These are not his only appearances, but the apostle John built his theme of faith by selecting particular events.

Sights of Super Sunday

I. INTRODUCTION

Super Sunday

*S*ome time in late January each year, millions of people are glued to their television sets to watch the NFL's annual "Superbowl," the most heavily viewed television program of the year and the most expensive for commercial advertising. The hoopla leading up to this usually covers at least a week with special programming, heavy gambling of both legal and illegal dollars, and the selling of a vast array of paraphernalia like T-shirts and team hats. In the vocabulary of the past two decades it has become known as "Super Sunday."

But the first Super Sunday took place hundreds of years before anyone invented football, much less the Superbowl. Approximately in the year A.D. 30, the Son of God rose from the grave never to die again. He broke the bonds of death on the first day of the week, thereby changing the worship schedule of the people of God and setting the theme for most New Testament preaching.

In this chapter we learn about eleven people who became eyewitnesses on that first Super Sunday, one woman and ten men whose story John recorded in this short chapter. They had all been intimate friends of Jesus, but none of them were emotionally or spiritually prepared for the dynamic of the resurrection. Who were these people? What did they see?

II. COMMENTARY

Sights of Super Sunday

MAIN IDEA: *The historical fact of the resurrection and its theological meaning will become the centerpiece of apostolic preaching in the Book of Acts. Perhaps from impetus provided by Peter and John, New Testament preachers claimed that the Savior is forever alive—a dramatic truth of the heart of the gospel to this very day. Our living Lord has conquered both sin and death. We can function in spite of trouble and heartache, knowing the ultimate victory is his and ours.*

◢ An Empty Tomb (20:1–9)

> **SUPPORTING IDEA:** *What sights awaited these two running men and one struggling woman? She saw the Lord; they found strips of linen and reacted with hesitation and uncertainty. Surely it was obvious that no grave robbers had been in this tomb; the orderly scene evidenced God's hand in delivering his Son from death. When John went in, he believed. He perceived the reality of the resurrection for the first time.*

20:1–2. We know from Matthew's account that Mary Magdalene was not alone on this visit (Matt. 28:1). If we follow the flow of Matthew's text from 27:55 through the burial and resurrection, it would appear that "the other Mary" refers to Jesus' mother who had already taken a secondary place before the resurrection, hardly elevated in the New Testament to the worship many afford her today.

Luke tells us it was early. This word refers to the last of the watches, probably between 3:00 and 6:00 P.M. John did not give us the details available in the other Gospels, but used the word *blepo* (**saw**), indicating that Mary Magdalene glanced at the tomb. Consider the larger report from Luke:

> On the first day of the week, very early in the morning, the women took the spices they had prepared and went to the tomb. They found the stone rolled away from the tomb, but when they entered, they did not find the body of the Lord Jesus. While they were wondering about this, suddenly two men in clothes that gleamed like lightning stood beside them. In their fright the women bowed down with their faces to the ground, but the men said to them, "Why do you look for the living among the dead? He is not here; he has risen! Remember how he told you, while he was still with you in Galilee: 'The Son of Man must be delivered into the hands of sinful men, be crucified and on the third day be raised again.'" Then they remembered his words (Luke 24:1–8).

Startled, Mary ran to the disciples. John mentions Peter by name while implying he was the other recipient of this message. Luke tells us her report was rejected (24:11), so unbelieving were the disciples regarding Jesus' promise to rise again. Mary's fear and frustration must have propelled her back to the disciples' hiding place. We find it interesting that she recorded her findings to the person who had betrayed the Lord at the fire of the enemy. With no thought of a miraculous resurrection, Mary must have entertained all kinds of possibilities, none of which seemed to her a happy outcome.

Two questions surface in these verses. First, we wonder why John mentioned only one woman when we know Mary was not alone in her visit to the garden. Some speculate that Mary made two trips, one alone and another bringing other women with her. Others suggest that the women came together, but Mary became separated from them in the darkness and was alone when she saw Jesus.

This kind of conjecture is interesting, but not helpful. John must have known exactly who was there and also what the synoptic Gospel writers had written. But his focus and mission did not consider some details important, so he centered on the one woman who spoke with Jesus and who was also named first in all the synoptic accounts.

The second question has to do with the need for additional spices after the efforts of Nicodemus and Joseph. Once again, speculation is our only option and we wonder whether the women even knew of what had been done on that terrible night of the crucifixion. "More probably," says Morris, "in view of the lateness of the hour and the nearness of the Sabbath, Nicodemus was not able to use all the spices he had brought in the way he intended. Something remained to complete the process of burial, and the women came to do this" (Morris, p. 831).

20:3–5. This passage talks a lot about running. Mary ran back to the disciples. Although John made it sound as though they immediately dashed off to the tomb upon hearing her report, Luke gives a slightly different picture: "They did not believe the women, because their words seemed to them like nonsense. Peter, however, got up and ran to the tomb" (Luke 24:11–12a).

All this is quite interesting since in first-century Palestinian culture, grown men did not run. In fact, the only other literal New Testament use apart from these verses appears in Matthew 28:8, describing the same event. The disciples had walked hundreds, maybe thousands, of miles with the Lord for three and one-half years. Now an empty tomb accelerated their pace.

John was certainly younger than Peter, and he may have been faster. He reached the tomb first and **looked at** the strips of linen. The text uses the same word for *saw* that appears in verse 1 describing Mary. Like Mary, John did not enter the tomb. We sense a certain hesitation and uncertainty, perhaps even fear. What lay beyond in that darkness? What horror might they find in the shadows of the burial cave? John was the only disciple to have seen the crucifixion, so we need not wonder at his unwillingness to look at that broken body again.

20:6–7. Whether motivated by shame or just acting according to character, Peter plunged into the darkness. We assume one of the men carried some kind of lantern or torch. The text says that Peter **saw** what John had seen and in addition, the burial cloth. But the word changes to one with a slightly different meaning, perhaps best translated as "noticed" rather than "looked at."

Notice that the burial cloth **was folded up by itself.** This was obviously an intentional act on the part of someone. All the evidence at the tomb itself that Super Sunday supports every claim the disciples made about the resurrection as well as the record of the four Gospel writers.

How clearly Peter must have remembered this night years later at the home of Cornelius: "We are witnesses of everything he did in the country of the Jews and in Jerusalem. They killed him by hanging him on a tree, but God raised him from the dead on the third day and caused him to be seen. He was not seen by all the people, but by witnesses whom God had already chosen— by us who ate and drank with him after he rose from the dead. He commanded us to preach to the people and to testify that he is the one whom God appointed as judge of the living and the dead. All the prophets testify about him that everyone who believes in him receives forgiveness of sins through his name" (Acts 10:39–43).

20:8–9. So three of Jesus' followers **saw** the empty tomb, but John was not finished with his report. He wanted his readers to know that after Peter entered the tomb, John himself **finally** found enough courage to follow him. Now we have yet another use of the English verb **saw** and yet a third Greek word appearing in the original text. This time John uses a word that means "to perceive with understanding." That is why our text reads that John **saw and believed.**

But lest readers of this Gospel get the wrong idea about the quality of the disciples' faith at this point, John appended a parenthesis telling us that neither he nor the rest of the disciples yet understood the connection between scriptural prophecy and the resurrection. That would await Jesus' post-resurrection teaching followed by the infilling with the Holy Spirit at Pentecost.

What Scripture might John have had in mind when he wrote verse 9? Quite possibly Isaiah 53:10–12 or even Psalm 16:10. What did he actually believe if he did not understand the biblical background of resurrection? Perhaps the best option in the text is to conclude that John believed Jesus was alive but could not figure out why or what would happen next. That fits well with the great surprise of the disciples at post-resurrection appearances. Nevertheless, once they understood, the message of the living Savior permeated their preaching throughout the next thirty years. This had been for them— and for us—a genuine Super Sunday.

Morris has this observation: "It is clear from the New Testament that the early Christians saw the resurrection as foretold in the Old Testament. But this verse shows plainly that it was belief in the resurrection that came first. The believers did not manufacture a resurrection to agree with their interpretation of prophecy. They were first convinced that Christ was risen. Then they came to see a fuller meaning in certain Old Testament passages" (Morris, p. 835).

B A Living Lord (20:10–18)

> **SUPPORTING IDEA:** *How beautiful to learn that though the cross may have killed faith and hope, it could not destroy love. Jesus told Mary not to hold on to the past. Now there would be a new relationship, and she would be the first witness to other disciples that Jesus was alive.*

20:10–12. The phrase "you will be my witnesses" or "we are witnesses" does not appear in this chapter of John, but the Lord used it in Acts 1:8 and we see it repeated in Acts 2:32; 3:15; 5:32; 10:39. In all four of those passages, it is always spoken by Peter, and the context always describes the crucifixion and resurrection.

But here the primary witness was not Peter but Mary. Peter and John had left, but Mary stayed at the tomb and John offered this loving and passionate account of the first post-resurrection appearance of our Lord.

Mary wept as we would over the loss of a dear friend. Then suddenly two angels appeared, and a fascinating conversation took place. We know from Luke's record that Mary had been cured of demon possession (Luke 8:2) and also had helped support the Lord financially. We must not confuse her with the prostitute of Luke 7 or with Mary the sister of Martha and Lazarus. Empty tomb or not, her grief was unbearable—so deep that she could not take her eyes off the grave to perceive the living Lord.

No Bible reader is surprised to find angels at the empty tomb. From the birth of Jesus (Luke 1:11,26) to the announcement of the Holy City (Rev. 22:8–9) we find angels announcing God's plan. They not only heralded the resurrection and showed up at the ascension; they even prophesied the second coming (Acts 1:11). One of the major duties assigned these "ministering spirits" was to appear at crucial times and places to announce God's plan to individuals or groups. This is the only place where John mentioned angels in his Gospel.

Tenney points out: "No description is given of the angels. When angels appear in the Bible, they are usually recognized by their powers rather than by any significant difference from human form. Mary did not respond to them in any unusual way, possibly because her eyes were clouded with tears, or because she was preoccupied with the loss of Jesus' body. The sole feature noted in the text is that angels were clothed in white" (Tenney, *EBC*, p. 190).

20:13–14. John records that Mary **saw** Jesus. She noticed a person standing there, but she had no idea who it was. Many interpreters have wondered about this passage. How could she not recognize Jesus? Certainly there are many plausible explanations.

She had experienced deep trauma; her eyes had filled with tears; it was still dark; she was very confused. But perhaps most important, she had not considered the resurrection a possibility. So the idea that she might be talking to a living Christ never occurred to her. She was looking for a body; she did not expect a resurrection.

20:15–16. Mary finally asked the person she thought to be the gardener where the body might be so she could retrieve it. Then Jesus spoke her name and tragedy turned to triumph. The early words of verse 16 remind us of John 10:4 where Jesus said that "his sheep know his voice." This first appearance to a woman shows us the grace and openness of the gospel. This historic narrative describes what really happened. Jesus did not show himself to Peter and John but spoke first to Mary. So much for gender discrimination in the Bible.

Hughes notes, "It is highly significant that Christ appeared first to a woman and that this appearance is recorded by all four Gospels. It was not only to a woman, one who in that culture had been oppressed, but to a person who had known great sin. What a great comfort this should be to us. Christ always comes first to the poor in spirit" (Hughes, p. 160).

20:17–18. Many ideas have been put forth to explain the words, **do not hold on to me.** But such conjecture is unnecessary, since Jesus told us this statement was connected with his ascension. The people who love Jesus on earth—beginning with Mary—must learn to live without the physical support of his presence.

Dods states the idea eloquently: "There must be no more kissing of His feet, but homage of a sterner, deeper sort; there must be no more sitting at table with Him, and filling the mind with His words, until they sit down with Him in the Father's presence. Meanwhile His friends must walk by faith, not by sight—by their inward light and spiritual likings; they must learn the truer fidelity that serves an absent Lord; they must acquire the independent and inherent love of righteousness which can freely grow only when relieved from the over-mastering pressure of a visible presence, encouraging us by sensible expressions of favour, guaranteeing us against defeat and danger" (Dods, vol. 2, p. 361).

Mary thus witnessed the resurrection, and her first act upon leaving Jesus was a report to the disciples. It is difficult to know from John's account whether this report or the one in verse 2 was rejected by the disciples. But for whatever reason, the women who believed the reality of the empty tomb could not convince the other disciples what had happened.

The lesson we must learn here centers in the rock-solid *unbelief* of Jesus' closest friends. We shall learn in a few verses that all reports of a risen Lord failed to convince the one absent disciple (Thomas) that Jesus had made a second appearance. The disciples had no faith in a resurrection.

◀C A Lasting Peace (20:19–23)

SUPPORTING IDEA: *The troubled disciples needed peace, and that is what Jesus brought in the first group appearance. He had promised to relieve the disciples' grief by replacing it with joy (John 16:20), and now he fulfilled that promise. He also gave them a measure of the Holy Spirit, probably to enhance their learning times between the resurrection and the ascension.*

20:19–20. The scene now moves from predawn hours to the evening of the same day. The disciples were locked in and riddled with fear in spite of what Peter and John had seen and what Mary had reported. Miraculously, instantly, the Lord appeared to offer them a warm "Shalom." Before they could respond, he showed them the nail prints in his hands and the spear scar in his side. Why such a display? These fearful believers had to grasp that the same Jesus who died now lived again and stood before them.

In the disciples' minds the locked doors protected them to some extent against Jewish authorities who might want to do to them what they had done to their Lord. But in John's view, the locked doors served as a symbolic reminder that nothing can stop or hinder the resurrection body of Jesus.

There is some discussion regarding the number in the group to which Jesus appeared in this chapter. John had used the term **the disciples** throughout his book to identify the Twelve when it appears with the definite article. In this situation there would have been ten. Judas was dead and Thomas was absent.

But many reliable interpreters take a wider view of inclusion, largely by linking the text in John 20 with Luke 24:33. Carson says, "How large a group is referred to by *the disciples* is not certain, but in the light of the circle at the last supper (made up of Jesus plus the Twelve, and then, after Judas Iscariot left, the Eleven), and in the light of the fact that Thomas is singled out as not having been present (v. 24)—though doubtless there were countless other 'disciples' less tightly connected with the Lord who were also not present— we should probably think of the Ten (i.e., the Twelve, less Judas and Thomas)" (Carson, p. 646).

20:21–23. Again the Father became the center of Jesus' words. He had been a servant on a mission, and now he sent his people out to witness. Most evangelical scholars believe this reception of the Holy Spirit was temporary— an illumination of their hearts for the next fifty days before Pentecost.

Gromacki notes: "This impartation of the Spirit was not the fulfillment of Christ's prayer and promise given earlier on the night before his crucifixion (14:16–17,26; 15:26–27; 16:7–15). That fulfillment occurred on the Day of Pentecost. Why then did Christ impart the Spirit before His ascension and the actual descent of the spirit? As John Walvord has suggested, 'apparently a temporary filling of the Spirit was given to provide for their spiritual needs prior to Pentecost.' In that sense they received a prechurch age filling of the Spirit in anticipation of the Day of Pentecost so they could fully understand the Savior's instructions" (Gromacki, pp. 141–42).

Of greater difficulty in this context is verse 23. On what basis could human beings forgive the sins of others? Obviously, much has been made of this in some segments of the Christian faith. Perhaps the best interpretation emphasizes the difference between absolution and proclamation. The duty of the disciples was to proclaim the forgiveness of sins; the actual forgiving would take place in heaven by the Lord who paid for those sins. Nevertheless, the claims of the gospel are clear—forgiveness only on the basis of Jesus' death on the cross.

Morris notes, "It should also be borne in mind that, according to the best text, the verbs 'are forgiven' and 'are retained' are in the perfect tense. The meaning of this is that the Spirit-filled church can pronounce with authority that the sins of such-and-such men have been forgiven or have been retained. If the church is really acting under the leadership of the Spirit it will be found that her pronouncements on this matter do but reveal what has already been determined in heaven" (Morris, p. 849).

🄳 A Genuine Invitation (20:24–31)

SUPPORTING IDEA: *The account of Thomas appears immediately before John's mission statement in verses 30–31. The goal of John's Gospel is always evangelistic. He wanted people to understand the truth about Jesus, to believe that he is the Son of God, and thereby to experience the life of which we have been reading in this Gospel. Faith itself is not an end but a means to an end.*

20:24–25. Are Christians gullible? Some may be, but John wanted to tell us about one who was not. Thomas the Twin was the original "show me" man from Missouri, long before that state existed. If Judas depicted betrayal and Peter denial, Thomas demonstrated skepticism.

In the Greek language, tense is very important. The word translated **told** in verse 25 appears in the imperfect tense. The disciples *kept on telling* Thomas they had seen the Lord. Thomas, fed up with such nonsense, grew weary of holding on to a faith that had crumbled. He took the old motto "seeing is believing" to frightening dimensions. He removed himself from the disciple band, telling them he wanted to hear no more about this ridiculous notion of a resurrection. Thomas used strong language with his friends, indicating the frustration to which the events of the past week had driven him.

Tasker offers an interesting paragraph in explanation of verse 25: "In place of the second reference to the *print* or mark (*tupon*) of the nails, some ancient MSS read 'the place' (*topon*). This variation should probably be adopted. Thomas wants not only to see the scar made by the nails in the hands, but also to put his finger into the place where the nails had been . . . There is no mention in this Gospel, or in Matthew and Luke, of the piercing of the feet. That the feet of Jesus may have been nailed to the cross rather than fastened with a rope which was the common practice, is an inference from Lk. xxiv. 39" (Tasker, pp. 226–27).

20:26–27. But John moved on to show us doubting alleviated. In spite of what he had said, Thomas at least joined the Sunday evening service a week later. Again, in spite of locked doors, Jesus appeared and greeted them exactly as he had a week earlier. But rather than showing his hands and side to the entire group, he turned to Thomas and invited empirical investigation. Sincere Christianity has always welcomed sincere research. Jesus did not scold Thomas or condemn his hesitation. He provided the evidence. Only then did he say to him, **Stop doubting and believe.**

20:28–29. In the flow of this wonderful story, John next offered us a record of doubting abandoned. Thomas moved quickly from rough-talking skeptic to willing worshiper. In the New Testament, no one had yet said to Jesus, **My Lord and my God.** Here again the theme of our study looms large—believing is seeing. Thomas saw and believed—and that was fine. But happy are the millions who since that day have not had the opportunity of Thomas and the other ten **and yet have believed.** More than 375 times in the Old Testament and 100 times in the New Testament, the Bible talks about *blessing.* This one is related to faith and especially faith in the resurrection.

Boice has these observations: "What convinced Thomas? Some have suggested that it was Christ's obvious knowledge of what Thomas had said, though Jesus had not been physically present when Thomas said it. To do that, so the argument goes, Jesus would have had to be God. But logical as this is, I do not find myself believing that this is what really got through to Thomas. What finally got through to him was the presence of Christ, identified by the wounds in his hands, feet, and side. It was the Christ of the cross who reached Thomas" (Boice, V, pp. 322–23).

20:30–31. Scholars remain hopelessly divided on how many miracles Jesus did **in the presence of his disciples,** but thirty-five seems a reasonable approximation. John recorded only ten at the most. The number was of little concern to John. He chose the works and words of Jesus that would prompt readers to faith. That faith would give meaning to experience as believers found life in the name of Jesus.

G. Campbell Morgan calls the resurrection "faith's anchorage" and tells us: "The living risen Christ is the Centre of the church's creed, the Creator of her character, and the Inspiration of her conduct. His resurrection is the clearest note in her battle-song. It is the sweetest, strongest music amid all her sorrows. It speaks of personal salvation. It promises the life that has no ending, it declares to all bereaved souls that 'them also that are fallen asleep in Jesus will God bring with him,' and therefore the light of his resurrection falls in radiant beauty upon the graves where rest the dust of the holy dead" (Morgan, p. 341).

> **MAIN IDEA REVIEW:** *The historical fact of the resurrection and its theological meaning will become the centerpiece of apostolic preaching in the Book of Acts. Perhaps from impetus provided by Peter and John, New Testament preachers claimed that the Savior is forever alive—a dramatic truth of the heart of the gospel to this very day. Our living Lord has conquered both sin and death. We can function in spite of trouble and heartache, knowing the ultimate victory is his and ours.*

III. CONCLUSION

Raise the Flag

A small Norwegian vessel lay in an English port for several days. One of those days happened to be Good Friday, and the chief officer carelessly said to the captain, "Shall I hoist the flag at half mast today?" The captain had no context for the question, and asked the officer why he would do that. "Well," said the officer, "they say Jesus died on this day."

An interesting gesture, and one certainly more common to an earlier era of human life, but in this particular case the captain was a Christian. He immediately responded, "Jesus, my Savior is a living Savior, not a dead one; if you put the flag out at all, you must hoist it right to the top of the mast."

The twentieth chapter of John contains a twofold message. To unbelievers it says, "Stop doubting and believe." There is no question that John's powerful Gospel aims its primary ammunition at people who need to come to faith, and this chapter is clearly the capstone.

But while offering an apologetic for consideration by unbelievers, John also provided an affirmation for his fellow believers. We are reminded of our witnessing role, a representation of the Savior in life. I think often of the wonderful words of Margaret Clarkson built on the twenty-first verse of this chapter.

> So send I you to labor unrewarded,
> To serve unpaid, unloved, unsought, unknown.
> To bear rebuke, to suffer scorn and scoffing.
> So send I you to live for me alone.

PRINCIPLES

- When it comes to spiritual truth, be prepared to believe what you have not seen.

- Know the difference between noticing something in God's Word and perceiving it.
- Full acknowledgement of the resurrection means taking your eyes off the empty tomb and placing them on the Lord.

APPLICATIONS

- Allow the reality of the living Lord to handle your hesitation to obey him in everything.
- When believers gather, be present in faith and expectation.
- In the tough days remember that Jesus said, "Peace be with you!"
- Never forget Jesus' promise, "Blessed are those who have not seen and yet have believed."

IV. LIFE APPLICATION

Get the Message

In Shakespeare's play *Henry V*, he shows us how Henry and John Falstaff had entered into a deep friendship until Henry became king, at which time he turned away from his old friends. Jesus did not do that in this chapter but emphasized through three post-resurrection appearances how close he remained to his disciples and friends. Mary had to understand the new relationship with him and with the disciples, but in one short verse (v. 17) Jesus linked the family by referring both to the Father and to his brothers, obviously not his physical half-brothers, but the disciples. The message is brief, precise, and clear, unlike so much human communication.

British military lore contains a story about the Duke of Wellington fighting for the crown on the European mainland. When the battle was won, he ordered a blinker sent from the coast of France across the English channel relaying the message, "Wellington defeated the enemy." But such a message took time to convey in that archaic mode of communication. A fog closed in after the first two words had been received. With defeat news ringing in their ears, the nation panicked and the stock market crashed until three days later when the fog lifted and the full message got through.

John wanted the full message to get through in this chapter. He also wanted his readers not only to understand and believe it, but to be willing to share it with others.

V. PRAYER

Father, thank you for the resurrection of Jesus and the promise of our own eternal life through faith in him. Thank you also for John and his faithful record of the works and words of Jesus. May we not only believe and receive but also share this clear record of life with others. Amen.

VI. DEEPER DISCOVERIES

A. I Send You (20:21)

Frequently when we encounter some form of the word *send* in the New Testament, we anticipate finding behind it the Greek word *apostello*, which emphasizes being sent with a message and serves as the base from which our English word *apostle* derives. But that is not the word we find here. This is *pempo*, used thirty-two times in this Gospel and seventy-nine times in the New Testament.

> The Greek verb *pempo* is an old and common term meaning *to send*, reaching all the way back to the writings of Homer (eighth century B.C.). In John's Gospel, however, *pempo* emphasizes that someone is being sent by another of higher rank to perform a special task. Those who questioned John the Baptist had been sent (1:21) by the Pharisees (cv. 24), but John explained that he had been sent by God (v. 33). The Father will send the Holy Spirit (14:26), and so will Jesus (15:26; 16:7). On two occasions Jesus stated that he sends his disciples (13:20; 20:21). The dominant function of *pempo* is found in Jesus' use of the term to explain that the Father had sent him. This aspect of *pempo* occurs twenty-three times in John's Gospel and has two connotations: first, to remind us of Jesus' divine origin, that he came from heaven where he had been with the Father (5:23; 6:38–39; 7:33; 8:16; 16:5); second, to emphasize that the Father gave him a special task that only he could accomplish, the task of redemption (4:34; 6:44; 7:16,28). In the latter case, *pempo* takes on the meaning *commission* or *appoint* (Blackaby, p. 58).

The disciples never forgot this commission which was augmented significantly by the pre-ascension challenge of Acts 1. They understood clearly throughout the remainder of the first century that they were "sent ones" in the same manner that the Father had sent Jesus.

The missionary hymn cited earlier ("So Send I You") was written by Margaret Clarkson and set to music by John Peterson. Clarkson wrote the words as a twenty-three-year-old schoolteacher in a gold-mining camp in northern Ontario earlier in the 20th century. She meditated on John 20:21 one evening, and God spoke to her with a phrase from that text. She realized that she was just as much a missionary as her friends who were serving in Africa and Asia because she was in the place where God had sent her with his message.

The words were published some six years later, and Miss Clarkson went on to Toronto to assume numerous other duties in education. Over the years many people have been challenged to hear the Lord's call through this inspiring hymn.

B. Forgiving Sins (20:23)

Sinclair Lewis once remarked, "Everyone says forgiveness is a lovely idea until they have something to forgive." The Greek word here is *aphiemi,* which means "to put away or apart." In the Greek Old Testament, the word is often used to describe the release of a prisoner or the remitting of a debt. In the New Testament, the word appears 142 times, of which 139 are in the Gospels (Matthew, 47 times; Mark, 34 times; Luke, 34 times; John, 14 times). The message is clear: forgiveness is tied to the life, ministry, death, and resurrection of Jesus Christ.

The word was also well known in secular literature. Detzler tells us that "it was used to indicate the sending away of an object or a person. Later it came to include the release of someone from the obligation of marriage, or debt, or even a religious vow. In its final form it came to embrace the principle of release from punishment for some wrongdoing" (Detzler, p. 168).

No Christian doubts the authority of the Father or the Son to forgive sins on the basis of Christ's death on our behalf. But a huge debate rages over what human role might be played in the forgiving of the sins of others. One of the world's major religions rests on the authority of religious officials to forgive sins, based to a great extent on this verse. I have stated an interpretive position in the "Commentary" section at the point of this verse. But I want to expand our study by presenting several versions of the text and a sampling of commentator opinions.

> *NIV:* "If you forgive anyone his sins, they are forgiven; if you do not forgive them, they are not forgiven."
>
> *HCSB:* "If you forgive the sins of any, they are forgiven them; if you retain the sins of any, they are retained."
>
> *KJV:* "Whose soever sins ye remit, they are remitted unto them; and whose soever sins ye retain, they are retained."
>
> *CEV:* "If you forgive anyone's sins, they will be forgiven. But if you don't forgive their sins, they will not be forgiven."

Admittedly, there is not much help in the variety of texts. The grammar is important, indicating that Christ's earthly messengers proclaim what Christ does in actuality in heaven. But let me allow a few evangelical commentators to speak for themselves:

> *Barclay:* "This sentence does not mean that the power to forgive sins was ever entrusted to any man or to any men; it means that the power to proclaim that forgiveness was so entrusted; and it means

that the power to warn that that forgiveness is not open to the impenitent was also entrusted to them. This sentence lays down the duty of the Church to convey forgiveness to the penitent in heart, and to warn the impenitent that they are forfeiting the mercy of God" (quoted in Morris, p. 848).

Morgan: "To whom have I the right to say, 'Thy sins are forgiven'? To any man, to any woman, to any youth, or maiden, who, conscious of sin, repents towards God, and believes on the Lord Jesus Christ . . . And when, for some reason of supposed intellectual pride, more often of moral delinquency, the soul has persisted in sin, saying, No, I can not give this up; then I have had to say to that soul, Your sins are not forgiven; they are retained, they remain with you" (Morgan, p. 321).

Carson: "The Christian witnesses proclaim and declare, and, empowered by the Spirit, live by the message of their own proclamation; it is God who *effectively* forgives or retains the sin" (Carson, p. 656).

Boice: "There's no instance in any of the New Testament books of any apostle taking on himself the authority to absolve or pardon anyone. This is important because it relates to a fundamental rule of Scripture interpretation, namely, that every text must be interpreted within its historical and biblical context, and never in isolation. To interpret this text correctly we must ask what Jesus meant by it and what the disciples understood Him to be saying" (Boice, p. 313).

The essential difference is the distinction between preacher and priest. In the confessional booth, a priest offers absolution from sins for individuals. Preachers, on the other hand, proclaim the biblical boundaries and procedures by which God through Christ forgives sins. Not the sins of individual people, but the sins of those who repent as a theologically definable group.

When we proclaim the gospel, we say explicitly that only those who trust Jesus Christ as personal Savior and accept his death on the cross as payment for their sins may receive God's forgiveness. Those who refuse to do so retain their sins.

VII. TEACHING OUTLINE

A. INTRODUCTION

1. Lead Story: Super Sunday
2. Context: We have mentioned it several times, but it may be useful to say again that John spent nearly half his book (chaps. 12–21) on the last week of Christ's life. It began with the triumphal entry and it

ended not with crucifixion but with victorious and triumphant resurrection.

3. Transition: The chasm between chapters 19 and 20 in John may be the most significant distinction in the book. From the burial scene ending with the words "they laid Jesus there" (19:42) to the trumpets of resurrection which announce "early on the first day of the week" (20:1), John has arrived at where he has been headed theologically throughout the book.

B. COMMENTARY

1. An Empty Tomb (20:1–9)
    a. Mary saw a displaced stone (20:1–2)
    b. John saw strips of linen (20:3–5)
    c. Peter saw a folded burial cloth (20:6–9)
2. A Living Lord (20:10–18)
    a. Recognition of the Lord (20:10–16)
    b. Return to the Father (20:17)
    c. Report to the disciples (20:18)
3. A Lasting Peace (20:19–23)
    a. The peace of salvation (20:19–20)
    b. The peace of service (20:21–23)
4. A Genuine Invitation (20:24–31)
    a. Doubting announced (20:24–25)
    b. Doubting alleviated (20:26–27)
    c. Doubting abandoned (20:28–31)

C. CONCLUSION: GET THE MESSAGE

VIII. ISSUES FOR DISCUSSION

1. How is it possible that even at the empty tomb Peter and John "still did not understand from Scripture that Jesus had to rise from the dead"?
2. In what ways does Jesus get our attention today the way he did by speaking Mary's name in the garden?
3. What lessons can we learn from Thomas that will help us defeat negative thinking and skepticism in our own lives?

John 21

Jesus Is Lord!

"He is Lord! He is Lord!

He is risen from the dead and He is Lord!

Every knee shall bow, every tongue confess

that Jesus Christ is Lord."

Anonymous

John 21

IN A NUTSHELL

As John brought his Gospel to a close, he left his readers with one thought beyond the oft-repeated emphasis on faith. He wanted to show us that these disciples, once mystified and confused, at last began to sense the depth of commitment they must have to their Master. To make this point, he chose a personal conversation between the Lord and Peter—words that John may have heard, and words to which Peter probably referred on many subsequent occasions.

Jesus Is Lord!

I. INTRODUCTION

Sent by God

He opened up more of the world's terrain than any man in history, driven on by the need for his medicines, a love for people he met, and a burning faith in his Savior. His traveling equipment included his medical chest, his Bible, and his "magic lantern," a crude slide projector used for missionary messages. He challenged the slave trade, chartered his findings, and channeled a treasury of important information back to the Royal Geographic Society in London.

David Livingston was born in 1813 in Blantyre, Scotland. As a teenager he worked twelve hours a day in a spinning mill, paying his way through medical school to become a missionary doctor in China. The Opium Wars dashed that hope, so at the age of 27 he determined to go to Africa. He explored that vast continent, virtually unknown in his day, by foot, canoe, and on the back of oxen. In 1851 he discovered the Zambezi River and in the next few years traveled from the Atlantic coast of Angola to Mozambique. He was the first white man to cross Africa.

Livingston was fascinated by the challenge of exploration and discovery, but his driving force centered on fulfilling God's commission to proclaim the gospel. Sent out again in 1866 to search for the source of the Nile, Livingston was plagued with a variety of problems, including personal health struggles with malaria and dysentery. But he finally hunkered down in the village of Ujiji on the eastern shore of Lake Tanganyika. This is where Stanley found him on November 10, 1871.

The famous lines from Stanley are well-known to those who have read the history of either exploration or evangelization: "I walked up to him, and doffing my helmet, bowed and said in an inquiring tone—'Dr. Livingston, I presume?' Smiling cordially, he lifted his cap and answered, 'Yes.' This ending all skepticism on my part, my face betrayed the earnestness of my satisfaction as I extended my hand and added, 'I thank God, Doctor, that I have been permitted to see you.' In the warm grasp he gave my hand, and the heartiness of his voice, I felt that he also was sincere and earnest as he replied, 'I feel that I am most thankful that I am here to welcome you.'"

Livingston refused Stanley's invitation to return to London in triumph. He pressed ahead with his search for the Nile. His health would not permit it, however, and after wandering for some eighteen months he came to a village in the Ilala District on the edge of a swamp. There his bearers found him on the morning of May 1, 1873, kneeling by his bedside in apparent prayer, his head resting on his hands. They were unable to rouse him; the messenger sent by God had gone home for the last time.

Peter's story is not quite as glamorous or as well known by people today, but he was no less called of God to specific ministry. In fact, we do not know for sure how Peter died, since we have only the fragmentary records of the ancients—no biblical information on the subject. What we do know from this chapter is that Jesus singled him out to call him to a life of discipleship and sacrifice that depended on his full recognition of a central Christian fact— "Jesus is Lord."

II. COMMENTARY

Jesus Is Lord!

> **MAIN IDEA:** *Jesus is Lord of our lives; Jesus is Lord of our service; Jesus is Lord of our future. He allows no selfishness to stand in the way of those who would follow him in full obedience.*

A Jesus Is Lord of Our Lives (21:1–14)

> **SUPPORTING IDEA:** *John has now recorded three post-resurrection appearances of Jesus: to Mary, to the disciples that first Sunday night, and a second time to the disciples with Thomas present. Now we see a different scene as Jesus visited his spiritual brothers as they followed their vocation. He demonstrated his friendship at a seaside breakfast with seven disciples present. Jesus disclosed himself to them through a miracle, and John announced to Peter, "It is the Lord" (v. 7).*

21:1–3. Seven of the disciples participated in this event: Peter, Thomas, Nathanael, James, John, and two unnamed disciples. If we consider geography and occupation, on the basis of chapter 1 we might plug Andrew and Philip into those vacant slots. This was no important event. They were just "hanging out," and for them, that meant fishing. But it was not a good night for the nets: in fact, **they caught nothing.**

Only John used the name **Sea of Tiberias** for the Sea of Galilee, and he even corrected himself on the title in 6:1. As we have noted earlier, this body of water was also called the Lake of Gennesaret (Luke 5:1). We should not hurry over the word **appeared** in verse 1. John used it and similar words to identify the self-revelation of Christ (John 1:31; 2:11; 9:3). He also used these words in his first epistle to describe the incarnate Christ (1 John 1:2; 3:5,8; 4:9) and the Lord's return (1 John 2:28; 3:2). Already in the first three verses of this chapter, Peter has emerged as the dominant personality among the post-resurrection disciples.

Tenney observes: "The leadership of Simon Peter is apparent at this point. Whether he was motivated by the need of earning money for his family or whether he simply wanted some activity to relieve the mental tension after the preceding fortnight in Jerusalem is speculative. The others assented to Peter's proposal; so they embarked in a boat that was available for a night of fishing. The presence of the definite article 'the' (*to*) with the 'boat' (*ploion*) suggests that the boat was Peter's. Their enthusiasm ended in frustration, for no fish were caught" (Tenney, EBC, p. 199).

John's central emphasis in this futile fishing foray was to set up the miracle he described in verse 6. Nevertheless, the metaphor had been established by both Matthew and Mark: "Follow me . . . and I will make you fishers of men" (Matt. 4:19; Mark 1:17). In the symbolic spiritual reality, we recognize the reappearance of John 15:5—futility without the presence and power of Christ.

21:4–6. Here we find a scene similar to what we saw in chapter 20 with Mary. These disciples, having seen the risen Lord twice, did not recognize him on shore. Let us not read anything mystical into the text. It could have been dark, or at least dusk. Perhaps there was some mist on the water. The text says they saw someone on the shore but could not tell who it was.

John would never forget the suggestion by this stranger to **throw your net on the right side of the boat.** How many times that night they had dropped the net on the right side of the boat, then the left, then the right, then the left again—all to no avail. With nothing to lose, they dropped the net and hauled in what some interpreters have suggested would have been over three hundred pounds of fish. Presumably that figure represents what first-century fishing nets might hold.

Was this another miracle? Jesus did not say, "Why not try your luck one more time on the right side of the boat?" He knew exactly what would be there, and he exercised divine omniscience for his friends. Tenney, however, is unconvinced: "The command to cast the net on the right side of the ship may be interpreted in two ways. Either Jesus was testing their faith by recommending a procedure the Galilean fishermen never used, or he could discern the presence of a school of fish from the more advantageous viewpoint of the shore" (Tenney, *EBC*, p. 199).

But there are more than two interpretations of this event, since I have already offered a third. Carson also suggests that Jesus may have just been reciting a generally known sign of good luck in Greek culture by emphasizing the right side, but just as quickly rejects it. Indeed, Carson finds "primary evidence of 'secondary' features in the story, prompting many to conclude that this is a variant account of the episode described in Luke 5:1–11" (Carson, p. 670).

This view has its problems, however, since the Luke account includes two boats and John clearly seemed to refer to one. The phrase "with the people crowding around him" from Luke 5:1 hardly fits the intimate breakfast with the disciples of John 21.

Morris twice uses the words "the miracle" to describe this amazing catch (Morris, pp. 863–64), and Boice says, "Why the right side? Because that was the side they were directed to by Jesus! If He had said the left side, there would have been fish there. They would have swarmed there from every part of the Lake of Galilee, so anxious would they have been to be caught" (Boice, p. 347).

Perhaps the strongest argument for recognizing a miracle here is the immediate response of John upon seeing the full net: **It is the Lord!**

21:7–9. Notice that the disciples put the net down without knowing who had suggested the right side. As soon as they saw the results, they responded in character—John with a word to Peter and Peter jumping into the water. The Greek word for **outer garment** is used only here in the New Testament. We should not presume that Peter was naked before this moment, though some have surmised that.

Morris suggests, "The probability here is that the word means that parts of the body normally covered were exposed so that Peter was not naked but rather 'stripped for work' (RSV, cited in Barclay). This may mean that he wore a loin cloth, or perhaps a sleeveless tunic which would not impede his movements" (Morris, pp. 864–65).

The act of putting on this cloak seems precisely the reverse of what we might do before jumping into the water from a boat. But the cultural significance of the outer garment seems important here for the Jews. Greeting in general was a religious act which required that a person be clothed. The greeting of the resurrected Son of God surely compelled Peter to follow the best protocol he could muster in an awkward situation.

21:10–14. The eight friends enjoyed breakfast together that day. The menu required some of the freshly caught fish in addition to what Jesus had already prepared. John, a professional fisherman, seemed amazed that they could pull in 153 large fish without the net breaking (another distinction from Luke 5). What a wonderful morning that must have been. These disciples (Thomas among them) experienced a new level of rest and comfort with the Lord's resurrection and presence.

Christians often eat together in groups. When they do, they portray scenes like this as well as many others throughout Luke's record in Acts where eating frequently reflects friendship, followership, and fellowship. At times like this we agree with one another that Jesus is Lord of our lives.

Let me give another warning against speculation here, this time in reference to the 153 fish. As a professional fisherman, John found great delight in the number and the size. But to assume that he intended some metaphysical significance in the number is valueless and perhaps even dangerous. Some interpreters have suggested, for example, that the total number of kinds of fish counted by the ancients was 153 and therefore the number symbolizes the universal appeal of the gospel.

"Another suggestion rises from the fact that 153 is a sum of numbers from 1 to 17. That is to say, it is the sum of 10, the number of the commandments and hence of the Law, and 7, representing the sevenfold gifts of the spirit. Some point out that 153 dots can be arranged in an equilateral triangle with 17 dots along each side" (Morris, p. 867). Another view claims that the 153 represents the total known languages in the world at that time. I agree with Morris: "Such explanations of the number may carry conviction to some, but I must confess to remaining completely unimpressed . . . it is much simpler to see a fisherman's record of a fact" (Morris, p. 867).

B Jesus Is Lord of Our Service (21:15–17)

SUPPORTING IDEA: *After he ate with his friends, Jesus turned his attention to Peter, probably because of the dominant role that he would play in the early church. Three times Peter had denied the Lord, so three times Jesus asked him, "Do you truly love me?"*

21:15. Embarrassing as it must have been at the time, this tender exchange restored Peter to leadership—a role he exercised early in Acts. Throughout the history of the church, thousands have been scattered on the roadside of good intentions for ministry; they traded God's call for something else—like fishing. Even though this night of fishing may have been just a casual outing with the guys, as a professional fisherman Peter could have entertained thoughts of going back to his former work. Being with Jesus had been great, and it must have felt wonderful to have him alive again. But who knows what might be next? A fellow has to make a living.

For the next nine verses, John brought his Gospel to a close with the clear enunciation of Peter's call to ministry. Jesus asked Peter almost the same question three times. This could reflect the three denials, but whether it did or not, the command was similar each time: **Feed my lambs . . . Take care of my sheep . . . Feed my sheep.** A quick glance at 1 Peter lets us know the disciple never forgot this moment.

Several questions jump at us from the text of these three verses. Even if we agree that the threefold reference probably does connect with the three-fold denial, specific questions remain unanswered:

1. What is the meaning of the words **more than these?**

2. Why did the Lord change the command after each of Peter's responses? Some indicate specificity in both the noun and verb changes such as a reference to children's ministry (lambs) and service to adults (sheep). Also the varied ministries of apostleship and later eldership would include spiritual feeding and care of the flock. Perhaps all of this is implied in the text; perhaps none. The point is that Jesus called Peter to shepherding rather than fishing. His future work would involve ministry to people.

21:16. The shepherding call continued a second time as Jesus used Peter's old name (Simon), reverting to "pebble" rather than "rock." The flow of the text emphasizes humility and service rather than primacy over the other apostles. According to Carson, "It is true that the figure of the shepherd can be used to picture authority. But this passage does not establish that Peter has relatively more authority than other 'shepherds' of the flock of God. When close comparisons are made with Acts 20:28 and 1 Peter 4:1–4, it becomes clear that *each* shepherd of the flock of God, of Jesus' sheep, of the church of God, is to mirror *both* authority *and* a certain brokenness that is utterly exemplary . . . In the context of the Fourth Gospel, these verses deal with Peter's reinstatement to service, not with his elevation to primacy" (Carson, pp. 678–79).

21:17. At this point in the text there is a change of verb in Jesus' question while the verb in Peter's answer stays the same. We also learn that Peter was **hurt** by the third question. In Jesus' first two questions he used the word *aqapao;* hence the NIV translation "truly love." In the third we find the word *phileo* and the NIV drops "truly."

Most interpreters find no significant difference in the words, particularly since the conversation took place in Aramaic. Nevertheless, John's record in Greek did, under the guidance of the Holy Spirit, adopt a different word. It seems difficult from the grammar of the text to argue that Peter's **hurt** was brought about only by the connection of a third question with his three denials. We might conclude that Peter was hurt because the question had been asked three times. But one should not dismiss the possibility that his discomfort lay in Jesus' use of a lesser word.

On this point, Westcott observes:

> Just as the idea of comparison was given up before, so now the idea of the loftiest love is given up. It is as if the Lord would test the truth of the feeling which St. Peter claimed. The three questions could not but recall the three denials; and the form of this last question could not but vividly bring back the thought of the failure of personal devotion at the moment of trial so *Peter was grieved* not only that the question was put again, but that this *third time* the phrase was changed; that the question

was not only put once again, but at the same time put so as to raise a doubt rather he could indeed rightly claim that modified love which he had professed (Westcott, p. 303).

Carson takes a different view in claiming, "When Peter is particularly grieved (v. 17), it is not because Jesus has changed verbs, but because the same question is being asked for the third time" (Carson, p. 678).

The preponderance of contemporary scholarship sees no difference between the words, but the careful Bible student should consider all the options. And before we leave this verse let us notice the brief but clear reference to omniscience in Peter's reply, **Lord, you know all things.** Peter switched words here as well. **Know** translates *ginosko* instead of *oidas*, which he has used twice before. Again, one must decide whether a conversation that probably took place in Aramaic using different words could possibly have any significant difference in the Greek translation—weighed against the exactitude of biblical words, particularly key words in John's Gospel like *know* and *love*.

According to Morris:

> There can be little doubt but that the whole scene is meant to show us Peter as completely restored to his position of leadership. He has three times denied his Lord. Now he has three times affirmed his love for Him, and three times he has been commissioned to care for the flock. This must have had the effect on the others of a demonstration that, whatever had been the mistakes of the past, Jesus was restoring Peter to a place of trust. It is further worth noting that the one thing about which Jesus questions Peter prior to commissioning him to tend the flock is love. This is the basic qualification for Christian service (Morris, p. 875).

Ⓒ Jesus Is Lord of Our Futures (21:18–25)

SUPPORTING IDEA: *Called by his Lord to be a dedicated follower, Peter could not resist comparing how Jesus dealt with John. He seemed to say, "If I have to be a martyr, why doesn't John receive the same fate?" So the Lord told Peter something you and I need to recall every day of our lives. Paraphrased, verse 22 might go like this: "What I choose to do with other people is none of your business; you follow me."*

21:18–19. Having established the motivation for service, Jesus went on to describe the turns that Peter's life would take. This brash, independent, vocal fisherman would one day be dependent, presumably a prisoner, and, many believe, a martyr. Only the Son of God could tell someone that following him would lead to death and then immediately say, **Follow me!**

All interpreters agree on the general tone of the prophecy. But the text gets difficult when we compare the words **stretch out your hands** with John's explanation of the event: **Jesus said this to indicate the kind of death by which Peter would glorify God.** Many see here a specific prophecy of crucifixion for Peter, but I remain unconvinced by the evidence.

In favor of the crucifixion interpretation, I offer this paragraph by Hughes: "While there are differing interpretations of this prophecy, I believe Jesus was saying that despite his aged infirmity, Peter would die a martyr's death by crucifixion. The give away is that John's description of Peter's death in verse 19, as something that would glorify God, used a phrase which was standard Christian language for martyrdom. The church fathers—including Iraeneus, Justin Martyr, and Cyprian—all viewed the phrase 'you will stretch your hands' as a description of crucifixion" (Hughes, p. 175).

Against that view is the syntax of verse 18 where the stretching of the hands precedes the leading **where you do not want to go.** In the words of Morris: "If this understanding of the expression goes back to the time of Christ then we have a prophecy of the exact mode of Peter's death. But unless we can be sure of this we cannot hold that the verse points to more than martyrdom in some form. Against it is the word order, for the 'carrying' would necessarily precede the crucifixion (though the order may be determined here not by the sense, but by the parallelism with the first part of the verse)" (Morris, p. 876).

21:20–21. We must not forget that Jesus spoke to a pre-Pentecost Peter. When he learned about his own death, Peter apparently glanced at John and asked a question about which he may have felt embarrassment for the rest of his life: **Lord, what about him?** He might have meant, "I'm more concerned about my brother John." More likely, however, the Peter we know and love would have responded to the prophecy by saying, "If I have to die, so does John."

Parents and teachers of children about 9–11 know this attitude only too well. Whether it is a test in the classroom or a game on the playground, kids love to complain, "It's not fair." In Tasker's words, "Peter and John have different vocations; but neither is to question why the other's vocation should be different from his own. *What is that to thee?* (21:22) is Jesus' rebuke to Peter when he shows himself idly curious about the future of his friend; and the last word of Jesus to Peter is similar to his first, *Follow thou me*" (Tasker, p. 231).

21:22–23. Jesus' response took the form of a mild rebuke and the command to follow. He allowed no comparison with how God leads others or what he gives them while we feel we may have endured great sacrifice. John would live longer than Peter, though there is no reason Peter would infer this from the text. The key is not how long John would live nor that he would live until the Lord's return (the **if** looms large here). The main thing is that each Christian should follow Christ in whatever manner he or she is called.

Nevertheless, **rumors spread among the brothers**—a malady that has worsened in the church over two thousand years. John felt the need to correct it, so he stated the exact words of Jesus. John lived into his nineties, history tells us, but he certainly did not have an exemption from death. The argument had nothing to do with longevity or death; it focused exclusively on Peter's attitude regarding God's will for his life.

21:24. Without naming himself, John indicated he was the one referred to in that conversation. Now he wrote down what he saw and heard—an eyewitness record, hand-written and accurate. The words **we know that his testimony is true** may represent a possible affirmation by the early church. The **we** could actually refer to the Ephesian elders, or it might be the editorial pronoun we still use today to avoid choosing the first person.

Morris notes: "It is a pity that there is no clue as to the identity of the 'we.' It would be a help to know who these people were who speak so confidently about the authorship of the Gospel. All that we can say is that the words (and hence their authors) must be very early, for there is no textual doubt about these concluding verses. Barrett regards the plural as very important. 'The "we" is to be taken with full seriousness; there exists an apostolic Church capable of verifying and affirming the apostolic witness'" (Morris, p. 881).

21:25. The last verse of the Gospel of John represents what we call *hyperbole,* a deliberate exaggeration for dramatic effect. John wanted his readers to know that he had just begun to tell the story. The words and works of Jesus were much greater than the record contained in his Gospel, the other Gospels, or the entire Bible. Nevertheless, on the basis of what he had written, John reminded us that Jesus expects his people to believe and to make him Lord of their lives, their service, and their futures.

> **MAIN IDEA REVIEW:** *Jesus is Lord of our lives; Jesus is Lord of our service; Jesus is Lord of our future. He allows no selfishness to stand in the way of those who would follow him in full obedience.*

III. CONCLUSION

Clear Warning

In this litigation-oriented society, commercial packaging has gone over the edge with bizarre warnings to consumers intended to thwart even the most ridiculous lawsuit. Consider the following actual examples:

On a bag of Fritoes: "You could be a winner! No purchase necessary. Details inside."

On a bar of Dial soap: "Use like regular soap."

On a hotel shower cap: "Fits one head."

On a package of Nytol sleeping aid: "May cause drowsiness."

On a string of Christmas lights: "For indoor or outdoor use only."

On the packaging of a Rowenta iron: "Do not iron clothes on body."

These represent just a small sampling of the ridiculous statements we find on all kinds of products. Today everyone has a right to compensation for any unpleasantness. If consumers are inconvenienced in any way, it is clearly the manufacturer's fault. Americans and Westerners in general have convinced themselves that *rights* and not *responsibilities* should determine their relationship with the world.

Such an attitude stands in stark contrast to the New Testament, and particularly John 21. In this chapter Jesus informed Peter that he must surrender whatever rights he had in complete obedience and submission to his Lord. Furthermore, Jesus issued a warning of what was ahead for Peter. Only after explaining the struggles and pain of the future did he say, "Follow me."

This chapter is about discipleship and the price that must be paid for accepting it. This is not a new theme in Jesus' teaching. But after his focus on evangelism throughout the book, John settled on this theme for his conclusion.

Our studies in the Fourth Gospel have led us on a spiritual odyssey through one of the greatest books of the Bible. We have learned about faith from this Spirit-inspired record of the life, ministry, death, and resurrection of Jesus, God's son.

John's purpose has been clear: to point people to faith in the Savior by showing both the historical record and the interpretation of his life and ministry. John alone among the Gospel writers recorded his own personal testimony about the Lord, the visit of Nicodemus, the raising of Lazarus, and the detailed prayer of chapter 17. He carefully selected those words and works of the Lord that he calculated would lead his readers to faith. And having led them to faith, he wanted those readers to become a part of the movement he himself had joined—followers of Jesus who would serve him to the death.

PRINCIPLES

- Serving Christ in the energy of the flesh alone will bring futility and frustration.
- Whenever the Lord tells you to do something, just do it.
- Discipleship means following Christ without asking questions about other people.

APPLICATIONS

- Reject everything in your life that is not the will of God.
- Never forget that love is the centerpiece of ministry to other people.
- Follow the Lord regardless of what happens in the lives of others.

IV. LIFE APPLICATION

View from the Balcony

On December 4, 1954, I had an important date. As a college junior, I took a beautiful young freshman girl to a basketball game. We continued dating and after some months began to talk about the possibility of marriage. But we faced a problem. In September, four months before that first date, I had committed my life to Christ for full-time Christian ministry wherever God would lead. Though she was a dedicated Christian, the young lady had no intention of spending her life in some missionary outpost or struggling through the problems of a local church pastorate. The match did not seem right.

One day I sat in the balcony during a chapel service at Taylor University where we were both students. The speaker was Dick Hillis, creative missionary statesmen on the Asian frontier, who challenged the student body to complete commitment in discipleship. At the end of his message, he invited to the front of the auditorium any students who wanted to give their lives unreservedly to Christ.

Tears filled my eyes as I watched my beloved friend move forward and kneel at the front of that room, declaring in her heart, "Jesus is Lord." We were engaged the next Christmas and married the following September. She is still the light of my life as we approach forty-four years together.

As you study John's Gospel and help others to improve their understanding of this great book, you cannot dodge the call to complete commitment. The question at the end of our study centers not on John's purpose or even on the splendid content of his book. The real issue is what we will do in response.

Has God brought us to greater faith through this study? Do we understand more of the light and life of which this apostle wrote? Are we prepared to respond to the Lord's command to Peter, to follow without reservation or complaint? Each time we open this Gospel, we are forced to admit that Jesus is Lord and to face the demands that this truth makes upon our own lives.

V. PRAYER

Father, thank you for the wonders of your Word, especially this magnificent Gospel that gives us such a personal look at our Lord. Amen.

VI. DEEPER DISCOVERIES

A. Post-Resurrection Appearances (21:14)

Though scholars are not in complete agreement on the number, one can identify at least nine appearances of Christ after his resurrection gathered from the following texts: Matthew 28:9,17; Mark 16:9; Luke 24:15,36,50; John 20:19,26; 21:1; Acts 1:1–8; 9:5; 1 Corinthians 15:5–8. As Tenney puts it, "The record of Jesus' post-resurrection ministry is as fragmentary as that of his career prior to the Resurrection, and the Gospel emphases on it differ. Matthew, Mark, and John 21 speak of a Galilean manifestation; Luke and John 20 deal only with Jerusalem" (Tenney, *EBC*, p. 198).

The word *appeared* in verse 1 is the same word translated "happened" later in that same verse. John used it again here in verse 14, and it characterizes his writings. It is the best word John could find to describe the self-revelation of Christ.

Lewis picks up on the importance of immediate belief in the resurrection because of these multiple appearances:

> The Acts of the Apostles shows that belief in the Resurrection did not emerge gradually in the early church, but that from the very beginning (within seven weeks of Jesus' public death) the resurrection event was being preached loud and clear by Peter at the Feast of Pentecost as part of the central message of Christianity (Acts 2:23–24; cf. 3:15; 4:10; 5:31–32). The whole of the New Testament witness, in all its strata, its different writers, and its various books, is united on the matter: The gospel accounts, passion narratives though they are, are all unequivocally clear on the matter of Jesus' resurrection as witnessed historical fact (Matthew 28:1–20; Mark 16:1–8; Luke 24:1–53; John 20:1–21) (Lewis, p. 360).

B. More Than These (21:15)

Jesus asked Peter whether he loved him "more than these." These what? Some believe Jesus meant more than the other disciples loved him, while others claim Jesus wanted to know if Peter loved him more than he loved the others in the group. Yet a third possibility would see the Lord asking Peter whether he loved him more than the fish. Interpreters can be lined up on each of the three views, though the preponderance of evidence falls on the side of the first because of Peter's boastful claims about his great devotion to the Lord (Matt. 26:33; Mark 14:29).

The Greek pronoun translated as "these" offers no solution, and the context would allow any of these three viewpoints. In my opinion, the second is least likely, since Peter's love for the other disciples had never been a point of discussion over the past three and one-half years. Certainly his love for Christ was an issue, and his love for fishing was contextually active in this chapter. We do well to remember Peter's words in John 13:37, "Lord, why can't I follow you now? I will lay down my life for you." But the fishing comparison does hold a certain realistic attraction in view of some modern distractions.

C. Peter's Death (21:18–19)

Much has been made of Peter's death by crucifixion, although biblical evidence for such a conclusion is flimsy. Tradition claims that Peter eventually ended up in Rome, served Christ there, and was martyred by crucifixion under Nero. A more embellished story tells us he served as bishop of Rome for twenty-five years, but there is not a shred of New Testament evidence to support such a view.

Carson asks us to focus on what the text says rather than what we think we know: "Later accounts of Peter asking to be crucified upside down, because he felt unworthy to be crucified as his Lord was, are too remote and too infected with legendary accretions to be reliable. What is undisputed is that the indelible shame Peter bore for his public disowning of the Lord Jesus Christ on the night he was sentenced to death was forgiven by the Lord himself, and subsequently overwhelmed by the apostle's fruitful ministry and martyrdom" (Carson, p. 680).

VII. TEACHING OUTLINE

A. INTRODUCTION

1. Lead Story: Sent by God
2. Context: John 21 seems an unlikely way for John to end a book devoted to evangelism. But as we have already noted, the ultimate conclusion to the crucifixion and resurrection of the last two chapters is devotion and discipleship to the living Lord.
3. Transition: The events of this chapter apparently took place between the beginning of the second week after the resurrection and the day of the ascension. John introduced the chapter with the interesting word *afterward,* which he has used in different forms in 2:12; 3:22; 5:1,14;

6:1; 7:1; 11:7,11; 13:7; 19:28,38. He used this word to move the text along, but it implies no more than some indefinite passing of time.

B. COMMENTARY
1. Jesus Is Lord of Our Lives (21:1–14)
   a. Friendship (21:1–3)
   b. Followership (21:4–9)
   c. Fellowship (21:10–14)
2. Jesus Is Lord of Our Service (21:15–17)
   a. "Feed my lambs" (21:15)
   b. "Take care of my sheep" (21:16)
   c. "Feed my sheep" (21:17)
3. Jesus Is Lord of Our Futures (21:18–25)
   a. Martyrdom predicted (21:18–19)
   b. Selfishness rebuked (21:20–25)

C. CONCLUSION: VIEW FROM THE BALCONY

VIII. ISSUES FOR DISCUSSION

1. What is involved in leaving one's occupation to serve Christ?
2. What do you mean when you say or sing, "Jesus is Lord"?
3. How would you describe what you understand to be God's will for your life and the ways in which he wants you to follow as a disciple?

Glossary

angel—A messenger from God, either heavenly or human, who delivers God's message of instruction, warning, or hope

apostles—Men chosen by Jesus as his official messengers; this term refers generally to his twelve disciples

atonement—God's way of overcoming sin through Christ's obedience and death to restore believers to a right relationship with God

Christology—The technical term describing a study of the nature and work of Jesus Christ

church—The community of those who believe in and follow Jesus Christ; used to designate a congregation, a denomination, or all Christians

covenant—A contract or agreement expressing God's gracious promises to his people and their consequent relationship to him

cross—Two wooden beams shaped as a letter t or x used as an instrument to kill criminals by the Roman government; the wooden beams on which Jesus was killed and thus a symbol of Christian faith and responsibility

crucifixion—A form of execution by affixing a victim to a cross to die; Jesus' death on the cross for sinners

disciple—A follower and learner of Jesus Christ

election—God's gracious action in choosing people to follow him and obey his commandments

eternal life—The quality of life that Jesus gives his disciples and unending life with God given to those who believe in Jesus Christ as Savior and Lord

faith—Belief in and personal commitment to Jesus Christ for eternal salvation

forgiveness—Pardon and release from penalty for wrongdoing; God's delivery from sin's wages for those who repent and express faith in Christ; the Christian act of freeing from guilt and blame those by whom one has suffered wrong

glorification—God's action in the lives of believers, making them able to share the glory and reward of heaven

gospel—The good news of the redeeming work of God through the life, death, and resurrection of Jesus Christ

Gospels—The four New Testament accounts of the life of Jesus Christ; Matthew, Mark, and Luke are called synoptic Gospels because they relate many of the same events and teachings of Jesus; John is the fourth Gospel and tends to be more theological in nature, telling events and teachings not in the Synoptics

grace—Undeserved acceptance and love received from another, especially the characteristic attitude of God in providing salvation for sinners

high priest—The chief religious official for Israel and Judaism appointed as the only person allowed to enter the Holy of Holies and offer sacrifice on the Day of Atonement

holy—God's distinguishing characteristic that separates him from all creation; the moral ideal for Christians as they seek to reflect the character of God as known in Christ Jesus

Holy Spirit—The third person of the Trinity; the presence of God promised by Christ and sent to his disciples at Pentecost representing God's active presence in the believer, the church, and the world

incarnation—The act of the divine Son Jesus becoming human and enduring all the experiences which tempt us and cause us to suffer, thus qualifying him to be the agent of God's saving plan for humanity

Glossary

inspiration—The breathing of God's Spirit on human speech and writing, producing the inspired text of the Bible

intercession—A prayer presenting one person's needs to another as Christians presenting the needs of others to God or as Christ or the Holy Spirit representing believers before God

interpretation—The human effort to understand the Bible with the guidance of the Holy Spirit and to apply its meaning to contemporary life

Jerusalem—Capital city of Israel in the Old Testament; religious center of Judaism in the New Testament; also name of the heavenly city John describes in Revelation (New Jerusalem)

Jesus Christ—The eternal Son of God; the Lord and Savior; the second person of the Trinity

joy—The inner attitude of rejoicing in one's salvation regardless of outward circumstances

judgment—God's work at the end time involving condemnation for unbelievers and assignment of rewards for believers

justification—The act or event by which God credits a sinner who has faith as being right with him through the blood of Jesus

Lamb of God—A title for Jesus that highlights his sacrifice for our sins and his victory over death

logos—Greek word meaning "word" used to describe the eternal ministry of Christ in creation and his appearance as the Son of God who became flesh

Lord—A title for God in the Old Testament; also used for Jesus in the New Testament; means "owner" or "master worthy of obedience"

Lord's day—The first day of the week (Sunday) on which most Christians have worshiped since Christ's resurrection on the first day of the week

love—God's essential quality that seeks the best interests of others regardless of the others' actions; love is commanded of believers

martyr—A person who bears witness to Jesus Christ and consequently suffers or dies rather than deny Christ

Messiah—the coming king promised by the prophets; Jesus Christ who fulfilled the prophetic promises; Christ represents the Greek translation of the Hebrew word "messiah"

miracle—An act of God beyond human understanding that inspires wonder, displays God's greatness, and leads people to recognize God at work in the world

new birth—God's work in the believer at conversion to create a new person empowered by the Holy Spirit

obedience—Hearing and following instructions and directions from God; expected of believers

omnipotent—God's unlimited power to do that which is within his holy and righteous character

omnipresence—God's unlimited presence in all places at all times

omniscience—God's unlimited knowing

parable—A short story taken from everyday life to make a spiritual point; Jesus' favorite form of teaching

passion—The suffering of Christ during his time of trial and death on the cross

Passover—The Jewish feast celebrating the Exodus from Egypt (Exod. 12); celebrated by Jesus and his disciples at the Last Supper

Pentecost—The fiftieth day after Passover celebrated by Jews as the culmination of the Feast of Weeks and by Christians as the anniversary of the coming of the Holy Spirit

preexistence—Existing always and before the creation of the universe; a characteristic of the trinitarian God alone

redemption—The act of releasing a captive by the payment of a price; Jesus' death provided our redemption from sin's power and penalty (Heb. 9:12)

repentance—A change of heart and mind resulting in a turning from sin to God that allows conversion and is expressed through faith

resurrection—The raising of Jesus from the dead to eternal life; the raising of believers for eternal life with Christ; the raising of unbelievers to eternal punishment

Sabbath—The seventh day of the week corresponding to the seventh day of creation when people in the Old Testament were called on to rest from work and reflect on God

sanctification—The process in salvation by which God conforms the believer's life and character to the life and character of Jesus Christ through the Holy Spirit

sin—Actions by which humans rebel against God, miss his purpose for their life, and surrender to the power of evil rather than to God

Son of God—Title for Jesus emphasizing his divinity as coexistent with the Father

Son of Man—The title Jesus most frequently used for himself that emphasized both his divinity as the prophesied One in the Old Testament and his identification with people

Trinity—God's revelation of himself as Father, Son, and Holy Spirit unified as one in the Godhead and yet distinct in person and function

universalism—The unbiblical belief that all people will ultimately experience salvation

Bibliography

Anderson, J. Kerby. *Moral Dilemmas*. Nashville: Word, 1998.

Andrews, Samuel J. *The Life of Our Lord* (rev. ed.). Grand Rapids: Zondervan, 1954.

Beers, V. Gilbert. *The Victor Handbook of Bible Knowledge*. Wheaton, Ill.: Victor Books, 1981.

Blackaby, Henry. *Experiencing the Word—Gospel of John*. Nashville: Broadman & Holman, 1999.

Blum, Edwin A. "John." *The Bible Knowledge Commentary*. Ed. by John F. Walvoord and Roy B. Zuck. Wheaton, Ill.: Victor Books, 1983.

Boice, James M. *The Gospel of John* (5 vols.). Grand Rapids: Zondervan Publishing House, 1977.

Borchert, Gerald L. *John*. The New American Commentary. Nashville: Broadman & Holman, 1996.

Brown, Colin, ed. *The New International Dictionary of New Testament Theology* (3 vols.). Grand Rapids: Zondervan, 1967.

Bruce, F. F. *The Gospel of John*. Grand Rapids: Eerdmans, 1983.

Carson, D. A. *The Gospel According to John*. Grand Rapids: William B. Eerdmans, 1991.

Denney, James. *The Death of Christ*. New York: Eaton & Mains, n.d.

Detzler, Wayne A. *New Testament Words in Today's Language*. Wheaton, Ill.: Victor Books, 1986.

Dods, Marcus. *The Gospel of Saint John* (2 vols.). London: Hodder and Stoughton, 1908.

Gangel, Kenneth O. *Acts*. Holman New Testament Commentary. Vol. 5. Ed. by Max Anders. Nashville: Broadman & Holman, 1998.

Gariepy, Henry. *100 Portraits of Christ*. Wheaton, Ill.: Victor Books, 1987.

Godet, Frederick L. *Commentary on the Gospel of John, Vol. II*. Grand Rapids: Zondervan.

Greene, Oliver B. *The Gospel According to John*. Greenville: The Gospel Hour, Inc. 1966.

Gromacki, Robert. *The Holy Spirit*. Nashville: Word, 1999.

Hastings, James, ed. *A Dictionary of Christ and the Gospels* (2 vols.). Edinburgh, Scotland: T&T Clark, 1913.

Hobbs, Herschel H. *An Exposition of the Gospel of Matthew*. Grand Rapids: Baker Book House, 1965.

Holloman, Henry. *The Forgotten Blessing*. Nashville: Word, 1999.

Hughes. *Behold the Man* (2 vols.). Wheaton, Ill.: Victor Books, 1984.

Inrig, Gary. *The Parables*. Grand Rapids: Discovery House, 1991.

Laney, J. Carl. *God*. Nashville: Word, 1999.

Lewis, Peter. *The Glory of Christ*. Chicago: Moody Press, 1997.

Lightner, Robert. *Angels, Satan, and Demons*. Nashville: Word, 1998.

Lightner, Robert P. *Sin, the Savior, and Salvation*. Nashville: Thomas Nelson, 1991.

Morgan, G. Campbell. *The Crises of the Christ*. London: Hodder and Stoughton, 1903.

Morgan, G. Campbell. *The Four Gospels*. London: Oliphants Ltd., 1956.

Morris, Leon. *The Gospel According to John*. Grand Rapids: Eerdmans, 1971.

Newman, Barclay M., and Eugene A. Nida. *A Transliterate Handbook on the Gospel of John*. London: United Bible Societies, 1980.

NIV Study Bible, The. Kenneth Barker, gen. ed. Grand Rapids: Zondervan, 1985.

Osbeck, Kenneth W. *Amazing Grace*. Grand Rapids: Kregel, 1990.

Pyne, Robert A. *Humanity & Sin*. Nashville: Word, 1999.

Swindoll, Charles R. *The Tale of the Tidy Oxcart*. Nashville: Word, 1998.

Tasker, R. V. G. *The Gospel According to Saint John*. Grand Rapids: Eerdmans, 1960.

Bibliography

Tenney, Merrill C. *John: The Gospel of Belief*. Grand Rapids: Eerdmans, 1948.

Tenney, Merrill C. *The Gospel of John*. Expositor's Bible Commentary. Vol. 9. Ed. by Frank E. Gaebelein. Grand Rapids: Zondervan, 1981.

Tenney, Merrill, C., gen. ed. *The Zondervan Pictorial Encyclopedia of the Bible*. Grand Rapids: Zondervan Publishing House, 1963.

Tozer, A. W. *The Pursuit of God*. Harrisburg, Penn: Christian Publications, 1948.

Trench, Richard C. *The Miracles of Our Lord*. London: Society for Promoting Christian Knowledge, 1904.

Westcott, B. F. *The Gospel According to John*. London: James Clarke & Co., Ltd., 1958.

Westcott, B. F. *An Introduction to the Study of the Gospels*. London: Macmillan & Company, 1895.

Westcott, B. F. *The Revelation of the Father*. London: Macmillan, 1884.

White, R. E. O. *The Night He Was Betrayed*. Grand Rapids: Eerdmans, 1982.

Witmer, John A. *Immanuel*. Nashville: Word, 1998.

Wuest, Kenneth S. *Great Truths to Live by in the Greek New Testament*. Grand Rapids: Eerdmans, 1953.